THE
LIFE
OF
JAMES FITZ-JAMES,
DUKE of *BERWICK,*

Marſhal, Duke, and Peer of FRANCE, General
of his Moſt Chriſtian Majeſty's Armies.

CONTAINING

An account of his Birth, Education, and military Exploits in

IRELAND,	The SEVENNES,
FLANDERS,	DAUPHINY, and
SPAIN,	On the RHINE :

With the Particulars of the Battle of ALMANZA,
and the Siege of BARCELONA.

GIVING A

General View of the Affairs of EUROPE, for theſe fifty
Years paſt :

The whole interſperſed with

Military and Political Reflections, and the Characters of
EMINENT MEN.

LONDON:

Printed for, and Sold by A. MILLAR, at *Buchanan's*
Head, over-againſt *St. Clement's-Church,* in the *Strand.*

MDCCXXXVIII.

PREFACE.

WE hope the following *Memoirs will be well received by the publick, on account of the connection they have with the principal wars, wherein Europe has been engaged for above these fifty years past: and those persons who are designed either for the command of armies, or to serve in them, will find in the character and conduct of Marshal* Berwick *a model capable of affecting and forming them.* This great man was always equal to himself, whether the affairs of England, France, or Spain *required him at the head of their armies, or whether some intervals of adversity obliged him to live in a private station.* He every where discovered the same wisdom, steadiness, uprightness and integrity, the same attachment to the interests of his master, and zeal for them, and the same spirit of piety and religion. You will not here meet with such events as at most serve only for amusement; things which are much to the taste of certain readers, whom after all it is of little consequence to please, or not to please. But the most remarkable transactions in Germany, Italy, Spain, France, England, *and* Holland, *as they have a natural connection with this subject, will here be related in their proper place.* These Memoirs

PREFACE.

moirs contain several particular accounts, which without being unintelligible to those who are not skilled in the art of war, will place, as it were, before the eyes of military men, the various actions which are here related. In a word, we have omitmitted nothing that might give an exact idea of the state of Europe *for these fifty years past; and know not any thing that could have been added to this work, either with regard to the different interests into which* Europe *is divided, or to whatever concerns the Life of Marshal* Berwick.

ADVERTISEMENT.

WHEN the Life of the Duke of *Berwick* first appeared in *French*, it was thought so interesting a subject to the *English* readers, that a translation of it could not fail being well received. However, as we were unwilling to offer to the publick any facts which we knew either to be false, or misrepresented, we have taken the liberty to make several alterations throughout this book, and have added notes to those places which could not be changed, or enlarged, without departing from the sentiments and character of the *French* writer.

THE

THE
LIFE
OF THE
Duke of *Berwick*.

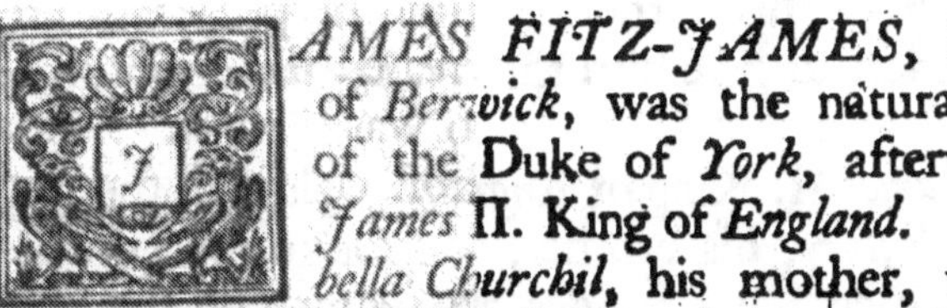

AMES FITZ-JAMES, Duke of *Berwick*, was the natural son of the Duke of *York*, afterwards *James* II. King of *England*. *Arabella Churchil*, his mother, was a lady diftinguifhed both by her beauty and wit, and fifter to *John Churchil*, who became afterwards fo famous under the name of the Duke of *Marlborough*.

He was born in the year 1671 at *Moulins* in the *Bourbonnois*, whither Mrs. *Churchil* had retired to conceal her pregnancy.

B

Being

Being brought from thence to *London*, the Duke of *York* bestowed on him an education worthy of the love which had given him birth. His early years gave that Prince the greatest hopes of him; and those sentiments which make men great and illustrious, sprung up in his mind at a time when we are employed in nothing but trifles and frivolous amusements. This young Lord was never fond of the diversions, and what they call the pleasures, of youth; but was wholly taken up either with his masters, or in reading good books. His sole view was to arrive at glory, and to render himself capable of performing the noblest actions.

From his tender age his heart was so full of that noble ambition, that his companions were struck with a respect and esteem for him, and could not help admiring him. He was exceeding serious and cool in his behaviour, and had from his infancy a great fund of piety and unfeigned religion, which increased the tender affection of his father, who was soon after in a condition to give him the most convincing proofs of it.

1685.   *Charles* II. King of *England*, dying on the sixth of *February*, his brother, the Duke of *York*, was proclamed King, under the name of *James* II, by the principal Lords of the kingdom, and without any opposition, though he professed the Catholick Religion. In the month of *April* following he was crowned at *Westminster*, the place where the Kings of *England* are usually crowned.

Soon

Soon after King *James* had afcended the 1685.
throne, the title of *Duke of* BERWICK was conferred on young *Fitz-James*, and he was invefted with the order of the Garter *. Lord *Churchil*,
Arabella's brother, was not forgot in the diftribution of the King's favours; but he afterwards
made ufe of his elevation with ingratitude and
infidelity to his King, his mafter, and benefa-
ctor.

King *James*, in the firft year of his reign,
was involved in a civil war; but it foon ended
in the deferved punifhment of him who had
raifed it. In this war the Duke of *Berwick* endeavoured to diftinguifh himfelf, though he was
yet only fourteen years of age: for this purpofe
he feveral times entreated the King to beftow
on him fome employment; but his Majefty being unwilling to expofe him fo early in a civil war,
where he run the greateft rifque, would only
give him leave to follow the Duke of *Albemarle*,
General of his army †, in the quality of Aide-
de-camp, and he ordered that General to fpare
and temper the courage of young *Berwick*.

* He was created Duke of *Berwick*, Earl of *Tinmouth*, and
Baron of *Bofworth*, *March* 19, 1686-7. *anno* 3. *Jac.* II. He was
invefted with the order of the Garter only in the year 1688, but
having fled to *France* with his father, he was never inftalled.

† The Duke of *Albemarle* being Lord Lieutenant of *Devonfhire*,
was fent down to raife the militia, and make head againft the
rebels; but the command of the King's regular troops was given
to the Earl of *Feverfham*, a *French* nobleman, and nephew to
Marfhal *Turenne*. It was this Earl, and Lord *Churchil*, who engaged the Duke of *Monmouth* at *Sedgemore* near *Bridgewater*.

 Let us here give an account of the motives
and particulars of this war, in which the Duke
of *Berwick* first served, and wherein he discovered a valour, capacity, and conduct above his
age, and worthy of his descent.

Mrs. *Lucy Walters*, a gentlewoman of *Wales*,
was one of the first mistresses of King *Charles* II,
and it was said that he had given her a promise
of marriage. By her he had a son whom he
created Duke of *Monmouth*, and distinguished
from the great number of his other natural children, by bestowing on him several lands, and
considerable employments. But King *Charles*
having afterwards had some reasons for being
displeased with his conduct, had banished him
into the *Spanish Netherlands*. He had likewise
solemnly declared, that he was never married to
the Duke of *Monmouth*'s mother.

Notwithstanding this, the Duke of *Monmouth*
pretended to be the lawful son of King *Charles* II.
and as soon as he had notice of his death, and
of King *James*'s accession to the *British* throne,
being then at *Brussels*, he immediately set out
for *Holland*, where he found several *English* malcontents who offered him their assistance, and
assured him that there were both in *England*
and *Scotland* many Protestants, to whom it was
a great grief and concern to see the Crown on
the head of a Roman Catholick; and who would
embrace his party as soon as he should appear.
He accordingly put himself at the head of those
who desired to follow him, and set out for *England,*

land, a little after the Earl of *Argyle*, who was
the moſt conſiderable man of his party, had embarked for *Scotland*.

1685.

King *James* being apprized of the Duke of
Monmouth's deſign to invade his kingdoms, ſent
to the States General a liſt of the *Engliſh* malcontents who were in *Holland*, and deſired that
they might be baniſhed out of theſe provinces.
But the enquiries of the States were too late;
for all thoſe mal-contents had already put to ſea,
and whatever diligence the *Dutch* uſed in purſuing them, they could overtake none of their ſhips,
except one ſmall frigat.

The Duke of *Monmouth* landed on the eleventh
of *June*, at *Lyme* in *Dorſetſhire*, with about two
hundred men, and arms for five thouſand more,
and eaſily got poſſeſſion of that ſmall town:
From thence he diſperſed manifeſto's, wherein
he declared that he had taken arms for the ſupport of the Proteſtant Religion, and of the privileges of *England*, to reſtore the laws of the land,
and deliver the kingdom from the uſurpation and
tyranny of the Duke of *York*.

The Parliament ſitting at that time, King
James acquainted them with the Duke of *Monmouth*'s landing. Whereupon a bill of attainder
paſſed againſt that Duke, and both houſes made
a loyal addreſs to the King, promiſing to ſtand
by him with their lives and fortunes, and to defend his Perſon and Crown againſt the Duke of
Monmouth, and all other rebels and traitors, and
all his Majeſty's enemies. Soon after, there iſ-

ſued

 sued a proclamation, forbidding all the King's subjects to read or disperse the Duke of *Monmouth*'s declaration, under pain of High-Treason. There issued likewise another, wherein a reward of five thousand pounds was offered to any person who should deliver up that Duke either dead or alive.

At the same time the King ordered his troops to march towards *Lyme*, under the command of the Duke of *Albemarle*. He had lately recalled three *English* and three *Scots* regiments, which were in the service of the States, and these joined with some new levies, made a more numerous army than was necessary to oppose that of the Duke of *Monmouth*.

The Duke, on his part, had sent some of his accomplices into the neighbouring counties, to excite a rebellion among the people. On the fourteenth of *June* he departed from *Lyme* with sixty horse, and a hundred and twenty foot; and after having marched two miles, he left them under the command of Lord *Grey*, who advanced as far as *Bridport*, a small town, about six miles from *Lyme*. These troops entered the town; but the inhabitants having gathered together, attacked them, killed seven, and made twenty three prisoners: whereupon the rest betook themselves to flight.

The Duke of *Monmouth* having now encreased his troops to four or five thousand men, marched them against the Duke of *Albemarle*, who advanced to give him battle. On the eighteenth

teenth of *June* he took poffeffion of *Taunton*, 1685.
where he was proclamed King. On the fifth
of *July* he arrived at *Wefton*, near *Bridgewater*,
where he lodged his infantry ; and he encamped
his horfe and dragoons about the town in a plain
oppofite to a morafs. Having advanced to the
morafs, he there found a free paffage, fo that
next morning he drew up his infantry in battalia,
and ordered Lord *Grey* to advance near *Sedge-*
more, where the King's army was encamped.

The Duke of *Albemarle* having notice of this,
immediately put his troops in a condition to receive them. His army confifted only of two
thoufand foot, and feven hundred horfe and dragoons ; for the King had fent the other troops
to furround the Duke of *Monmouth*, who, on
his fide, had refolved to come to an engagement,
becaufe he faw that all depended upon a victory,
that otherwife he could not advance, and that
if he retreated, or waited for new forces, he ran
the hazard of being furrounded.

He accordingly attacked the King's army; and
his troops began with loud cries, and a general
difcharge of their fmall arms. His cavalry were
ordered to advance, and were immediately put
to flight by the Duke of *Berwick*, who being at
the head of five hundred horfe, to whom he
had been fent with the Duke of *Albemarle*'s orders, laid hold of that opportunity to attack the
cavalry of the rebels, which he did with fo much
courage, and in fo good order, that he entirely
defeated them.

B 4

The

   The Duke of *Albemarle* was fo much furprifed
at the conduct and valour of young *Berwick*, that
he could not help approving what he had not ordered, and greatly commended him for the prudence he had fhewn in that action, which would
have done honour to the moft experienced officer.

As for the Duke of *Monmouth's* infantry, they
kept their ground without yielding in the leaft.
Whereupon there was a brifk firing on both fides.
The King's infantry were covered by a ditch.
As foon as their cannon arrived, the Duke of *Albemarle* ordered it to be fired on the infantry of
the rebels, and having at the fame time attacked
them in flank with his horfe, he utterly routed
them.

In this action he took three pieces of cannon,
which was all the artillery of the enemy. Of
the King's troops there fell only two hundred
men, and about as many were wounded; of
the rebels there were killed upon the fpot two
thoufand men, and many were made prifoners.
Next day, being the feventh of *July*, he marched with five hundred foot, fome horfe and dragoons, to *Bridgewater*, and having made himfelf mafter of that place, the rebels who were
there betook themfelves to flight, and difperfed
into feveral parts. Being informed that the Duke
of *Monmouth* fled with about fifty horfe, he fent
feveral parties in purfuit of him, as well as of
Lord *Grey*. The latter was taken the fame day

at

at *Ringwood*, on the frontiers of *Hampshire*, dif- guifed in the habit of a fhepherd.

As for the Duke of *Monmouth*, obferving that the horfe who fled with him made a body whofe march could hardly be concealed, he refolved to leave them. In the evening of the fame day fome fhepherds informed thofe who purfued him, that they had feen two of the fugitives en- ter a neighbouring wood: whereupon the ave- nues of it were ordered to be fhut up, and next morning a fearch was made after thofe who ab- fconded in it. For this purpofe they ufe blood- hounds, according to the cuftom of the *Englifh*, who make ufe of dogs to difcover robbers con- cealed in forefts. Thefe blood-hounds ftopt at a ditch, and barked; whereupon a man was found lying under a very thick hedge. This was a *German*, who afking quarter, promifed to fhew the place where the Duke of *Monmouth* was hid. That unfortunate Duke had made all poffible hafte to reach the fea-fhore, where he hoped to find fome bark in which he might ef- cape; but his horfe having failed him, he had been obliged to alight, and difguife himfelf in a very mean drefs. He was found lying under a bufh in a ditch, having in his pockets his Gar- ter, a watch and about fixty guineas. He was no fooner taken, than he fainted away, and it was fome time before he recovered.

The fear of death had feized him to fuch a degree, that he tried all poffible means of ob- taining the King's pardon. As foon as he was

appre-

1685. apprehended, he wrote to his Majesty a letter, wherein he expressed his grief and sorrow for the rebellion he had raised, and transferred his guilt upon those persons whom, he said, it had been his misfortune to know, and who had engaged him to take arms against his Majesty, contrary to his own inclination: he earnestly intreated the King to grant him the favour of speaking with him, alledging that he had matters of importance to discover to him.

The Duke of *Monmouth* and Lord *Grey* being brought to *London*, on the thirteenth of the same month they were interrogated in the council, and afterwards sent to the Tower, where the Duchess of *Monmouth*, the Duke's wife, was already imprisoned with her children. The Duke earnestly intreating that he might be admitted to speak with the King, it was granted to him at the request of the Queen Dowager.

As soon as he appeared before the King, being dressed in a velvet cloak, with his hands tied, he threw himself at his feet, confessed his crime in the most moving terms, conjured him with tears in his eyes to save him from the punishment he deserved; alledging that if the King put him to death, he would shed his own blood; and had even the weakness to beg the King to change his punishment of death into a perpetual imprisonment.

King *James,* who knew how necessary it was in the beginning of his reign to punish such rebellions by a severity contrary to his own inclination,

tion, would not suffer himself to be moved by 1685. this great submission. He told the Duke that he wished he could pardon him, but that his crime was of too great consequence to pass unpunished. Next day he signed the sentence of his death. On the fifth of *July* the Duke of *Monmouth* was degraded from the Order of the Garter, and on the fifteenth he was beheaded on *Tower-hill.*

The Earl of *Argyle* was not more successful in *Scotland.* He at first gathered together some troops; but they were quickly dispersed by the King's forces, which pursued that Earl into all the places whither he fled. A peasant and two servants wounded him, and took him in a water which he had entered for shelter. He discovered himself by crying out, *O unfortunate Argyle!* On the twenty first of *June* he was brought to *Edinburgh,* where he was beheaded on the thirtieth of the same month.

King *James* having extinguished a rebellion which had at first appeared dangerous, thought himself now above all fear, and that from henceforth, none of his subjects being powerful enough to oppose or withstand him, he had a favourable opportunity of effecting the design he had formed of rendering himself more absolute than the Kings his predecessors, of lessening the great power of the Parliament, and protecting the Catholick Religion.

He had used all his endeavours to make a strict union between himself and the King of *France :* it was even believed that King *James* made no

step

1685. ſtep in that affair, without acquainting that King with it, and that there was a ſecret treaty between theſe two Princes, whereby they had engaged to aſſiſt each other againſt their enemies, and to aboliſh the Proteſtant Religion in their reſpective kingdoms. What made this credible was, that the King of *France* had no ſooner ſeen King *James* well eſtabliſhed on the *Britiſh* throne, than he gave the laſt blow to his Proteſtant ſubjects, whoſe ruin he had till then endeavoured to compaſs only by indirect means.

For at that time his Moſt Chriſtian Majeſty revoked the edict of *Nantes*, made in the year 1598, and that of *Niſmes*, made in 1629, which the difficulties of thoſe times had engaged *Henry* IV. and *Lewis* XIII. to grant the *Calviniſts*. In like manner he revoked the other declarations made in favour of the Proteſtant Religion; which was the ſole and moſt expeditious way of extinguiſhing that hereſy in *France*.

1686.   King *James*, on the other ſide, was obliged by the laws of *England* to diſband his army, after the rebellion of the Duke of *Monmouth* had been ſuppreſſed. Notwithſtanding this, under pretence of providing for the ſecurity of the nation, both againſt the enterpriſes of foreigners, and inteſtine troubles, he not only continued the troops which were then on foot, but alſo made new levies, in order to maintain his authority, and effect the deſign he had propoſed.

For this purpoſe he called a parliament, whom he perſuaded into what he deſired. And now

thinking

thinking himfelf in a condition gradually to in-
fringe the privileges of the nation, he placed his
Catholick fubjects in all the chief employments he
could decently beftow on them. This, as will
appear in the fequel of thefe Memoirs, brought
about the great revolution which happened in
thefe kingdoms.

In the mean time, the Duke of *Monmouth*'s
rebellion being extinguifhed, and King *James* in
the peaceable poffeffion of his kingdoms, the
Duke of *Berwick* found no opportunities in *England* of gratifying his prevailing paffion for arms,
and therefore fought to fatisfy it elfewhere. At
this time *France* enjoyed a peace, but the Emperor was at war with the *Turks* in *Hungary*; and
it was thither the Duke of *Berwick* refolved to
go, with fo much more reafon, as he efteemed
it an act of religion to fight againft the enemies
of chriftianity. Accordingly he afked leave of
King *James* to go to the imperial army, which
his Majefty granted with great reluctance.

In the beginning of the year 1686 the Duke
of *Berwick* fet out for *Germany*. Being arrived
at *Vienna* he went to the houfe of the *Englifh*
ambaffador, to whom the King had fent notice
of the Duke's defign, and had recommended him.
Two days after his arrival, he was introduced to
the Emperor, who received him gracioufly, and
with marks of diftinction. He faid to the Duke,
that the defire of acquiring glory was commen-
dable in every man, but much more in one of
his age, and that by his prudent and wife deportment

1686. portment he could hardly believe he was so young as he pretended to be. Afterwards his Imperial Majesty talked with him concerning the Duke of *Monmouth*'s rebellion in *England*, and made him relate all the particulars of that war, and of the death of that unfortunate man.

The Emperor was so well pleased with the Duke of *Berwick*'s conversation, that in the evening he expressed his satisfaction to the whole court, saying, *We have got a new volunteer, the King of* England's *natural son; but his prudence and sentiments distinguish him more than his birth, and, in time, he will probably distinguish himself by his exploits.*

Whilst the Duke of *Berwick* staid at *Vienna*, there happened an affair to him, which, however inconsiderable, I relate because it is an instance of his great devotion and attention in prayer. He had been visiting Count *Stratman*, the Emperor's minister, who sent a gentleman next day to invite him to dinner. This gentleman went to the *English* ambassador's, where the Duke lodged; and not finding him there, he was informed that the Duke was at the church of the *Capuchine* Friars, where he went every morning to offer up his devotion. The gentleman went thither, and accordingly found the Duke of *Berwick* prostrate at the altar, and in so deep a meditation, that he mistook him for a candidate who desired to be admitted among the *Capuchines*; and this gave Count *Stratman* an occasion of rallying the Duke of *Berwick*:

It

It was thought at *Vienna* that the Duke of 1686.
Lorrain would command this year in *Hungary*, ⌇
as he had done the year preceeding. People
were much furprized when they knew that the
Elector of *Bavaria* was to have that command.
Some would have it that the Duke of *Lorrain*'s
health would not fuffer him to continue in that
poft; others pretended, that the Emperor was
difpleafed with him. But the true reafon of his
being fet afide was this: The court of *Vienna*
being informed that the Elector of *Bavaria* was
ftrongly follicited by the Marquis of *Villars* to
come into a ftrict union with the King of *France*,
the Emperor was willing to make him amends
for certain grievances he had complained of, and
attach him the more to his intereft, by beftow-
ing on him that honourable poft. The Duke
of *Lorrain*, who was wholly devoted to the Emperor, willingly yielded to that political reafon;
but afterwards, when the campaign was opened
in *Hungary*, he went into that kingdom, though
without going to the army, that he might give
no umbrage to the Elector of *Bavaria*, being
content to watch the operations of the campaign.
However, this became afterwards a new reafon
for the Elector of *Bavaria*'s complaints againft
the Emperor.

As foon as his Electoral Highnefs was informed
that the Emperor had appointed him General of
his army, he fet out for *Vienna*. Upon his arrival,
the Duke of *Berwick* went to vifit him, as did
alfo the great number of volunteers who waited

for

1686. for the opening of the campaign, among whom
were many young *French* noblemen. The Elector ſtayed but a ſhort time at *Vienna*, and ſet
out to take upon him the command of the army, being attended with all thoſe volunteers,
who made his court very ſhining. While theſe
young men, during the journey, gave a looſe to
the gaiety of their youth, the Duke of *Berwick*,
by his ſedate and mild behaviour, appeared a-
mong them like their *Mentor*; and the Elector
of *Bavaria* was ſo greatly ſurprized to obſerve
in the Duke, at the age of fifteen years, ſo much
diſcretion and wiſdom, that he took particular
notice of him, and gave him ſeveral proofs of his
favour and kindneſs.

Being arrived at the army, the Elector reviewed it, and immediately took the field. He began with inveſting *Buda*, a city where the
Turks kept all their warlike ſtores. The beginning of this ſiege was not ſucceſsful; the Elector,
according to the advice of the engineers, having
attacked *Buda* on its ſtrongeſt ſide, and neglected
the weakeſt, by which it received ſuccours from
the *Ottoman* army. After he had made a ſufficient breach in the walls of the town, he gave the
aſſault; but the Imperial troops were ſo vigo-
rouſly repulſed, that he was forced to raiſe the
ſiege.

This diſadvantage did not diſcourage the Elector of *Bavaria*; for ſome days after he began
a-freſh to carry on the ſiege on another quarter.
He went to it himſelf, in order to animate the

troops

troops by his prefence, and pufh the attacks 1686.
with more vigour and fuccefs.   In thefe attacks
he fucceeded; for *Buda* was now fo clofely invefted, that it could take in no more fuccours,
and was therefore forced to furrender.

In this fiege, which was the firft the Duke
of *Berwick* had feen, he might be faid to have
been every where, in order to inftruct himfelf
in the leaft operations.   The Elector of *Bavaria*
obferving how much he expofed himfelf to dangers, defired him one day not to hazard his life
fo much as he did, and intreated the Duke not
to bring upon him any reproaches from the King
of *England*, and to be more affiduous about his
perfon.

After the taking of *Buda* the Elector advanced
with his army, in order to find an opportunity
of giving battle to the *Turks*, and, by gaining a
victory over them, to facilitate the fiege of *Belgrade*, with which he defign'd to put an end to
to the campaign.   Two miles from *Buda*, he
met the *Turkifh* army, which, at his approach,
drew up in *Battalia*.   The Imperial army did
the fame, and without much difficulty engaged
them to fight.   The battle was obftinate and
bloody on both fides.   The Duke of *Berwick*,
who behaved with great valour, was wounded
by a *Bacha*, whom he afterwards made a prifoner.   The fuccefs was doubtful for fome time,
but declared at laft for the Imperialifts, who
gained over the *Turks* a compleat victory.   However the Imperial troops were fo greatly fatigued

1686. by the siege of *Buda* and this engagement, that it was impossible for the Elector to push his conquests farther at that time; he was therefore obliged to defer till the following year the siege of *Belgrade*, which put an end to this war against the *Turks*.

Though the Duke of *Berwick*'s wound was not dangerous, it was nevertheless very painful. When the Campaign was ended, he was brought to *Vienna*, where the Emperor sent some of his court to visit him, and recommended him to the care of his first surgeon.

1687. As soon as his wound was cured, he waited upon the Emperor to thank him for the proofs he had received of his favour; and his Imperial Majesty spoke to the Duke in so gracious and obliging a manner, as manifested that he was highly pleased with his behaviour in the army, and had a particular esteem for him.

While he was preparing for the next campaign against the *Turks*, and hoped to be present at the siege of *Belgrade*, which was publickly talked of at the Court of *Vienna*, he received a letter from the King his father, wherein his Majesty acquainted him that his presence was now become necessary in *England*, and ordered him to come home.

Being now obliged to think of nothing but returning to *England*, he went to see the Emperor, who was much surprised to know his design of departing so suddenly; but being informed that it was by King *James*'s command, he pre-

sented

fented the Duke with his picture fet with dia- 1687.
monds, and faid, *You do well to obey the King*
your father ; but fince I cannot keep you here, ac-
cept of this picture, which I prefent you with as a
token of my particular efteem for you.

Being arrived at *London*, he found King *James*
in the greateft perplexity. *Lewis* XIV, King
of *France*, had acquainted him that he had been
informed by Count *D'Avaux*, his Embaffador at
the *Hague*, that the Prince of *Orange* was me-
ditating fome great defign againft him in *Eng-*
land, and that notwithftanding all the enquiries
he made into that affair, it was conducted with
fo much fecrecy, that he could not make any
difcovery : which was the more uneafy to him,
as it was by this means out of his power to prevent the defign.

The year which we are now entering difclofed 1688.
the whole myftery. The project of the Prince
of *Orange* appeared, and brought about fo great
a Revolution in *England*, that we hope the reader will be well pleafed to find here an account
of the motives and circumftances of that great
event. For this purpofe we fhall begin a little
higher.

The *Englifh* obferving with great difcontent
that King *James*, prompted by his religion, had
invaded their privileges, and fearing left he fhould
by degrees deprive them of their boafted liberty, began to enter into fecret correfpondences
with *William*, Prince of *Orange* : Whereupon
this Prince, having brought the *Dutch* into their

C 2

interefts,

1688. intereſts, and knowing that he would certainly be ſupported by the Princes of the *Augſburg* league, formed that great deſign wherein he had ſo extraordinary ſucceſs.   In order to. oppoſe it, King *James* brought together great forces both by ſea and land; while the King of *France*, who ſeconded him in his deſign of rendering the Parliament leſs abſolute, and of re-eſtabliſhing the Catholick Religion in *England*, equipped a great fleet, under pretence of chaſtiſing the *Algerines*, who took many *French* ſhips in all the ſeas.

In the beginning of theſe troubles the Queen of *England* was delivered of the Prince of *Wales*. It is well known what rumours the partiſans of the Prince of *Orange* ſet about concerning this birth, as if the child had been ſuppoſititious: they gave out that the King was of too weak a conſtitution, and too unhealthy to have any children.   But this was diſproved by the birth of a Princeſs, of whom the Queen of *England* was afterwards delivered in *France*.

In the mean time the new-born Prince alarmed a great part of *England*, and gave the Prince of *Orange* an opportunity of augmenting his party. As ſoon as he was in a condition to diſcover his deſign, and put it in execution, he embarked at *Helvoet-ſluis* with Marſhal *Schomberg*, who had left *France* on account of religion.

His fleet conſiſted of about fifty men of war, twenty-five frigates, as many fire-ſhips, and about five hundred tranſports, and carried fifteen thouſand diſciplined troops, ſeveral volunteers

and

and about three hundred *French* officers, who 1688.
had left *France* for their religion, together with
the neceſſary horſes, artillery and ammunition.

On the nineteenth of *October* he put to ſea,
and about three or four hours after there aroſe a
violent ſtorm which ſcattered the ſhips, and
obliged them to put in where they could.   They
were all driven to the place from whence they
had ſet ſail, excepting a few which were driven
as far as *Norway*, from whence they returned
ſome time after into the *Dutch* harbours; and
only one frigate was loſt.

On the firſt of *November* the Prince of *Orange*
having now repaired the damages which his fleet
had ſuffered in the ſtorm, and having a favourable wind, again ſet ſail for *England*.   King
James believing this fleet would ſail to the north
of *England*, had ſent a great body of his troops
into thoſe parts: but on the fifth of *November*
the Prince of *Orange* arrived at *Torbay* in *Devon-
ſhire*, where he landed his army without oppoſition.   Lord *Dartmouth*, who commanded the
Engliſh fleet, could not engage that of the *Dutch*
by reaſon of the contrary wind; beſides, few of
his captains would conſent to it.

As ſoon as the Prince of *Orange* landed, he
publiſhed his declaration, wherein he ſet forth
the deſign for which he entered *England* with an
army, namely, to call a free Parliament, and to
preſerve the religion and liberties of the nation.

On the eighth of *November* he arrived at *Exe-
ter*, where he refreſhed his troops; from thence

he

1688. he difperfed feveral copies of his declaration, and took care to fpread them over the whole kingdom. Many people of all ranks came into his army, and whole counties joined with him in demanding a free Parliament. Some of King *James*'s regiments went over to him; *George*, Prince of *Denmark,* who was to command the King's army, joined him; and the Princefs *Anne*, his wife, King *James*'s daughter, retired f.om court. All this could not induce the King to depart from his defign of giving battle to the Prince of *Orange*. Accordingly he fet out from *London* to *Salifbury* to take upon him the command of his army; but the weak condition in which he found it broke all his meafures, and obliged him to return, and think of calling a Parliament. Mean while the Prince of *Orange* continued his march towards *London*, and on the nineteenth of *November* his army arrived at *Salifbury*.

What greatly afflicted King *James* was, that Lord *Churchil*, who had been indebted to him both for his elevation and fortune, to which of himfelf he could never have pretended, was among the firft who abandoned him, and went over to the Prince of *Orange*. Lord *Churchil* did more; for not content to be guilty of that infidelity and ingratitude, he fomented a revolt among feveral noblemen who were attached to the King's intereft, and even endeavoured to feduce the Duke of *Berwick* his nephew. The latter was always near his Majefty, and watched

over

over his perfon with all that zeal, love and affi-
duity which became a dutiful fon and faithful
fubject. *Churchil* not finding any opportunity
of fpeaking with him, thought fit to write a
letter to him, and demand a conference, wherein he hoped to withdraw him from the King's
party. The Duke of *Berwick*, who would hold
no correfpondence with his uncle after he knew
his infidelity, received that letter with a real in-
dignation, and without reading or opening it, he
went and delivered it to the King, who, upon
perufing it, could not help melting into tendernefs at this proof of the Duke's fidelity, and being highly offended at Lord *Churchil's* conduct.

King *James* feeing himfelf abandoned by moft
of the nobles of his kingdom, and the greateft
part of his troops, and judging from thence that
there was no longer any fecurity for his perfon,
or for the Queen and Prince of *Wales*, began
now to confult how he might convey them to
France, being refolved to follow them himfelf
foon after; yet not doubting but that there
were many fpies about him, he gave, as ufual,
the neceffary orders both for his land and fea-
forces, and all the general affairs of the kingdom.

In the mean time, being obliged by the pe-
tition which was prefented to him by the chief
of the clergy and nobility, to fend a deputation
to the Prince of *Orange*, in order to know the
defign of his coming into the kingdom; he received for anfwer, that it was for the fecurity of
the Proteftant Religion, and to hinder him from
C 4

invading

1688. invading the liberties of the people, at the insti-
gation of the enemies of his crown; that to put
a speedy end to these disorders, it was necessary
to call a free Parliament, wherein both the religious and civil liberties of the kingdom might be
secured; that as this was the sole design of his
coming into *England,* he was willing not to advance nearer *London* with his army than thirty
miles, provided the King would remove to the
same distance; but that if his Majesty persisted
in staying in *London* he would likewise be there
with an equal number of guards.

The populace, which had before committed
a great many disorders, even at a time when the
whole nation appeared to be attached to the
King, became as it were furious at the sight
of this change: they pulled down houses under
pretence that they belonged to Papists, and de-
molished all the Catholick Chapels, which had
yet escaped their rage. King *James* being informed of these tumults, sent for the mayor and
aldermen, and commanded them to suppress them;
but they answered that the rioters were so numerous, that it was dangerous to attempt it, and
besides, that the rest of the city, not being well-
affected, would perhaps make use of such a
pretext to shew their ill will. Having dismissed
them, he gave notice to the Constable of the
Tower, that it was time to intimidate the city
by firing some cannon. But when he was going
to put these orders in execution, the garrison re-
belled,

belled, and threatned to kill him, if he obeyed 1688. them.

Being now fully determined to retire into *France*, King *James* ordered Count *Lauzun*, who was about his perfon, to make the neceffary preparations for the departure of the Queen and the Prince, whom he intended to fend away before him. He went to bed that night, (being the ninth of *December*) at the ufual time, without letting the Queen know his intention; two hours after, Count *Lauzun* came in and acquainted his Majefty that all things were now prepared for the Queen's departure. Whereupon he arofe, and went to awaken the Queen. As foon as he acquainted her with his defign, fhe fell at his feet, and, with tears in her eyes, begged he would allow her to partake of the danger which threatned him. But he made her fenfible that it could not be done, and people were fent to awaken the young Prince's two Nurfes. The Infant being brought into the Queen's chamber, the King embraced him, and with the greateft expreffions of love and tendernefs, charged Count *Lauzun* to be moft careful of fo precious a truft.

By this time it was between three and four o'clock in the morning, when the Queen of *England*, with the Prince of *Wales*, and a few attendants ftole by the privy-ftairs to the waterfide, croffed the *Thames* in a dark ftormy night, and being got to the other fide, waited under a wall till the coaches were made ready

in

1688. in the next inn. The Queen and her retinue having taken coach, were attended by a ſtrong guard to *Greenwich*, and from thence to *Grave-ſend*, where ſhe embarked in a yacht, which lay ready to carry Count *Lauzun* to *France :* ſhe had a very quick and ſafe paſſage, having landed next day at *Calais* about four o'clock in the afternoon.

The whole *French* coaſt was informed of her coming ; for Count *Lauzun*, whom King *James* had commanded to make the neceſſary preparations for her departure, had ſent a bark to *Calais*, to give notice of it. The garriſon of that town was under arms, and the cannon pointed ; there were alſo ſome brigantines at ſea to favour the Queen's arrival. The Duke of *Charoſt*, Governor of *Calais* went to receive her Majeſty and the Prince of *Wales* at the yacht, and conducted them to the town under the diſcharge of the cannon.

The King of *France* having notice of her landing, ſent the Marquis of *Beringhen*, the ſon, with his coaches, to bring her to St. *Germains :* but ſhe intreated his Moſt Chriſtian Majeſty, in a moving letter which ſhe wrote to him on her misfortune, to permit her to ſtay at *Boulogne*, that ſhe might be nearer King *James*.

Mean while, the Queen and the Prince of *Wales* not appearing in *London*, there aroſe a general murmur and diſcontent, and ſome Lords met on that account. King *James* having notice that the Queen was ſafely embarked, and
that

that difaffectednefs and tumults were daily in- 1688.
creafing among his fubjects, made all poffible
hafte to follow her: accordingly on the eleventh
of *December*, about two o'clock in the morning,
his Majefty went in difguife to *Feverfham*.
There he met with a new misfortune, being
feized and rifled by the populace, who took him
for a Prieft, and Chaplain to one of his attendants; for which reafon he fuffered many grofs
indignities. At laft, among others who croud-
ed about the King, there came one who knew
his face, and prefently fell at his feet, begging
his Majefty to pardon the rudenefs of the mob,
and bidding the Fellows return the jewels and
gold which they had taken from him. But
the King would only receive the jewels, and
fuffered the populace to fhare among them the
gold, being about four hundred guineas. From
thence he was conducted to *Rochefter*, where
he was guarded till word came from the Prince
of *Orange*.

In the mean time the lords, who were at
London, having made themfelves certain of the
King's flight, had deputed to the Prince of
Orange the Earl of *Pembroke*, and fome other
Peers, to demand his protection in favour of the
Church of *England*, and in fupport of their pri-
vileges.

Being afterwards informed that the King was
at *Rochefter*, they fent a deputation to him, inviting his Majefty to return to his capital. The
Prince of *Orange* was by this time advanced to
Windfor,

1688. *Windsor*, and having notice of this proceeding of the Lords, which he greatly disliked, he sent a messenger to the King to desire him to continue at *Rochester*. But the messenger coming too late, the King returned to his palace, and was received in *London* with great demonstrations of joy. No sooner had the Prince of *Orange* notice of this, but he sent another message to the King, desiring him to remove from *London*. This message did not arrive till midnight, and was delivered to King *James* when he was a-bed; and now reflecting that his subjects were disaffected, that his army had deserted him, and that he was forsaken even by his favourites, and his own children, all except the Duke of *Berwick* and one more, he at last resolved to comply with this message, and accordingly he went back to *Rochester*: there he continued till the twenty third of *December*, when about two o'clock in the morning, taking only with him the Duke of *Berwick*, one Mr. *Selden* and Mr. *Labadie*, a *Frenchman*, he went towards the river, and having immediately put to sea with a favourable wind, he soon landed at *Ambleteuse*. A servant whom the Duke had dispatched to *Boulogne*, and who was already arrived there with some *English* gentlemen, had given notice that King *James* was landed: whereupon the Duke of *Aumont*, Governor of the *Boulonnois*, made all the necessary preparations for his reception; and the Marquis *Beringhen* immediately set out to meet him with the King of *France*'s coaches,

the

the officers belonging to his table, and the ftew- 1688.
ard of his houfhold to ferve him upon the road :
his Moft Chriftian Majefty fent Count *Armag-
nac,* mafter of the horfe, to compliment him,
and afterwards went himfelf to meet him, being accompanied by the Dauphin, the Duke of
Orleans, and all the other Princes of the blood,
as he had formerly met the Queen ; and he conducted King *James* to *St. Germains,* where the
Queen with the Prince of *Wales* had arrived fome
days before.

During this time the Prince of *Orange,* who
had favoured the King's flight, that he might
the better effect his defigns, call'd a Parliament,
which declared him King of *England.*

This revolution will appear to future ages the
more aftonifhing, as we have no inftance of a
Prince in the lawful and peaceable poffeffion of
his kingdoms, forced to abandon them, without
any refiftance made in his favour by any of his
fubjects, or officers who had taken an oath of
allegiance and fidelity to him. This fhews how
dangerous it is to make any attempt upon the
religion and privileges of a nation fo fickle and
inconftant as the *Englifh,* even though their religion is heretical, and their privileges are ufurped.

The King of *France* being no longer able to
conceal his refentment againft the *Dutch,* who
had been the abettors of this revolution, and had
furnifhed the Prince of *Orange* with an army
and a fleet to effect it, refolved to keep no meafures

1688. fures with them, judging that both his glory and the intereft of *France* required it. Accordingly on the fixteenth of *November* he declared war againft the *Dutch*.

1689. *Ireland* having continued in its allegiance to its lawful fovereign, King *James* refolved to pafs into that kingdom, and the King of *France* furnifhed him with fhips and troops to accompany him. He accordingly embark'd at *Breft* in the beginning of *March* 1689, being attended by the Duke of *Berwick*, who was always near him. Having landed in *Ireland*, he found more than fixty thoufand men, who offered him their fervice, and relying upon whofe fidelity, he refolved to preferve at leaft one of his kingdoms.

About this time *Lewis* XIV endeavoured to prevail with the King of *Spain* to take arms in favour of his *Britifh* Majefty, and join in reftoring him to his kingdoms, or at leaft to keep an exact neutrality: but being informed that the Catholick King had entered into the *Augfburg* league, and was already making warlike preparations againft *France*, he refolved to be beforehand with him, and accordingly declared war on *Spain*.

Befides, *Lewis* having much at heart the reftoration of the King of *England*, and judging that the troops and fhips which he had fent with him to *Ireland* might not be fufficient to maintain him in that kingdom, refolved to fend over new fupplies of both. Thefe fhips, to the number of twenty four, *viz.* fifteen third rates, and

nine

nine fourth rates, with two frigats, and two fire- 1689.
ships, sailed in a hazy weather from *Breft* on the
sixth of *May*, N. S. carrying the troops designed for King *James*'s army in *Ireland.* On the
ninth of *May*, N. S. they came within sight of
land, between *Kinsale* and *Cape Clear.*

This fleet was commanded by Count *Chateau-
renault*, who ordered three ships which came up
to him to be pursued, and learned that they belonged to the van-guard of the *English* fleet,
which had been fifteen days on the coast of *Ireland.*

On the same day our fleet arrived over against
Rofs, and the people who came aboard informed
us that some hours before they had discovered a
fleet of twenty five sail. About five leagues from
the harbour one of our frigats and a fire-ship
took a small *Oftend* bark. Admiral *Herbert*,
who commanded the *English* fleet, had forced
this bark to keep to sea, and had placed some
English in it under a *Spanish* flag, to observe our
fleet; for he did not yet know that war had
been declared between *France* and *Spain.* By
this bark we learned that four ships which were
seen cruizing about *Kinsale* had separated from
the *English* fleet (consisting of twenty eight or
thirty sail) with a design to hinder the landing
of our men in *Ireland.* Three of these ships,
which were on guard, were sent off in the morning, and came within three leagues of our fleet
to reconnoitre us, but they retired before we
could come up with them.

Count

1689.   Count *Chateau-renault* having sent a sloop to
land, she was received with great joy by the inhabitants of the place where she arrived; and an *Irish* Colonel immediately came aboard of her, to acquaint our Admiral that the three ships, which had been seen, were the van-guard of the enemy's fleet.

Toward the evening we discovered a flute with an *English* flag. One of our ships pursued this flute for some time, but not thinking it proper to go farther, she returned: upon which the flute returned likewise, drew nearer, was brought upon the stay, and after observing our fleet for a considerable time, she run towards *Kinsale*.

At the same time Count *Chateau-renault* received advice from land, that the enemy had anchored between *Cork* and *Kinsale*. Our fleet was now ten leagues off to the leeward of this last place. A council of war being held, it was resolved to sail to *Bantry-Bay*, and there to land the troops designed for King *James's* services. Pursuant to this resolution we anchored on the tenth of *May*, *N.S.* at two o'clock in the afternoon, five leagues off from *Bantry*.

Count *Chateau-renault*, who did not doubt but that the enemy would come up and attack him while the fleet was employed in landing our men, stationed two ships at the mouth of the bay as a guard, and foreseeing that he might be shut in, he resolved not to enter it.

Immediately after he embarked in six fireships and four frigates, or merchant-ships, which
had

had followed the fleet from *Breſt*, the arms, ſad- 1689.
dles, bridles, powder, ball and money which
belonged to King *James*'s troops, and would
have embarraſſed him in an engagement.

Though the wind was contrary, yet theſe fire-
ſhips, being favoured by the tide, ſailed on the
ſame evening, and were conducted to *Bralegab-
benne*, in the bottom of the bay, ſeven leagues
from the place where our fleet had anchored.

About nine of the clock in the evening, whilſt
they were preparing to ſail, we heard the report
of the guns of the two ſhips on guard. This
was the ſignal agreed on to give notice that the
Engliſh fleet appeared. Theſe two ſhips having
rejoined our fleet, brought an account that they
had reckoned twenty five ſail of the enemy.

As we had been only five hours employed in
the debarkment, Count *Chateau-Renault* did not
think proper to continue it, but landed at the
neareſt ground the reſt of the troops which could
not be embarked in the ſhips of burthen, and
now put his whole fleet in readineſs to engage.

Next day, being the eleventh of *May, N.S.*
about five or ſix in the morning, one of our
ſhips, which had been on guard, gave a ſignal
that the enemy was in ſight. Soon after the
Engliſh fleet appeared off *Miſſenhead*. We began
to ſee them on the eaſt point, and reckoned
twenty eight ſail, among which we obſerved
twenty one great ſhips, four of which were
larger than any in our fleet, one frigat, and
ſeven ſaicks, that were taken for fire-ſhips.

D

All

 All our men were not yet landed, and there was reason to fear that, if any of the *English* frigats could get a passage into the bay, they might take the two ships which were laden for *Brallegabbenne*, and had already sailed to that place. To prevent this, Count *Chateau-Renault* lay with the fleet at the mouth of the bay till half an hour after eleven, and then gave the signal to call in the van-guard.

At last our fleet came to an engagement with the *English*. The fight was very sharp and obstinate. But the detail of it being foreign to our subject, we shall only say that the *French* fleet gained over the *English* a compleat victory, having obliged them to retire towards *Kinsale* in great disorder, and very much disabled.

On the fourteenth of *May*, N. S. our fleet put to sea, and steered to *Kinsale* in quest of the *English*, but could discover none of their ships. On the fifteenth, sailing along the coast of *Kinsale*, they perceived four ships and one galliot, which were hastening to land. On the sixteenth, early in the morning, being at the point of the isle of *Ushant*, they discovered a fleet of seven *Dutch* ships which came from the island of *Curassow* in *South America*. Whereupon Count *Chateau-Renault* sent some ships, which seized them. On the eighteenth, at break of day, our fleet arrived at *Brest* with this capture. This voyage lasted only twelve days; during which time they landed in *Ireland* as many men and warlike stores as they possibly could; they

beat

beat the *English* fleet, and made the capture 1689.
abovementioned. Our fleet confisted of two
ships more than the *English*, but the ships of the
latter were much larger.

The fuccours which the King of *France* fent
to King *James* fufficiently declared how much
he had at heart the reftoration of that Prince;
but as he had not yet an opportunity of entering into a war with the *English*, he did not
difcover his fentiments till the twenty third of
June, N.S. when a manifefto was publifhed,
declaring that his Moft Chriftian Majefty would
have long before proclaimed war againft the
Prince of *Orange*, who had ufurped the Crown
of *England*, had he not been afraid left he fhould
confound King *James's* faithful fubjects with
the partizans of that Prince; the King having
always hoped that thofe perfons who were well
affected to his *British* Majefty, would preferve
an averfion and horror at the unjuft and tyranni-
cal proceeding of the Prince of *Orange*, and returning to their allegiance and duty, would for-
fake his party, and fupport the interefts of their
lawful Sovereign: but being informed that the
Prince of *Orange* had prevented him, and declared war againft *France*, his Majefty ordered
all his fubjects to treat as enemies not only the
Dutch, but alfo the *English* who were rebels to
King *James*.

Let us now return to *Ireland*. King *James*,
upon his arrival in that kingdom, had formed an
army of thirty thoufand men; but they were

bad

1689. bad troops, ill paid, and undisciplined. Nevertheless, being joined by the *French* succours, he
marched this army very far into the country, and
seized all he met with in his way. The Protestants retiring to *Londonderry*, he followed them,
took fort *Culmore*, and expected to make himself
master of *Londonderry* by means of Colonel *Lundee*, the Governor of that place, who lying under several obligations to the Duke of *Berwick*,
had promised to deliver it to him.

The conspiracy being discovered, the Protestants sent *Lundee* to *Scotland*, and chose in his
room a clergyman named *Walker*, who being a
man of courage, and having some skill in the
art of war, answered the hopes they had conceived of him : for King *James*, who had invest-
ted *Londonderry* on the twentieth of *April*, was
at length forced to raise the siege of that Place : a
siege which he had undertaken contrary to the
advice of the Duke of *Berwick*, who represented
to him that since his correspondence with *Lundee* was discovered, it would be hazarding too
much to attack a well fortified and garrisoned
town with troops which were fatigued and undisciplined.

In effect, the new Governor made such good
regulations, and both by his discourse and example inspired the besieged with so much courage
and resolution, that they made very frequent
sallies, which greatly annoyed King *James*'s army,
and the place held out after it was reduced to
great extremities.

The

The Duke of *Berwick* was continually in the 1689.
midſt of the greateſt dangers, and endeavoured
to animate the King's troops, and inſpire them
with bravery and courage. Though he ſaw that
his utmoſt efforts could not put a ſtop to the advantages of the beſieged, yet he hoped the army
might ſtill reduce that place, if he could hinder
any ſuccours from entering it. For this purpoſe,
as the beſieged could only be relieved from the
river, he lined both ſides of it with two thouſand muſqueteers, and contrived in the narrow
part of it where the ſhips which were to come
to their relief muſt paſs, a kind of Staccado, being a boom of timber joined by iron chains, and
ſtrengthened by a cable of twelve inches thick-
neſs twiſted round it.

During this ſiege King *James* went to *Dublin,*
whither he had called a Parliament, in order to
receive the neceſſary ſupplies for carrying on the
war: but the ſupplies which this Parliament
granted, were very inconſiderable, amounting
only to twenty thouſand pounds a month.

The ſiege of *Londonderry* had now been carried on for a conſiderable time, and the ſuccours
which Major General *Kirk* had brought from
England were now lying in the *Lough,* not far
from the town, but could not enter it by reaſon
of the Staccado; ſo that the beſieged began to
be in great want of proviſions, and were forced
to live for ſome weeks on horſe-fleſh, dogs, cats,
and the moſt loathſome things imaginable: they
would ſoon have been forced to ſurrender, as the

Duke

1689. Duke of *Berwick* expected, had not a party of
these succours, by an extraordinary success,
made their passage into the town: for some
ships laden with provisions had the good fortune
to break the Staccado, notwithstanding the great
iron chains, the strong cable, and the continual
firing from fort *Culmore*, and both sides of the
river.

The ships surmounted all these obstacles, and
suffered only a very inconsiderable loss: so that
on the last of *July* King *James*, despairing of
taking the place, raised the siege, after having
blown up fort *Culmore*, and lost a great number
of officers and soldiers in the frequent sallies made
by the besieged. It was computed that seven
thousand people died of famine and sickness in
Londonderry during this siege.

The day before the siege of *Londonderry* was
raised, King *James*'s troops received a check
from the garrison of *Inniskilling*. *Makarty* who
commanded a body of his forces, which the Duke
of *Berwick* would have commanded, if his Majesty had permitted it, was attacked by the Protestants of that garrison, to the number of twelve
hundred horse, and above fifteen hundred foot,
lost upon the spot two thousand men, and was
himself taken prisoner, with four hundred more.

These advantages, and the arrival of the Duke
of *Schomberg*, whom the Prince of *Orange* had
sent over with some troops to join the rebels,
greatly incouraged them, and put them in a condition to make head against the royal army.

The

The new supplies which the King of *France* 1689.
sent to King *James* consisted of eight thousand
men, commanded by Count *Lauzun*; which induced the Prince of *Orange* to go over to *Ireland*
himself, in order to reduce that kingdom.

In the month of *March* Colonel *Woolsley* gained
a considerable advantage over the *Irish* near *Bel-
turbat*, with a detachment of seven hundred
horse and three hundred foot.

On the twenty third of *May* the Duke of
Schomberg, whose army amounted to forty thousand men, took *Charlemont* by surprise, a place
which he had blocked up for some time, and
which was necessary for marching his army to
Dublin, as he intended.

On the same day Colonel *Woolsley* made himself master of the castle of *Balingargy*, one of
the strongest places in *Ireland*. This officer
formed a design to surprise King *James*'s troops
at *Dungannon*. The Duke of *Berwick* having
notice of it, went strait to their assistance.
Woolsley marched his men during the night; and
though he had been informed that the Duke of
Berwick was arrived at *Dungannon* with two
thousand men, who joined with the garrison,
made a considerable body, posted before the
town, yet he resolved to attack them. The fight
was very bloody, and lasted above an hour; after
which the *Irish* abandoned their post, notwithstanding the efforts of the Duke of *Berwick*, who
greatly distinguished himself on this occasion by
his valour and undaunted courage: he had a

horse

1689. horfe killed under him, and received a wound in his thigh.

Though this wound greatly indifpofed him for action, yet without thinking of having it dreffed, he mounted another horfe, rode after the *Irifh* who fled, reproached them with their cowardice, rallied them, and obliged them to make amends for their fault.

Thefe troops being recovered out of the panic which had feized them were afhamed of having abandoned that poft, and the Duke of *Berwick*, for whom they had a great efteem and veneration, and expreffed an earneft defire of returning to the charge. The Duke laid hold of that favourable opportunity, rallied and brought them back to the engagement; and finding *Woolfley's* troops employed in pillaging, he charged them fo brifkly, that he foon put them in diforder, recovered the poft, and killed the greateft number of the enemy, among whom the Colonel himfelf had much difficulty to efcape.

The Duke of *Berwick's* wound would not have been dangerous, had it been dreffed fooner; but the great fatigue he fuffered in this action, and the blood he had loft, weakened him to fuch a degree, that when he was taken off his horfe, he was fpeechlefs. No body was more concerned for him than King *James*, who every day either fent or came himfelf to fee him.

1690. In the beginning of the year 1690 Count *Lauzun*, who commanded under King *James* the *French* troops, took *Charlemont* and fome

other

other confiderable places, whereby he opened 1690.
the paffage to the *Boine*. On the feventh of
July, N. S. King *James*, accompanied by the
Duke of *Berwick*, who was now entirely cured
of his wound, march'd with his whole army to
Dundalk, and encamped on the ninth at *Atber-
dee*. On the tenth he advanced within cannon-
fhot of *Drogheda*, where he pofted his army a-
long the river.

The Prince of *Orange* fet out from *London* on
the fourteenth of *June*, N. S. being accompanied by Prince *George* of *Denmark*, the Duke
of *Ormond*, the Earl of *Oxford*, and feveral o-
ther perfons of diftinction. Having fent before
him the greateft number of his forces, he embarked on the twenty firft at *Highlake*. Two
days after he landed at *Carrick-fergus*, from
whence he went by land to *Belfaft*, where he
joined his army, commanded by Marfhal *Schomberg*, and immediately gave orders to pay them.

His army confifted of fixty two fquadrons of
horfe and dragoons, and of fifty two battalions
of foot, the whole amounting to about thirty fix
thoufand men. The van was commanded by
Lieutenant General *Dowglas*, the right wing by
Major General *Kirk*, the left wing by the Earl
of *Oxford* and Count *Solmes*, and the main body
by the Prince of *Orange*. On the feventh of
July all this army began to march towards *Dundalk*.

The Prince of *Orange*, having under him
Marfhal *Schomberg*, refolved to pafs the *Boine*
in

 in fight of King *James*'s army, relying upon the superior number of his forces. For this purpose he went himself to view the fords of that river. It was upon this occasion he was wounded by a cannon ball, which grazed upon his shoulder, but did not indispose him for action.

Next morning, being the eleventh of *July*, *N. S.* the Prince of *Orange* attempted to pass the *Boine*. Count *Maynard Schomberg* at the head of the horse, and Lieutenant General *Dowglas*, who commanded the foot of the enemy's right wing, began the action, and having got over, attacked and defeated eight squadrons of King *James*'s army. Soon after the rest of the enemy passed the *Boine* in several bodies. The horse on the right of the King's army made a very brave resistance, and forced the left wing of the enemy to give ground, and several of them to cross the river again. The *Irish* foot, commanded by the Duke of *Berwick*, bore the enemy's attacks for some time with great courage, but were at last broke, and fled in disorder. All the efforts the Duke of *Berwick* made to rally them proving unsuccessful, he went over to the horse, who maintained the fight for a considerable time: but being at last overpowered, and *Hamilton* their General being made a prisoner, they were also forced to give ground; and King *James*'s whole army was routed, and pursued till it was night.

The Duke of *Berwick*, who received a slight wound in this action, the Duke of *Tyrconnel*,

and

and Count *Lauzun*, discharged all the duties of 1690.
able Generals: but, excepting the troops sent
by the King of *France*, this army consisted only of the militia, and of men gathered together
from divers parts, and too little enured to war,
to bear the attacks of a compleat army of regular forces.

In this action Marshal *Schomberg* was killed
by King *James*'s Guards *; and as it was some
time before the Prince of *Orange* appeared, there
went a report that he was also slain.

After the loss of this battle King *James* retired to *Waterford*; and seeing it impossible for
him to maintain himself in *Ireland*, he resolved
to return to *France*, whither he went soon after with the Duke of *Berwick*.

The Prince of *Orange*, to improve this victory, took the proper measures to reduce the
whole kingdom of *Ireland*: for which purpose
he sent a detachment of his men to secure *Dub-*

---

* The Duke of *Schomberg* seeing the *French* Protestants in some
disorder, and left exposed without a Commander, after Mr. *La
Caillemote* was slain, passed the river in order to head them, and
could not be persuaded to take time to put on his armour.
Whilst he was encouraging them by this short harangue, *Allons,
Messieurs, voilà vos persecuteurs*; (*Come on, Gentlemen, behold
your persecutors*) pointing to the *French* Papists in the *Irish* army,
fifteen or sixteen of King *James*'s guards, who returned full
speed to their main body after the slaughter of their companions,
fell furiously upon the Duke, and gave him two wounds over
the head, which however were not mortal. Whereupon the regiment of *Chambon* firing rashly upon these guards, shot the Duke
through the Neck, of which wound he instantly died. Not long
before, Dr. *Walker*, so famous for the defence of *Londonderry*, received a wound in the belly, which he survived but some few
moments.

lin

1690. *lin*; he took *Waterford*, and afterwards invested *Limerick*, whither King *James*'s troops had
retired after this defeat, and his Majesty's withdrawing to *France*.

Boi*ffelat*, a Captain of the King of *France*'s
guards, who had been sent into *Ireland* as Major General of the army, was Commander in
this place, and defended it with great bravery
and resolution, though it was weak of itself, and
ill fortified, and besieged by the whole army of
the Prince of *Orange*. *Limerick* being open on
several quarters, bore many assaults; but Count
Sarsfield with a body of six hundred horse and
dragoons having taken and blown up the enemy's artillery, as it was upon the road from
Kilkenny to their camp before *Limerick*, the
Prince of *Orange* was forced to raise the siege of
that place, after having suffered a considerable
loss.

1691.   In the beginning of the year 1691 we were
informed that the Prince of *Orange*, after having
been forced to raise the siege of *Limerick*, had
left his army in *Ireland* under the command of
Lieutenant General *Dowglas*, and had sent thither Lord *Churchil*, now created Earl of *Marlborough*, with fresh troops, in order to compleat
the reduction of that kingdom; that he was
gone to *London*, and set out from thence to the
Hague, where he had made a very magnificent
entry on the fifth of *February*, *N. S.*

His design in this journey was to have a conference with all the Princes and Ministers of
                                          the

the allies againſt *France.* The Elector of *Bran-*
denburg was among the firſt who appeared at the
Hague : the Elector of *Bavaria* arrived there
on the ſixteenth of *February*, and was followed by the Marquis of *Caſtanaga*, Governor of
the *Spaniſh Netherlands*, the Landgrave of *Heſſe-
Caſſel*, and ſeveral other Princes, and perſons of
diſtinction.

This congreſs was ſo numerous, that there
were reckoned at the *Hague* above fifty either
Princes or Counts, Generals, and other Perſons
of quality, and more than thirty Embaſſadors,
beſides ſeveral ladies of diſtinction; which formed one of the moſt ſplendid courts that ever appeared.

In this interval the Duke of *Berwick* was at
King *James*'s court at *St. Germains*, where the
whole diſcourſe ran upon the congreſs at the
Hague, and the preparations the King of *France*
was making for the next campaign in *Flanders*,
whither he had determined to carry the main
ſtreſs of the war. This was very comfortable
news to the Duke of *Berwick*, who now reſolved to quit the inactive life he led at *St. Germains*,
and return to the field.

Accordingly he expreſſed to King *James* his
earneſt deſire of ſerving in the enſuing campaign.
The King approved of it, but told him at the
ſame time that as he might afterwards have occaſion for him, he would not have him attach
himſelf wholly to the *French* ſervice, nor accept
of any employment which he could not lay down
in

 in cafe it was neceffary to follow him into *Ire-land.*

The Duke having affured him that his intention was only to ferve as a volunteer, King *James* intreated his Moft Chriftian Majefty to be pleafed that the Duke of *Berwick* fhould ferve next campaign as a volunteer in his army in *Flanders.* *Lewis* XIV, who knew how great a reputation the Duke of *Berwick* had acquired both in *Hungary* and *Ireland,* anfwered that he would not only be glad to have him in his army, but would alfo beftow on him an employment fuitable to his merit, was he not afraid of doing an unkindnefs to his *Britifh* Majefty, knowing how necef-fary the Duke of *Berwick* was to his fervice.

A few days after, being prefented to the King of *France* to return his Majefty his thanks, the King faid to him, *I am obliged to the King of* England *for giving me fuch a volunteer as you, whofe courage will be an example to others, and whofe merit renders you worthy of the greateft employments.*

Having prepared his equipage for this campaign, the Duke fet out foon after for *Flanders,* and arrived at the army on the thirteenth of *March.*

Two Days after, the Marquis of *Boufflers,* who then had the command of the *French* army, invefted the city of *Mons.*

The defign of the King of *France* to lay fiege to *Mons* was not known till now it was invefted. Never was enterprife conducted with more fecrecy, though we had brought together about a
hun-

hundred thousand men, and the necessary pro- 1691.
visions for so great an army at a barren time of
the year, together with a great quantity of artillery and warlike stores.

What is surprising, all these great preparations
were made without the enemy's having notice of
it, or even suspecting the design upon *Mons.* The
Prince of *Orange* was the first who was deceived;
for by the continual motions which he observed
our troops were making, he imagined they were
going to raise contributions, or that they intended
to besiege *Charleroy,* or *Ostend.*

On the twenty first of *March* the King of
France arrived before *Mons,* being accompanied
by the *Dauphin,* the Duke of *Orleans,* and all
the Princes and Lords of his court; and next
day the trenches were opened. Marshal *Luxembourg* was appointed with his army to cover the
siege, and to hinder all succours from entering
the town. This was one of the most memorable sieges in the reign of *Lewis* XIV, but
without giving here the detail of it, we shall
only speak of those actions wherein the Duke of
Berwick had the greatest share.

On the first of *April,* about two of the clock
in the afternoon, the ditch of the hornwork being quite filled up, the Marquis of *Boufflers,* who
commanded that day, sent the Prince of *Turenne*
to acquaint the King that the bridge over the
ditch was ready, that we were lodged on the
Berm, and that if his Majesty pleased, the regiment of guards might attack the hornwork.
There

1691. There was reason to believe they would be able to carry it, the besieged having only made a slight resistance, when we were filling up the ditch. Mr. *de Vauban*, who had the direction of this siege, and had till now deferred this attack, to prevent the slaughter of the troops, having likewise believed they would be successful, had asked the King's permission to make an assault upon that outwork when he should think it proper; which his Majesty had granted.

The regiment of the *French* guards which was yet in the trenches, and was to be relieved by the *Swiss*, being informed that Mr. *Vauban* had obtained leave to attack the hornwork, pressed him to permit the attack to be made before they should be relieved; besides Marshal *Feuillade*, their Colonel, desired to have the honour of making it.

The attack being resolved upon, and appointed to be made at five of the clock in the evening, the two companies of the grenadeers of the *French* guards, commanded by Messieurs *Beauregard* and *Saillans*, and three other companies of the grenadeers of the King's regiment were ordered to begin it, and the troops which were in the trenches were to follow and support them.

As soon as the Duke of *Berwick*, who was continually in the trenches, had notice of this, he went to Mr. *Beauregard*, and asked leave to accompany him in the attack, alledging that as he was a volunteer in the army, and consequently fixed to no particular post, he would be exceeding

ceeding glad to be among the foremoft in the at- 1691.
tack of the horn-work, and a witnefs of the glory
which Mr. *Beauregard* was going to acquire in
that action. The latter anfwered that he would
efteem it an honour to be accompanied in that
enterprife by a man of his rank and merit,
whofe fkill and example would be of great af-
fiftance to him.

All things being in readinefs for this attack,
the Duke of *Berwick* advifed Mr. *Beauregard*
not to begin it till the grenadeers of the King's
regiment fhould arrive; neverthelefs Marfhal
Feuillade thought fit to begin it without waiting
for them, and Mr. *Vauban* himfelf told Meffieurs
Beauregard and *Saillans* what they were to do
when they fhould enter upon the horn-work.

Mr. *Beauregard* advanced firft with his men,
being accompanied by the Duke of *Berwick*;
and Mr. *Saillans* followed with his: the grenadeers mounted with great vigour and courage,
being following by the battalions: the befieged
fuftained the attack for about half an hour;
after which they abandoned the horn-work. As
foon as our men entered it, the pioneers began
the lodgement; but their number being infuffi-
cient, our grenadeers were expofed defencelefs,
and obliged to undergo a terrible firing from
all the works and ramparts of that place.

The Duke of *Berwick* was one of thofe who
expofed themfelves to the greateft dangers; his
hat and his coat were fhot through in feveral
places.

E The

1691.

The befieged perceiving the error we had committed, appeared on the gorge of the horn-work, the greateft part of them being armed with fcyths helved infide-out, fell fuddenly on the grenadeers of the guards, and obliged them to abandon the horn-work. This would not have happened, had Mr. *Beauregard* followed the Duke of *Berwick*'s advice, inftead of that of Marfhal *Feuillade*, and waited for the grenadeers of the King's regiment.

The King expreffed fome difpleafure at this, faying, he would fend troops upon that attack who fhould maintain their ground; and being informed of the Duke of *Berwick*'s advice, which had been rejeded, and how bravely he had expofed himfelf; *Had I known*, faid the King, *that the Duke of* Berwick *was defirous to be in that attack, I would have given him the command of it, and it would not have mifcarried; and though he went there only as a volunteer, yet his advice ought to have been of great weight, and fhould have been followed; for there are certain perfons of a diftinguifhed merit, whofe charaɛter fupplies the want of the greateft employment.*

Afterwards the King retired to his tent with Mr. *Vauban*, and made a new difpofition for the attack of that outwork: next morning he fent for Meffieurs *Maupertuis* and *Jauvelle*, who commanded the mufqueteers, and ordered them to draw out a detachment of 1500 of their men, who were to fupport two companies of the grenadeers of the King's regiment, two of the
Dauphin's

1691.

Dauphin's, two of the marines, two of the *Tou-louse*, and the *Swiss* who were in the trenches.

On the fame evening, being the firft of *April*, the mufqueteers received their orders, and affembled next morning at fix of the clock at the head of their camp: twelve men were taken from each detachment to make a forlorn-hope, which was commanded by *d'Alifart*, Quarter-mafter of the firft company.

The Duke of *Berwick*, who had been the evening before at that attack of the horn-work which had mifcarried, was defirous to be pre-fent alfo at this, being well affured by the mea-fures which were taken, that it would be as brifk as the former, and more fuccefsful. Ac-cordingly he came up to Mr. *Maupertuis*, who was at the head of the mufqueteers, and faid to him, *I hope, Sir, you will be pleafed that I ferve among your men.* Mr. *Maupertuis*, who knew after what manner the King had fpoken the day before concerning the Duke of *Berwick*, anfwer-ed, *I wifh, my Lord Duke, I could yield my com-mand to your Grace: I fhall at leaft account it an honour to follow your advice, which I fhall obey as my orders ;* and with mutual compliments and civilities they arrived with the troop at the trenches.

Some hours before the affault was made, our artillery made a terrible fire on the horn-work which was to be attacked, and on the works which defended it, while we threw a great many bombs on thofe places.

E 2

The

1691. The besieged having expected this attack, had taken all possible precautions, in order to make a vigorous defence. The Prince of *Bergues* had posted in the horn-work between three and four hundred men, who waited for us in battle order, most of them being armed with partisans and scyths helved inside-out.

The troops appointed for the assault being now in readiness, and the pioneers within call with all the instruments for making a lodgement on the horn-work, they began their march about ten of the clock in the morning, after the thirteenth bomb had been thrown, which was the signal agreed upon.

The enemy, fighting with their partisans and scyths, disputed the height of the breach for a long time with the King's grenadeers. Mr. *Vauban*, who had an eye every where, perceiving the resistance made by the besieged in that quarter, drew off a company of grenadeers, whom he ordered to pass over a flood-gate belonging to the curtain, where there was a narrow pass. Having entered this pass in file, they fell upon the flank of the besieged who defended the breach, and being assisted by the grenadeers who attacked the enemy in front, they made them give ground, and slew a great number of them.

We had planted some pieces of cannon which played upon the bridge of communication between the place and the horn-work. These cannons firing incessantly on this passage, by

which

which alone the enemy could send fresh suc- 1691.
cours to the place attacked, did great execution,
and cut off many of the besieged.

The pioneers presently came up, and made
the lodgement in a very short time, notwithstanding the great fire of the enemy from their
ramparts and other pieces of fortification, which
commanded the horn-work.

During this action, the motions of the besieged
were carefully watched, that in case they sal-
lied out, as they had done the day before, they
might be vigorously repulsed.

But a mistake happened which occasioned a
considerable loss to a body composed of most of
the nobility of the kingdom, whose valour, if
we may presume to say it, was attended with
too much heat and impetuosity ; I mean the
King's musqueteers, the first detachment of
whom, under the command of *d'Alifart*, waited for orders at the bridge of fascines, while the
other, under the command of *Artagnan*, was
posted along the *Boyau*, as well as the rest who
were commanded by *Rigauville*.

While they were in this disposition, a musque-
teer, whom Mr. *Maupertuis* had ordered to follow Mr. *Vauban*, came and told him to bring
up the musqueteers: whereupon his detachment
passed the bridge of fascines, and bravely mounted
the parapet of the horn-work, where *Maupertuis*
stopt them the very moment they were going
to rush in, remembering that the King had ordered them not to advance, unless the besieged,

who

 who had now been driven off, fhould attempt to return, as they had done the day before.

At the fame time Mr. *Artagnan* halted with his detachment at the foot of the horn-work on the bridge of fafcines, and *Rigauville* was about the ravelin with the reft of the mufqueteers.

Prefently after, one was heard calling for the mufqueteers: there were in that place thirty one of them, twelve of the grey, and the reft of the black. Whereupon *Trebans*, Quarter-mafter of the black, and *Lanofe*, a Brigadeer, having headed them, they immediately paffed the bridge and the ravelin.

The Duke of *Berwick* obferving this dangerous and rafh ftep, gave notice of it to Mr. *Maupertuis*, who in vain cried out to ftop the mufqueteers. The Duke of *Berwick* ran after them, and endeavoured to temper their ardour, but to no purpofe; and was even carried on by their impetuofity.

They entered through the curtain fword in hand, croffed all the horn-work, and advanced as far as the bridge which the enemy had broken in their retreat; and then finding nothing but a ditch full of water, and very deep, they bore a terrible firing from the works which were ftill poffeffed by the befieged, who were then upon the ramparts of that fide. The firing was fo thick and frequent, that the like was not feen during the whole fiege. In this attack a great many of them were killed, and few returned without fome wound or bruife. The Duke of *Berwick*

had

had only in his clothes the marks of his valour, 1691.
and of the dangers to which he had expofed
himfelf.

The King, who was prefent at this attack,
beftowed great encomiums on the troops which
had engaged, and chiefly on the mufqueteers,
who notwithftanding might be cenfured for temerity ; and hearing that the Duke of *Berwick*
was prefent at this action, he fent for him, and
faid to him, *It was not neceffary to expofe your
felf fo much as you have done in that attack, to
give proofs of your courage; that was known before ; and I befeech you to take more care of your
felf for the future.*

After the taking of the horn-work, the befieged held out fome days, in hopes of being relieved by the Prince of *Orange*, as he had promifed them. In effect, this Prince appeared
with an army on the eighth of *April*, but obferving that it was impoffible to draw near the
place, by reafon that Marfhal *Luxembourg*, with
his army of obfervation, had fhut up the paffes, he was obliged to return to his camp at
Hall; and the fame day, the befieged lofing all
hopes, were forced to furrender.

After the conqueft of *Mons*, the King having
given orders to repair the fortifications of that
city, and to provide it with the neceffary ftores,
gave the command of his army to Marfhal *Luxembourg*, and on the twelfth of *April* his Majefty fet out for *Verfailles*.

E 4

After

 After the King's departure, Marshal *Luxem-bourg*, being now Commander in chief of the *French* army, told the Duke of *Berwick*, that it was not fit a person of his rank should serve only as a volunteer, and therefore entreated him to be near his person in all the actions of this campaign. The Duke presently understood by this, that Marshal *Luxembourg* was desirous he should be near him as his Aid-de-camp; but having resolved to serve only as a volunteer, that he might be at full liberty to follow King *James* into *Ireland*, when his Majesty's Service should require it, he made as if he did not understand the Marshal's intentions, and only said that he would esteem it an honour to be always near his person, and to behold and imitate his great acti-ons.

The first attempt made this campaign, after the King's departure, was upon *Hall*, not far from *Bruffels*, which our army took by surprise: but the engagement at *Leuze*, or *Catoire*, was still more resolute and glorious. In this action the Duke of *Berwick* gave signal proofs of his great capacity, and skill in the art of war: for which reason we shall here give a particular account of it.

By the intelligence which Marshal *Luxem-bourg* received on the eighteenth of *September*, he understood that the enemy, who were then at *Leuze*, intended to decamp next morning. This gave him hopes that if they marched towards *Ath*, or *Chambron*, he might find an opportunity
of

of attacking one part of their troops, after the 1691.
others had paffed a little river which was in their
way to either of thefe two places; and, if they
continued at *Leuze*, he intended to come towards
Antoin, and take poffeffion of the pofts in that
country, which he well knew, and afterwards
to bring his whole army from *Leffines* into thofe
parts.

Accordingly towards the evening he detached
two hundred horfe of the King's houfhold, and
two hundred carabineers and light horfe, under
the command of *Marfilli*, whom he ordered to
draw as near as poffible to the enemy's camp,
and to fend him frequent advices of their motions.

Next day, being the nineteenth, Marfhal
Luxembourg having fent before him the body of
troops under the Marquis of *Villars*, began to
march the King's houfhold, the Gendarmery, the
regiment of *Merinville*, the horfe, and the regiments of the King's dragoons and of Teffes;
advancing towards *Leuze*, and leaving *Antoin* on
his right.

Being half-way between *Leffines* and *Leuze*,
he received advice from *Marfilli* and the people
of the country, that the enemy had decamped
two hours before day-light, and were marching
towards *Chambron*. This induced him to haften
his march, left all their troops fhould pafs the
rivulet *Blequy* before he came up with them,
or leaft he fhould find fo few of them on this
fide the rivulet, as to render this march more
fatiguing

1691. fatiguing to his army, than hurtful to the enemy.

Marſilli ſent advice a ſecond time, that he ſaw ſeveral troops of the enemy not far off drawn up in battle order. By this time he had been joined by the troops under the Marquis *Villars*. Not-withſtanding, Marſhal *Luxembourg* immediately ſent him orders not to make any attempt upon the enemy till his arrival ; at the ſame time he rode up himſelf, and obſerved a line of fourteen or fifteen ſquadrons, which was their rear-guard.

This body being too ſtrong for the troops under the command of the Marquis *Villars*, Mar-ſhal *Luxembourg* thought it proper to wait for the arrival of the King's houſhold, to whom he diſpatched orders to march up with all poſſible diligence : being then only at the diſtance of half a league, they ſoon arrived, and immediately he drew them up in battalia upon a favourable ground, which was now filled with a number of men equal to that of the enemy.

While our General was thus employed, the regiments of the King's and of Teſſé's dragoons arrived ; whereupon he turned to the Duke of *Berwick*, and ſaid, *Where think you, my Lord Duke, theſe dragoons ought to be placed? Sir, I am perſuaded,* anſwered the Duke of *Berwick, you will place them on the right among theſe hedges,* pointing them out to him, *where they will do their duty better than the three ſquadrons of horſe whom you will place on the left.* The Marſhal re-plied, *That was my deſign, and I perceive, my*
Lord

Lord Duke, that you know more of these matters than a young man like you ought to know.

The dragoons were accordingly placed on the right in the hedges, and the three squadrons of the *Merinville* cavalry were posted on the left. The Duke of *Choiseüil* commanded the right, and Mr. *Dauger* the left. In this situation the Marshal waited some time for the Gendarmery. As soon as they arrived, he placed them in the second line, with the brigade of *Coade*'s horse.

We have been informed since, that the enemy observing the Marquis *Villars*'s troops, mistook them for those commanded by Mr. *de Bezons* at the siege of *Mons*, and that having had notice that Marshal *Luxembourg* had set out from *Lessines* only on the seventeenth instant, at ten in the morning, they did not imagine he could be near *Catoir* on the nineteenth at noon with any considerable body of troops. But as soon as they saw our line formed, and perceived the King's houshold, they found their mistake. Whereupon the Prince of *Waldeck*, who commanded the enemy, ordered the left wing of his army, which was just landed on the other side of the *Blequy*, to repass that rivulet with all expedition.

He formed them, as they came up, into a second line behind his rear-guard, and placed in the hedges and morasses on his left five battalions which had been posted at the rivulet to support his rear. These battalions were opposite to the regiments of dragoons above mentioned, who were posted on our right.

Marshal

1691. Marſhal *Luxembourg* perceiving that the ene-my increaſed, reſolved not to wait the arrival of our left wing, which was under the command of Mr. *de Roſen*, and was marching up to join him; but to advance immediately, and attack the enemy. Accordingly his firſt line, compoſed of the King's houſhold, and of the three ſquadrons of *Merinville*, marched towards the enemy, who being covered by a little brook, waited for their attack with great boldneſs, and did not fire their pieces till our men were very near them. The King's houſhold bore the fire with their uſual intrepidity, and paſſed the brook to come at them.

This firſt attack was one of the fineſt and moſt vigorous that ever were ſeen, and worthy of that renowned body. The enemy gave ground, and the King's houſhold drove them to the ſecond line, which they likewiſe attacked with the ſame vigour, broke, and put into diſorder.

But while our troops continued to drive them towards the rivulet, Marſhal *Luxembourg* perceived the enemy had ſtill a conſiderable body drawn up in battalia: for which reaſon he ordered the King's houſhold to halt, and brought them back to their lines.

Afterwards he ordered the Gendarmery and *Coade*'s brigade to paſs into the intervals. As ſoon as this was done, he went himſelf along the line, within half piſtol-ſhot of the enemy, and ordered the commanders of the troops to move forward,

forward, whenever they should see the right 1691.
advance. The fierceness with which the Gendarmery marched up to the enemy struck them
with terror, and made them fly as soon as they
had discharged their pieces. The Gendarmery
pushed them for some time in good order: but
Marshal *Luxembourg* observing some of their infantry, which arrived upon an eminence, and
and began to descend into the plain, ordered
the troops not to proceed farther, and thought
fit to retire at a slow pace.

However the enemy did not repass the brook:
so that our troops continued above an hour in
the field of battle, to carry off the dead and the
wounded.

Several circumstances rendered this action glorious both with regard to our troops in general,
and to particular persons: the former behaving
with the most undaunted courage, and the latter
performing actions of unparallelled valour and
boldness.

Marshal *Luxembourg* discharged all the duties
of a great warrior and able commander. The
Duke of *Chartres* went over in the beginning
of the action to the life-guards, and advanced
at the head of them to engage the enemy: but
Marshal *Luxembourg* was obliged to use his authority as General, to make them retire. However towards the end of the battle he joined the
Duke *du Maine*, and charged the enemy at the
head of the squadrons which rallied, in order to
break the last line of the enemy.

All

1691. All the time this battle lasted, the regiments of the King's and *Tessé's* dragoons were employed in skirmishing with the five battallions which lined the hedges on the left of the enemy; and by thus amusing them during the action, they were a great support to our right wing, which had otherwise been very much annoyed from these hedges.

Never was greater intrepidity than appeared on this occasion among our troops: twenty two of our squadrons attacked seventy two of the enemy. Never was so great an action performed with so much coolness, nor did ever troops engage in finer order, and keep their ranks better, or closer.

During this action the Duke of *Berwick* was always near Marshal *Luxembourg*, and consequently in the most dangerous places; for that General exposed himself like a grenadeer. The Marshal having desired the Duke of *Berwick* to cause the Gendarmery to advance towards the left, the Duke of *Berwick* rode up to them, and while he was speaking to the Prince of *Bournonville*, who commanded them, an officer of the enemy, who was an *Englishman*, came up with a pistol in his hand to shoot the Duke; but having missed him, the Duke immediately attacked and killed him.

While the Duke of *Berwick* run this danger, Marshal *Luxembourg* escaped such another. One of the Prince of *Orange's* guards, of the Duke of *Ormond's* company, having perceived the Mar-

shal,

fhal, advanced with great fpeed with his piftol 1691.
in his hand, and his fword hanging at his arm,
in order to kill the General, who was attended
by ten or twelve perfons; but he turned afide
the piftol with his cane, and ftruck the foldier
with it feveral times, who prefently fuffered for
his temerity, being killed upon the fpot.

The battle at *Leuze* was the laft action of
this campaign. The King fent Mr. *de Chamlay* to
confer with the General about the winter quarters of the army, which were allotted to the
troops on the twentieth of *October.*

This campaign being ended the Duke of *Berwick* returned to *St. Germains,* where he found
King *James* deeply afflicted, on account of the
ill fuccefs of his affairs in *Ireland.*

The King of *France* had fent this year into
Ireland new and powerful fuccours, befides fome
troops commanded by Lieutenant-general *St.
Rhuë;* and the Duke of *Tyrconnel,* who came
to *France* in the beginning of this year, to take
the proper meafures with King *James* for preferving *Ireland,* had returned thither with feveral *Englifh* and *Irifh,* who continued faithful to
their King.

Notwithftanding all this, the Prince of *Orange*'s
army made new conquefts in that kingdom: they
took *Ballimore, Athlone, Galloway,* and *Limerick,* befides feveral other towns which opened
their gates to him. They likewife gained over
King *James*'s army a battle near *Kilcommodon,*
which was loft by a mifunderftanding between
Mr.

1691. Mr. *St. Rhuë*, and Count *Sarsfield*, who were joined together in command. The former was killed in this action by a cannon ball: and the Duke of *Tyrconnel*, so valuable on account of his attachment to his rightful sovereign, died at *Limerick*, on the twenty second of *August*, partly of regret to see his Majesty's affairs in so desperate a situation.

The Duke of *Berwick*, who had been informed at the army of part of this melancholy news, could not see King *James* so deeply afflicted, without being greatly concerned. One day this unfortunate Prince talking with the Duke concerning the infidelity of his subjects, and the ill success of his affairs in *Ireland*; the latter represented to his Majesty, that he ought not for all this to despair of re-ascending the throne; that the *English* were a fickle and inconstant people, and would soon grow weary of the Prince of *Orange*, who exhausted their treasures to satisfy his ambition; and that a new revolution might deprive him of those crowns which he had usurped with so much ease.

King *James* answered almost in the words of our Saviour. *My kingdom is no more of this world, and my hopes are only for the world to come:* an expression worthy of a Christian King!

1692. In the beginning of the year 1692, most of King *James*'s subjects who had continued faithful to him, being no longer able to maintain themselves in *Ireland*, after the principal towns of that kingdom had fallen into the hands of the enemy,

enemy, and the battle at *Kilcommodon* had been 1692.
loft, embarked from thence, and arrived at *Breft*,
to the number of fourteen thoufand men.
Whereupon King *James* fet out from *St. Germains* with the Duke of *Berwick*, and having arrived at *Vannes*, he there reviewed thefe troops,
and divided them into regiments, the moft confiderable of which he beftowed on the Duke of
Berwick, calling it by his name. Thofe who
were brought over to *France* by Count *Sarsfield*
were not fo numerous, and arrived only fome
time after. King *James* went likewife to review them, and difpofed them into regiments.

About this time, the regulations were made
at the court of *France* for the operations of the
enfuing compaign. It was refolved to be upon
the defenfive in *Germany* and *Piedmont*, and to
carry on the war in *Catalonia*, and efpecially in
Flanders, with great vigour. We likewife began to equip a numerous fleet, which was to act
on the ocean, and to be commanded by Count
Tourville; and Count *Etrées* was appointed to
command the fleet for the *Mediterranean*.

Marfhal *Luxembourg* had likewife this year
the command of the army in *Flanders* under
the King, who went to it; and Marfhal *de Lorges* that of the army in *Germany*. The Marquis
Boufflers was appointed to command a body of
men which was to act between the *Sambre* and
the *Meufe*. The Duke of *Noailles* was chofen
to command in *Catalonia*, and Marfhal *Catinat*
had orders to continue in *Piedmont*.

F

Befides,

 Besides, Marshal *de Bellefonds* went into *Normandy*, and there headed an army of eight or ten thousand *French* troops, and fifteen battalions of *Irish*, which were appointed to make a descent upon *England*, in hopes of being supported by the interest which King *James* still preserved in that kingdom.

While the King of *France* invested *Namur*, his fleet put to sea, in order to make a descent upon *England* in favour of King *James*. This Prince came to the coasts of *Bretagne*, accompanied by the Duke of *Berwick* and all his court, and there he met the *Irish* troops, with some *French* regiments.

Three hundred transports were appointed to carry them over, with a large store of all sorts of warlike provisions. Twelve men of war, commanded by Count *Etrées* were ordered to escort them, while the great fleet under Count *Tourville* were to cruise in the channel.

King *James* published a manifesto to encourage the *English* who had continued faithful to him, and incline them to receive him. All things seemed to be so well concerted and conducted hitherto, that this enterprise was looked upon as infallible. But the winds did not suffer Count *Etrées* to join King *James* with his squadron, and also detained Count *Tourville* in the haven of *Berteaume*.

This unfortunate accident gave the Princess of *Orange* time to make all the necessary preparations for defeating the enterprize. The Prince

of

of *Orange* likewife, being then in *Holland*, had ha-ftened the equipment of the *Dutch* fleet, which by this time was put to fea, and had joined that of the *Englifh.*

It was pretended that there was a confpiracy in *England* to feize that Princefs, with the principal Lords of her party; and that King *James* had gained to his intereft a confiderable number of the officers in the fleet.

As this is one of the moft remarkable expeditions in the hiftory of King *James*, and as the Duke of *Berwick* was prefent in it, we think proper to give here a particular account of it; that it may the better appear what unexpected misfortunes attended all the enterprizes of this Prince, for whom Heaven referved a more folid blifs than what the fuccefses of this life can afford.

Notwithftanding the unfortunate accidents a-bove-mentioned, Count *Tourville*, who had orders to enter the channel and engage the enemy, whether weak or ftrong, weighed from the haven of *Berteaume* on the twelfth of *May* with thirty feven men of war, and feven fire-fhips, fteering to the channel. The wind was north-eaft at feveral times; neverthelefs, on the twenty fifth inftant, he arrived over againft *Plimouth*, where he received a reinforcement of feven men of war and four fire-fhips, which were brought to him by the Marquis of *Villette :* and now this fleet amounted to forty four men of war, and eleven fire-fhips.

F 2

The

1692.   The *English* and *Dutch* fleet confisted of eighty one men of war, and eighteen fire-fhips, and
carried thirty five thoufand fix hundred and fixty
one men, and five thoufand eight hundred and
forty fix guns; *viz.* of the *English*, fix fhips of
100 guns, ten of 96 guns, twenty three of 70,
fix of 67, and five of 50, in all fifty men of war,
carrying twenty four thoufand feven hundred and
thirty fix men, and three thoufand fix hundred
and eighty guns.   Of the *Dutch*, five fhips of
92 guns, five of 82, fix of 72, ten of 60 to 64,
and five of 50, in all thirty one men of war,
carrying ten thoufand nine hundred and twenty
five men, and two thoufand one hundred and
fixty fix guns.   This fleet was joined by feven
fhips more, when the engagement began.

They fet fail from the bay of St. *Helens* on
the twenty feventh of *May*; but as it fell
calm, they could get no further than a little beyond the ifle of *Wight*.   On the twenty eighth
they fet fail again, and the twenty ninth at fun-
rife they perceived the *French* fleet at the diftance
of about three leagues.

On our fide, Count *Tourville* difcovered this
fleet on the fame day, the wind being fouth eaft,
and our fhips feven leagues at full fea between
Cape la Hogue and *Cape Barfleur*.

It being then a hazy weather, he could not
reckon the number of their fhips; befides, he
had received no intelligence of their ftrength:
for he was not joined by the ten long barks which
had been fent to him from *la Hogue* and *Cher-*
bourg,

bourg, to give him advice that the enemy had 1692.
brought together almoft all their fhips at the ifle
of *Wight*, and to carry new orders not to advance
on that fide, but to lie at the mouth of the
channel, or near the ifle of *Ufhant*, till the arrival of Count *Eftrées* and the other fhips which
were ordered to join him.

Count *Tourville* not having received this advice, followed his former orders. Accordingly
he called a council of war, and laid his inftruéti-
ons before them. Afterwards he gave the fignal
for the order of battle, and our fhips made all
poffible hafte to take their feveral ftations.

In this difpofition, having come up pretty near
to the enemy, we reckoned in their fleet eighty
eight fhips of the line, of which more than thirty
fix were of three decks. Notwithftanding this
great fuperiority of their numbers and ftrength,
and though our Admiral, having the wind-gage of
the enemy, might perhaps have avoided an engagement, yet he thought it moft advifeable to
fight; as he had pofitive orders to that purpofe,
and had now drawn fo near their fhips, that if
he declined to fight, and fhould afterwards be
obliged to it, which might happen, his retreating would infallibly ftrike his men with fo much
terror, as would give the enemy a greater advantage over him than the fuperiority of their
numbers. He therefore bore up to them in the
following order.

The Marquis of *Amfreville* in the *Formidable*,
which carried ninety two guns, commanded the

van-

1692. van-guard, or the white and blew squadron, con-sisting of fourteen ships.   Count *Tourville* in the *Royal Sun*, with a white flag, carrying an hundred and six guns, commanded the centre.   The rear was under the command of Mr. *de Gabaret* in the *Marvellous*, which carried ninety four guns.

On the side of the enemy, the centre, or squadron of the red, was commanded by Admiral *Russel*, who had for his Vice-admiral Sir *Ralph Delaval*, and for his Rear-admiral Sir *Cloudesly Shovel*.   The van-guard, consisting of *Dutch* ships, was commanded by Vice-admiral *Allemond*; and the rear-guard, or squadron of the blew, by Sir *John Ashby*, who had for his Vice-admiral *Rook*, and for his Rear-admiral *Caster*.

As soon as Admiral *Russel* perceived our fleet bearing upon him, he sailed his ship as far as he could to the wind-ward, that every ship of his fleet might see his signals, and have time to take the stations allotted to them.   By eight in the morning his line was formed, reaching from south-west to south-east.

Count *Tourville* having resolved, as we have said above, to fight the enemy, and observing that some of his ships had not yet entered the line, made a second signal to call them up; and afterwards advanced, with a fore-wind, steering directly upon the *English* Admiral, whose motions he carefully watched, not to lose an opportunity of engaging him.

The

The Marquis *Villette,* Vice-admiral of the 1692.
white fquadron, fixed in like manner upon the
Englifh Vice-admiral, carefully watching all his
motions. The Marquis *Langeron* who commanded the third divifion of our main body,
likewife entered the line, where he took his
proper ftation.

As for our Van-guard, the weather being
calm, the Marquis *Amfreville* ordered his boats
to tow him forward. *Nemond* and *Relingue,* who
commanded the firft and third divifions of our
van-guard, did the fame. But the former being before the other two commanders, bore up
fooner and nearer to the enemy than they, ftanding directly at the head of them; fo that the
Bourbon, the firft fhip of his divifion, which
was commanded by *Perinet,* lay over-againft the
headmoft *Dutch* fhip.

This was of great fervice to our fleet : for the
line of the enemy being much longer than ours,
the Marquis *Nemond,* by thus ftanding over-
againft the headmoft of their fhips, prevented
their paffing our line on that fide.

At the fame time, the Marquis *Amfreville*
obferving a large empty fpace in the enemy's
line between the laft divifion of his van-guard,
which was that of Mr. *de Relingue,* and the firft
divifion of our main body, being that of the
Marquis *Villette,* and fearing left the fhips which
fhould have filled that fpace were wheeling
about in order to intercept him, he refolved
not to advance farther, and ftood, as well as

Mr.

1692. Mr. *Relingue*, fo as to have always the windward of the enemy : this was likewife very ferviceable to our fleet.

In our rear-guard, commanded by Mr. *Gaba-ret*, Mr. *Coëtlogon* brought his divifion into the line, all his fhips bearing together upon thofe of the enemy which were oppofite to them. But Mr. *Pannetier*'s divifion, which was the laft of our rear-guard, being the hindmoft when our fhips began to form the line of battle, could not arrive fo foon as the reft, though he made all the fail he could.

On the other fide, the enemy had put them-felves upon the ftay, to wait the arrival of our fleet, having formed themfelves into a line that was not fo ftrait as it ought to have been ; but the like defect was on our fide, which was ow-ing to the want of wind.

The divifions of Meffieurs *de Tourville*, *Vil-lette*, *Langeron*, *Coëtlogon*, *Gabaret*, were now within mufquet-fhot of the enemy. Such was the difpofition and pofture of both fleets, without any firing on either fide, when a *Dutch* fhip of the enemy's van-guard fired upon the *St. Louis* in our van, being commanded by Mr. *la Roque*, and killed one of her gunners. Whereupon one of our fhips haftily fired a gun, which was, as it were, the fignal for both fleets : for on a fudden (it being now about ten of the clock in the morning) there was a moft terrible firing throughout the whole line, but efpecially in the centre.

There

There was not one ship in the *French* fleet 1692. which did not engage two or three of the ene- my's, especially in the divisions of Count *Tour- ville*, and the Marquis *Villette* : for whereas the *English* Admiral who attacked the former, and their Vice-admiral of the red who engaged the latter, had in their divisions sixteen of the largest ships in their fleet, Count *Tourville* and the Mar- quis *Villette* had in theirs only six.

Never was a brisker or longer engagement, the two fleets having fought from morning till night with very little interruption. Ours was too in- feriour both in number and strength to gain the victory: yet we lost none of our ships, and if in this engagement several of ours were distressed, several ships of the enemy's fleet suffered like- wise.

The engagement being over, each of our ships put herself, without distinction, under the first flag she met. The ebbing of the tide happening about one of the clock in the morning, Count *Tourville* took this occasion of retiring from the enemy, and fired a gun, as a signal for our ships to put to sail: accordingly he bore off, having only eight ships with him: part of the rest having joined him next morning, he had now thirty five sail, and wanted only nine, *viz.* six which had steered under Mr. *Nemond* to the *Hogue*, and the three ships of Messieurs *Gaba- ret, Langeron,* and *Combes,* which had taken their course towards the *English* coast, in order to put in at *Brest.*

Having

 Having failed all the night of the twenty ninth, on the thirtieth at ten in the morning he found he was a league in the wind of the enemy. This advantage might have been fufficient to bring him off; but his fhip the *Royal Sun*, which had greatly fuffered in the engagement, failing ill, retarded the whole fleet: about ten in the evening fhe was obliged to come to an anchor near *Cherbourg*, and to wait for the tide in a place about half a league from the enemy.

For this reafon Count *Tourville* refolved to go aboard another fhip, which he had hitherto been unwilling to do, left the *Royal Sun*, if he left her, fhould fall into the enemy's hands. Accordingly he went aboard the *Ambitious*, commanded by the Marquis *Villette*, and made towards the *Ras de Blanchard*, hoping to pafs it by means of the ebb, and with the help of the currents to get before the enemy, who fteered towards *Cafquets*.

The *Ras de Blanchard* is a channel formed on one fide by the coaft of the *Cotentine* from *Cape la Hogue* to *Flamanville*, and on the other by the Ifles of *Origny* and *Guernfey*: it is about five leagues in length, and one and a half in breadth; the current is there very ftrong, and the mooring dangerous.

Having weighed anchor from *Cherbourg* about eleven in the evening of the thirtieth, he entered this channel. This courfe had almoft brought him off; for about five of the clock next morning he was four leagues before the enemy,

and

and of his thirty five ſhips, twenty had already 1692.
paſſed the channel: the other fifteen, in which
number was the *Ambitious*, were within cannon
ſhot of it, when the tide coming, they were
obliged to caſt anchor; and as the mooring was
there very bad, they trailed with their anchors,
and were bore away by the currents, ſo that
theſe ſhips were in the wind of the enemy, ſe-
perated from the reſt of our fleet.

Of theſe fifteen ſhips, reduced to this extremity, three which had ſuffered moſt continued
at *Cherbourg*, leſt they ſhould fall into the hands
of the enemy: the firſt entered the ditch of *Ga-
let*, and the other two came into the harbour of
Cherbourg. With the remaining twelve Count
Tourville, having no anchors, and not being able
to ſail much farther, reſolved to retreat to the
Hogue, where he arrived on the thirty firſt in
the evening, being chaſed by forty ſhips of the
enemy, who ſhut him up in that harbour.

Upon his arrival, King *James*, who was then
at the *Hogue* with the Duke of *Berwick*, Marſhal *Belfonds*, and Mr. *Bonrepos*, conſulted with
the General Officers what meaſures were to be
taken at this criſis. After they were well aſſured
that theſe ſhips could not be ſaved, and that even
if they attempted to defend them, they run the
hazard of being carried off by the enemy; it was
reſolved, in order to ſave the ſeamen, cannon,
and tackle, to run them a-ground, and arm
ſome ſloops to keep the enemy from burning
them.

In

1692.   In purfuance of this refolution, fix of thefe fhips were run a-ground near fort *Liffet*, and the other fix behind fort *la Hogue*. Afterwards they took off as much of their tackle as they could, and prepared the floops appointed to keep off the enemy. But as there were only twelve of thefe floops, as the boats which joined them were unfit for failing, and both were armed with men vanquifhed and difheartned, they could not hinder the enemy, who fent a detachment of two hundred light floops well armed, from burning, toward the evening of the fecond of *June*, the fix fhips run a-ground at fort *Liffet*; notwithftanding that Meffieurs *Tourville, Villette,* and *Coëtlogon*, with feveral Sea-captains and Officers, went aboard thefe floops to animate our men.

Next day at the morning tide, which came at ten of the clock, the enemy having entered the little harbour of the *Hogue* with a number of floops and boats ftill greater than the day before, and fupported by a frigate with oars carrying thirty pieces of cannon, and a galley mounted likewife with cannon, together with two fire-fhips, they could not be hindered from burning the fhips run a-ground in that place: they fet fire alfo to fome merchant-fhips which lay near them.

Such was the iffue of an enterpize which in its beginning had promifed great fuccefs. The unfortunate confequences of this fea-engagement defeated all the defigns upon *England*, and obliged

ed his *British* Majesty to return with the Duke 1692.
of *Berwick* to St. *Germains*, imputing this mighty loss which *France* had sustained to his own
unlucky star, as he expressed himself in a moving letter which he wrote to the King of *France*
on that subject. After this action the *Irish* troops
were sent into *Germany*.

King *James* having returned to St. *Germains*,
found his Queen brought to bed of a Princess,
born on the twenty eighth of *May*. This infant
was baptized on the fourth of *August* in the chapel of the old castle of St. *Germains*. The King
of *France* and his sister-in-law the Duchess of
Orleans held this Princess over the baptismal font,
and named her *Mary-Louisa*, after the Queen
of *England* and the King of *France*.

On the twenty third of *August* King *James*,
who was greatly afflicted by the death of the
Duke of *Tyrconnel*, and had a particular regard
for his memory, caused a solemn service to be
performed for the repose of his soul in the church
of the *English* nuns in the suburb St. *Antoin*. To
this ceremony he invited the most considerable
persons both at Court and in *Paris*. *Richard*,
Duke of *Tyrconnel*, was *Lord Lieutenant of* Ireland, *Captain Lieutenant General of all his* British *Majesty's forces, one of his most honourable
Privy Council, and Knight of the most noble order
of the Garter*. But these honours and high offices distinguished him less than his merit and
virtue, his zeal for his sovereign, and inviolable
attachment to his person and interests.

The

1692.   The Duke of *Berwick* being returned to St. Germains, and seeing that nothing could be attempted this year for King *James*'s service, as there was no probability that *France*, after the great loss which had befallen her at the *Hogue*, would soon make a second attempt upon *England*; and knowing besides, that he would still be in time for the campaign in *Flanders*, if Marshal *Luxembourg*, who commanded our army in that country after the King's departure, should make any enterprize this year, as he had done the year preceeding; he asked leave of the King of *England* to go to the campaign in *Flanders*.

King *James* being now no longer in a condition to reward the Duke of *Berwick* for his fidelity and attachment to him, on which account he had quitted *England*, and lost all his estate, was extremely glad to see him ambitious of serving in our armies. His Majesty had great reason to hope that the Duke would soon distinguish himself in the field, and easily obtain a rank suitable to his birth and merit; which induced King *James* to consent very willingly to his serving in *Flanders*.

As soon as the Duke of *Berwick* arrived in *Flanders*, he went to visit Marshal *Luxembourg*, who expressed a great satisfaction at his return to the army, highly commended his design, and gave him several proofs of an unfeigned esteem for him.

To give an idea of the posture of our army, and of the enemy at this time, we must begin

a

a little higher. After the reduction of *Namur*, 1692. our troops having been reinforced at the camp of ᨉ *Gerard* with several battalions and the King's houshold, went to pass the *Sambre* near *la Buffiere*, and took possession of the camp of *Mierbe la Potterie*, from thence to observe the motions of the enemy, who were encamped at *Fleurus*.

The Prince of *Orange*, very much vexed at the taking of *Namur*, formed great designs to make up that loss. There went a report in his camp that he intended to invest *Namur*, and that he would the more easily take it, as the people of *Liege* had promised to supply him with every thing necessary for the subsistence of his horse, and the transporting of his artillery to that place; and had engaged to send whatever he should want by the *Meuse* in four thousand boats which it was given out were now ready, and even laden.

In the mean time Marshal *Luxembourg* refreshed his troops in his camp, and endeavoured to repair the great damage they had suffered during the siege of *Namur*. The scarcity of forrage had weakened the cavalry, and the infantry were not in a better condition, being greatly distressed by the high price of provisions, by marches and encampments in hard weather, and very heavy rains.

Whilst our army refreshed themselves under shelter of the laurels which the King had gathered, the enemy decamped from *Fleurus*, and came to *Genap*, extending their right as far as *Niville*.

By

1692.   By this motion it appeared that the Prince of *Orange*, far from intending to befiege *Namur*, was in fears for *Charleroy*, and endeavoured to prevent its having the fame fate with *Namur*; as he only took poffeffion of this camp, in order to confume all the forrage thereabouts, and deprive our army of the means of fubfifting in that country, in cafe Marfhal *Luxembourg* fhould attempt the fiege of *Charleroy* during this campaign.

Such a precaution was very prudent: a General accuftomed to be worfted, ought rather to think of warding off the blows with which he is threatned, than threaten thofe who have worfted him.

Whilft the Prince of *Orange* was encamping his army at *Genap*, Marfhal *Luxembourg* marched to take poffeffion of that of *Soignies*, to be within reach of difturbing his forrage, and make him apprehend fome enterprife of greater importance than the fiege of *Charleroy*.

The Prince of *Orange*, who was always more alert upon his receiving alarms than his loofing towns, immediately fent a detachment of eight thoufand men to *Anderlecht*, in order to cover *Bruffels*, and prevent the enemy from confuming all the forrage of *Brabant*: another wife precaution, but truly not very effectual, fince that detachment did not hinder Marfhal *Luxembourg* from forraging even within fight of *Bruffels*, and confuming, during his encampment at *Soignies*, all the forrage of *Hall*, *Tubife*, and *Braine-le-Comte*.

Such

Such was the fituation of our army, and of 1692. that of the Prince of *Orange*, when the Duke of *Berwick* joined Marfhal *Luxembourg*. The whole month of *July* had been fpent in thefe motions, without our being able to fee into any defign of the enemy, except that of defending the country, to keep the people from complaining.

On the firft of *Auguft* the Prince of *Orange* marched from *Genap*, and encamped upon an eminence near *Hall*. The fame day Marfhal *Luxembourg* having intelligence of this march, went to take poffeffion of the camp of *Enghien*, which he had viewed fome days before: he placed his right at *Steenkerke*, his left at *Heri-nen*, and his center behind *Enghien*.

Next day the Prince of *Orange* paffed with his whole army the rivulet called *Senne*, placing his right near the village of *Tubife*, having *Hall* in his rear, and in his front the villages of *St. Martin Legniek* and *St. Pierre-lieu*: he encamped in two lines. The fame day the *Hanoverian* troops re-inforced his army with eight thoufand men, horfe and foot: they encamped in a third line.

The Prince of *Orange* received intelligence that Marfhal *Luxembourg* had fent his artillery to *Mons*, by reafon of the roads which were impraĉticable, and that he had none in his camp at *Soignies*. He had long flattered himfelf, that if he could bring on fome aĉtion where the horfe could not aĉt by reafon of the fituation of the country, he might have his revenge for the battle of *Leuze*, where all his horfe had been defeated. He now

G

thought

1692. thought he had a favourable opportunity for effecting his design: perhaps others would have judged in the same manner.

With this view he decamped from *Tubise* on the third of *August* about midnight, and marched his whole army towards our camp with so much secrecy and diligence, that about six in the morning he arrived upon the rising ground at *Steenkerke*, between the great and little *Enghien*.

At this time there happened a pretty odd accident, which had well nigh surprized Marshal *Luxembourg*, and gave the enemy a considerable advantage in the beginning of the action we are going to relate.

A musician belonging to the Elector of *Bavaria*, whom the Marshal employed to bring him intelligence of the enemy's designs and motions, was at this time detected and seized by the enemy. The Prince of *Orange*, to improve this opportunity in favour of his design, ordered the musician to write to the Marshal not to be surprized if he saw a large body of troops on the third instant, they being only a detachment of the enemy ordered to cover a great forrage which they were to make that day.

This letter was conveyed to Marshal *Luxembourg* by the same hand which the musician had employed before; and as this spy had hitherto given right intelligence, the Marshal made no difficulty to believe him.

Some time after, Mr. *Tracy*, who was that day upon duty with a detachment, having perceived

ceived a confiderable body of the enemy march- 1692.
ing towards the leffer *Enghien*, immediately gave
notice of it to the Marfhal, who fent him word
not to be under any concern upon that account, as
he knew what they were. Obferving that the
enemy increafed, he again fent notice of it to
Marfhal *Luxembourg*, who anfwered that it was
only a forrage the enemy were making. Our
General gave no farther attention to them, till
a Captain of carabineers, who was at the mill of
Haute Croix, fent him advice that he faw on his
fide a column of the enemy's cavalry.

Upon this advice, Marfhal *Luxembourg*, with
the Prince of *Conti*, the Duke of *Vendôme*, the
Duke of *Berwick*, Count *Auvergne*, the Duke
of *Elbœuf*, the Duke of *Villeroy*, the Marquis
Tilladet, and the Chevalier *Gaffion*, advanced between *Rebé* and *Steenkerke*, where the Duke of
Orleans, who was then upon duty, though fick,
arrived at the fame time.

Here Marfhal *Luxembourg* received a third advice from *Tracy*, acquainting him that he faw a
great body of foot and horfe upon their march,
leaving *St. Regnelde* on the right, and doubling
upon the rivulet of *Steenkerke*; that he believed
it was the whole army of the enemy, becaufe he
perceived they carried cannon along with them;
and that he was going to reconnoitre them, in
order to fend him furer intelligence.

Upon receiving this advice, the Marfhal advanced to a rifing ground, from whence he obferved a great number of the enemy's troops:

G 2

where-

1692. whereupon he prefently fent notice of it to the Marquis of *Boufflers*, and defired that officer to join him with all fpeed. At the fame time he obferved that the enemy halted upon a plain fo fmall that it could only contain a few troops in feveral lines, and that on their right a confiderable body of foot advanced to the wood.

This obliged him to order his whole army to arms, without his being yet able to judge on which fide the enemy defigned to attack him, as they could throw fome infantry into the wood on the right, as well as that on the left. He even believed they would attempt to make themfelves mafters of *Enghien*; for which reafon he fent thither a brigade, and defired Count *Auvergne* to return to the left, which was his proper poft.

Our General was not long in doubt; for he obferved that the enemy left the rivulet of *Steenkerke* on their left, that all their foot advanced to *Steenkerke*, and began to enter the wood.

This made him judge that it was near *Steenkerke* they defigned to make their real attack (for being covered there by the rivulet, they could not be difturbed in flank by our cavalry) and that while their horfe remained behind the wood, they intended to march all their foot to that fide.

Whereupon Marfhal *Luxembourg* brought thither the greateft part of his infantry, except that on the left, not being able to know what the enemy were attempting on his right, by reafon

of

of the woods and defiles. After having formed 1692.
his lines, he went to the church-yard of *Steen-*
kerke, whither the Duke of *Choiſeüil* had ſent
the horſe grenadeers to guard the bridge. From
thence he obſerved if the enemy were paſſing
the rivulet in order to plant their cannon on a
riſing ground, where they might have greatly
annoyed our infantry in flank. When he ſaw
they had not thought of this, he ſent Mr. *Lan-*
dournac with twenty horſe grenadeers to obſerve
if they were laying bridges over the rivulet; but
he brought advice that they did not attempt it.

As Marſhal *Luxembourg* was returning to the
infantry, he heard they began to ſkirmiſh, which
ſoon drew on the battle.

The enemy had cannonaded us long before
our artillery came up. As ſoon as it arrived, Mr.
Vigny ſeparated the brigades, and fired the firſt
battery. Part of the brigade of *Champagne* were
ſent to diſlodge ſome pieces of the enemy's cannon which played upon our dragoons.

The enemy by this time attacked us in good
earneſt. The dragoons on our right, under the
command of Count *Mailly* and the Marquis of
Alegre, ſuſtained their attacks for a conſiderable
time, and fought very bravely. The regiment
of *Orleans* on the left of the dragoons defended
and kept their poſt with equal bravery. That
of *Chartres* on the left, and the ſecond battalion
of the *Bourbonnois*, though both were quite expoſed to the enemy's fire, yet they kept their
poſt, and behaved with great courage.

<table>
<tr><td>G 3</td><td>Though</td></tr>
</table>

1692. Though the regiment of *Orleans* was reinforced only by that of *Chartres*, and the firſt battalion of *Bourbonnois* by the ſecond, in order to be covered from the great firing of the enemy who were poſted in the wood, yet the greateſt part of this firſt line kept their ground. However, the Prince of *Conti* thought fit to ſupport them by the brigade of *Stoppa*, the battalions of which were a little ſeparated, and to reinforce *Stoppa*'s brigade by that of *Porlier*, which advanced with great boldneſs. But the enemy coming up to the poſts we ſtill poſſeſſed, the regiment of *Porlier*, which was fronted by the opening in the wood, as well as the *Chartres* and *Bourbonnois*, cloſing to the right and left, received ſo great a fire, that they could hardly continue in the plain, notwithſtanding they had not advanced ſo far as they had deſired.

While things were in this poſture, the enemy ſallied out of the wood, and placed very near us their *Cheveaux de Friſe*, behind which they made a terrible firing.

Marſhal *Luxembourg* having deſired the Duke of *Berwick* to carry orders to the brigade of the *French* guards to advance to the enemy, the Duke ſaid to him, *I think, Sir, it would be fit to make them attack ſword in hand:* the other anſwered, *I approve your thought, give them in my name what orders you think proper; I rely wholly upon your judgment.* Mr. *Renold*, who commanded the *Swiſs* guards, being then preſent, intreated the

Marſhal,

Marſhal, and prevailed with him to give the *Swiſs* 1692. leave to do the ſame.

Immediately he led on the *Swiſs*, having made their files equal in number of men to thoſe of the *French* guards. The enemy, ſurpriſed at the fierceneſs with which theſe two brigades advanced, did not fire till they were joined by them: ſoon after they were worſted and put to flight.

Marſhal *Luxembourg* had intreated the Duke of *Chartres* to ſtay with the reſerve which was poſted behind *Enghien*, aſſuring him that he would find an opportunity of bringing him into the engagement, and ſatisfying his deſire of giving proofs of his courage. That Prince ſent him word that he would be glad to ſee the beginning of the action: but the Marſhal having again intreated him to continue at his poſt, he ſent to him his Governor, the Marquis of *Arcy*, who told the Marſhal that the Prince was ſo much concerned to remain in the reſerve, and was ſo deſirous of being witneſs to the battle, that he intreated him to grant his requeſt. Marſhal *Luxembourg* could not withſtand theſe ſollicitations; but the Duke of *Chartres* having received a muſquet-ſhot in the ſhoulder, the Marſhal obliged him to return to his brigade.

In the beginning of this action the Prince of *Conti* had a horſe killed under him, and afterwards another at the head of the regiment of *Perlier*, which occaſioned his ſaying, *The enemy aim at my horſes.*

G 4

After

 After the *French* and *Swifs* guards had defeated the enemy, recovered the cannon we had
loft, and taken four pieces of the enemy's, the
Prince of *Conti* haftened to his poft, which was
on the right, where he found the Chevalier
Gaffion, who having obferved that fome of the
enemy's horfe advanced to our right, had come
thither with the Chevalier *Angouleme*, and the
Dauphin's regiment of dragoons, and had put to
flight a battalion pofted behind the hedges.

About this time the Duke of *Berwick*, having
joined the Prince of *Conti*, made him obferve
that the enemy were fending fome troops to drive
away the Dauphin's dragoons: that Prince thanked him, and intreated him to come along with
him, in order to prevent it: accordingly they advanced with the regiment of *Provence*, which
being animated by their prefence, drove the enemy beyond the hedges with great vigour.

While we were thus fuccefsful on our right,
the regiments of *Champagne* and of *Nice* attacked
and defeated the *Englifh* guards. Mr. *Montal*
purfued the enemy, preffed them very vigoroufly,
and gained a great deal of ground upon them.

The King's brigade were ftill engaged, as well
as that of the Dauphin. The enemy were defeated and driven from the rivulet of *Steenkerke*
as far as the right of the wood: but at the entrance of that wood, where the country was narrow, and broken by a great many hedges, thefe
two brigades could not put to flight the brigades
of the enemy, which were continually fupported

by

by frefh battalions one after another. This occa- 1691.
fioned a very brifk engagement on that quarter,
while the reft of our troops continued in the
peaceable poffeffion of the pofts they had feized.

The firing was there very great; *Boufflers*
went thither to give orders very opportunely,
and found that Mr. *Montal* was doing the fame
on the right. In the mean time the enemy
lodged fome battalions in the hedges on their
left, and extended themfelves a confiderable way
towards the wood of *Triou*. They were even
gaining fome advantage over a battalion of our
left, which they had attacked both in front and
flank, when Mr. *Bufca* brought up a fquadron
of the King's guards of the *Lorges*, commanded
by Mr. *Baliviere*, fell upon the battalion of the
enemy which advanced, and obliged them to
retire with all fpeed.

It was now about feven of the clock in the
evening, when the Prince of *Orange* thought fit
to retreat, and accordingly made his men file off:
the moft advanced battalions returned to thofe
which lay behind, and by degrees found themfelves in the road between *Rebé* and *Steenkerke*,
which they had taken in the morning when
they came to attack us. Marfhal *Luxembourg*
followed them about two miles, without finding
an opportunity of charging them: their horfe
difappeared fo fuddenly, that when he advanced,
he could not fee any of their fquadrons. As for
their foot, which were in a hollow country, and
more favourable to them than to the horfe,
they

1692. they retired in good order; and the night coming on, our General thought it more advisable to bring back his army to their camp, than engage them in a fruitless pursuit.

Such was the battle of *Steenkerke*, from which neither side reaped any other advantage, except that of having tried their strength at the expence of a great many brave men who fell in it. *

The Prince of *Orange*, who during all this campaign had sought to bring on some action, where, by reason of the country, the foot alone could engage, felt in the battle of *Steenkerke* the strength and valour of the *French* Infantry, as in the battle of *Leuze* he had experienced that of our cavalry.

In all this war, there had not before been so long or so obstinate an engagement of the foot: for it began to be very fierce about noon, and continued till seven of the clock in the evening. There were in this engagement as many remarkable actions as there were hedges and ravines to pass. The field of battle was from right to left at most but half a league in extent; being bounded on our right by the rivulet of *Steenkerke*, and on our left by the avenue to the castle of

---

* In this battle the confederates lost the brave Lieutenant-general *Mackay*, Sir *John Lanier*, Sir *Robert Douglas*, the Earl of *Angus*, and several other gallant officers; above two thousand men were killed, and three thousand wounded or made prisoners. On the side of the *French*, the Prince of *Turenne*, the Marquis of *Bellefonds*, the Marquis of *Tilladet*, the Marquis of *Firmacon*, and several other men of distinction, and two thousand private soldiers were killed, besides about as many wounded.

Warete.

Warete. On this Ground we formed with the enemy above twelve lines of Infantry, without mentioning the horfe who were pofted behind. 1692.

Never was attack better projected, or be-gun with better order: and according to all appearances it ought to have been moft advantageous to the enemy; efpecially fince Marfhal *Luxembourg* relying, as we have faid above, on the intelligence he received from his fpy, was not on his guard when it began. But what was very furprifing, the fame troops which had gained fo great an advantage at the firft onfet, and were almoft victorious in a country where the roads were impracticable, were repulfed and driven from hedge to hedge, and obliged to fly with fo much precipitation and diforder, that they could never rally till they returned to the main body of their army.

The Duke of *Chartres*, the Duke of *Bourbon*, the Prince of *Conti*, and the Duke of *Vendôme*, gave on this occafion fignal proofs of their great valour: to thefe we partly owe the fuccefs of this battle; for the example of thefe four Princes fired our troops with fo much courage and bravery, that all of them, even the meaneft foldiers, vied with each other in bold and gallant actions. The Duke of *Berwick* was among thofe who diftinguifhed themfelves moft, and gave remarkable proofs of his intrepidity, and of a capacity worthy of the moft able commander. Marfhal *Luxembourg* writing to the King of *France* a detail of this battle, thought himfelf obliged to

give

1692. give his Majefty an account of the Duke of *Ber-wick*'s gallant behaviour, and mentioned with great encomiums the fervices he had done in this action.

After this battle the Prince of *Orange* retired to his camp at *Hall*, as Marſhal *Luxembourg* did to his. Next day the latter went to the field of battle, and gave the neceſſary orders for removing the wounded, and burying the ſlain: he continued eight days after this in his camp, during which time the enemy did not move from theirs, and conſumed all the forrage about *Hall*.

During the reſt of this campaign, though the Prince of *Orange* had received from *Oſtend* and *Nieuport* a conſiderable reinforcement of troops, which had been defigned to make a deſcent upon the coaſts of *France*, yet he could gain no advantage over Marſhal *Luxembourg*. It is true, a detachment from the troops of *Liege* defeated a party of the garriſon of *Namur*: but this diſadvantage was fully repaired by the check which the Marquis of *Harcourt* gave the enemy near *Marche en famine*, by the attempt which Count *Guiſçard* made upon the ſuburbs of *Stat* near *Huy*, and the bombarding of *Charleroy* by Mr. *Boufflers*.

The King of *France* finding that this campaign had not brought his enemies to the end which he had in view, namely, of giving peace to *Europe*, and terminating a bloody war which he had not occaſioned, his Majeſty was ſenſible that he muſt force them to it by the ſtrength of his arms.

arms. Accordingly, in the month of *September,* 1692.
he augmented his troops with twelve new regiments of foot, befides that of *Breffey,* and one
of *Huffars*; and ordered the Governors of towns
and forts to levy free companies compofed of
people of the refpective countries, the better to
know the roads. His Majefty further ordered
the levying of feveral regiments of the militia in
Alface, and three companies of fufileers of a
hundred men each, under the name of the fufileers of *Flanders.* They likewife negotiated in
Switzerland a permiffion to levy fome new regiments.

Befides, in order to repair the lofs which
France had fuftained this year at fea, the King
ordered new fhips to be built in all the maritime
towns of the kingdom, and the others to be repaired; and fent Mr. *Bonrepos* to *Denmark* in
the room of Mr. *Martangis* (whofe health did
not agree with the air of that country) to negotiate a permiffion to buy or build fome fhips.
Towards the end of the year his Majefty made
a general promotion of Sea-officers.

The Duke of *Berwick* being returned to *St.* 1693.
Germains, expreffed to King *James* his earneft
defire to engage in the fervice of *France,* and accept of fome poft that might enable him to fupport his expences. His Majefty was overjoyed
that the Duke had prevented him in an affair
which he himfelf had greatly defired, ever fince
it was out of his power to beftow on him fome
poft fuitable to his merit: he therefore acquainted

1693. ed the King of *France* that the Duke of *Berwick* had ferved in *England* as Lieutenant-general, that he had always diftinguifhed himfelf, and that he (King *James*) would prefent his Moft Chriftian Majefty with fo worthy a fubject, if he would be pleafed to grant the Duke the favour of employing him in his armies. *Lewis* XIV. anfwered, that after the teftimony which Marfhal *Luxembourg* had given of the courage and merit of the Duke of *Berwick*, he would have prevented his *Britifh* Majefty by afking that Duke of him, had he known that it would have been agreeable to his Majefty; that he accepted with pleafure fo worthy a fubject; that hereafter he fhould belong to them both, fince his fervice fhould never be inconfiftent with the zeal and fidelity he owed to his lawful fovereign; and that in the promotion he was going to make of General Officers he would give him fuch a rank as was due to his merit.

This anfwer gave great joy to the Duke of *Berwick*, who could now hope to ferve in the next campaign, and to have a rank in the *French* army: but this joy was fomewhat difturbed by the uncertainty he was in of the rank which was to be beftowed on him. He was Lieutenant-general in the army of the King of *England*, and wifhed to have the fame rank in that of *France*. Yet he could not hope for this, feeing that the Princes of the blood had in their firft campaign only the rank of Marefchal de Camp, and that the Duke *du Maine*, *Lewis* the fourteenth's natural

tural

tural fon, had obtained no other rank. He re- 1693.
mained all winter in this uncertainty; however
he prepared for the campaign, and had his equipage ready to be fent away, as foon as he fhould
know his fate.

In the mean time the whole difcourfe at Court
ran upon the promotion of General Officers which
was foon to be made, and all thofe who thought
they deferved to be included in that number,
were making great intereft not to be forgot.

The Duke of *Berwick* alone waited calmly at
St. Germains for his Majefty's pleafure; when
on the feventh of *March* there was a promotion
of feven Marfhals of *France*, without any mention of other General Officers; namely, the Duke
of *Villeroy*, the Marquis of *Joyeufe*, Count *Tour-*
ville, the Duke of *Nöailles*, the Marquis of *Bouf-*
flers, Count *Choifeüil*, and Mr. *Gatinat*.

They now began to defpair of feeing any other
promotion this year. The Duke of *Berwick* was
the only perfon who did not lofe hopes, confid-
ing in the King's promife. At laft, in the beginning of *April*, when it was no longer expected, there was made a promotion of twenty eight
Lieutenant-generals, in which number was the
Duke of *Berwick*, of twenty fix Marefchals de
Camp, twenty fix Brigadeers of horfe, and thirty feven Brigadeers of foot.

The King having publickly declared this promotion, fent to King *James* at *St. Germains* the
commiffion of Lieutenant-general for the Duke
of *Berwick*, which his *Britifh* Majefty delivered
to

1693. to him.   Immediately the Duke went to *Ver-*
failles to thank the King of *France*.   As foon as
he came thither, he was informed that his Majefty had named thofe who were to have the
command of his armies in the enfuing campaign,
and the officers who were to ferve in them, and
that he was appointed to ferve in the army of
Flanders, which was to be commanded by the
Marfhal of *Luxembourg*, and under him by the
Marfhals *Villeroy* and *Joyeufe*; that Marfhal
Boufflers was to command the army on the
Meufe, Marfhal *Lorges* that on the *Rhine*, Marfhal *Catinat* that in *Piedmont*, and Marfhal *No-*
ailles that in *Catalonia*.   It was likewife faid, that
his Majefty intended to go this campaign to the
army in *Flanders*.

Marfhal *Luxembourg* prefenting the Duke of
Berwick to the King, faid to him, *Sir, the Duke*
of Berwick *is come to exprefs to your Majefty the*
great fenfe he has of the honour you have conferred
on him, and I dare affure your Majefty, after be-
ing witnefs to his Grace's behaviour in the battle
of Leuze, *and in the battle of* Steenkerke, *that*
your Majefty gains a worthy fubject; for he already
deferves and is able to command an army.   The
King, addreffing himfelf to the Duke of *Ber-*
wick, faid, *My Lord Duke, I am glad, according*
to the King of England's *intentions, to engage in*
my fervice a man of your merit.

Some days after, that is, on the tenth of *May*,
the King created a new Order of Knighthood,
under the name of *the military Order of St. Lewis*,

to

to be conferred as a reward upon thofe officers 1693.
who fhould diftinguifh themfelves in the field.
His Majefty declared himfelf the Sovereign,
Grand-mafter and Founder of this Order, and
united and incorporated the Grand-mafterfhip of
it with the Crown of *France*, making it impoffible to be alienated at any time from that Crown
for any reafon whatever.

The Duke of *Berwick* returned to *St. Germains*, but haftened to depart from thence, that
he might be one of thofe who came earlieft to
the army. He ufed to fay that an officer could
not be too forward in attending his duty, and
fhould always be prefent in the army before his
General arrived. In the fequel of thefe Memoirs
it will appear, that when he commanded in chief
he never pardoned any officer who was guilty of
this neglect; and, without regard or diftinction,
punifhed all thofe who were not in the army before him. If this great ftrictnefs has been cenfured by certain perfons, it has been admired by
many others, who have gained from fuch a rigorous difcipline confiderable advantages and much
glory.

On the fourteenth of *May* the Duke of *Berwick* arrived at Marfhal *Luxembourg*'s army,
which at that time met at *Eftines* and *Givry*,
between *Binch* and *Mons*. The army under
Marfhal *Boufflers* was then encamped at *Haine*,
which is a league north-eaft of *Binch*.

On the fifteenth the King fet out from *Verfailles* to head his troops, having refolved to com-

H   mand

 mand in perſon the army under Marſhal *Bouf-flers*: but being detained at *Queſnoy*, where his Majeſty fell ſick, and was blooded twice, he did not arrive at *Haine* till the ſecond of *June*. The King was accompanied by the Dauphin, the Duke of *Orleans*, the Duke of *Chartres*, and all the Princes and ſeveral Ladies of the Court.

Next day his Majeſty reviewed his army ; and that under Marſhal *Luxembourg* decamped from *Eſtincs*, advancing towards *Nivelle*: the horſe of the ſecond line paſſed by *Haine*, where the King's army ſaw them file off.

On the fifth of *June* the King encamped at *Harlemont-Capelle*, near the rivulet of *Pieton*, and Marſhal *Luxembourg* at *Sekey* about a league from *Nivelle*. On the ſixth the King marched to *Thimeon*, and on the ſeventh to *Gemblours*, where his Majeſty took his quarters, and conti-nued for ſome days.

Whilſt people we e now in expectation that the King's deſigns wonld quickly appear, and in ſuſpence where they would break out, they were much ſurprized when his Majeſty declared his intention of returning to *Verſailles*, and ſending the Dauphin to *Germany* with a detachment of twenty ſeven battalions, and forty ſix ſquadrons.

So ſudden a change occaſioned much talk, e-very one labouring to diſcover the reaſon of it. But in vain do we endeavour to penetrate the de-ſigns and projects of Sovereigns, which are known only by the event, or a conſiderable time after. It appeared afterwards that the King of *France*'s

deſign

defign was upon *Liege*; but that the ftay his 1693.
Majefty had been obliged to make at *Quefnoy* by
reafon of his indifpofition having given the enemy time to fecure that place, he had therefore
refolved to abandon that project, and return to
Verfailles; and that having received a courier
from Marfhal *Lorges* acquainting him with the
taking of *Heidelberg*, his Majefty had for that
reafon refolved to fend the Dauphin with the detachment above mentioned into *Germany*, in order to pufh his conquefts in that country.

After the King's departure, and that of the
Dauphin, Marfhal *Luxembourg*, to whom his
Majefty had left the command of the reft of the
troops in *Flanders*, united both the armies together, which now confifted of ninety nine battalions and twenty two fquadrons. He encamped at *Torine les Ardens*, from whence he removed, and marched between *Tilmont* and *Judoigne*,
at the diftance of a league from the enemy's army, which was yet at *Park-abbey*; fo that the
advanced guards were within fight of each o-
ther.

This General meditated enterprizes of great importance; but his camp fuffered fo much for
want of provifions, that it was not in his power
to put them in execution: nor was he in a condition to attack, before the arrival of a great convoy which he expected: it confifted of feven hundred waggons laden with corn and two chefts
of money, and had arrived at *Mons* feveral days
before, but was forced to lie in that place, be-
H 2   caufe

1693. caufe it was feared that the enemy having notice of the preffing occafion we had for it, and how impatiently it was expected, would make their utmoft efforts to carry it off, efpecially as the garrifon they had in *Charleroy* could facilitate the means of doing it.

The Prince of *Orange* feeing that Marfhal *Luxembourg* durft not venture the tranfporting of this convoy, laid a fnare for him. He weakened the garrifon of *Charleroy*, that the Marfhal might take this as an opportunity of receiving the convoy. The latter, not being aware of this ftratagem, gave into the fnare, and had no fooner notice that the garrifon of *Charleroy* was leffened, than he fent word to Count *Vertillac*, Marfhal de Camp and Governor of *Mons*, to lay hold of this opportunity; and that as the welfare of the army depended upon it, he fhould not think the convoy was fafe till it was in his own hands. Count *Vertillac* was ordered to deliver it to Count *Guifcard*, Lieutenant-general and Governor of *Namur*, who was to receive it at *Beaumont*, and they were to continue together with all their troops, if the latter thought it proper.

Vertillac fet out from *Mons* on the night of the fecond of *July* with fix hundred horfe, and arrived fafely at *Beaumont*, where he met Count *Guifcard*, to whom he delivered the convoy.

Next morning *Vertillac* with his troop of horfe fet out on their return to *Mons:* but foon after his departure Count *Guifcard* fent him a meffage defiring him to return with all fpeed, becaufe he

had.

intelligence that the enemy intended to attack 1693.
him, in order to carry off the convoy. *Vertillac*
flew to his affiſtance, and though both their troops
together were far inferior in number to thoſe of the
enemy, yet he thought proper to attack them,
and to amuſe them by ſkirmiſhes, that the convoy might have time to file off, and arrive at
Namur.   But this attack ſoon became very briſk
and important.   Never was a more bloody and
obſtinate fight.

We ſaved the convoy; but it coſt us dear:
for in this action we loſt Count *Vertillac*, an officer of uncommon merit, who haſtened to follow the ſteps of the greateſt men.

The convoy being arrived at *Namur*, Marſhal *Luxembourg* decamped from *Judoigne*, and
marched to *Truyen*, where he received advice on
the ſixth of *July* from the Chevalier *Neſle*, whom
he had ſent out with a party that Count *Tilly*,
brother of Prince *Tſerclas de Tilly*, was encamped under *Tongeren* with a large body of troops.
Whereupon he reſolved to attack this camp. To
conceal his deſign, he ſent next morning the left
of his army to forrage, and about noon he gave
orders to eight ſquadrons of the King's guards,
two of the Gendarmery, two of the light horſe,
and that of the horſe grenadeers, and of the light
horſe of the right wing, to ſet out between ſix
and ſeven in the evening, in order to join him at
the village of *Houthem*, where he waited for them
with other troops both horſe and foot, all which
compoſed a body of ten thouſand men.

H 3

Theſe

1693.   Thefe troops, being commanded by the Duke
of *Berwick*, arrived about eight of the clock in
the evening within four miles of the camp of
Heilifheim, where Marfhal *Luxembourg* had continued after the forraging was ended.   The foot
had marched before ; for we knew not that Count
Tilly had none.   The Duke had orders to guard
a pafs on the *Jecker*, at about four miles from
Tongeren.

About eleven of the clock at night Marfhal
Luxembourg at the head of the cavalry marched
them in two columns, one of which was led by
Marfhal *Villeroy*. They continued to march very
faft during the whole night, and arrived at three
in the morning within two miles of the place
whither they intended to go.

Whereupon they haftened to gain an eminence, from whence they difcovered within the
diftance of a quarter of a league Count *Tilly*,
who having received advice about midnight of
Marfhal *Luxembourg*'s defign, was now retiring :
but as he had only begun to fend off his baggage,
he had not time enough to efcape us.

Marfhal *Luxembourg* detached feveral fquadrons to attack him, while the reft of our troops
followed with great fpeed.   Thofe which were
the foremoft drew near him, after having paffed
fome ravines ; but whilft they were expecting to
attack him, they found between them and the
enemy another ravine which our horfe could not
pafs.   There were only about a hundred of our
horfe and others who got over, and flanking a
                                                    body

body of the enemy which was poſted on a riſing 1693.
ground, began to ſkirmiſh with them. This body
conſiſted of ſix or ſeven ſquadrons, which were
very cloſe, and having had poſitive orders not
to come to an engagement, only fought as
they were retreating, whilſt the main body of
their troops filed off by a village, in order to paſs
the *Jecker* and eſcape us.

In this interval, the Duke of *Berwick* diſco-
vered a place on the right, from whence he might
take them in flank ; but as ſoon as he arrived on
the eminence, he found only a ſmall number of
the enemy. They were driven above two
leagues very near *Maeſtricht*, whither Count
Tilly was obliged to retire, the paſs to *Liege* being blocked up.

About ſix in the evening our troops returned
from this chace, which was of eighteen or twenty
leagues, and brought to the camp more than a
thouſand cows, and ten thouſand ſheep.

Soon after this action, Marſhal *Luxembourg*
reſolved to beſiege *Huy*; for which purpoſe he
decamped from *Heiliſheim* with his whole army,
and drew near that place.

The Prince of *Orange* being informed of this
deſign, decamped from *Park-abbey* : having ſent
his heavy baggage to *Dieſt*, he encamped at *Tilmont* ; from thence he marched to *Wangen*,
where he continued, after having ordered his
army to be in readineſs to march.

In the mean while Marſhal *Luxembourg* ordered Marſhal *Villeroy* to beſiege *Huy*, which

did

1693. did not hold out long, having furrendered five days after it was invefted.

The Prince of *Orange*, who was now between *Truyen* and *Tongeren*, being informed of the taking of *Huy*, immediately fent ten battalions to *Liege*, and encamped next morning at *Neerhef-pen*, where he continued in order to have intelligence of Marfhal *Luxembourg*'s motions. Being informed that the lines we had made in *Flanders* to cover our conquered countries from the *Scheld* to the *Lys*, and from thence to *Ypres*, *Berg St. Winnox*, and to the fea by *Dunkirk*, were guarded only by a few troops, he fent on the eleventh of *July* the Prince of *Wirtemberg* with a ftrong detachment to attack thefe lines in three feveral places.

The Marquis *la Vallette*, who commanded in our lines, was forced to abandon them for want of troops, and they were rafed by the Prince of *Wirtemberg*, who, upon this fuccefsful attempt, fent a detachment towards *Doway*, which put the country of *Artois* under contribution, took fome pofts and caftles, and made themfelves ma-fters of a large extent of ground in the open country.

The Prince of *Orange* continued in his camp at *Neerhefpen* till the eighteenth of *July*, intend-ing to return next day to *Park-abbey*: but Mar-fhal *Luxembourg* feeing that the detachments which that Prince had fent to *Flanders* and to *Liege* had weakened his army, he refolved to have his revenge for the expedition againft our

lines,

lines, and to attack him before he returned to his former post. For this purpose he marched to *Lesquy*, in order to oblige the Prince of *Orange* to draw nearer *Liege*; and made a feint of besieging that place, having sent a strong detachment, composed of the King's houshold, of carabineers, dragoons and grenadeers, as it were to examine the country and posts about *Liege*.

Marshal *Luxembourg*, who went himself at the head of this detachment, being accompanied by the Duke of *Berwick*, observed that the troops commanded by Count *Tilly* were intrenched in the lines that were near the town. As soon as he returned, he ordered four thousand fascines to be made ready against the following day; and the better to conceal his design, on the twenty eight of *July*, he ordered Marshal *Joyeuse* to march with a strong detachment and ten pieces of cannon, under pretence of going to the assistance of the Marquis *la Vallette*, against the Prince of *Wirtemberg*. This detachment set out at break of day, and entered the plains at the head of the *Jecker*.

These orders, together with the various marches which Marshal *Luxembourg* had made, surprised every body. It could not be conceived what was their purpose: the Duke of *Berwick* alone saw into the designs of our General.

Having several advices that the Prince of *Orange* was encamped on this side the *Geet*, Marshal *Luxembourg* marched his army in seven columns

with

1693. with fo great diligence, that having fet out by break of day from *Helle*, which is feven leagues from the enemy's camp, his van-guard came within fight of it at four in the afternoon. He at firft headed the left wing which in this march made the right column. But being arrived at the mill of *Varem*, he had advice from *Tracy*, the Chevalier *Nefle*, and *Dufour*, whom he had fent out by different ways, that the enemy were ftill in their camp: whereupon he halted, to give the reft of his army time to pafs the *Jecker*; and Marfhal *Joyeufe*, who had been detached under pretence of affifting the Marquis *la Vallette*, as we have faid above, having joined our army with his troops, Marfhal *Luxembourg* committed to him the charge of making them pafs that river, and went himfelf to head the right wing which was led by the Marfhal *Villeroy*, and was already between *Lens-les-Beguinez* and *Avernas*.

While the infantry under the Prince of *Conti*, the Duke of *Berwick* and *Rubantel*, were paffing over feveral bridges, Marfhal *Luxembourg* advanced at the head of the King's houfhold, being followed by the reft of the column, and haftened to arrive in view of the enemy, with a defign either to oblige them to continue in their camp, or to charge their rear-guard, if they fhould repafs the river.

He fent orders to the Prince of *Conti* and the Duke of *Berwick* to advance with the columns of foot; but this could not be done without

great

great trouble, by reafon of the long march they 1693.
had made. And now the defign of the feveral
motions which Marfhal *Luxembourg* had ordered
began to appear.

The Prince of *Orange* could not have timely
notice of this march, and was far from thinking
that we came to attack him.

As foon as the head of our army, which was
commanded by the Marfhal himfelf, came in
view of the enemy, being at the diftance of
half a league, he took poffeffion of the villages
of *Landen*, *St. Gertruydenland* and *Overwinden*,
in order to command the country which lay before him. After this, he gave the neceffary
orders for putting our troops in battalia as they
arrived in the plain, which was within reach of
the enemy's cannon.

When the head of our army appeared, the
Generals of the Allies being perfuaded that *Luxembourg*'s defign was upon *Liege*, could not believe that our whole army was come to attack
them, and imagined it was only a detachment
fent by our General to cover his march; but the
Prince of *Orange* having got on horfeback, with
the Elector of *Bavaria*, and the chief officers of
their army, foon difcovered the Marfhal's real
defign: whereupon he immediately drew up
his men in battalia, at the head of their camp;
and held a council of war, wherein, notwithftanding moft of the general officers were for repaffing the *Geet*, they refolved to wait for us,
and venture a battle.

Had

1693.   Had we been in a condition to attack them on that day, we might have eafily defeated them : but that was impoffible, for all our troops were not yet arrived.

On the twenty ninth of *July*, as foon as it was day, we difcovered the enemy drawn up in battalia, againft the expectation of many who thought they would have retired. They had made in the night feveral bridges over the rivulet *Beck* pretty near *Leuwe*, to which place they fent all their baggage. At the fame time they had pofted a ftrong body of infantry in the hedges on the other fide of the *Beck*, in order to facilitate their retreat in cafe of need. The left wing of their army extended from the village of *Heilifheim* and the caftle of *Wau* on the *Geet*, to the village of *Overwinden*, and was covered by a brook and feveral hedges and hollow ways. They had likewife made in the night a retrenchment, behind which they pofted a part of their infantry. Their left wing being covered by the *Beck*, reached from the village of *Dormal* to *Neerlanden*, and from thence formed an arch behind the infantry in the retrenchment, in order to fupport them.

Marfhal *Luxembourg* having viewed both wings of the enemy's army, and feeing it was neceffary to make himfelf mafter of one of thofe two villages in order to defeat the Allies, he fent to *Overwinden* fix brigades in the firft line, and two in the fecond, to fupport the former, under the command of the Duke of *Berwick* and Mr. *Rubantel.*

At

At the same time he sent six brigades under 1693.
the command of the Prince of *Conti* and the
Marquis of *Crequi* towards *Neerlanden*, which
was on his right.

Mean while the enemy having planted eighty
pieces of cannon on their rentrenchment, fired
them upon our troops; and as they were lodged
upon an eminence, and saw our troops under
them, their cannon put our horse in great disorder.

Whereupon Marshal *Luxembourg* brought up
his artillery, which consisted of seventy pieces
of cannon, and planted them before his army;
though we could only play them on the enemy's
batteries, by reason of the eminence, yet they
were pointed so justly that they did great execution.

Both armies were in this posture about nine of
the clock in the morning, when Marshal *Luxembourg* ordered the Duke of *Berwick* to attack the
village of *Overwinden*; and as the taking of *Neerlanden* on our left was impracticable, he contented himself with amusing the enemy on that
side.

The Allies, who had only these two posts to
maintain, all the rest of the ground being almost inaccessible, placed their best troops in
them, and fired so violently, that our men
could hardly bear it; and as the villages were
full of hollow ways, stopped up with great trees
hewn down for that purpose, and defended by
retrenchments, we were obliged to make extra-

ordinary

 ordinary efforts, and repeat our attacks three times, before we could drive the enemy from thefe pofts.

At laft, by the conduct and valour of the Duke of *Berwick*, whofe example animated the troops under his command, the attack made on the village of *Overwinden* proved fuccefsful: but the Prince of *Orange*, knowing how important it was to recover that poft, fent a detachment of frefh troops, which came to attack the village with great fury. The Duke of *Berwick* feeing this, prepared to make a vigorous defence. Upon the falfe intelligence he had received that the Prince of *Orange* was with thofe troops, he expofed himfelf with the utmoft temerity; for as he perfonally aimed at this Prince, he fought him out on this occafion, in order to encounter him: thus, as foon as the enemy began the attack, he rufhed upon them, aud forced his way to their third line, where, being overpowered by their numbers, he was obliged to yield himfelf a prifoner.

Immediately our troops loft their ardour upon lofing their General, and being unable to fupport the furious onfet of the enemy, they abandoned the village.

The Duke of *Berwick* being taken prifoner was brought to the Prince of *Orange*, who having notice that his troops had recovered *Overwinden*, and thinking the victory would be on his fide, afked him whether Marfhal *Luxembourg* did not repent his having come to attack him?

The

The Duke anfwered very fiercely, that his High- 1693.
nefs might in a fhort time repent his having
waited for him.

In effect, Marfhal *Luxembourg*, after we had
loft *Overwinden*, immediately fent the brigade of
Guiche, and fome others, to recover it: the
Duke of *Orleans* headed them, and attacked that
village a fecond time with fo much valour,
that he drove the enemy from thence, and lodged in it the brigade of *Guiche*.

The Prince of *Orange*, who made it his chief
point to maintain that poft, fent a new detachment to recover it: they repulfed our men,
not wholly out of the village, but to fome hedges
at a confiderable diftance from the firft, which
the enemy poffeffed. After this, a brigade was
detached from our fecond line to fupport the
troops at *Overwinden*; but the enemy's fire was
fo hot, that our troops could advance no farther
than the lower part of the village, which we
ftill maintained.

And now, all our horfe and foot went in front
to the enemy's retrenchments: this fierce ftep
began to aftonifh them; but as they ftill poffeffed
the villages on their right and left, and their retrenchments were yet entire, they did not move
for all this.

The King's houfhold, with the reft of the
horfe and foot, having drawn near them, found
ravines and parapets which the horfe could not
pafs; upon which account, the firft lines continued in a narrow hollow ground, in order to
avoid

1693. avoid the enemy's batteries, which greatly annoyed our army.

Towards noon, there had yet happened nothing decisive; and moſt of the General Officers ſeeing that all the efforts which had been made upon the two villages could not force the enemy to abandon them, were of opinion that ſuch an enterprize ought to be given up : nay, the Prince of *Conti* propoſed it to Marſhal *Luxembourg*, alledging that the King's army muſt ſuffer greatly if we perſiſted in attempting to drive the enemy from ſo advantageous a poſt.

The Duke of *Bourbon* was of a different opinion, and inſiſted upon our attacking once more the village of *Overwinden* with battalions which had not yet ſuffered, and even intreated the General to give him the charge of making that attack.

Marſhal *Luxembourg* liſtened to this propoſal with pleaſure, told the Duke of *Bourbon* that he ſpoke like the worthy grandſon of the great Prince of *Condé*, and intreated him to put in execution what he had propoſed, ſaying, that he was perſuaded the troops which were to fight under his command would make their utmoſt efforts to ſurmount the greateſt obſtacles, being animated by the brave example of ſo great a Prince.

This attack proved ſucceſsful, and brought on the victory, which ſoon after appeared on our ſide. This engagement was one of the moſt remarkable and bloodieſt that ever happened. The enemy loſt twelve thouſand men in the field of

battle.

battle. Our lofs amounted to fix thoufand : and 1693.
on both fides many officers of diftinction were
killed or wounded *.

As for the prifoners of diftinction, there were
only on our fide the Duke of *Berwick*, Count
Coffé, and Mr. *de Salis* Brigadeer of foot. On
the fide of the Allies there were the Duke of
Ormond, Lieutenant-general and Captain of the
Prince of *Orange's* life-guards, General *Syrauve-
more*, Count *Brouay*, the Earl of *Montfort*, and
Major-general *Waleftein*.

After the battle of *Landen*, both armies carried off their wounded. Afterwards they exchanged their prifoners. The Duke of *Berwick*
was exchanged for the Duke of *Ormond*.

On the twentieth of *Auguft* the Duke of *Berwick* joined Marfhal *Luxembourg* at *Nivelle*,
where he was encamped with his army, and
continued till the twenty ninth, when he decamped for *Soignies*, from whence he marched
on the ninth of *September*, and encamped between
Binch and *Eftines*.

The Prince of *Orange* was encamped between
Hall and *Tubife*, having his quarters at the caftle
of *Lambec*, and the Elector of *Bavaria* having
his at *Hall*: he continued in this camp till the

---

* As for the lofs of men, the Confederates owned but fix thoufand killed, wounded or taken prifoners ; and the *French* could
not deny but that they had two thoufand officers killed or wounded. The Confederates gave out that the *French* loft eighteen
thoufand men in the battle, which affertion feems to be counte-
nanced by *Luxembourg's* not purfuing the victory, and continuing
a forthnight at *Waren* without attempting any thing.

I

thirtieth

1693. thirtieth of *August*; he then went to encamp at *St. Quintin Linnik*, where he stopped in order to act according to the motions of the *French* army.

During all these marches, Marshal *Luxembourg* had given orders for preparing great quantities of warlike stores, and bringing together a great many waggons.

He gave some umbrage to *Liege*, in order to conceal his design of attacking *Charleroy*, the siege of which place had been resolved upon after the battle of *Landen*. The artillery and pontoons were embarked upon the *Sambre* at *Namur* and *Maubeuge*. Mr. *Megrigny*, with several engineers, was ordered to go to *Mons*; and the pioneers necessary for making the lines of circumvallation were appointed.

On the ninth of *September* Count *Guifcard*, Governor of *Namur*, set out from thence to *Charleroy* with fix battalions of his garrison, and a regiment of dragoons, with which troops he invested *Charleroy* on the side of *Chaftellet*, while Mr. *Ximenes* invested it on the side of *Marchienne* with fixteen squadrons of horse and one of dragoons.

On the tenth of *September* Marshal *Villeroy* at the head of thirty two battalions and thirty four squadrons detached from the army, arrived before *Charleroy*, while Marshal *Luxembourg* encamped with the rest of his troops at *Hairlemont Capelle*.

On

On the night between the fifteenth and six- 1693.
teenth, Mr. *Rubantel* and the Duke of *Roquelaure*
opened the trenches. We feized an advanced
poft called *la Maifon de la Garenne,* which was
advantageoufly intrenched: we there took fifty
prifoners, and killed a hundred and twenty men.
Afterwards we took a redoubt in a Morafs on
that fide of *Charleroy* which is towards *Mons,*
near *Fontaine l'Evéque*; and weformed two at
tacks.

On the fixteenth Mr. *de Rozen* and Mr. *Wag-
ner* mounted the trenches on the left, and the
Marquis of *Crequi* on the right: the fame day
the befieged fallied out, but were repulfed.

On the night between the feventeenth and
eighteenth the Duke of *Berwick* relieved the
trenches on the left, and the Duke of *Elbeuf*
thofe on the right; we continued the works
with fuccefs, and without any difturbance.

On the eighteenth the Prince of *Conti* mounted the trenches on the left, and the Baron *Breffey* on the right: we advanced the works for the
general attack as far as a ftone redoubt at the foot
of the glacis of the body of the place, before the
Bruffels port.

On the nineteenth the Prince of *Conti* was relieved by the Duke of *Berwick,* and Baron *Breffey* by the Marquis of *Gaffion:* the Duke planted
a battery of forty pieces of cannon, which put
a ftop to the cannon of the enemy.

On the twentieth Mr. *Ximenes* relieved the

 Duke

1693. Duke of *Berwick*, and Count *Marcin* relieved on the right.

Marſhal *Luxembourg*, who had decamped the day before to obſerve the motions of the Prince of *Orange*, lay this night at *Mons*: he had ordered the Duke of *Berwick* to join him, as ſoon as he ſhould be relieved from the trenches. Accordingly the Duke joined him at *Mons*, and next day he was ſent by the Marſhal with ſeventeen battalions to reconnoitre the enemy's army as near as poſſible, and to bring certain intelligence of their motions.

On the twenty fourth Marſhal *Luxembourg* returned from *Mons* and encamped at *Vanderbeck*, waiting the Duke of *Berwick*'s return. The latter went as far as the advance-guards of the Prince of *Orange*'s camp, which was then at *Ninoven*, and learned from the deſerters that the Electeor of *Bavaria* had marched towards *Flanders*, with a deſign to draw Marſhal *Luxembourg* into that country, and thus to have an opportunity of going by a counter-march to the relief of *Charleroy*; but that not being able to ſucceed in this deſign, he had been obliged to repaſs the *Schelde* and return to the camp at *Ninoven* on the twenty ſecond inſtant.

Marſhal *Luxembourg*, like an able General, had diſappointed the enemy's expectations, and was content to obſerve their army, and diſpoſe his men into columns, that he might be ready to follow the Elector of *Bavaria*, or the Prince of *Orange*, whatever courſe they ſhould take.

This

This made the Prince of *Orange* apprehend 1693. that if he ventured to pafs the *Scheld*, in order to join the Elector of *Bavaria*, Marfhal *Luxembourg* would fall upon his rear.

The Elector of *Bavaria*, being returned, was obliged to repafs the river, that he might be at hand to affift the Prince of *Orange*, in cafe Marfhal *Luxembourg* fhould attack him. Thus all their meafures were broken, without our making any ftep whereof they could take advantage.

The Duke of *Berwick* being returned, continued fome days in Marfhal *Luxembourg*'s army : but growing weary of remaining inactive, he intreated and prevailed with the General to give him leave to return to the fiege of *Charleroy*.

On the eight of *October* he mounted the trenches on the left. The fame day the Marquis of *Vateville* relieved thofe on the right; and we lodged fome troops on the top of the covered way of the whole front that was attacked.

On the tenth Marfhal *Villeroy* fummoned the Governor to furrender, and upon the refufal he made, we prepared for giving the affault, after the mines fhould be blown up. But the befieged obferving thefe preparations, and expecting no relief, beat the *Chamade* on the eleventh at eight of the clock in the morning, after having defended that place twenty feven days from the opening of the trenches. Hoftages were exchanged, the capitulation was figned, and the garrifon obtained all the honourable terms that

I 3

were

1693. were due to men who had fo bravely difcharged their duty.

The day after the furrender of *Charleroy*, Marfhal *Luxembourg*, who had lain with his army at *Vanderbeck* to cover that fiege, decamped from thence, and cantoned his troops.

On the fixteenth the enemy moved from *Ninoven*, and the Prince of *Orange* began to detach feveral fquadrons and battalions, which he fent into divers garrifons. Some days after, both armies broke up and went into winter quarters.

The Duke of *Berwick* went as ufual to pafs the winter at *St. Germains* with King *James*: he came fometimes to *Verfailles* to make his court to the King, and to procure the favour of the minifter.

1694. In the beginning of the year 1694 we made the neceffary preparations for the enfuing campaign. In the month of *April* the King of *France* declared his intention of fetting out on the feventeenth of *May* to head his armies, without mentioning to which fide his Majefty defigned to go ; and they were preparing his equipage. The Duke of *Orleans* was to command in *Bretaigne*, as he had done the preceeding year, and Marfhal *Humiers* was to ferve under him ; but fome days after the King declared that he did not intend to go to the campaign in *Flanders*, nor to fend the Duke of *Orleans* to *Bretaigne*; and that the Dauphin was to command his army in *Flanders*, having under him Marfhal *Luxembourg* and Marfhal *Villeroy*: at the fame time his Majefty named all the

general

general officers who were to ferve under the Dau- 1694.
phin, and the Duke of *Berwick* was of that number.

Marfhal *Boufflers* was appointed to command
an army of twenty thoufand men, which was.
to act on the *Meufe*, and join either the army
in *Flanders*, or that in *Germany*, as occafion
required. Marfhal *Lorges* was appointed to
command that on the *Rhine*, and under him
Marfhal *Joyeufe*; Marfhal *Catinat* that in *Italy*,
which the King had weakened by fending fome
detachments from thence to *Catalonia*, where his
Majefty intended to act with greater vigour, and
to have the main ftrefs of the war. Marfhal
Noailles was appointed to command the army in
that country.

On the twenty feventh of *May* the Duke of
Berwick came to the army in *Flanders*: the
fame day Marfhal *Luxembourg* fet out from
court for the fame place, and was foon after followed by the Prince of *Conti* and Marfhal *Villeroy*.

The Dauphin did not leave *Verfailles* till the
thirty firft. All the troops of his army were cantoned about *Maubeuge*, till the forrage was more
advanced; whilft the army which was to be
commanded by Marfhal *Boufflers* was cantoned for the fame reafon about *Namur* and
Charleroy.

In the mean time the enemy met at *Betlehem*
near *Louvain*, to be within reach of fuccouring
Bruffels, or *Mechlin*, of covering *Louvain*, and
preferving *Liege*, for which place they were the
moft apprehenfive. They likewife brought to-

gether

1694. gether a small army at *Tongeren*, under the command of General *Tettau*, to cover *Maestricht*, or to throw succours into *Liege*. Some time after, the Earl of *Athlone* joined this army, and took the command of it. On the eleventh of *June* the Prince of *Orange* arrived in the main army of the Allies, and took his quarter at *Betlehem*.

Marshal *Luxembourg* having assembled his army the day before, ordered several regiments commanded by the Duke of *Berwick* to pass the *Sambre*. Within three days after, the whole army passed that river, and encamped at *Fleurus*; from thence they moved to *Gemblours*, and afterwards to *Boneff*, where they continued for some time. At this camp Marshal *Boufflers* joined our army with the body of troops which he commanded. Mean while the Prince of *Orange* marched to *Dorn*, from thence to *Betum*, and advanced as far as *Tilmont*.

Both armies continued in this situation till the tenth of *July*, and all that time was spent in forraging, and sending out detachments.

On the tenth the Dauphin's army decamped from *Boneff*, marching upon two columns always in a plain country, and arrived at *Orelle* on the *Jecker*, where the general quarters were appointed.

The Prince of *Orange* having notice of this march, dispatched a courier to the Elector of *Bavaria*, who was encamped at *Neer-Yche*, to desire him to come and join him on the thirteenth.

teenth. When that Prince was preparing to 1694.
march, he was informed that the Dauphin had
changed his camp only for the convenience of
forraging ; whereupon he continued in the fame
pofts till the twenty fecond of *July*.

As he now was in no fear for *Leige*, he refolved to decamped and poffefs himfelf of a poft
which would have cut off all communication between our army and *Namur*, though there was
fome danger of our falling on his rear-guard,
when part of his army fhould have paffed the
Scheld.

On the twenty fecond of *July* he fet out in the
night, and after a march of fix hours his army
arrived at *Mont St. André*, not far from the *Mebaigne*, and there they began to encamp. But the
Dauphin and Marfhal *Luxembourg* made fo fpeedy
a march as broke his meafures : for having advice
of the enemy's motions, and feeing into their defign, the Dauphin decamped from *Tongeren* on the
twenty fourth, drew near *Huy*, paffed the *Jecker*,
and encamped on the *Mebaigne*, his right wing
being at the diftance of two leagues from the Allies, and covered by the rifing ground of the abbey *Vau Nôtre Dame*. The Dauphin took his
quarters at *Norre*, and Marfhal *Luxembourg* at
Vignamont. The heavy baggage was fent beyond
the *Meufe*, and fome bridges were laid over this
river, not only for the tranfporting of the baggage, but for the convenience of forraging in the
Condrotz, and receiving the convoys from *Namur*.

The

1694.   The body commanded by Marſhal *Boufflers* encamped at *Varline* on the right of our army, facing *Liege*. All *Europe* knowing the ſituation of theſe two armies, expected ſome great event.

The Prince of *Orange*, who was highly pleaſed with having gained the poſt he had taken, had ſent to the Allies ſeveral couriers to acquaint them of it, and to aſſure them that he would oblige our army to repaſs the *Meuſe*, as it was impoſſible for us to ſubſiſt long in our camp; he even aſſured them that the Dauphin could not paſs the *Mehaigne* to go towards the *Sambre*, without running the hazard of being attacked at a great diſadvantage, by reaſon of the rivers and brooks he muſt croſs within ſight of the right wing of the Allies; and that if he ſhould make ſuch a motion, they might attack him on any quarter.

The Dauphin foreſeeing all the Prince of *Orange* could do, ſecured his army, and put it in a condition to forrage on the other ſide of the *Meuſe*, after they ſhould have conſumed the forrage about *Liege* and the plain of *Acoche*. He fortified the head of his camp with retrenchments covered by a large ditch, and extending from the left of his foot to the flank of his right. His left was ſecured by ravines which were before it, and by the *Mehaigne* which covered its flank and rear as far as *Huy*. He afterwards made ſeveral other bridges upon the *Meuſe*, in order to ſend over that river thoſe troops he ſhould appoint to forrage, and he ſecured them by a body under the command of the Marquis of *Harcourt*,

which

which was encamped upon the rifing ground at 1694.
Huy.

On the twenty ninth of *July* we made a great forrage on the fide of the enemy's army: the Dauphin and all the Princes were on this party. Two days after, we made another on the fide of *Leige*, within fight of the enemy's camp which covered that place. The Dauphin and Marfhal *Luxembourg* fearing fome oppofition from that camp, gave the command of this party to the Duke of *Berwick*, though it was not his turn; for which reafon feveral Lieutenants older than the Duke of *Berwick* murmured at this diftin-ction.

This forrage was made without any difturb-ance, except a few fkirmifhes which were of no confequence; and till the eighteenth of *Auguft* we did nothing but forrage about *Huy* and *Liege.*

The Prince of *Orange* had flattered himfelf, as we have faid above, that our army would be obliged to decamp for want of forrage; but he was miftaken, and had the mortification to de-camp firft. He fent his heavy baggage to *Lou-vain*, and on the eighteenth of *Auguft* moved from *Mont St. André* to *Sombref*, where he en-camped next day: continuing his march towards *Fehuy* and *Arguennes*, he arrived between *Soignies* and *Brain-le-Comte*, from whence he advanced to *Chambron*, after having ordered a ftrong de-tachment under the Elector of *Bavaria* to march with great diligence to *Pont Efpieres*, and make
them-

1694. themfelves mafters of it, before the troops which we had in that poft could be reinforced. He defigned to make his army pafs the *Scheld*, and to penetrate afterwards into *Flanders*.

The Prince of *Orange* continuing his march, encamped on the twenty third at *Frefnes*, near *Peufe*, and fent another detachment under General *Tettau* to attempt to poft themfelves on the *Scheld*, making likewife towards *Pont Efpieres*.

The Dauphin waited only till the Prince of *Orange* decamped, to quit the neighbourhood of *Huy*. He was informed of it at nine of the clock in the morning; and knowing how important it was to prevent the enemy's defigns, he immediately gave orders to decamp. In the evening he came to *Froidmont*, next morning to the caftle of *Soy* on the *Sambre*, afterwards to *Aufart-Letang*, and from thence to *Mons*, where he ftopt to give his troops time to come up : he continued his march towards *Tournay*, from whence he fent Marfhal *Villeroy* to *Pont Efpieres* with a ftrong detachment.

Marfhal *Villeroy* having marched feventeen hours without interruption, arrived at *Pont Efpicres* before the Elector of *Bavaria*, who drawing near it with his detachment, was greatly furprifed to fee on the other fide of the *Scheld* eighty fquadrons in battalia, and even believed that all our infantry was arrived there likewife; for Marfhal *Villeroy* had the precaution to difplay a great many colours, in order to deceive the enemy. Some hours after the Dauphin arrived with

the

the King's houfhold and fome regiments of dra- 1694.
goons.

The Elector of *Bavaria* found it impoffible to obey the Prince of *Orange*'s orders; and after each fide had cannonaded the other for fome time, he thought fit to pafs the *Scheld* near *Oudenarde*, which ftopt the enemy two or three hours, and gave our army time to arrive. On the twenty fifth at eleven of the clock in the morning the greateft part of our infantry came up in two co-lumns, one led by the Prince of *Conti*, and the other by the Duke of *Berwick*.

On the fame day the Prince of *Orange*'s army filed off in fight of ours, the *Scheld* running between the two armies, and encamped within a fhort league of *Oudenarde*, while the Elector of *Bavaria*, who went before, was advancing with his detachment to pafs the *Scheld* near the fame place. The next morning the whole army of the enemy followed, and encamped between the *Scheld* and the *Lys*, having *Deynfe* on their right, and *Oudenarde* on their left.

This great diligence of the Dauphin, who marched forty two leagues in five days, though he had five rivers to pafs, broke the meafures of the enemy. They had expected to pafs the *Scheld* before us, having had only twenty leagues to march in a ftrait line, and being fet out a full day before our army : whereas we had been obliged to make a large circuit, and pafs feveral rivers, which is always a great delay to the march of an army. Their defign was to enter

our

1694. our lines and to make themfelves mafters of *Courtray*, which the Prince of *Orange* would have
effectually done, notwithftanding the extraordinary diligence of our troops, had his march been
as fpeedy as ours; but he could not imagine that
this was poffible, and he was extremely furprifed
when he was affured that we had paffed the
Scheld before him. This march did great honour
to the Dauphin: it is indeed one of the moft remarkable that ever were known, and may ferve as
an inftructive example to all Generals of armies. *

Nothing elfe confiderable happened during this
campaign in *Flanders* †. In the room of con-

---

* This hafty march coft the *French* a great many men and
horfes: but that lofs was inconfiderable in comparifon of the
advantage they gained by hindering the Allies from penetrating
into *French Flanders*, where, confidering their ftrength, they
would, in all probability, have made fome important conqueft,
or at leaft fecured winter-quarters. The King of *France* was
fo fenfible of the great advantage of this march, that he wrote a
letter, which he ordered to be read at the head of the army,
wherein he returned thanks in the firft place to the Princes of
the Blood, next to the Marfhal of *Luxembourg*, as having had a
principal fhare in the conduct, then to the reft of the Marfhals of
France, and all the General Officers; and laftly, to the *French* and
Swifs infantry, regiment by regiment, acknowledging how much
he was beholden to their zeal and incredible diligence.

† King *William* finding it impoffible to attempt any thing on
the fide of *French Flanders*, laid hold of this occafion to difpoffefs
the *French* of the town and caftle of *Huy*. This place was invefted by Prince *Tferclas de Tilly* at the head of a party of *Brandenburg* horfe and fome battalions of foot. About the middle of *September*, when the Duke of *Holftein Ploen*, who was appointed to
command the fiege, approached the town with feventeen regiments of foot, it immediately furrendered. On the twenty feventh the *French* Governor, who had retired to the caftle, beat
a parley, and furrendered that fortrefs next day. By this conqueft the *French* were totally expelled the Bifhoprick of *Liege*.

quefts

quefts the Dauphin was content to defeat all the 1694.
enemy's defigns.   On the eighteenth of *Septem-*
ber he returned to *Verfailles*, where his Majefty
gracioufly received him.

As long as the Prince of *Orange* remained in
his camp at *Roufelaër*, Marfhal *Luxembourg* lay
encamped near *Courtray*; but on the feventh of
October he was no fooner informed that the
Prince had fet out for *Holland*, and left the command of his army to Mr. *Overkerke*, than he
decamped from thence, and fent his army into
winter quarters.

The Duke of *Berwick* being returned to *St.* 1695.
Germains, his ufual abode in winter, found that
King *James* had refolved to marry him.   His
Britifh Majefty had two motives for it; one
was, that he might ftill more attach to his intereft the family of the Earl of *Clanrickard*, which
had continued faithful to him; and he judged
the moft effectual way of doing this was to beftow on the Duke of *Berwick* a Daughter of
that Family, who was of late a widow, and attended his Queen: the other was, that he might
reward the faithful fervices of the Duke of *Ber-*
wick; for as that family had a very large eftate
in *Ireland*, the King faw that this marriage
would bring an ample fortune to the Duke, if
ever any favourable revolution fhould reftore him
to the *Britifh* throne.

The Duke of *Berwick* had no thoughts of
marrying: but the will of his Sovereign determined him.   He faw the young widow, was
taken

1695. taken with her perfon and merit; and about the beginning of this year he married in the chapel of the caftle of *St. Germains*, in the prefence of the King and Queen, *Honora Bourk*, daughter of *William Bourk*, Earl of *Clanrickard*, and the widow of *Patrick Sarsfield*, Earl of *Lucan*.

Never was a more happy or more focial marriage; but it was of fhort continuance, for this lady died three years after. The Duke of *Ber-wick* could not but be deeply afflicted at his lofs, and always preferved the moft tender remembrance of fo worthy a confort.

Toward the beginning of this year Marfhal *Luxembourg* died of a pleurify. The Duke of *Berwick* who had enjoyed the friendfhip, efteem and confidence of that great man, was fenfibly afflicted at his death. The lofs which *France* fuftained thereby could only be made up by the many able Generals who were formed under him, among whom the Duke of *Berwick* is one of thofe who have done the greateft honour to his memory.

While his Chriftian Majefty ufed all his endeavours to reftore the peace of *Europe*, the Prince of *Orange* alone went about to defeat them. However, the credit which that Prince had acquired with the allies againft *France* began to decline. Far from making any conquefts upon *France*, a profpect which he had prefented to their view when he brought them into the *Augfbourg* league, they found that there hardly

paffed

paffed one campaign, wherein they did not lofe 1695.
fome important battle, or important town.

They began to complain loudly againft the
laft campaign, efpecially the *Englifh* and *Dutch*,
who bore almoft alone the burthen of this war.
The latter publickly demanded a peace, and the
former did the fame, though with lefs noife for
fear of the Parliament, which hitherto had been
devoted to the will of that Prince.

The Houfe of Commons, backed by fome
members of the Houfe of Lords, made a ftrict
enquiry into the frauds and extortions committed
in the army, and briberies in Parliament; they
expelled their Speaker out of their houfe, imprifoned fome of their chief members, impeach-
ed the Earl of *Danby*, * Prefident of the Prince
of *Orange*'s Privy-council, and continued to profecute him till the Parliament was prorogued.

Such proceedings, carried on in the face of all
Europe, and under the eye of that Prince, againft
his moft devoted creatures alarmed him greatly,
and made him apprehenfive of a revolution: befides, the Princefs of *Orange* dying about this
time, he became exceeding jealous of the intrigues of the Princefs *Anne* of *Denmark*, and
feared every thing that could befal him from
thofe who continued faithful to King *James*.

However, the Prince of *Orange*, like an able
politician, concealed the vexation which all thefe

* King *William* had created him Marquis of *Carmarihen* and
Duke of *Leeds* in the year 1694.

K

affronts

1695. affronts had given him, left nothing undone to
appeafe the Parliament and the people, and exerted his utmoft efforts to keep the Allies in the
Augfburg league.

He knew that the moft effectual way of maintaining his power in *England*, and his credit with
the Allies, was to perform fome great action in
the enfuing campaign; and the death of Marfhal *Luxembourg* gave him hopes of fucceeding.
With this view he induced the *Englifh* and
Dutch, and the other Allies, to augment their
warlike preparations againft *France*, and went
over to *Holland* earlier this year than he had done
the year preceeding.

The King of *France*, on the other hand, to
prevent the defigns of the enemy, appointed betimes thofe who were to command his armies,
and the General Officers who were to ferve in
them. The Duke of *Berwick* was named to
ferve in the main army in *Flanders*, which was
to be commanded by Marfhal *Villeroy*. Marfhal
Boufflers commanded this year, as he had done the
year preceeding, on the *Meufe*; Marfhal *Lorges*
in *Germany*, having under him Marfhal *Joyeufe*;
Marfhal *Catinat* in *Italy*, and Marfhal *Noailles*
in *Catalonia*; but the latter having fallen fick
during the campaign, his place was fupplied by
the Duke of *Vendome*. Marfhal *Choifeüil* commanded on the coafts of *Bretagne*, Marfhal
Etrées in the country of *Aunis*, and Mr. *Vauban* at *Breft*.

When

When the Duke of *Berwick* arrived in the 1695.
army in *Flanders*, it was in different places between *Turnes* and the *Meuse*. Marſhal *Villeroy*
arrived in it two days after, and immediately ordered the troops about *Kieurain* to paſs the *Haine*
and march to *Blaton* in the enemy's country,
about two leagues from *Condé*: at the ſame time
he ſent orders to all the troops which were cantoned to march to *Leuze*, and there to encamp; while the army under Marſhal *Boufflers*
advanced to *Goſſeliers* on the *Pieton*, being two
leagues from *Charleroy*.

Marſhal *Villeroy* having notice of the arrival of
the Prince of *Orange* at his army, which was
then at *Aerſeele*, decamped from *Leuze*, and
marched to *Cordes*, and next day to *Potte*, between *Tournay* and *Oudenarde*; on the ſame day
he viewed the lines between the *Lys* and the
Scheld, and between *Ypres* and the *Lys*.

The Prince of *Orange* upon his arrival, reviewed his horſe, and detached twelve ſquadrons
under the command of the Marquis *la Foreſt*,
which paſſed the *Lys* at *Machelin* upon three
bridges, to join the Elector of *Bavaria* who encamped with his army at *Ninoven*.

Theſe motions ſeemed to threaten *Menin*,
Ypres, *Kenoque* and *Furnes*; though the real deſign of the Prince of *Orange* was not to attack
any of our towns on the ſea-ſide: however
Marſhal *Villeroy*, who had orders to guard thoſe
parts preferable to the country about the *Meuſe*
having notice of this, decamped from *Potte*.

K 2

Our

 Our army paſſed the *Scheld* on ſeveral bridges, the foot being led by the Prince of *Conti* and the Duke of *Berwick*, and the horſe by the Duke of *Bourbon* and the Duke *du Maine*. Next day they arrived at *Houthain:* whereupon Marſhal *Villeroy* ordered the hedges and thickets which ſtopped the communication of our troops in their marches to be cut down, appointed workmen to finiſh the lines, and drew up his army in battalia, that they might know the places where they were to be poſted, in caſe the enemy ſhould come to attack us: he afterwards pointed out to every ſquadron the battalion which they were to ſupport, and diſtributed powder and ball.

Theſe orders and precautions made it believed that Marſhal *Villeroy* had received ſecret intelligence that the Prince of *Orange* deſigned to attack him; but it ſoon appeared that the real deſign of that Prince was to beſiege *Namur*.

The better to conceal it and to put Marſhal *Villeroy* on a wrong ſcent, he attacked *Kenoque*, as if he intended to penetrate into *France* on the ſea-ſide, and advance as far as *Dunkirk:* the command of this attack was given to the Duke of *Wirtemberg*, who did not meet with all that ſucceſs which the Prince of *Orange* had expected. Count *la Motte*, who commanded on that ſide, ſent a reinforcement to *Kenoque*, whither he went afterwards in perſon.

The attack was very briſk, but Count *la Motte* made ſo vigorous a defence that he obliged

the

the enemy, after having loſt ſeveral of their 1695.
men, to abandon that enterpriſe, and to retire in
diſorder, and with precipitation.

About this time the Prince of *Orange* ſent the
Earl of *Athlone* and the Baron *Heyden* to inveſt
Namur. Marſhal *Boufflers* having notice of the
enemy's deſign paſſed the *Sambre* at *Solre*, arrived at *Philippeville*, and next morning before it
was day-light paſſed the *Meuſe* at *Dinant*, where
he was joined by the Marquis of *Harcourt*: at
the diſtance of a league from thence he halted
for ſome time to reſt the horſes, and afterwards continued his march towards the bridge of
Namur, being reſolved to force his paſſage, if
the enemy had troops to oppoſe it on that ſide;
but as they had none, he entered the town
without oppoſition, at ten of the clock in the
evening, with ſeven regiments of dragoons.

On the eleventh of *July*, the enemy having
finiſhed their lines of circumvallation, and their
great cannon being arrived, the Prince of *Orange*
opened the trenches before *Namur*. The Prince
of *Vaudemont* commanded a flying camp to obſerve Marſhal *Villeroy*, and hinder him from relieving the town.

Marſhal *Villeroy* being informed of this, repaſſed the *Scheld*, and encamped at *Potte*; at the
ſame time he ſent ſome horſe to *Mons*, *Charleroy*,
Maubeuge, and *Philippeville*, to harraſs the enemy in their convoys and forrages, and afterwards
reſolved to attack the army which was under the
command of the Prince of *Vaudemont*: for which

K 3

purpoſe

1695. purpofe having formed his troops into four columns, which were led by the Duke of *Bourbon*, the Prince of *Conti*, the Duke *du Maine*,
and the Duke of *Berwick*, he fet out from *Potte*
on the twelfth of *July* at ten of the clock in the
evening, and marched his army with fo much
diligence, that after having paffed four rivers, he
arrived next morning at *Roofbeecke* on the *Man-
del*, which was only four miles from the enemy,
who were then encamped at *Denterghem*.

In this march, the Duke of *Berwick* at the
head of his column forced the caftles of *Ingelmunfter*, *Meulebeeck*, and *Marckeghen*, and made
their garrifons prifoners at difcretion. They confifted of four hundred men.

The Prince of *Vaudemont* being apprifed by the
attacking of *Ingelmunfter*, that Marfhal *Villeroy*'s
troops were advancing, and knowing that they
had been encamped two days before at *Potte*,
could hardly believe that the whole *French* army
was fo near him, and imagined it was only a
detachment fent to amufe him, while Marfhal
Villeroy marched to the relief of *Namur*. However, as he had received orders from the Prince
of *Orange* to return with his troops to the main
army, in cafe that Marfhal fhould advance to
attack him, he endeavoured to get fure intelligence of it, and in the mean time continued in
his poft, where he had narrowly efcaped being
furprized.

Having feen our van-guard at fix in the evening on the rifing ground near *Dentreghem*, where
his

his right wing was pofted, and being now affur- 1695.
ed it was the whole *French* army which advanced againft him, he immediately changed the difpofition of his camp, placing his right at *Aer-*
feele, and his left at *Grammen*, near the *Lys*; at
the fame time he ordered retrenchments to be
made on both fides. Count *Noyelles*, who had
the command of thefe works for part of the center and the whole left wing, caufed his General's orders to be executed with fuch extraordinary diligence, that on the fourteenth, by break
of day, he made a very defenfible line; the rifing grounds upon the right of *Aerfeele* were alfo
fortified by ten of the clock in the morning:
whereupon the artillery was placed in the right
flank, and in the whole front of the line. In
this pofture the enemy paffed the whole day.

The Prince of *Vaudemont* perceiving by the motions of the Duke of *Berwick*, whom Marfhal
Villeroy had detached with a body of horfe and
fome regiments of dragoons, that we defigned to
befet him on all fides, and to fall upon his rear,
at the fame time that we fhould attack him in
front, thought it high time to provide for a retreat.

Thereupon he ordered the intrenchments to
be perfected every where; fome advanced houfes
to be fet on fire, left our troops fhould take poffeffion of them when they advanced againft him;
and the cannon of his left wing continually to
play upon us, that we might imagine he was rather difpofed to fight than to retreat.

K 4

     In the mean time he caused the cannon of the right and front to be silently drawn off, and to march towards *Deynse*, and ordered Mr. *Overkerke*, with the right wing of the horse interlined with some battalions, to make a line, extending from the mill of *Aerseele* towards *Winck*, as if he intended by this line to hinder the Duke of *Berwick* from attacking his rear : but Marshal *Villeroy* ordered the Duke soon after to return to the army.

Afterwards the Prince of *Vaudemont* suddenly ordered the horse and battalions under Mr. *Overkerke* to march by *Winck* and *Nivelle* directly to *Ghent*, and the foot, which was now marching along the entrenchments, to take the road to *Wouterghem*. The Earl of *Rochford*, who was posted with the left wing of horse and two battalions of foot towards the *Lys*, made the rear-guard towards the left, retiring to *Deynse*. The *Dutch* infantry commanded by Count *Noyelles*, made the rear-guard of all the foot.

After the foot of the right wing had marched off, the Prince of *Vaudemont*, the Prince of *Wirtemberg*, and the General Officers of the *English* troops, with their domesticks and attendants, formed a rank of horse, as if it had been a squadron, and continued some time in their camp, to observe what motions our army would make upon this retreat, and afterwards followed their troops.

Our General Officers observing these motions, were of opinion, especially the Duke of *Berwick*,

that

that we ought to march to the enemy, without 1695.
waiting for Marſhal *Villeroy*'s orders, time being
now precious, and the occaſion very favourable.
Though the Duke of *Bourbon*, and the Prince of
Conti, were of this opinion, yet they would not
take it upon them to attack the enemy without
the orders of the General, who was at this time
in the right of our army, and therefore notice
was ſent to him of the poſture of the enemy :
but a conſiderable time was loſt, for it was ſeven
of the clock in the evening before he was acquainted with it.

It was now too late, and the opportunity was
miſſed. However, Marſhal *Villeroy* immediately ordered ſome foot to march directly to the
retrenchments, which they found abandoned, and
detached ſome dragoons and the King's houſhold
to follow the enemy. Though this detachment
marched with great ſpeed, they could only come
up with a ſmall number of the enemy's rear-guard,
and gave but little diſturbance to their retreat.

It is a neceſſary rule in military affairs, that
an officer ſhall not undertake any thing without
the order of his ſuperior. Nevertheleſs, there
are certain favourable moments when this rule
may be diſpenſed with. An officer ought not
to be afraid of anſwering for the event of an
action undertaken without the authority of his
ſuperior, if that action is important and deciſive,
if the opportunity is extremely favourable, and
muſt either be preſently ſeized, or is preſently
over.

We

 We have an instance of this in the present case: for it is certain that if the Duke of *Berwick*'s advice had been followed, the Prince of *Vaudemont* had been defeated, and the Prince of *Orange* forced to raise the siege of *Namur*.

Marshal *Villeroy*, having missed so fine an opportunity, resolved to attempt the siege of *Newport*, where he knew there was a weak garrison: but being informed that Major-general *Elenbergher*, a *Dane*, was encamped under *Dixmude*, with twelve battalions and some squadrons of dragoons, to relieve either of these two places that should be attacked, he resolved first to hinder these succours from entering *Newport*. For this end he detached *Rubantel* to seize a redoubt which was in the road between *Dixmude* and *Newport*, and kept a communication between these two places. *Rubantel* having possessed himself of this redoubt, continued to march towards *Newport*, whither Marshal *Villeroy* followed him with part of his army, leaving the rest at *Rouselaer*.

He encamped within half a league of *Newport*, and took his quarters at *Saerback*. Next day he viewed the avenues and posts about the place; but being informed that the Prince of *Vaudemont* had detached Lieutenant-general *Bellasyse* with twelve battalions to secure *Newport* and the canal of *Plassendal*, that they were encamped near that place, that they were followed by twelve battalions and thirty two squadrons commanded by the Prince of *Wirtemberg*, and

that

that befides, the enemy had put the country a-   1695.
bout *Newport* under water, he gave up this enterprize, decamped from *Newport*, and went to
befiege *Dixmude*.

This place was garrifoned by eight battalions
and a regiment of dragoons under Major-general
Elenbergher.   It was invefted on the twenty fifth
of *July*, and the trenches were opened the next
day in the prefence of Marfhal *Villeroy*, the
Princes and General Officers.   The day after,
the Marfhal left the conduct of the fiege to
Count *Montal*, and returned to *Roufelaer*, where
the main army was encamped.

Dixmude held out only two days from the
opening of the trenches, and the Commander
and garrifon were made prifoners of war.   The
Marquis *Feuquieres* and Baron *Alfeld* having appeared before *Deynfe* on the fame day, the Commander of that place furrendered immediately at
difcretion, with a garrifon of two thoufand four
hundred men. *

All this could not oblige the Prince of *Orange*
to abandon the fiege of *Namur*. By this time
the town had capitulated, and Marfhal *Boufflers*
had retired to the caftle.   Whereupon Marfhal

* Major-general *Elenbergher*, who delivered up *Dixmude* to
the *French*, after a flight refiftance of thirty fix hours, though
he might have held out a forthnight, was on that account condemned by a Court Martial to be beheaded ; and Brigadeer *Of-
farel*, Governor of *Deynfe*, who delivered up that town without
making any refiftance, was condemned to be cafhiered with in-
famy, and imprifoned during the King's pleafure. *November* 30.
Elenbergher was beheaded at *Ghent*.

Villeroy,

1695. *Villeroy*, having left Count·*Montal* with five or six thousand men to guard the lines, went to encamp at *Avelghem* on the *Scheld:* the next morning part of our army passed that river, took provisions for six days, and proceeded to *Benay*, where they continued for some time: afterwards they advanced between *Steenkerke* and the lesser *Enghien*, from whence Marshal *Villeroy* sent the heavy baggage into the neighbouring garrisons.

The Prince of *Vaudemont* being informed of this march, sent word to the Prince of *Wirtemberg*, who was on the side of *Newport*, to provide for the security of the towns and forts in that country, and to follow him with the rest of his troops.

In the mean time the Earl of *Athlone* arrived at *Waterloo* with a thousand horse. The Prince of *Orange*, on his side, fearing that Marshal *Villeroy* designed to bombard *Bruffels*, set out on the twentieth of *Auguft* from his camp before *Namur* with a body of troops to join the Prince of *Vaudemont*, leaving the conduct of the siege to the Elector of *Bavaria*. The same day he arrived at *Waterloo*, where his army amounted to forty thousand men. The troops of the Allies were disposed in such a manner about *Bruffels*, that in less than six hours they could bring together sixty thousand men.

Mean while Marshal *Villeroy* waited at *Enghien* for the great convoy which had set out from *Mons*, escorted by the Marquis of *Harcourt*: it

arrived

arrived in the army at *Haute-croix* near *Enghien*. 1695.
From thence we marched to *Hall*, and arrived
the next day in the plain of *Anderlight*. Our
army halted for some time, till the necessary
dispositions were made for investing *Brussels*.
But Marshal *Villeroy* finding he was too far from
the town, passed a brook not far from it and encamped in two lines. The enemy's foot which
was encamped on the banks of that brook, had
retired almost as soon as our army appeared :
whereupon we planted batteries on the heights
of *Anderlecht*, where were the general quarters.

The enemy fired upon us from two batteries,
one in the town, and the other in their camp.
The ramparts were lined with citizens who
having at their gates an army of sixty thousand
men well retrenched, thought they had nothing
to fear. The front of the town was put under
water from the place where the *Senne* enters it
to fort *Montery*. Within pistol shot of their
batteries they had made a strong intrenchment
above three fathoms high, upon a great hollow
way which served as a ditch to it, and extended more than five hundred fathoms into the
country.

Besides, they had fortified three mills on our
left along a small canal, and thereby hindered
us from drawing near enough to the town to
bombard it. In the afternoon we attacked these
posts with several pieces of cannon, and towards
the evening we opened the trenches in two places.
The Duke of *Berwick* mounted the trenches at
the

1695. the attack of the place under water on the right, with the regiments of *Piedmont* and *Provence*, supported by ten battalions; he ordered a fortified mill and a redoubt to be attacked, that we might approach nearer the town in order to bombard it. The enemy being driven from the mill and the redoubt, were purfued to the gates of the town, where five of our grenadeers entered with them and were made prifoners.

Mr. *Rubantel* opened the trenches on the left. This day and the next were employed in advancing the trenches, and preparing batteries of mortars and cannon for firing bombs and red-hot bullets. When thefe batteries were ready, Marfhal *Villeroy* wrote a letter to the Prince of *Berghen*, Governor of *Bruffels*, to acquaint him that the King his mafter had fent him an order to bombard that town, by way of reprifals for the bombarding of the maritime towns of *France* by the *Englifh* and *Dutch* fleets, and at the fame time to declare that fuch kind of hoftilities gave fo much reluctance to his Majefty, that if the Allies would abftain for the future from making war in that manner, his Majefty would do the fame. That his Majefty had refolved upon the bombarding of *Bruffels* with fo much the more concern, as the Electrefs of *Bavaria* was there: that the Governor would be pleafed to let him know in what part of the town fhe was, the King his mafter having ordered him not to fire there; concluding, that he expected in fix hours

a prea precife anfwer, and fuch as he could depend 1695. upon.

The enemy were glad of this delay of fix hours, that the Electrefs of *Bavaria* might have time to retire to the fuburbs. The time allowed being elapfed, the Prince of *Berghen* fent word that the Elector of *Bavaria* was juft arrived, on occafion of the Electrefs's being ill, and that if Marfhal *Villeroy* would wait one hour more, the Elector himfelf would fend an anfwer. The Marfhal waited an hour and a half, without any body coming from the town; for which reafon he ordered five or fix bombs to be thrown into it, one by one. Whereupon the Prince of *Berghen* fent him a letter to let him know that the propofal which the King of *France* had made could only be anfwered by the Prince of *Orange*; that he would acquaint that Prince with it, to have an anfwer in twenty four hours, if Marfhal *Villeroy* would agree to it; and afterwards thanked the King of *France* for the confideration his Moft Chriftian Majefty had for the Electrefs of *Bavaria*, and told him that fhe was in the King of *Spain*'s Palace.

Marfhal *Villeroy* underftanding that the enemy wanted only to gain time, ordered fome bombs to be thrown into the town one by one, to oblige them to fend a more definitive anfwer; afterwards we fired by way of falvo twenty five at a time, and continued firing without intermif-fion all that night, the day following and the night after that. The effect was fo violent, that

a great

 a great part of the town was seen in flames. After having thrown three thousand bombs into *Bruſſels*, which was the number ordered to be fired into that town, Marſhal *Villeroy* drew off the artillery and ſent it to *Haute-croix* on the ſide of *Enghien*.

On the ſeventeenth of *Auguſt* our army marched to *Soignies* in ſix columns, which were commanded by the Duke of *Bourbon*, the Prince of *Conti*, the Duke *du Maine*, the Duke of *Berwick*, Mr. *Rubantel*, and Mr. *Feuquieres*, moving towards *Namur*, where Marſhal *Bouf-flers* was making a vigorous defence in the caſtle, but was in great anxiety, not having heard from Marſhal *Villeroy* ſince the twenty fifth of *July*. The latter waited for the return of Mr. *Champlay*, whom he had ſent to the King to receive his Majeſty's laſt orders, as to what was to be done in the preſent juncture. Mr. *Champlay* having re-turned and brought the King's orders that Mar-ſhal *Villeroy* ſhould make his utmoſt efforts to preſerve a place of ſo great importance, our ar-my decamped from *Soignies*, marched to *Ni-velle*, and from thence to *Fleurus* and to *Marbay*, where it arrived on the twenty ſixth of *Auguſt*. Towards the evening Marſhal *Villeroy* gave *Boufflers* a ſignal of our approach, by a ſalvo of ninety pieces of cannon, which the latter an-ſwered by a great fire ſet on the higheſt part of the caſtle.

The Prince of *Orange* being informed of the approach of Marſhal *Villeroy*, left the direction

of

of the fiege to the Elector of *Bavaria*, and re-
paired to his army of obfervation, which was encamped at *Mazy*, to take upon him the command of it. He took his quarters at the caftle
of *Boüeffe*, near the village of *St. Dennis*, and
having brought up his right wing to *Boüeffe*, he
ordered the retrenchments to be 'finifhed, and
fome trees to be cut down along the wood of
Argenton. From thence he went to order the
fame to be done towards the farms of *Bruyeres*
and *Oftin*, where the troops under Prince *Vaudemont* were arrived.

Thereupon Marfhal *Villeroy* went to view the
avenues to the enemies camp at *Mazy*, with a
thoufand grenadeers and a detachment of the
King's houfhold, being accompanied by the
Princes, the Duke of *Berwick*, and Mr. *Rubantel*. They obferved that the paffage to the enemy was very narrow, and blocked up by a great
intrenchment mounted with artillery and troops;
that before our men could arrive at that intrenchment, they muft pafs feveral ravines and moraffes; and that it was impoffible to maintain a
communication between the right and the left.
Having gone to view their camp on another fide,
he took no other General Officer with him but
the Duke of *Berwick*, who obferved to him the
fame difficulties: for which reafon, having returned to his army, he held a council of war,
where all the General Officers agreed that it
was in vain to attack the enemy in fo advantageous a fituation.

L

This

 This council was neceffary for the reputation of Marfhal *Villeroy*, as it ferved to prove that it was impoffible to relieve *Namur*.

On the thirtieth, Marfhal *Villeroy* went to encamp beyond *Perwys*, having the *Mehaigne* before him along the great caufeway, his right at *Cinq Etoiles*, and his left at *Cenfe du Soleil*, and behind his center the village of *Grand-Rofier*. It was there that he was informed of the furrender of the caftle of *Namur*, the garrifon having capitulated on the fecond of *September*. Whereupon he decamped from the banks of the *Mehaigne*, and towards the evening arrived at *Couilley* near *Charleroy*, in order to cover that place, and at the fame time to obferve the troops of *Brandenburgh* and *Hanover* which had marched towards *Louvain*. In this pofture he continued till the fifth, when he marched his infantry, and encamped the left wing on the *Sambre*. The Prince of *Conti* and the Duke of *Berwick* commanded the firft line. The artillery was fent to *Ham* on the *Heufe*. Mr. *Rubantel*, who commanded the fecond line, marched to *Marbay*, between *Thuin* and *Marchienne*. At the fame time Marfhal *Villeroy* marched with all the horfe to encamp at *Binch*.

On the fixth, the Prince of *Conti* and the Duke of *Berwick* encamped at *Grandreng*, and Mr. *Rubantel* at *Buffiere* and *Mierbe-Poterie*: there they continued the feventh and the eighth, and arrived on the ninth near *Mons*. On the twentieth they arrived at *Chambron* within two leagues of *Ath*: the fame day Marfhal *Villeroy* joined them

with

with the horfe, and continued his march to *Leufe.* 1695.

Thefe motions were neceffary, becaufe the enemy having quitted *Namur,* had arrived on the tenth between *Hall* and *Bruffels.* On the twenty third they went to *St. Quintin Linnick,* from whence the Prince of *Orange* fent feveral detachments, and ordered his battalions which were the moft fatigued to winter-quarters. On the twenty fourth he fet out for *Holland,* leaving the command of his army to the Elector of *Bavaria.*

The *French* army broke up fome days after: our troops were fent into the winter-quarters which the King had allotted to them, and Mar-fhal *Villeroy* returned to *Verfailles.*

At the fame time the Duke of *Berwick* fet out for *St. Germains,* where he found that feve-ral *Englifhmen* were importuning King *James* to improve the prefent opportunity of re-afcending the *Britifh* throne.

We have already feen that the *Englifh* and their Allies began to complain of the continuance of the war, and that the Prince of *Orange* had been very much vexed by his pretended fubjects. The advantages which the enemies of *France* had gained this laft campaign, and which they highly exaggerated, rendered them more obfti-nate in refufing any propofals of peace. By the taking of *Namur,* the Prince of *Orange* had re-gained his credit with the Allies, but efpecially with the *Dutch:* however, the people, whofe in-tereft it was that a peace fhould be made, and who greatly defired it, feared that it would be

 put

1695. put off by this firſt advantage which the Allies had gained. They were drained, and the commerce of the *Engliſh* and *Dutch*, wherein their riches confiſt, had been greatly diſtreſſed by the *French* privateers, who had taken many of their ſhips. Beſides, money was become ſcarce in *England*, the greateſt part of their current money was clept, and the recoining of it according to the eſtabliſhed ſtandard had lately put them to a vaſt expence. Moreover, the Prince of *Orange* had at this time very few land-forces in *England*, and but a few ſhips to guard the coaſts; all his troops were in *Flanders*, his great fleet was at *Cadiz*, and a ſquadron of large ſhips had lately ſailed from the *Downs* to join it.

Such was the ſituation of affairs in *England*, when thoſe who adhered to King *James* thought they had a favourable opportunity of reſtoring him to his throne.

His *Britiſh* Majeſty was then employed in nothing beſides the care of his ſoul, and had no thoughts of recovering a Crown which he had ſacrificed to GOD; but being unable to withſtand the follicitations of his Queen, the tenderneſs he had for his ſon the Prince of *Wales*, and the preſſing intreaties of his faithful ſubjeĉts, he was obliged to comply with the propoſals which ſeveral *Engliſh* Lords had made him.

The Duke of *Berwick* being informed of theſe favourable circumſtances, propoſed to King *James* to give him leave to go over to *England* in diſguiſe, that by the aſſiſtance of the Ducheſs of *Berwick*'s

relations,

relations, he might encourage and encreafe the 1695.
number of his Majefty's faithful fubjects. His
zeal met with applaufe, and his propofal was
approved. Accordingly towards the end of this
year the Duke of *Berwick* went in difguife to
England.

The King of *France,* who had much at heart 1696.
the interefts of King *James,* was eafily induced
to furnifh him with fhips and troops. Befides the glory which his Moft Chriftian Majefty
would have acquired by reftoring a King to his
throne, had this enterprize proved fuccefsful, he
would have likewife delivered the fubjects of that
King from an expenfive war. For this purpofe
the King of *France* gave the neceffary orders;
and the preparations for this expedition were carried on with great fecrecy in all the ports of the
Mediterranean and of the ocean, and with fo
much diligence, that by the month of *February*
there were in the port of *Toulon,* or in the road
of *Hieres,* fifty one men of war ready to put to
fea, with feveral fire-fhips and galliots. The
fame preparations were carried on in the ports of
Breft, Dunkirk, Calais, Rochefort, and *St. Malo.*

The fecret could not be fo well kept, but that
the enemy fufpected at leaft that the King of
France was preparing for fome great defign. E-
very politician was making his conjectures, when
the King declared that all thefe preparations concerned *England.* There were by this time between four and five hundred fhips ready at *Calais*
and *Dunkirk,* to tranfport the troops, horfes,

and

1696. and all the neceſſary ſtores for this expedition.
The troops conſiſted of eighteen regiments of
foot, three of horſe, and two of dragoons, all
experienced men, to the number of ſixteen thouſand, and were commanded by the Marquis of
Harcourt. They were to be eſcorted by two
ſquadrons, one under the command of the Marquis *Neſmond*, and the other under that of the
Chevalier *Bart.* Beſides, ſome troops had been
ordered to advance towards the ſea-coaſt, and to
ſupport, in caſe of need, the firſt which were to
embark.

King *James*, who in the month of *January*
had permitted the *Engliſh* who attended him to
go over to *England*, ſet out from *St. Germains* in
a poſt-calaſh on the twenty eighth of *February*.
The next day he arrived at *Montreüil*, and on
the firſt of *March* at *Calais*, where he found an
Intendant of the Marine, and ſome Commiſſa-
ries and Engineers who were ordered to embark
with him.

Beſides an hundred thouſand louis-d'ors which
the King of *France* had given his *Britiſh* Majeſty, and ſix millions which he had promiſed him,
King *James* had pawned jewels for five hundred
thouſand livres.

The Prince of *Orange* being appriſed of theſe
preparations againſt him, took the neceſſary meaſures to hinder the deſcent of our troops in *England.* He had been informed even from ſome of
King *James*'s party, that this Prince deſigned to
land near *Dover*, or *Rye*, where all thoſe who
adhered

adhered to him were to aſſemble, in order to 1696.
favour his landing, and ſupport the enterprize.
Whereupon he gave notice of the intended inva-
ſion to his Parliament, and took jointly with
them all the precautions he judged neceſſary to
defeat it. He ordered all the Catholicks who
were above ſixteen years of age to depart from
London, and not to come within ten miles of that
city; and thoſe who lived at a greater diſtance,
to depart from their reſpective abodes, and not
to come within five miles of them.

At the ſame time he ſent orders throughout
the whole kingdom, to diſarm all perſons who
were ſuſpected of being in the intereſt of King
James: beſides, he ſent from the Tower ſeveral pieces of cannon towards *Dover*, with ſome
regular troops and ſome militia. By the eighth
of *March* his fleet was ready to ſet ſail, and
weighed about this time from the *Downs*, being
followed by forty eight men of war and frigats,
under the command of Admiral *Ruſſel*. It ſtood
over towards *Graveling*, where it was joined by
ſeveral other men of war and fire-ſhips, the whole
fleet amounting now to near ſixty men of war.
The deſign of the enemy was to ſecure the ſea
on that ſide, and thus to cut off the communication between *Dunkirk* and *Calais*.

The *Dutch*, who had feared that our troops
were deſigned to inſult their coaſts, being informed that theſe preparations were made againſt *England*, ordered fourteen battalions, under the command of the Prince of *Wirtemberg*, to embark

L 4
in

1696. in five tranſport-ſhips, and to ſail directly to *Eng-land*, under the convoy of five men of war. Beſides, the *Dutch* ſent over the troops which were at *Oſtend*; ſo that the Prince of *Orange* received a reinforcement of about twenty battalions of choſen troops, while his fleet was reinforced by fifteen *Dutch* men of war which had put to ſea on the ſixteenth, under the command of Vice-admiral *Lallemberg*.

At the ſame time a report was ſpread of a conſpiracy to aſſaſſinate the Prince of *Orange*, entered into by ſeveral private perſons, and, as it was pretended, fomented by King *James*. All *England* was convinced by the concurring teſtimonies of the conſpirators who were apprehended and examined, that it was not only without his Majeſty's orders they had engaged in ſo black a deſign, but likewiſe without his privity. It was however the intereſt of the Prince of *Orange* to render King *James* as odious as poſſible. But the religion and eminent virtue of that Monarch have been ſo conſpicuous, that it would be unneceſſary to clear him from ſuch an aſperſion. It is true, when he engaged the King of *France* in this enterprize, he relied upon the aſſiſtance of a great number of his faithful ſubjects, who groaned under the domination of the Prince of *Orange*, and waited only for a ſupport from *France* to ſhake off his yoke, and appear for their rightful ſovereign. But it is manifeſt that there was no need of recurring to ſuch methods, to give ſucceſs to this enterprize;

for

for if the winds had been favourable, fo that King 1696.
James's fleet could have failed in time, and if
certain traytors had not early apprifed the Prince
of *Orange* of the danger which hung over him,
fo that he had time to render this enterprize utterly impracticable, he had infallibly been driven
out of *England*, and King *James* had been re-
inftated in the *Britifh* throne.

Mean while the Duke of *Berwick* was already
affured of a confiderable party in *England*, which
he daily augmented; he only waited for the arrival of King *James*'s fleet to appear for him;
when he was informed by a letter from his Majefty, that the contrary winds had detained him,
that he was betrayed, that the Prince of *Orange*
had taken fuch meafures as rendered the enterprize impracticable; and that befides, as the Parliament of *England* had lately declared that they
would make all their efforts to fupport the ufurper,
it was neceffary to fubmit to the will of God,
which fo manifeftly appeared; concluding, that
he defired him to return as foon as poffible, and
to take the utmoft care of doing it fafely, and
that he would wait for him fome time at *Calais*.

Upon the receipt of this letter, the Duke of
Berwick immediately prepared to fet out for
France, and as he was expofed to greater danger
in returning, the Prince of *Orange*, who had
notice of his prefence in *England*, having iffued a
proclamation, and promifed a reward of a thoufand pounds fterling for apprehending him, he
thought fit to difguife himfelf like a failor, and

put

1696. put to fea in a fifher's boat, wherein by the favour of a very dark night he efcaped the *Englifh*
and *Dutch* fleets, which were cruizing at that
time in the channel. Having landed at *Calais*,
he returned with King *James* to *St. Germains*,
where that unfortunate Prince gave over thinking
of his kingdoms, and minded nothing but his
falvation.

The Duke of *Berwick* upon his return found
his Confort was delivered of a fon, to whom King
James ftood Godfather, and who was named
James-Francis Fitz-James. He is now Duke of
Liria and *Xerica*, Grandee of *Spain* of the firft
clafs, Knight of the Order of the Golden Fleece,
and of the *Ruffian* Orders of St. *Andrew* and St.
Alexander, Chamberlain to his Catholick Majefty, and Lieutenant-general of his armies.

Upon this occafion the Parliament of *England*
manifefted the greateft concern and zeal for the
Prince of *Orange*, and the fafety of his perfon :
they declared that he alone was their rightful and
lawful King, they framed and fubfcribed an af-
fociation, whereby they obliged themfelves to
maintain his government, and in cafe he fhould
come to a violent death, to revenge it upon his
enemies, and to fupport the fucceffion of the
Crown as they themfelves had fettled it. The
Prince of *Orange* being thus fecured at home,
and having given the proper orders for the adminiftration of *England* in his abfence, went to
Holland, and from thence to *Flanders*, where
he headed the army of the Allies.

In

In the mean while the King of *France* gave 1696.
the neceffary orders for fecuring the coafts of
his kingdom. Marfhal *Etrées* was appointed to
guard thofe of *Bretagne*, Marfhal *Tourville* thofe
of the country of *Aunis*, and Marfhal *Joyeufe*
thofe of *Normandy*. At the fame time his Majefty augmented his troops, and made great preparations for carrying on the war this campaign
with more fuccefs than in the preceeding; intending to oblige the enemy to accept of a peace,
either by the force of his arms, or by negociations, or by withdrawing fome Princes from the
alliance againft him; and in this he fucceeded,
as will appear hereafter.

In the beginning of this year he made a promotion of General Officers, namely, of feventeen
Lieutenant-generals, forty three Marfhals de
Camp, thirty three Brigadeers of horfe, and
thirty five Brigadeers of foot. Marfhal *Villeroy*
had likewife this year the command of the principal army in *Flanders*, and Marfhal *Boufflers*
the command of that on the *Meufe*. Befides,
there were appointed four flying camps; two on
the fide of the fea, commanded by Count *Montal* and Count *la Mothe*; the third near *Luxembourg* commanded by the Marquis of *Harcourt*,
and the fourth near *Dinant* by Count *Guifcard*.
Marfhal *Lorges* being fick, and therefore not
able to command this year the army on the *Rhine*,
as he had done the year preceeding, the King
gave the command of that army to Marfhal
Choifeüil. Marfhal *Catinat* was fent to *Italy* with
an

1696. an order to negociate a peace at *Turin* with the Duke of *Savoy*, by the mediation of the Pope's Nuncio, and of the Envoy of the *Venecian* Republic. The Duke of *Vendôme* had the command of the army in *Catalonia*.

At the same time the King appointed the General Officers who were to serve in his armies: the Duke of *Berwick* was ordered to serve under Marshal *Villeroy*. He used to be among those who came earliest to the army; but this year he could not arrive in it till the nineteenth of *May*, when it was encamped at *Machelen*, the right at *Graveshanten*, and the left between *Deynse* and *Machelen*, being covered by the river *Lys*. He was no sooner arrived in the army, than Marshal *Villeroy* gave him the command of a small body of foot encamped at *Peteghem*, near *Deynse*, and designed to secure our left. Marshal *Villeroy* had in like manner placed some regiments of foot and dragoons to cover his right, which lay about the castle of *Graveshanten*. This camp was very convenient by reason of its situation upon the *Lys*, and of the great quantities of forrage which were found near it. The next day Marshal *Villeroy* ordered some bridges to be made over the river for the convenience of forraging, and even to send over his whole army when occasion required; and being informed that the enemy had brought together under *Ghent* a body of troops commanded by the Prince of *Vaudemont*, he ordered a camp to be marked out on the other side of the *Lys*, which had *Grammen*

QD.

on its right, and *Aerseele* on its left, and faced 1696.
Caneghem, with a design by possessing that camp,
to prevent the enemy, should they march to
that side. On the night between the last of
May and the first of *June*, he sent a detachment
of grenadeers and horse to burn the forrage
which was on the counterscarp of *Oudenarde*;
this was put in execution with pretty good success. Having afterwards advice that the enemy
had placed a guard of horse at *Mariekerke*, near
Ghent, beyond the canal of *Bruges*, he sent
Jannet, a Captain in the regiment of *Bourgundy*
with a detachment of sixty troopers and fifty
dragoons, to surprise it. This officer went
through the defiles with great speed, attacked
the enemy with vigour, killed about twenty of
them, pursued the rest to the pallisades of *Ghent*,
and returned to our camp with all his men.

Some days after, it was thought that the main
stress of the war was to lie upon the Elector of
Bavaria's army. It had been lately reinforced
by fourteen battalions sent from *Namur*. On
the twelfth the Prince of *Orange* joined it with a
detachment from the army at *Ghent*, and viewed the ground about *Genap*. The Prince of
Wirtemberg advanced to *Appel* with fifteen regiments, most of them *English*, to observe the
Marquis of *Courtebonne*, whom Marshal *Villeroy*
had detached with twelve squadrons and six
battalions: that Prince took his quarters at *Ber-
ner*, from whence he marched to *Vilvorden*,
that he might be at hand to join the Prince of
Orange

1696. *Orange* when it fhould be neceffary. The latter having ordered fome bridges to be made over the *Scheld*, above and below *Waure*, and fent his heavy baggage to *Louvain*, advanced to *Corbais*, where he encamped.

Upon the enemy's approach, Marfhal *Boufflers* reinforced the garrifon of *Charleroy*, and not being in a condition to make head againft them, he paffed the *Sambre*, and encamped at *Goffeliers*, from whence he moved to *Fleurus*. His army poffeffed fo many different pofts, that the Elector of *Bavaria* having afked a trumpeter where Marfhal *Boufflers* was encamped, of which he could get no intelligence; the trumpeter anfwered that his right was on the *Meufe*, and his left at the fea. Marfhal *Villeroy*, on his fide, fent twenty one battalions and eighteen fquadrons, with ten pieces of cannon, under the command of Mr. *Artagnan*, to encamp at *Helchin* till further orders; befides, he fecured all the paffes to *Dunkirk*.

Such was this year's campaign in *Flanders*, where the enemy's army being much ftronger than that of *France*, we were content to keep them from gaining any advantages. All the motions they made could not deceive our Generals, who took fuch juft meafures as rendered all their defigns ineffectual, efpecially that upon *Dinant*. The Prince of *Heffe* being weary of thefe marches and counter-marches, returned home with his twenty two thoufand men: but as we doubted that this was another feint, and that the

enemy

enemy defigned to make fome attempt on the 1696.
fide of the *Rhine*, the Marquis of *Harcourt* was
fent to obferve him.

The Allies now began to make loud complaints, and the Prince of *Orange*, to difculpate
himfelf, only alledged that what paffed in *Piedmont* had obliged him to be very circumfpect *,
meaning the fecret negociation which Marfhal
Catinat had begun with the Duke of *Savoy*, and
which, after a private peace concluded in *Italy*,
foon brought on a general peace in *Europe*. Befides it was known that Mr. *Calliere* was gone
incognito to *Holland*, and that Marfhal *Boufflers*
had held feveral conferences with the Earl of
Portland.

The Duke of *Berwick* upon his return to *St.
Germains* found King *James*'s court in that perplexity and agitation, which the reports of a
peace naturally occafion among thofe who muft
fuffer by it. King *James*, though lefs difturbed
than his court, being one day in his clofet with
the Duke, faid to him; Berwick, *all Europe is
now inclined to a peace, and it is their intereft to
put an end to this war. The King of* France *in
particular wifhes it, by reafon of the views which
he has upon* Spain. *The Prince of* Orange *has*

---

* As for the inaction of this campaign, King *William*, in his
fpeech to the Parliament, alledged the difappointment in the funds
given at their laft meeting, and the difficulties which had arifen
upon the recoining of the money; and it is well known that
both the *French* army, and that of the Allies fuffered equally this
year for want of pay.

1696. *room to hope that he will be acknowledged King of England, and I am alone going to be a victim to this peace. I say it before God, was it not for the sake of the Prince of* Wales, *and of those faithful subjects who have adhered to me, I should not be concerned for it : I need not tell you that I wish it was in my power to convince you, my dear* Berwick, *of my affection for you. You cannot doubt of my heart. But my hopes are no longer in this world. Your merit and virtue, which have gained you the esteem of the King of* France, *will supply what I cannot do for you. May Almighty God hear the prayers which I shall daily offer up that he may bless and prosper you.*

The Duke of *Berwick* was not in a condi-
to make any answer. The Queen coming in very opportunely, he retired overwhelmed with grief, and went to pour out his heart before God. He saw his King dethroned, and a victim to the blackeſt ingratitude ; had come from the preſence of a father full of tenderneſs for him, which tenderneſs even ſerved to increaſe his afflictions. He was deeply affected with thoſe Chriſtian ſentiments which the King had expreſſed, and found only in his religion that reſource for his diſtreſs, which was at this time ſo neceſſary to his noble and generous ſoul. Such was all his life, the worthy ſon of a Prince, whom God ſanctified by the ſevereſt trials, and who in our days has been the conſolation of the Church, and the ornament of Religion.

The

The year 1697, which we are now entering, 1697. was remarkable for a general peace: however, the armies took the field, and even made conquests: for it is a maxim of policy that to attain a peace, Princes muſt make their utmoſt efforts in the field, in order to conſtrain their enemies to conſent to it, and to procure more advantageous conditions. According to this principle, the King of *France* ordered in the winter the neceſſary preparations to be made, for putting in execution the deſigns which he had formed againſt the enſuing campaign.

After having made a peace with the Duke of *Savoy*, he withdrew his troops from *Italy*. They amounted to more than thirty thouſand men: with theſe troops he augmented his armies in *Flanders* and *Catalonia*, countries dependent on *Spain*, where he intended to make new conqueſts. Of the three armies which he ſent to *Flanders*, the command of the greateſt was given to Marſhal *Villeroy*: this was the army of Obſervation to which the Duke of *Berwick* was ſent. Marſhal *Catinat* commanded the ſecond army, which was to form the ſieges, and Marſhal *Boufflers* the third, which was to act on the *Meuſe*. Beſides Marſhal *Choiſeüil* commanded on the *Rhine*, the Duke of *Vendôme* in *Catalonia*, Marſhal *Joyeuſe* in *Normandy*, Marſhal *Tourville* in the country of *Aunis*, Marſhal *Etrées* in *Bretagne*, and Count *Grignan* in *Provence*.

The enemy not having forces enough to oppoſe us in *Flanders*, and fearing the loſs of ſome

of

 of their towns, reinforced their garrifons, and with the reft of their troops formed their main army commanded by the Prince of *Orange* and the Elector of *Bavaria*.

In the mean time all preparations were making for a peace. Mr. *Calliere* was already in *Holland*, and had induced the *Dutch* to enter into a conference. Upon this difpofition towards a peace, the King of *France* had named his Plenipotentiaries.

The Emperor and the King of *Spain* deferred fending their Plenipotentiaries as long as they could. They at firft ftarted many difficulties before they would agree to the place of congrefs; but they were at laft obliged to acquiefce in that which the King of *France* and the Republick of *Holland* had chofen, which was the caftle of *Ryfwick* near *Delft*. The pafs-ports of the States General arrived at *Verfailles* on the fifteenth of *February*, and the next day they received thofe of the King of *Spain*, the Elector of *Bavaria* having fent them from *Bruffels*.

Meffieurs *Harlay* and *Crecy*, two of our Plenipotentiaries who had prepared long before for this journey, fet out from *Verfailles* fome days after, and arrived at *Delft* on the eighteenth of *March*, where they met Mr. *Calliere* our third Plenipotentiary. The Minifters of the Princes allied againft *France* arrived at *Ryfwick* much about the fame time, and the conferences were oon begun.

The

The Duke of *Berwick* knowing that the cam- 1697.
paign would begin earlier this year than the year
preceeding, went betimes to the army, where
he arrived on the eighth of *April*. Our troops
met at divers places. On the tenth Marfhal
Catinat arrived at *Tournay*, and after having viewed the fortifications of the town and citadel, he
went to *Helchin*, where he ordered bridges to be
made over the *Scheld*. From thence he came to
Calandre, about a league from *Helchin*, in the
way to *Pont Efpieres*, and had there a conference with Marfhal *Villeroy*. The latter, after having ordered the gates of *Tournay*, on the right of
the *Scheld*, and facing the *Spanifh* countries, to
be fhut, fent in the beginning of the night four
thoufand horfe, under the command of the Prince
Camille, to inveft *Ath* on the fide of the lines;
while Marfhal *Catinat* did the fame on the other
fide; afterwards he went to encamp at *Leuze*.
The Marquis of *Montrevel* was ordered to guard
the lines of *Flanders* from the *Scheld* to the fea-
fhore: he could be joined, when occafion required, by the Marquis of *Crequi*, who had been left
at *Celles* on the *Haie* with eight battalions and nine
fquadrons, to prevent the incurfions of the garrifon of *Oudenard*. Marfhal *Boufflers* was to cover
the fiege: he had encamped on the fifteenth near
Binch on the river *Haine*, between *St. Waft*
and *Haine St. Pierre*. The lines of circumvallation being finifhed, the trenches were opened
on the twenty fecond in the prefence of the Marfhals *Villeroy* and *Catinat* in two places, namely,

1697. at the front of the *Bruffels* port, and on the left. Count *Teffé* commanded in one, and Count *Marcin* in the other. The town capitulated on the fifth of *June*.

Marſhal *Villeroy* being informed that the Elector of *Bavaria* had left *Deynfe* ſome days before, and advanced towards *Ghent* to join the Prince of *Orange*, ſent the Marquis of *Crequi* to encamp near *Oſtiche*, and the Marquis of *Montrevel* to ſupply the place of the former at *Celles*; whilſt Marſhal *Boufflers* advanced his left to *Chambron*; ſo that theſe three armies could eaſily join together, when occaſion required. After the ſurrender of *Ath*, Marſhal *Catinat* having repaired the fortifications of that place, our Generals formed a deſign which would have greatly diſconcerted the enemy, had it ſucceeded. The deſign was to ſeize the poſt of *Anderlecht* near *Bruffels*, to take that town, and likewiſe *Vilvorden*, with the fort of the *three towers*, and thus making themſelves maſters of the canal, to cut off all communication between the enemy's army and the countries of *Brabant* and *Holland*. But the Prince of *Orange* prevented them, and obliged them to retire.

Marſhal *Catinat* was now encamped at *Vive St. Eloi*, where he was joined by the Marquis of *Montrevel*: from thence he moved to *Zulte*, about four miles from the Elector of *Bavaria*'s camp. It was at this time that Marſhal *Boufflers* had a conference with the Earl of *Portland* in a caſtle ſituated in the plain of *Brakom.*

kom. They afterwards had frequent meetings, 1697.
fometimes on the fide of *Hall*, fometimes at *Bra-*
kom, fometimes at *Tubife*, and removed feveral
difficulties which would have occafioned much
delay at *Ryfwick*, where the peace was at laft
concluded. One of the conditions which the
King of *France* refufed, was to acknowledge the
Prince of *Orange* King of *England*, and to promife not to give any affiftance for the future to
King *James*. But the latter was the firft who
removed this difficulty : he faid to *Lewis* XIV.
feveral times, that it was enough for him to enjoy an azylum in *France*, and that he did not
defire that the peace and advantage of *Europe*
fhould be delayed upon his account. Accordingly the treaties were figned, and orders were
fent for a ceffation of hoftilities.

Towards the end of *September* our troops withdrew from the countries of *Spain*; Marfhal *Bouf-*
flers decamped from *Soignies* and retired behind
Mons; Marfhal *Villeroy* marched from *St. Lieven-*
fhaufen towards *Leuze*, and Marfhal *Catinat* retired
to *Dixmude*, and entered the lines. On the fide of
the Allies, the troops of *Hanover*, *Munfter*, and
the other auxiliaries, fet out on the fourth of
October, and returned to their refpective countries.

On the twenty firft of *October* the peace was
proclaimed in *Holland* and at *Paris*; and towards
the end of this year the Duke of *Burgundy* married the Princefs of *Savoy*.

M 3

The

1697. The reader will perhaps be surprised that the Duke of *Berwick* did not appear in all the last campaign, though he was in the army commanded by Marshal *Villeroy*. The reason of it is, that there was a secret order from the Minister not to employ him. The Marquis of *Barbezieux* had no kindness for him, and was no-ways disposed to gratify his desires.

The Court of *St. Germains* was at this time in a melancholy condition, being full of *Englishmen* who wanted the means of subsistence: what the King of *France* annually gave to King *James* was not sufficient to support so many people. The Duke of *Berwick* being now out of employment, no longer received the pay of Lieutenant-general, and was involved in the common want.

It was said, that during the peace some General Officers would be employed on the frontiers: whereupon King *James* intreated the King of *France* not to forget the Duke of *Berwick*; and the Duke went to *Versailles* to sollicite in person the favour of being employed. He knew not yet that the Marquis *Barbezieux* was not his friend, and had imputed his not being employed during the last campaign, to the indifference which Marshal *Villeroy* might have for him, and to the liberty he had taken in delivering his opinion with relation to the relief of *Namur*. The manner in which the Minister received him did not in the least serve to undeceive him; for he made him very fair promises. The Prince of *Conti*, who ever since the battle of *Landen* had

a great

a great confideration for the Duke, prefented him 1697.
to the King, and his Majefty affured him that he
would have a regard to the requeft which the
King of *England* had made in his behalf. The
King promifed very fincerely; but the Marquis
Barbezieux reprefented to him, that care fhould
be taken not to irritate King *William*, who could
not well bear to fee a natural fon of King *James*
meet with fo much diftinction. Thus it frequently happens, that the difaffection of a private man becomes a matter of ftate. The Duke
of *Berwick* was given up, and the Minifter would
have made him believe that we were engaged by
a fecret treaty to employ none of thofe perfons
who were attached to King *James*. The Duke
had almoft believed it, when one day meeting
the Prince of *Conti*, and having made his complaint to him, the Prince, who knew the Court
better than he, let him into the myftery. *Since
then I have nothing to hope for here*, faid the
Duke, *my circumftances do not allow me to live
in this place, and I will retire to the country. If
you are of that mind*, anfwered the Prince of
*Conti, you cannot chufe a better place than the
town of* Pezenas *in* Languedoc; *I am the Lord
of it, and I will give orders for your having
all the conveniencies you can defire.* The Duke
of *Berwick* expreffed the utmoft gratitude for
this offer, accepted it, and after acquainting King
James with all that had paffed, fet out for *Pezenas* with the Duchefs of *Berwick* and his
fon.

M 4

In

1698.   In his journey to that place, the Duke of *Ber-wick* gave an inftance of his charity which well deferves to be mentioned. Being arrived at *Moulins*, a woman who lived in that town, and whofe hufband had become a bankrupt, finding herfelf and her only daughter reduced to great want, applied to him for relief, and expreffed her indigence in the moft moving terms. The Duke was not in a condition to make prefents; yet he had too compaffionate and generous a foul not to be pleafed, even at this time, with an opportunity of relieving the diftreffed. He gave this woman the half of all the money he had, and exhorted her and her daughter to continue to lead virtuous lives, and to truft in the Providence of God, which would not be wanting to them.

He lived at *Pezenas* like a private man, being folely employed in the duties of a Chriftian, paffing the greateft part of the day in his devotions, and only making himfelf known in that town by his exemplary piety and religion. The inhabitants of *Pezenas* have even at this time a veneration for his memory.

The tranquillity which the Duke of *Berwick* enjoyed here was not of long continuance; his virtue was foon put to the trial by a fevere affliction. The Duchefs his wife fell fick, and his moft tender care for the prefervation of her life, with which his happinefs was fo clofely united, proved ineffectual. She died with that firmnefs and refignation of mind, and with thofe Chriftian fentiments which had gained her the efteem

and

and love of the Duke of *Berwick*, and juftified the
excefs of his grief, to which he gave no other bounds
than thofe which religion prefcribed. His grief
could not be calmed, and the wound which the
lofs of this lady had given him, could never be
thoroughly healed. He caufed her heart to be
placed in a filver box, which he always kept
with the utmoft care, and during his ftay at *Pezenas* he fpent feveral hours every day in praying
at her tomb, which was in the church of the Fathers of the Oratory.

Towards the end of the year 1699, an *Englifh* Lord of King *James*'s Court paffing by *Pezenas*, fpent two days with the Duke of *Berwick*, and being returned to *St. Germains*, he
gave his *Britifh* Majefty an account of the affliction the Duke was in, and of the retired life
which he led. Whereupon King *James*, fearing left he fhould impair his health, thought fit
to recall him to *St. Germains*, and defigned to
marry him again. He wrote to him in fuch
tender and preffing terms, that the latter could
not avoid complying with his Majefty's invitation,
and accordingly fet out for *St. Germains*, where
he arrived in the beginning of the year 1700.

They were exceedingly affected with feeing
the Duke of *Berwick* fo much altered and ema-
ciated. The King, in order to divert his grief,
obliged him to marry *Anne Bulkley*, the Daughter of *Henry Bulkley*, and of *Sophia Stuart*, who
was related to his Majefty. This Lady's character perfectly fuited that of the Duke of *Berwick*,

1698.

1699.

1700.

1700. *wick*, and her perfon, merit and virtue made amends for his former lofs.

In the mean time *Charles* II, King of *Spain*, was dying, and both the Courts of *Verfailles* and of *St. Germains* were folely attentive to that event. The King of *France*, King *William*, and the *Dutch* had at firft concerted meafures together, to hinder the fucceffion of *Spain* from falling to the Arch-duke, and to fettle it on the Electoral Prince of *Bavaria*, grandfon of *Marguerit Therefa* of *Auftria*, fecond infanta of *Spain*, daughter of *Philip* IV. and younger fifter of *Mary Therefa* of *Auftria*, Queen of *France*. This *Margueret Therefa* had been married in the year 1651 to the Emperor *Leopold*, by whom fhe had an only child, *Mary Antonina*, married to *Maximilian*, Elector of *Bavaria*. But to make amends to the Dauphin, and to the Arch-duke the Emperor's fecond fon, fome of the *Spanifh* dominions were difmembered in their favour. This treaty had been figned on the eleventh of *October* 1698. but the Emperor had refufed to accede to it.

The Electoral Prince of *Bavaria* dying on the fixth of *February* 1699, another treaty of partition was made, which alfo the Emperor refufed to ratify. Thefe partition-treaties were likewife difrelifhed by the Duke of *Lorrain* and the Princes of *Italy*. as for the *Spaniards*, they could not bear the mentioning of them. The difmembering of their Monarchy not only leffened the grandeur and potency of *Spain*, but likewife

hurt

hurt their particular interefts, as it deprived them 1700.
of the hopes of feveral Governments and Vice-
royalties.

It was not doubted but that the war would
foon break out a-new; and as it was King *William*'s intereft to unite himfelf with the Emperor, the Court of *St. Germains* hoped that the
article in the treaty of *Ryfwick* which concerned
them, would no longer be obferved by *France*
than the peace continued. Thefe hopes were
increafed by the death of the Duke of *Gloucefter*,
only fon of Prince *George* of *Denmark*, and of the
Princefs *Anne*, King *James*'s Daughter by his
firft marriage, and fifter-in-law to King *William*,
who looked upon him as his fucceffor.

Mean while the *Englifh* and *Dutch* took the
proper meafures for effectuating the partition-
treaty upon the death of the King of *Spain*.
The King of *France* ufed all his endeavours for
the fame purpofe, and ordered his Minifters in
all the Courts of *Europe* to procure the ratification of this treaty, as the fole foundation of the
peace and liberty of *Europe*.

On the firft of *November* the King of *Spain*
died, having difpofed of his dominions by a Will
made on the fecond of *October*. This Will being
opened in the council of *Caftile*, it appeared that
his Catholick Majefty had appointed the Duke
of *Anjou*, fecond fon of the Dauphin, his univerfal heir; and in cafe he died without iffue,
his younger brother the Duke of *Berry*; failing
him and his line, the Arch-duke *Charles*, fecond

fon

1700. fon of the Emperor *Leopold*; and failing him and his iffue, the Duke of *Savoy*. The Council of Regency appointed by the Will immediately difpatched a courier to give notice thereof to the King of *France*: the next day they difpatched another courier with a letter, wherein they intreated his Chriftian Majefty to grant them the Duke of *Anjou* for their King, and expreffed their earneft defire of feeing him fpeedily feated in the throne.

All *Europe* was attentive what courfe the King of *France* would take upon this occafion. His Majefty called a council on the eleventh of *November*, where the Dauphin and the Duke of *Burgundy* were prefent, and, after various opinions, it was refolved that the Duke of *Anjou* fhould accept the Crown of *Spain*. However, this refolution was not made publick till the fixteenth, becaufe the King was willing to give the *Spanifh* Ambaffador time to fend the firft advice of this to the regency, in a letter which his Majefty wrote to them. On the fame day the Duke of *Anjou* was declared King of *Spain*, and acknowledged as fuch by the *Spanifh* Ambaffador, who faluted him upon his knee, and kiffed his hand. Soon after King *James* paid a vifit at *Verfailles* to the new King of *Spain*, being accompanied by the Duke of *Berwick* and all his Court.

About this time we were informed that Count *Tallard*, Ambaffador to the King of *England*, was arrived at *London*, that he had obtained an

audience

audience of King *William*, wherein he had sig- 1700.
nified to him that the late King of *Spain*'s will
was accepted by the King of *France*, and acquainted him with his reason for doing so: that
King *William* had answered in general terms,
and so as to make it known that he was not
pleased with this proceeding: that he had given
orders for fitting out ships in all the ports of
England, held councils every day, and took measures for renewing the war. We were likewise
informed that there was arrived at *London* a Minister from the Emperor, with whom King
William had frequent conferences which were
kept very secret. Mean while the King of
France used all his endeavours to avoid the war,
and with this view he began to negociate on all
sides. Such was the situation of *Europe* towards
the end of this year.

It was thought fit presently to secure the King 1701.
of *Spain*'s dominions in *Italy*: for which purpose
Count *Tessé*, who resided at *Venice*, was ordered
to pass through *Turin*, where he had several
conferences with the Duke of *Savoy*, and engaged this Prince to own *Philip* V as King of
Spain, and to make a treaty with the King of
France, by which it was stipulated that his Catholick Majesty should marry the Duke's second
daughter, and that his Royal Highness should
furnish the King with eight thousand foot and
two thousand five hundred horse of his own
troops, in consideration of which *France* should
pay him fifty thousand crowns a month. To
this

1700. this fum were added afterwards, twenty five thou=
fand livres upon his being made Generaliffimo
of the army of the two Crowns in *Italy*. Befides, the Duke of *Savoy* engaged to grant a free
paffage through his dominions to the *French*
troops which were appointed to defend the *Mi-
laneze*. By virtue of this treaty feveral troops
were fent to join thofe which the ftate of *Milan*
had raifed, but which were not fufficient for the
defence of that country.

Whilft the King of *France* took thefe meafures to hinder the Imperialifts from penetrating into *Italy*, and left nothing unattempted
to withdraw the *Dutch* from the league which
was forming againft him; King *William* being
now come to *Holland* ufed all his endeavours to
increafe the grand alliance.

Thefe difpofitions to an approaching war a-
wakened the hopes of the Duke of *Berwick*; but
the death of the King his father plunged him
anew into the deepeft affliction; for on the fixth
of *September* King *James* II. of *England* and VII.
of *Scotland* died of a lethargy at *St. Germains en
Laye* in the fixty eighth year of his age. By
his firft marriage with the Lady *Anne Hyde*,
Daughter of *Edward* Earl of *Clarendon*, and
Great Chancellor of *England*, he had two daughters: *Mary* the eldeft was married in the year
1677 to *William* Prince of *Orange*, afterwards
King of *England*: *Anne* the youngeft was married in the year 1683 to *George* Prince of *Denmark*. Both thefe Princeffes have wore the
Crown

Crown of *England.*   By his second marriage 1700.
with *Mary*, daughter to *Alphonso de Este*, Duke
of *Modena*, he had two children ; namely *James-
Francis-Edward*, Prince of *Wales*, born on the
twentieth of *June* 1688, who after his father's
death took the title of King of *England*, under
the name of *James* III, and *Louisa-Maria-The-
resa*, born at *St. Germains en Laye* on the twenty eighth of *May* 1692, who died in the year
1712.

King *James*, some time before he expired,
said in the presence of his Court, that as he was
going to render an account of his actions to GOD
the Sovereign Judge, who sees into the inmost re-
cesses of our hearts, he thought himself obliged
to declare that all that his enemies had published
to withdraw from him the affection of his subjects, was nothing but mere artifice, and intended
only to deprive him of his dominions ; that by
granting a liberty of conscience, he had had no
other design but to secure the peace of his people,
and to render his kingdoms flourishing ; that what
was accounted a virtue and a wise policy in the
States of *Holland*, and other countries, where a
diversity of religions was tollerated by law, was
deemed in him a crime ; that as his people had
put no constraint upon his conscience when he
came to the crown, he had thought that he
might and ought to grant a liberty of conscience
to all his subjects, leaving it to GOD to bring
back, when it should be his good pleasure, those
who might have departed from the true faith ;
that

1701. that our Savior had not given him an example of putting any reſtraint upon men's conſciences, and had taught him to bear his Croſs with re-ſignation; that he moſt humbly prayed his Savior to pardon him, if through human frailty he had harboured any ſentiments of diſcontent and impatience; that he forgave from his heart, and as he wiſhed GOD might forgive him, the Prince of *Orange* his ſon-in-law, his two daughters, the Emperor, the *Dutch*, and all the authors and abettors of the violences which had been offered to him, or intended to be offered.

Afterwards, he ſaid to his ſon the Prince of *Wales*, that if GOD ſhould think fit ever to reſtore him to the kingdoms of his anceſtors, he (the Prince) ſhould remember not to ſhew any reſentment of the inju-ſtices which had been done to his father: that thoſe of his ſubjects who had ſuffered themſelves to be carried down by the torrent, were ſufficiently puniſhed by the inward remorſes of their own conſciencies; that he was ſo far from wiſhing them any ill on account of thoſe misfortunes which they had brought upon him for more than theſe twelve years paſt, that he eſteemed himſelf happy in having had thereby an oppor-tunity of ſacrificing to GOD the grandeurs and vanities of this world, and the ſplendor of royal-ty.

He afterwards expreſſed a real tenderneſs for the Duke of *Berwick*, and died with a Chriſtian firmneſs of mind, and with all thoſe ſentiments which the true religion inſpires. He had ordered

'dered that he fhould be buried without pomp, 1701.
like a private gentleman, in the church of the
Englifh Benedictines at *Paris*, and that there
fhould only be engraven on his tomb

HERE LIES JAMES THE SECOND,
KING OF GREAT BRITAIN.

The King of *France* having come to fee him
fome days before he died, he entreated his Chriftian Majefty to acknowledge the Prince of *Wales*
as King of *England*, when GOD fhould pleafe to
call him into the other world; to continue his
kindnefs and protection to that Prince, to the
Queen his confort, and the young Princefs his
daughter. He likewife recommended to him
the Duke of *Berwick*. *Lewis* XIV was exceedingly affected with this melancholy fcene, promifed all that his *Britifh* Majefty afked of him,
and kept his promife.

Four days after the death of King *James*, the
King of *France* went to fee the Queen of *England* and the Prince of *Wales*, and declared to
them in the moft obliging terms that he acknowledged this Prince as King of *England*, *Scotland*,
and *Ireland*, and that he would continue to give
him the fame penfion which he had given the
King his father (namely, fifty thoufand livres a
month) and the fame number of officers and
life-guards, with the ufe of the caftle of *St.
Germains*; declaring at the fame time that
he did not mean to difturb King *William* in

1701. the poffeffion of the Crown of *England*. In effect, his Chriftian Majefty wrote to King *William*, that King *James* having died at *St. Germains*, and the Prince of *Wales* having thereupon taken the title of King, as being fon and heir of the late King his father, he had made no difficulty to acknowledge him as fuch; fince having always treated him as Prince of *Wales*, it was natural to own him as King of *England* after the death of his father: that in this there was nothing contrary to the treaty of *Ryfwick*, in the fourth article of which it was only mentioned that his Moft Chriftian Majefty fhould not difturb the King of *Great Britain* in the peaceable poffeffion of his dominions, nor affift with his troops, fhips, or any other fupplies, thofe who fhould go about to difturb his government: that he intended punctually to obferve this article: that the title of King of *England*, which the Prince of *Wales* muft inevitably take, fhould not procure from the King of *France* any other affiftance to that Prince, than that which the King his father had received fince the peace of *Ryfwick*, which it would be very hard to refufe to his fon: that befides, he could not pretend to judge between King *William* and the fon of King *James*; and that to refufe the latter a title which he claimed by his birth, would be deciding againft him: that for the reft, the conduct of the King of *Great Britain* and of the States General, the equipment of their fleets, the fecret affiftance which they gave to the Emperor, the declarations

tions they made in favour of that Prince, and 1701.
their levying troops on all fides, might with much
more reafon be deemed real infractions of the
treaty of *Ryfwick*.

These reafons, fupported by feveral inftances
of parallel cafes, did not fatisfy King *William*,
who immediately expreffed his refentment of this
proceeding, and fent an order to the Earl of *Man-
chefter*, his Ambaffador at the Court of *France*,
to come away forthwith without taking his audience of leave. Charmed with this pretext of
breaking with *France*, and of juftifying his engagements with the Emperor, he made ufe of
it to obtain from the Parliament of *England* the
neceffary funds for effecting the defign which he
had formed, in concert with the *Dutch* and feveral Princes, to deprive the houfe of *Bourbon* of the *Spanifh* Crown. Whereupon the neceffary preparations were made in *France* for fending feveral armies into the field, one on the *Mofelle*, one in *Flanders*, one on the *Rhine*, and one
in *Italy*.

In the beginning of this year died the Marquis
of *Barbezieux*, Minifter and Secretary at War.
He was fucceeded in his office by Mr. *Chamillard*,
who was already Minifter of State and Controller
General of the Finnances. As thefe two employments were very weighty, efpecially at a time when
all the Princes of *Europe* were leagued together
againft *France*, Mr. *Chamillard* entreated his Majefty to give him leave to lay down one of them;
but the King, who put great confidence in him,

 infifted

1701. infifted upon his keeping both, and faid to him, *I grant thefe two employments are very burthenfome; but let not that difcourage you: I my felf will bear a part of the fatigue.*

The Duke of *Berwick* did not fuffer by this change. He went to fee Mr. *Chamillard*, and met with a very favourable reception. *I know, my Lord Duke,* faid the Minifter to him, *that the King intends to employ you in his armies: and if his Majefty fhould forget you, I fhould take a real pleafure to put him in mind of you, and to fuggeft to him that a perfon of your merit and diftinction is always ufeful, and may do great fervice.*

On the third of *May*, the King named the Generals of his armies, and the officers who were to ferve in them. Marfhal *Boufflers* was appointed to command the army in *Flanders*, Count *Tallard* that on the *Mofelle*, Marfhal *Villeroy* that on the *Rhine*, and Marfhal *Catinat* that in *Italy*, of which the Duke of *Savoy* was Generalliffimo.

Our affairs began very unfuccefsfully in *Italy*, notwithftanding the wife precautions of Marfhal *Catinat*: he was always prevented by the enemy, who had intelligence of his moft fecret defigns. Upon this account he fufpected that there were fome treacherous perfons about him, and wrote a letter to the King, wherein he did not conceal the fufpicions he entertained of the Duke of *Savoy*. His Majefty could hardly give credit to thefe fuggeftions, and befides having reafons for not breaking with that Prince, he concealed
his

his refentment, and only fent Marfhal *Villeroy* to 1701.
Italy in the room of Marfhal *Catinat*, having appointed the Marquis *d'Uxelles* in the place of the
former to command his army on the *Rhine*.   It
is well known that our affairs were not mended
by this change.

The Duke of *Berwick* ferved this year under
Marfhal *Boufflers* in *Flanders*, where the campaign paffed on both fides in taking the neceffary
meafures, and making the neceffary difpofitions for
the war, without any act of hoftility.   There were
ftill fome people in *Holland* who feemed difpofed
to continue the peace : however, without relying upon that, both fides put themfelves in a condition to renew the war with great vigour.

All the lines which the King had ordered to
be made being finifhed by the month of *October*,
fifteen battalions and fix fquadrons were fent to
guard them during the winter.   Thefe troops
were to be relieved once in fix weeks : for which
purpofe they had built cazerns and ftables.   The
Duke of *Berwick* was one of the Lieutenant-generals appointed to command in the lines.

On the other fide, King *William* having fent
the troops of the Allies into winter quarters,
went to the affembly of the States-General, where
he agreed upon and figned the projects of war
for the enfuing campaign, and afterwards embarked for *England.*

The King, who did not rely on the pretended 1702.
negociations of King *William* and the *Dutch* for
the prefervation of the peace, well knowing that

N 3   their

1702. their real bufinefs was to prepare for renewing the war, continued to take the neceffary meafures for fupporting it. In the beginning of *January* 1702, his Majefty ordered a hundred regiments to be levied, each confifting of one battalion; and on the twenty ninth of the fame month he made a promotion of feventeen Lieutenant-generals, forty nine Marfhals de Camp, and eighty one Brigadeers.

His Majefty was aware that both *England* and *Holland* would inevitable declare againft him. King *William* wifhed for a war, and the *Dutch* being intirely devoted to that Prince, he eafily brought them into his defigns. It was his intereft to be always in arms in order to maintain the authority which he had affumed over the Parliament of *England*, and over *Great Britain* *. He had only confented to the peace of *Ryfwick* becaufe he was forced to it by the *Englifh* and *Dutch*; and if he feemed to have had at heart the partition-treaty, it was only becaufe he forefaw that it could not be put in execution without plunging *Europe* into a new war. It is not therefore furprifing that King *William* made ufe of the King of *Spain*'s teftament in favour of the Duke of *Anjou*, as a pretext for forming a

---

* The *French* Writers being unwilling to own that the *Britifh* nation was well affected to King *William*, pretend that it was the intereft of that Prince to be always at war abroad, in order to maintain his authority at home: whereas it appears that his Parliaments always fupported him both againft his declared and fecret enemies.

new alliance against *France* : this alliance was 1702.
signed and ratified towards the end of the year
1701 by *England, Holland,* and the Emperor.
But King *William* did not live to have the satisfaction of seeing the success of it; for on the seventh of *March* as he was riding from *Kensington*
to hunt near *Hampton court,* he was thrown
from his horse, and broke his collar bone; and
a fever coming on, he died at *Kensington* on the
nineteenth of the same month.

This Prince was a great General and an able States-
man, but much more distinguished in the cabinet
than in the field : could the severity with which
he sacrificed to his ambition the King his father
in-law and the Prince his brother-in-law be justi-
fied, he might be compared with the best of
Princes : however, from this severity he always
claimed great merit and praise. A boundless
ambition bears down the sentiments of nature and
humanity, and the success of unwarrantable projects stifles those inward remorses which they
naturally beget.

Upon his death-bed he called for the Princess
Anne his sister-in-law, informed her of the engagements he had entered into with the Emperor and the *Dutch* against *France,* and recommended to her to observe them; he named to
her those of his Privy-council whose advice
she should follow, and told her that if she would
maintain her authority she must always keep
her people employed : that a foreign war would
therefore contribute to secure her government,

N 4

especially

1702. efpecially a war with *France,* as fhe would thereby gain the Proteftant party and the houfe of
Aufiria : that in certain conjunctures the fentiments of nature muft give place to political reafons, and that therefore fhe muft avoid holding
any correfpondence with her brother, as it might
give occafion to believe that fhe was inclined to
the Catholick Religion : that the hopes given to
the houfe of *Hanover* of arriving one day at the
Crown of *Great Britain* would attach to her intereft all the Princes of the houfe of *Brunfwick,*
and all the Proteftants of *Germany.* He afterwards recommended to her to take all opportunities of favouring the Republick of *Holland,* to
which he was indebted for the Crown he was
going to tranfmit to her; advifed her to fupport
the Prefbyterians, or Nonconformifts, to put an
end to the divifions between them and the
Church of *England,* and to unite *England* and
Scotland into one kingdom, and under one Parliament.   After this, he delivered to her a me-
morial containing a fhort account of the art of
government, and efpecially of the conduct which
a King of *England* muft hold in order to maintain his authority, and avoid all differences with
his Parliament; and then embraced and took his
laft farewell of her.   It was midnight when the
Princefs withdrew; but King *William* finding
that he grew weaker, immediately fent for the
principal Lords of his Privy-council, among
whom were the Earl of *Portland* his favourite,
the Earl of *Marlborough,* whom he had defigned
for

for the command of the troops which were to 1702.
be fent into *Holland*, and the Earl of *Godolphin*,
who had the adminiftration of the treafury. He
told them, that as he had now but a few moments to live, he fent for them to let them
know, that as the Princefs of *Denmark* was to
fucceed him, he had informed her of his defigns;
that he relied upon their zeal and attachment to
her fervice, and had therefore intreated her to
continue them in their employments, and to put
an entire confidence in them: that he exhorted
and commanded them by the authority which
he yet held, to refpect, honour and obey her
after his death as their rightful Sovereign, and
the heir of his kingdoms; to affift her by their
advice in following the meafures which he had
concerted, and fupporting the engagements he
had entered into with the Allies, all which were
well-known to them; but efpecially not to fuffer any perfon fufpected of holding a correfpondence with *France*, or with the Prince whom
the King of *France* had acknowledged as King
of *England*, to be near that Princefs: laftly, he
recommended to them always to act in concert
with the States-General. Thus King *William*
endeavoured to reign even after his death.

Having difmiffed his Privy-counfellors he fent
for the Archbifhop of *Canterbury* and the Bifhop
of *Salifbury*, who adminiftered the Communion to
him about five of the clock in the morning, and
about eight he expired, aged fifty one years four
months and five days, being born at the *Hague*
on

1702. on the fourteenth of *November* 1650. He reigned in *England* thirteen years, having been crowned in the year 1689 with *Mary Stuart*, his
Wife, daughter of the Duke of *York*, afterwards
James II. King of *England*.

Upon the death of King *William*, the Princeſs
Anne ſummoned the Lords of the Privy-council,
declared to them that ſhe intended to follow exact-
ly the plan which the late King had formed, and
ordered them to continue the preparations which
had been begun. She made the like declaration
to all the Allies. On the ſame day ſhe was proclaimed with the uſual ſolemnity Queen of *England*, *Scotland*, and *Ireland*; but ſhe was not
crowned till the fourth of *May*.

Queen *Anne* at firſt made no change either in
the miniſtry or in the publick employments.
This joined with the readineſs of the Parliament
in giving the ſupplies which the late King had
aſked, was the reaſon why his death, which
had at firſt alarmed the Princes of the Alliance,
made no change in the ſituation of affairs; ſo
that both ſides continued their preparations for
the bloody war which broke out ſoon after.

The Queen of *England* ſent the Earl of *Marlborough* to the States-General, to renew the treaties of alliance which the late King and the
Kings her predeceſſors had made with that Republick. The Earl ſet out for *Holland* on the
twenty fifth of *March*, having the character of
Ambaſſador Extraordinary and Plenipotentiary,
which

which was the more suitable to him, as he had 1702.
negociated and signed in King *William*'s name the
treaty of Grand Alliance concluded on the seventh of *September* in the preceeding year, by which
it was resolved to make war against *France* and
Spain. At last the Allies began hostilities by cut-
ting to pieces forty four *French* dragoons who had
been sent by the Marquis of *Montreüil* to *Bruel*
near *Dragen*, and by laying siege to *Keyserswert*
on the nineteenth of *April*. The *Dutch* pretended that they were not parties in the war,
alledging that they had only lent their troops.
By this artifice they hoped to secure their commerce; and in case we should have the advantage,
they meant to keep their country from being over-
run by our army, which was earlier in the field
than that of the enemy. But the King of *France*
was not deceived by it, and on the twenty second of *April* ordered all his subjects to fall
upon the *Dutch*, as having committed acts of
hostility against the troops of *France* and *Spain*
in his Majesty's dominions.

At the same time the King gave the command of his army in *Flanders* to the Duke of
Burgundy, and as it was the first campaign of
this Prince, he appointed Marshal *Boufflers* to
serve under him, and to use all the care, vigilance and precaution which were necessary for
executing his orders. The Duke of *Berwick*
was appointed to serve as Lieutenant-general in
this army.

The

 The Duke of *Vendôme* had been sent into *Italy* by the month of *March*. The affair of *Cremona* wherein Marshal *Villeroy* was taken prisoner had happened on the first of *February*. It is well known that Prince *Eugene* having formed a design to surprise *Cremona*, had conveyed into that town, by means of an aqueduct, about a thousand men, who having made themselves masters of *St. Margaret*'s *Gate*, admitted into *Cremona* a considerable body of *Imperialists*, who fell upon our men with great fury, but were at last obliged to retire and abandon that enterprize: on this occasion our troops behaved with such undaunted courage, as can hardly be paralleled in history.

Marshal *Catinat* had the command of the army in *Germany*. The Emperor had sent the King of the *Romans* to command on the *Rhine*, and under him the Prince of *Baden*.

The right wing of the army under the Duke of *Burgundy* was encamped at *Santen* (in the Dutchy of *Cleves*) where Marshal *Boufflers* had posted himself. That Prince arrived in his army on the third of *May*, and on the same day he went to view his left, which was at *Soesbeck*: next day he viewed his right. On the fifth he went a forraging with a party commanded by the Duke of *Berwick*. All means were tried to bring the enemy into the plain behind *Cleves*, in order to engage them. The Prince detached Count *Coigny* with three hundred of the life-guards and two thousand seven hundred horse to

reconnoitre

reconnoitre them, reinforced his army with all 1702.
the detachments which had been drawn from it,
and ordered Count *Tallard* to join him with a
party of the troops of his flying camp.   Afterwards there was a general review of the army,
which was overjoyed to fee that Prince enter
into the minuteft details.   The Elector of *Bran-*
denburgh, who was in the neighbourhood, fent
him a prefent of a brace of live-bucks.   The
Duke of *Burgundy* gave fifty *Loüis d'Ors* to
thofe who brought them, and made a confiderable prefent to the officer of the Elector who
prefented them.

Four battalions of the enemy having pofted
themfelves over-againft our camp on the other
fide of the *Rhine*, we raifed during the night
a battery of twenty pieces of cannon, without
the enemy perceiving it, and with fo much diligence, that it was ready to play upon them by
two of the clock in the morning.   The fire of
this battery put them into great diforder, killed a
confiderable number of them, and obliged the
reft to retire behind the caufey which runs along
the *Rhine* to hinder that river from overflow-
ing the adjacent country, which lies very low.
In purfuance of the defign we had to attack the
enemy, who were at the diftance of feven or
eight leagues from us, the Duke of *Berwick*
was ordered on the eight of *June* to fet out at
fix of the clock in the evening with twelve hundred horfe and five hundred grenadeers, to march
along the river *Niers* between *Goch* and *Gennep,*
and

1702. and to obferve if there were any paffes through
the Wood of *Cleves*, behind which the enemy
were encamped. The Prince of *Bournonville*,
Meffieurs *Souternon*, *Villaine*, *Silly*, and *Def-
fourneaux* were detached with him. The Duke
advancing along the *Niers*, was informed that
there was a defile near a morafs between two
paper-mills, within four miles of the enemy's
camp : whereupon he refolved to penetrate to
the enemy on that fide. At the fame time he
had advice that his defile was guarded by a hundred and twenty men, fupported by fix hundred
more, who poffeffed fome pofts which lay behind; but as he knew not whether they were
intrenched or not, he fent Mr. *Lifle* with a hundred and fifty grenadeers and a hundred dragoons
to force this paffage, and marched the reft of his
troops to fupport him. Mr. *Cliffon*, Lieutenant of
the grenadeers of the *French* guards attacked this
defile at the head of no more than fourfcore
grenadeers, and carried it notwithftanding the
great fire of the enemy. The Duke of *Berwick*
having afterwards advanced beyond the defile,
faw that it was impoffible to penetrate on that
fide with the army, nor even with a large detachment, by reafon of the multitude of other
defiles which were guarded by troops intrenched,
and within reach of being fupported by each
other, and by the main of their army. He
therefore returned from thence, and fent Mr.
Rofers, Lieutenant-general of dragoons, and an
Enfign of the body-guards to view the paffage

on

on the fide of the wood of *Cleves*. They ad- 1702.
vanced very near to the enemy's camp, drove
away one of their guards, and took fome ma-
rauders, but found on this fide ftill greater obftacles to the march of our army.

The Duke of *Berwick* being returned to give
an account of this to the Duke of *Burgundy*, met
the Prince with his whole army at *Narguena*,
whither he had advanced in hopes that the
Duke of *Berwick* would find one of thefe two
paffes practicable. Upon the report which the
Duke made, the Prince immediately fent him
along the wood with the fame detachment augmented with four hundred men, to obferve if
we could advance to the enemy by the heath
of *Meock*, which lies at the extremity of that
wood, on the fide of *Grave* and *Nimeguen*.
About eight of the clock in the evening, he
found within four miles of the enemy's camp a
defile which he feized : but as the night was
coming on, he did not think proper to advance
further without being well informed of the
number of the enemy who were behind; and
this could hardly be difcovered, becaufe they
were pofted on an eminence. This defile was
of great ufe to him, and gave him an opportunity of detaching Brigadeer *Silly* with three
hundred horfe, whom he ordered to advance
to the entry of the heath of *Meock*. Mr. *Silly*
fent before him a captain of dragoons of the
regiment of *Liftenois* with a few men, by the
way of *Cranenburgh*; which could not have been
done,

1702. done, had we not been masters of the defile, lest the enemy should send some troops on that side to attack us in rear. They were so much disturbed at this, that they came twice or thrice in the night to observe if that defile was still occupied. At break of day, the Duke of *Berwick* was informed that we could not longer see the enemy upon the eminence beyond the defile: whereupon, having gone thither himself, he ordered some horse and dragoons to advance and post themselves on this eminence.

At the same time he had advice from the Captain of dragoons, whom Mr. *Silly* had detached, that the enemy were marching, and that about twenty platoons appeared on the heath at the distance of a mile from thence. Whereupon he immediately sent advice of this to the Duke of *Burgundy*, and to Marshal *Boufflers*, who was already advancing towards him at the head of the army. About the evening they arrived near the heath of *Moock*, famous for the battle between the *Spaniards* and the *Dutch*, in the beginning of the revolt of the latter. The left of our army was placed by the morass of *Moock*, and the right in the old camp of the enemy. After three hours rest, the Duke of *Burgundy* got on horseback, and entered the heath.

The Earl of *Athlone*, who saw into the design which the Duke of *Burgundy* had formed to cut off this communication with *Grave* and *Nimeguen*, sent a detachment of six squadrons of horse and two regiments of dragoons, to make themselves

felves mafters of the heights of *Moock* before us, 1702.
and afterwards decamped from *Clarinbeck*.   He
fent befides, another detachment of twelve fquadrons under the Duke of *Wirtemberg* to fupport the former, and followed them with the
reft of his horfe, ordering his foot to march the
fhorteft way to *Nimeguen*.   Upon his march he
received advice that fome of our fquadrons appeared: this was Mr. *Silly*'s detachment. Whereupon he advanced with Count *Tilly* to fupport
the Duke of *Wirtemberg*.   This Prince having
perceived the body of horfe under the Duke of
Berwick, immediately abandoned the heights of
Moock, according to the orders he received from
the Earl of *Athlone*, and joined him by the favour of fome fkirmifhes.   The Duke of *Berwick*
having informed the Duke of *Burgundy* of what
paffed, fent orders to the Marquis of *Silly*, who
was not half a mile off, to advance towards the
troops of the enemy which appeared: he afterwards followed him with his whole detachment,
and judging by the motions of the enemy that
they defigned to retire, he made great hafte to
come up with them.   Whereupon the Earl of
Athlone drew up his horfe in battalia, and retired in good order to his infantry.

The Duke of *Berwick* having detached fome
men to fkirmifh with and amufe the enemy,
came within a mile of them, and pofted himfelf
on fome heights, from whence he could not fee
what paffed behind him, but faw all the motions of their army: he extended his front, and

O

by

1702. by this ſtratagem kept the enemy in awe, making them believe that it was the head of our
army.

As ſoon as the Duke of *Burgundy* had advice
of all theſe motions, he ſent to the Duke of *Berwick* the Duke of *Guiche* with the regiment of
the Colonel-general of the dragoons and a brigade
of carabineers, to ſupport him in caſe the enemy
ſhould advance to him: he afterwards marched
the army with all poſſible diligence. But the
enemy having well judged that the Duke of *Berwick* would not have come ſo near them without being followed by all our troops, prepared
to retire towards *Nimeguen*, which was in their
rear; becauſe, had they continued their march
towards *Grave*, they would have been expoſed
to great danger. The Duke of *Guiche* ſent *d'En-
tragues* to acquaint the Duke of *Burgundy* that
the enemy appeared on the plain. Upon receiving this advice, the Prince ordered the artillery
to advance with great diligence, ſent word to the
foot to haſten their march, and rode up to join
the Duke of *Guiche*.

Our army found in their march a prodigious
defile on the left of a very deep lake, where they
loſt a great deal of time. It had then been eaſy
for the enemy to attack and defeat the Duke of
Berwick, and afterwards the head of our army;
upon this to make themſelves maſters of the
defile, and to hinder us from advancing further,
poſting their right at the *Meuſe*, and their left at
the wood of *Cleves:* but the bold countenance of
the

the Duke of *Berwick* having deceived them, they 1702. had no thoughts but of retiring to *Nimeguen*; fo that our army paffed this defile without oppofition, and came into the heath of *Nimeguen*.

The Duke *du Maine* arrived with the cavalry of the left of the firft line, which had made the van-guard: this line had marched in the fame order as it was encamped. The King's houfhold did not begin to march till after the infantry. The fecond line had likewife marched: but the horfe on the right were doubled, and having paffed the foot, arrived much about the fame fame time with the horfe on the left. The King's houfhold and the horfe of the firft line not having made this motion foon enough, could not arrive till a confiderable time after.

As foon as the head of our troops was within reach, and fome battalions were come up, the Duke of *Burgundy* gave orders to follow the enemy more brifkly, though they were pofted under *Nimeguen*. The troops under the Duke of *Berwick*, which formed a fort of line, began to fkirmifh with them. Five fquadrons of the enemy having advanced towards our left, we charged them: the attack was begun by a body interlined with the regiments of the King and of *Condé*, and fupported by the laft fquadron of the King's regiment. The regiment of *Duras* behaved with extraordinary courage, and charged two regiments of the enemy; and as more of their regiments were advancing, Lieutenantcolonel *La Beulaye* ordered his fquadron to halt,

and

 and draw their fwords. The officer of the enemy whom he encountered was killed at the firft
blow.

In this interval, the infantry being arrived
within four miles of *Nimeguen*, marched in battalia as far as the ground would permit: they
did not arrive near the glacis till eleven of the
clock, when they were drawn up in two lines,
and the horfe placed in two wings. The enemy
no fooner faw our infantry, than they fent
theirs into the town and the covered way. Their
horfe having continued on the glacis, the Duke
du Maine ordered the carabineers to charge them
on the left; and the Duke of *Burgundy* ordered
the King's houfhold to do the fame on the right.
This Prince advanced within piftol-reach of the
glacis, paffing with great calmnefs from right to
left at the head of a few horfe. As foon as the
artillery was arrived, two batteries were raifed
in the center, one confifting of twelve pieces of
cannon, and the other of ten; and one much
ftronger was raifed in the left. Thefe batteries
began at noon to make a terrible fire, and continued till two of the clock. The bullets fell in
the midft of the enemy's fquadrons, or in the
covered way upon their foot, and did great execution.

Afterwards we detached fifty fufileers out
of every battalion, from all the regiments of
the left of the firft line. This detachment advanced within piftol-reach of the enemy's horfe
and dragoons, and killed many of them; fo that

being

being no longer able to bear this onset, they re- 1702.
tired in disorder by the right and left, in the
roads between the town and the *Wael*.

The cannon which played from the ramparts
of *Nimeguen* greatly annoyed us, and we lay exposed to it for near two hours. But as soon as
the enemy's horse disappeared, our troops retired
out of the reach of their cannon. We passed
the night in great distress, by reason of the want
of water and forrage, the country hereabouts
being all over heath.

Afterwards we went to the camp which the
enemy had quitted; whilst they, on the other
side, passed the *Wael*, and went into isle of *Be-
thau*. In this action they lost twelve hundred
men, a great number of horses, an hundred waggons of artillery, and a great part of their baggage. Our soldiers pillaged in the neighbourhood of *Nimeguen* to the value of five hundred
thousand crowns, and carried off near twenty
thousand cattle.

This action was the more glorious to the Duke
of *Burgundy*'s army, as it consisted then only of
thirty six battalions and sixty one squadrons. This
Prince, though it was the first time he had been
in any action, shewed all the firmness of an experienced General. He continually exposed himself to the cannon of *Nimeguen*, notwithstanding
all the remonstrances which were made to him,
giving his orders with great calmness, and in the
most gracious manner, without appearing to be
discomposed by the number of people who were
                     slain.

1702. flain very near him.   Having met the Duke of
Berwick after the action, he faid to him, *My
Lord Duke, I fhall give the King an account of
your behaviour, and of the fervice you have done
in this affair; you have contributed very much to
the fuccefs of it, and I fhall fhew upon all occafions the value and efteem I have for you.*   It will
appear in the fequel of thefe Memoirs that this
was not a mere compliment.

Next day the Duke of *Burgundy* fent orders to
Count *Tallard* to advance on the fide of *Rhyn-
berg*, in order to cover that place; and feeing
that the enemy were retired, he went to encamp
at *Deafburgen*, between *Nimeguen* and *Cleves*,
where he found himfelf mafter of the whole
country, and eafily fubfifted his army.

Mean while the Earl of *Athlone* paffed the
Wael with all his horfe, and went to encamp
near fort *Skink*, where he received fome reinforcements.   He difpofed his army along the
Wael and the *Rhine* in fuch a manner, as to make
it impoffible for us to pafs either of thefe rivers.

The Duke of *Burgundy* fent a detachment to
poft themfelves between *Neleker* and *Vanten*, and
it was about this time that Mr. *Virieu* arrived,
and gave him an account of an action which had
paffed on the left, and which we think proper to
relate here.   On the twenty feventh of *June*, about
eight of the clock in the evening, Mr. *Philipe* an
Exempt in the life-guards, with the commiffion
of a Colonel, had detached Mr. *Curly*, Exempt
in the fame guards, to fcour the country about
                                        Nime-

Nimeguen. His detachment confifted of three hundred and ninety troopers, *viz.* fixty of the life-guards, ten of the King's Gen-d'armery, ten of the light horfe, ten mufqueteers, twenty horfe grenadeers, an hundred carabineers, and the reft of the light horfe of *France*, the *Walloon* troops and dragoons; the whole divided into eight troops. On the twenty eighth at break of day, they arrived on the eminence at *Grave*, when Mr. *Curly* found that his guide had miſled him. He returned towards the mill of *Croifbec*, where were thirteen troops of the enemy, who being more numerous, advanced to fire upon him and endeavoured to furround him, but to no purpofe. Each of his troops marched up with great boldneſs to the enemy, who halted firſt, and fired their pieces almoſt within piſtol-reach of our men, without killing or wounding any of them. Mr. *Philipe*, who by this time had joined Mr. *Curly*, immediately fell fword in hand upon the enemy, and charged them with fo much vigour, that he broke them, and pierced to their fecond line.

We then heard fome of them cry out, *We are loſt.* However, they rallied, came again to the charge, and put our dragoons on the right into diforder: but thefe dragoons being well fupported by our carabineers, who gave them time to rally, returned to the charge: the enemy again gave ground: they attempted to rally a third time; but obferving that Mr. *Philipe* advanced in good order to attack them, they thought pro-

                                    per

1702. per to retire, and quit the field of battle. Mr. *Philipe* followed them for some time, and left them near a wood, which he did not think fit to enter, left there fhould be any infantry concealed in it. Mr. *Curly*, who had his horfe killed under him, was taken prifoner in the fight, after having killed the Commander of one of the enemy's troops. His fon, a mufqueteer, miffing him, fought with furprifing boldnefs; he went fix times to the charge, mixed as many times with the enemy, pierced to their third rank, and he alone made a prodigious havock. Mr. *Philipe* faid to the Duke of *Burgundy*, that he looked upon it as a miracle that this brave young man was not flain a thoufand times. Two troopers having taken prifoner an officer of diftinction, difputed together which of them fhould have him; when to decide the matter, one of them killed him.

Mr. *Philipe*, who was flightly wounded in the hand, continued mafter of the field of battle, where he paffed above an hour in carrying off the wounded, whilft the enemy were in battalia without his reach, and durft not return to the charge, though their number was greater than ours by one half. This action happened on the heaths of *Moock*, near four miles from *Nimeguen*. The piquet of the left marched thither, but the action was over when they arrived.

The Duke of *Burgundy* having ordered Mr. *Lapara* to trace out a horn-work, in order to cover the head of two bridges over the *Meufe*,

drew

drew a detachment from each battalion to raise
it, and went thither himself. Three days after, this Prince went early in the morning to
examine the posts of the enemy, and to observe if the redoubt which was near *Wael* on
the other side of the *Niers* was entirely demo-
lished: from thence he went to *Hegen* on the
left to view the bridges over the *Meuse*, and to
see if the batteries which he had ordered to be
raised, and the horn-work, were quite finished.

On the eighth of *July* he detached from his
army, according to the King's orders, seven battalions and three regiments of horse, which were
sent into *Germany*. Mr. *Caraman* was appointed to command this detachment; but this officer falling sick, Marshal *Boufflers* proposed to
give the command of it to the Duke of *Berwick*.
The Duke of *Burgundy* did not approve of this
proposal, saying, *I am too well pleased that the
Duke of* Berwick *serves in my army, to send him
elsewhere; let the Marquis of* Surville *have the
command of that detachment, and conduct it to*
Namur. This was accordingly done.

On the same day the troops which had fought
under Mr. *Philipe* and Mr. *Curly* filed off in the
presence of the Duke of *Burgundy*, who ordered
a double share of provisions to be given them,
sent a gratuity to Mr. *Curly*, who could not
be removed from *Nimeguen* by reason of his
wounds, and ordered another to be given to his
son.

The

1702. The next day, being informed that the enemy had sent from *Grave* four thousand horse under the command of the Prince of *Wirtemberg*, he detached four hundred horse commanded by Mr. *Aremberg*, who passed the *Meuse* and took provisions for two days. Mean while the enemy had passed the *Wael*, and were encamped between *Nimeguen* and *Grave*. Their army, which was daily increasing, was commanded by the Earl of *Marlborough*, who arrived at *Nimeguen* on the second of *July*. This new General, who had never before appeared at the head of an army, had attained this high degree of honour by the great interest and favour his wife had long held with the Queen of *England*.

Soon after, we had advice from Mr. *Aremberg*, that being come up at *Lyndhoven* with an advanced guard of the Duke of *Wirtemberg*'s detachment, he had charged them, killed several of their men, made some of them prisoners, and driven the rest beyond the village of *Styp*; and that he had been informed by the curate and peasants that the enemy were returning to *Grave* by *Bois-le-duc*: he added, that having continued near *Styp* to observe the enemy, he had seized a courier going to *Maestricht*, and that he had sent the Letters unopened to the Marquis of *Surville*, who might reap some advantage from them.

Our army continued in their camp till the twenty sixth of *July*, when in the evening the Duke of *Burgundy* sent the second line and the

heavy

heavy baggage to *Venlo*, where they arrived the next day in the evening; the reſt of his army arrived at *Venlo* immediately after. The next day they croſſed the *Meuſe* at *Roermond*, and below that town upon three bridges, and marched to *Horn*, where they were reinforced with three regiments of horſe and two of foot, detached from the body under the command of Count *Tallard*.

On the thirtieth the enemy made a long march to *Achell*, where was their quarter general; their right wing was near *Hamont*, and their left at *Linderſtip*: beſides there arrived in their camp three regiments of dragoons, two *Swiſs* battalions, one *Engliſh* ſquadron, and a great quantity of artillery.

Our army decamped in the afternoon and marched till it was night, when they halted two or three hours, and afterwards continued their march: the dragoons were ſent before to take poſſeſſion of the poſt of *Breey*, whither all the army followed them.

The enemy were now joined by ten battalions taken from *Nimeguen* and *Grave*. On the firſt of *Auguſt* they encamped at *Bruegel*, between *Hamont* and *Peer*, towards *Breey*, and prepared to attack us. They now conſiſted of near ſixty thouſand men; but the Duke of *Burgundy* marched in the night towards *Haſſelt*, with a deſign to paſs the River *Demer*. The Earl of *Marlborough* having miſſed his aim, ſettled his

quarter

1702.

1702. quarter general at *Sill*, and the Earl of *Athlone* took his at *Bruegel*.

Our army paſſed between *Beringhen* and *Dieſt*, having its right at *Erkenronde*, its left near *Dieſt*, the river *Demer* in its rear, and ſome moraſſes in its front. We continued in this camp till the ninth, when about two of the clock in the morning we marched to *Balen*, where we were joined by three *Swiſs* battalions which came from *Liege*. The next day the baggage paſſed at *Moll*, and afterwards at *Ber-kay*, and the army encamped at *Rithoven* ; the enemy advancing towards *Sembde* to obſerve us.

Then it was that the Earl of *Marlborough*, not being able to make any advantage of the ſupe-riority of his forces, reſolved to beſiege towns. The Duke of *Burgundy* ſeeing into his deſign, ſent ſeveral detachments to reinforce the garri-ſons of the towns in *Guelderland*, entered the *Mairie* of *Bois-le-duc*, where he found abundance of forrage, and advanced within half a league of *Eyndhoven*; whilſt the enemy decamped, and poſted themſelves at *Cuerberg*, to favour the ſiege of *Venlo*, upon which they had reſolved.

On the eleventh the Duke of *Berwick* was ſent to *Eyndhoven* with two brigades of foot, one of horſe, and ten pieces of cannon. Three days after the Duke of *Burgundy* came thither and ordered bridges to be laid over the *Dommel*. A report being ſpread on the fifteenth that Count *Tilly* was on the other ſide of the little river *Aa* with ſix thouſand horſe, the Duke of *Burgundy* ordered

ordered the firſt line of the horſe of his left wing 1702.
and the ſecond line of the right, with ſome detachments of grenadeers and foot ſoldiers, the
command of which he gave to the Duke of
Berwick, to march in purſuit of them. But
Marſhal *Boufflers* having gone to reconnoitre the
enemy, and having obſerved that it was impoſſible to attack them, diſſuaded the Duke of *Burgundy* from purſuing this deſign.

Venlo was inveſted on the twenty ninth by General *Obdam*, on the ſide of *Fort St. Michael*, and
by Baron *Heyden* on the other ſide of the *Meuſe*.
General *Coehorn* had the direction of the attacks,
and the Prince of *Naſſau-Saarbruck* the command
of the ſiege. The Earl of *Marlborough* ſent a
detachment to attack the little town of *Weſt*,
and marched on the twenty ſecond to *Holchleen*.

The Duke of *Berwick*, who watched his
motions, charged one of the hindmoſt troops of
his rear-guards, took twenty priſoners, and retired in good order to give the Duke of *Burgundy*
advice of the enemy's march. Our army was
then a quarter of a league from *Echlet*, and
having arrived ſoon after on the heath of *Peer*,
it was drawn up in battalia. The enemy who
were on the upper part of the heath, drew forth
ſome troops and put themſelves likewiſe in battle order. Their batteries were ready ſooner
than ours, but they were not ſo well ſupplied.
The two armies cannonaded each other from
three of the clock in the afternoon till night.
Had the Earl of *Marlborough* ſtirred from his

camp

1702. camp, an engagement muſt have followed; but he would not loſe the advantage of his ſituation, in which it was impoſſible to attack him. Marſhal *Boufflers* having gone to view the moraſs on his right, was covered with earth by two bombs, and the enemy fired four cannons at him. The Duke of *Berwick* had the ſkirt of his coat carried off by a cannon-ball. Whereupon the Duke of *Burgundy* was pleaſed to compliment him.

Immediately after, this Prince ſet out for *Verſailles*, where he arrived on the eighth of *September*. Our army marched to *Balen*. *Venlo*, though ill fortified, held out fourteen days from the opening of the trenches, after having been inveſted near a month. The capitulation was ſigned by the Prince of *Naſſau-Saarbruck* on one ſide, and on the other by Count *Varo*, Governor of *Venlo* for the King of *Spain*, and Mr. *l'Abadie*, Commander of the *French* troops. On the twenty fifth of *September* the gariſon marched out at the breach with all the honours of war, and was furniſhed as well as the inhabitants of the town with the neceſſary boats for tranſporting the ſick and the wounded to *Antwerp*. *Venlo* coſt the Allies a great many men.

On the eleventh of *September* we had encamped near *Tongeren*, and the day following Marſhal *Boufflers* had ſent a detachment of ſix thouſand men towards *Liege*, under the command of Prince *Tſerclas*, while the enemy advanced within a league of *Maeſtricht*. After the taking of *Venlo*, the Earl of *Marlborough* detached Count

Tilly,

Tilly, Lieutenant-general of the *Dutch* cavalry, 1702. with twelve hundred horfe, to inveft *Roermond*, while fort *Stevenfwaert* was invefted by Count *Noyelles*, in order to open the way to *Maeftricht*. This fort, which is built on a fmall ifle of the *Meufe*, about a league fouth of *Roermond*, was attacked on the twenty feventh of *September*, and capitulated on the fecond of *October*. The garifon was conducted to *Namur*, with all their baggage, two pieces of cannon, twelve covered waggons, and all the ufual honours.

On the fame day Count *Tilly* opened the trenches before *Roermond*. Count *Horn*, Governor and Captain-general of the province of *Guelderland* for the King of *Spain*, commanded in the place, and defended it till the feventh of *October*, when he capitulated.

Marfhal *Boufflers* having fent the troops abovementioned to Prince *Tferclas* for the fecuring of *Liege*, advanced with his army near *Tongeren*, where he was obliged to entrench himfelf; the enemy being fo fuperior to him in number, that it had been a great temerity to make head againft them. Soon after he came within the lines, to cover *Brabant*. Whereupon the enemy held a great council of war with the deputies of the States-General, wherein it was refolved to march to *Liege*, and befiege that place. Accordingly on the twentieth of *October* they opened the trenches before *Liege*. Mr. *Milon*, who commanded there, not being in a condition to
make

1702. make a long refiftance, capitulated on the thirtieth.

Thus ended the campaign of the year 1702. On the twelfth of *November* Marfhal *Boufflers* received orders from the Court of *France* to fe-parate his army. Accordingly our army broke up, after the enemy had fent their troops into winter quarters. Our General continued at *Bruf-fels* with Mr. *Ximenes* and Mr. *Puiffegur*. Count *Gaffé* went to *Antwerp*, Mr. *d'Uffon* to *Louvain*, Count *Gaffion* into the country of *Waës*, Count *La Mothe* towards *Oftend*, and the Marquis of *Blainville* to *Namur*.

About this time we miffed a great advantage over the enemy. The Commander of a *French* party ftopped in a yacht the Earl of *Marlborough*, Baron *Obdam* and Mr. *Geldermalfen*, Deputy of the States-General, as they were going to *Holland*. One of them fhewed him a pafs-port; relying upon which this foolifh man fuffered them to efcape. *

The

---

* On the fourth of *November*, as the Earl of *Marlborough*, Baron *Obdam*, and Mr. *Geldermalfen*, were coming in a yacht, during the night, to a place two or three leagues below *Venlo*, where the horfe which efcorted them were obliged to march at a confiderable diftance from the river; a party of thirty five men from the garrifon of *Guelders* iffued from an ambufcade, and at-tacked the yacht. They prefently laid hold of the rope, dragg'd the veffel towards the fhore, making at the fame time a general difcharge of their fire-arms, throwing into it feveral grenado's, and at laft boarding and making themfelves mafters of the yacht, notwithftanding the refiftance of the twenty five foldiers who were in it. The Commander of the party having demanded if they had any pafs-ports, Mr. *Obham* and Mr. *Geldermalfen* produced

The Duke of *Berwick* not being employed 1702. this winter, returned to *Verſailles*, where he met with the Duke of *Burgundy*, who gave him publickly the moſt obliging, and at the ſame time the moſt ſincere proofs of his eſteem for him. This Prince was with the King when the Duke of *Berwick* was preſented to his Majeſty, and did not let ſlip this opportunity of giving him the higheſt character. The Duke of *Burgundy* had frequent conferences with him ; and he has been often heard ſay, that he knew few men of ſo ſolid and juſt an underſtanding, or ſo capable to give good advice, as the Duke of *Berwick.* They who know the diſcernment of this Prince, and how reſerved he was at the ſame time, will eaſily conceive what a high idea we ought to have of the Duke of *Berwick*, who had deſerved ſo glorious an encomium. The King diſtinguiſhed him on many occaſions; he was much reſpected by Mr. *Chamillard :* in ſhort, he found at Court all the ſatisfaction he could deſire, and began to enjoy a ſtate of proſperity, which muſt have been the more agreeable to him, as it neither expoſed him to envy nor jealouſy.

In the year 1703 two new Powers entered in- 1703. to the league againſt *France* and *Spain*, and gave a

duced theirs, which were according to form. The Earl of *Marlborough* had one which had been made uſe of by his brother General *Churchil*, but was now expired: however, he preſented it with ſuch preſence of mind, and ſo much calmneſs, that the partiſan took it for a good one ; and having ſearched their baggage, ſeized what ſilver plate he found, and made the eſcort of twenty five men priſoners, he allowed the reſt to purſue their voyage.

P

confi-

1703. confiderable diverfion to our arms, by reafon of the fituation of their dominions.   The King of *Portugal*, on one fide, broke the engagements he was under to the two Crowns; and what was ftill more furprifing, the Duke of *Savoy*, difregarding all the confiderations which, one would think, fhould have prevailed with him to adhere to *France* and *Spain*, declared for the Houfe of *Auftria*, and went about to dethrone his own daughter, who was married to King *Philip* V.

Neverthelefs, this year's campaign was very fuccefsful and glorious on our fide: and though *France* was obliged to divide her forces, though the Arch-duke *Charles* of *Auftria*, fecond fon of the Emperor, was acknowledged King of *Spain* by the Princes of the Alliance, yet we gained fignal advantages over the enemy in all the countries whither our armies were fent.

Towards the end of the preceeding year, the King had ordered his forces to be augmented with fome new regiments; and all things were prepared for opening the campaign betimes. It was refolved that there fhould be two armies in *Flanders*, one commanded by Marfhal *Villeroy*, and the other by Marfhal *Boufflers*, in concert with the former; that there fhould be a feparate body upon the *Mofelle*, under the command of Count *Tallard*; that Marfhal *Villars* fhould command on the *Rhine*, befiege fort *Khiel*, and after taking it, endeavour with a part of his army to penetrate into *Bavaria*, in order to join the Elector,

who

who had declared for us; that after Marſhal *Vil-* 1703.
lars ſhould have ſet out upon this junction, Count
Tallard with his troops ſhould join the remainder
of Marſhal *Villars*'s army on the *Rhine,* and
ſupply his place; that the Duke of *Burgundy*
ſhould go thither and command as Generalliſſi-
mo; and that the Duke of *Vendôme* ſhould be
continued in the command of the army in *Italy,*
where he was arrived before this time. The article which concerned *Bavaria* was kept very ſecret, as well as that wherein the chief command
of the army on the *Rhine* was conferred on the
Duke of *Burgundy:* for when, in the beginning
of this year, the equipage of this Prince was preparing for the campaign, it was generally believed that he was to command the army in *Flanders*; eſpecially as our principal forces were ordered to that country.

The King made afterwards a promotion of
twenty three Lieutenant-generals, twenty four
Marſhals de Camp, and thirty one Brigadeers.
This promotion was followed, on the fourteenth of *January,* by another of ten Marſhals
of *France*; namely, the Marquis of *Chamilly,*
Mr. *Rozen,* the Marquis of *Huxelles,* Count
Teſſé, Count *Montrevel,* Mr. *Vauban,* Count *Tallard,* the Marquis of *Harcourt,* Count *Château-
renault,* and Count *Etrées.*

The Duke of *Berwick* imagining, as many o-
thers did, that the Duke of *Burgundy* would
command in *Flanders,* entreated Mr. *Chamillard*
to let him ſerve in that country. His requeſt

was

1703. was granted, and he was appointed to ferve in Marfhal *Villeroy*'s army. Before his departure, which he had fixed on the firft of *April*, he went to pay his duty to the Duke of *Burgundy*, who faid to him, *You are going, my Lord Duke, to ferve in* Flanders, *as you have defired: I had indeed refolved that you fhould ferve in another country, but I was unwilling to oppofe your requeft. Sir*, anfwered the Duke of *Berwick*, *I defired to be fent to the army in* Flanders, *that I might have the happinefs of ferving under your orders.* The Duke of *Burgundy*, who perceived by this anfwer that the Duke of *Berwick* was not in the fecret, finiled, without faying any thing that might difcover it.

As the army was not yet affembled, the Duke of *Berwick* went to *Bruffels*. Marfhal *Villeroy* arrived there on the twenty fixth of *April*, and took meafures with Marfhal *Boufflers* (who had paffed the winter in that town) to prevent the enemy. He fent orders to the troops which were to compofe his army to begin their march, and to be at *Montenaken* and at *Niel*, above *Landen*, by the eighth of *May*. On the ninth, he marched his army towards *Tongeren*, to attack a body of fix thoufand men cantoned along the *Roer*. He fent the Duke of *Berwick* upon this enterprize with a body of eight thoufand men, and followed himfelf with the army. The Duke's march was fo fecret and expeditious, that the enemy were almoft befet, and had fo late notice

of

of our approach, that they were forced to leave all their baggage.

Advancing further towards *Tongeren*, where the enemy had two battalions, we chafed the regiment of horfe of *Chambleau*, which retired in great hafte to *Maeftricht*, and we took an officer and feveral troopers prifoners. The garrifon of *Liege* was all night under arms, and early in the morning they marched from thence with all their baggage to the army of the Allies, which met under *Maeftricht*.

Tongeren was invefted on the tenth. Baron *Delz*, Brigadeer of the foot, commanded in it. Upon his refufing to furrender, Marfhal *Villeroy* ordered eight pieces of cannon to be brought up, and to play upon a little tower in flank; and twenty companies of grenadeers, fupported by fome battalions, to ftorm it. This place being only fortified with earth, could not make great refiftance. The Commander furrendered himfelf and his garrifon prifoners of war; and almoft all the equipage of the Prince of *Wirtemberg*, which was in *Tongeren*, fell into our hands. The Duke of *Berwick* continued here for fome time to blow up the towers, and to undermine the walls. Before he went from it, he difcharged all the debt for forrage which Marfhal *Boufflers* had left unpaid in this place the preceeding year.

Mean while the enemy had brought together a part of their army under *Maeftricht*, while another part of it was employed in the fiege of

Bonn.

1703. *Bonn.* This place, which had been invested ever since the twenty fourth of *April*, and before which the trenches had been opened only on the third of *May*, was obliged to surrender on the fifteenth. The Marquis *Alegre* Lieutenant-general, commanded in it. The Duke of *Marlborough* set out from thence on the seventeenth, and on the nineteenth he arrived at the camp of *Maeſtricht*, where, in a few days after, he was joined by the troops which had been employed in the siege of *Bonn.* Whereupon he passed the *Jecker*, and encamped on the heights of *Viſet*, having the village of *Hentin* in his lines. On the same day the army under Marshal *Villeroy* marching up by the *Jecker*, extended itself along the great causey; which obliged the enemy to post their right at the brook of *Houten*, and their left at the village of *Tieſſen*, making their line pass through the village of *Neudorf.* We continued to march up by the *Jecker*, and afterwards encamped along the river, our right extending from the village of *Orell* above the wood of *Heer*, and our left, which was at *Orell*, extending to the village of *Wichmart.* On the twenty seventh, Prince *Tſerclas de Tilly* marched to *Liere* with a flying camp, to be within reach of preventing the enemy, in case they should gain some marches before us towards *Antwerp*, which Count *Guiſcard* had been ordered to possess.

On the same day, the enemy sent their heavy baggage to *Maeſtricht*; whereupon Marshal *Villeroy* ordered his army to be in readiness, and sent
the

the Duke of *Berwick* with a detachment of the 1703.
King's houfhold to obferve the enemy. Marfhal
Villeroy paffed this night at the head of the line
with Marfhal *Boufflers*. The Duke of *Berwick*
furprifed a party of four hundred *Huffars*, and
made them all prifoners of war, not one efcaped.
On the other fide, Count *La Mothe* lay near *Oftend*
with twenty battalions, to fecure that place.

On the thirtieth, the enemy advanced, and
found us drawn up in battalia; they durft not
pafs the *Jecker*. Marfhal *Villeroy* perceiving that
they pitched their tents, and had no defign to
attack him, made a motion on his right along
the *Jecker*, to take poffeffion of the camp of
Affelbruck: for as the enemy could march either towards *Huy*, *Liere*, or *Antwerp*, he was
fituated in this camp fo as that he could move
to either fide. However, all paffed in civilities,
and in prefents which the Generals made to each
other. The enemy retired about half a mile
from *Warfufee*, placing their right at *Remercour*,
and their left near *Rencau* and *St. Georges*, having a brook on their right, and a ravine towards
the left of their rear. As foon as Marfhal *Villeroy* had notice of this, he got on horfeback with
Marfhal *Boufflers* and the Duke of *Berwick*; and
they all three went to the banks of the *Jecker*, to
view the march of the enemy.

Whilft our army moved to *St. Gervais Lens*,
the Duke of *Berwick* went towards the village of
Tourine, to examine the ground; and upon the
report which he made, we ftopped about half a
P 4   league

1703. league before the right of the enemy, and within pistol-reach of their left, *Tourine* lying on the right of our center. Behind this village was placed the brigade of *French* guards, with two regiments of horse on their right, and two on their left, stretching towards the camp, that nothing might pass between them and the army. By this means we could easily march to occupy the camp which had been marked out, the right at *Falais* on the *Mehaine,* and the left within pistol-reach, before the castle of *Heloigne* on the *Jecker.* After all these measures had been taken, the heavy baggage was brought into the camp. There was only a plain between the two armies, without any rivulet or ravine. The Marshals *Villeroy* and *Boufflers* went with the piquets to an eminence about half a league off, from whence they saw the whole camp of the enemy. Our main design was to hinder them from entering the country of *Brabant*; and we chose rather to prevent this, than entirely to block up their way to *Huy.*

The Marquis of *Bay,* Lieutenant-general of the *Spanish* troops having acquainted Marshal *Villeroy* that two *Spanish* Captains affirmed that they could surprise the guards which were in the front of the enemy's camp, he gave each of them an hundred and fifty troopers. They marched like the enemy's troops, wearing green boughs in their hats, and entered their camp, where they were allowed to pass. After having cut off the guard on the left, which consisted of

thirty

thirty troopers, they attacked another confisting 1703.
of an hundred; thefe refifted, but were driven
very far into the camp. The picquets taking
the alarm, prefently got on horfeback, and
brifkly repulfed them to the place where the
Marquis of *Bay* was pofted. Whereupon the
latter charged, and purfued them pretty far,
and afterwards retired in good order: however,
as he faw that the enemy followed him, he faced
about and obliged them to give ground. The
Duke of *Guiche* was with eight hundred horfe
on the right; and this deceived the enemy. He
retired without being followed. The Marfhals
Villeroy and *Boufflers* having headed the picquets
came to meet the Marquis of *Bay*, who had
been for an hour and a half in battle order in
the enemy's prefence: but they did not think
proper to make any attempt; and both fides retired to their refpective camps.

All thefe motions kept the army of the Allies
in awe, though it was far fuperior to that of the
two Crowns. But the fole defign of the Duke of
Marlborough was to pafs into *Brabant*, and for
this purpofe to force our lines in the Country of
Waës. They were guarded by Count *La Mothe*
with fourteen battalions and four regiments of
dragoons. General *Coehorn* attacked them on
one fide, and Baron *Spar* on the other. The
former met with very little refiftance, becaufe
the lines being of a large extent, Count *La Mothe*
had not a fufficient number of troops to defend them: but Baron *Spar*, who had to do
with

1703. with seven battalions, could not paſs the lines till after a very long and obſtinate engagement. It was afterwards neceſſary for the enemy to force the lines of *Antwerp*, which were commanded by the Marquis of *Bedmar*, General of the *Low-Countries* in the Elector of *Bavaria's* abſence. My Lord *Marlborough* and Mr. *Overkerk* were to attack on the ſide of *Louvain* and *Mechlin*. Mr. *Coëborn* lay with his flying camp on the left of the *Scheld* towards *Dutch Flanders*, in order to draw the attention of the Marquis of *Bedmar* to that ſide, whilſt Baron *Obdam* with about fifteen thouſand men, went to encamp between *Ekeren* and *Capelle*, near *Antwerp*, in a ground that was very advantageous by reaſon of the moraſſes and canals with which the whole country is interſected. But theſe projects were diſconcerted by the reſolution which Marſhal *Villeroy* took in concert with Marſhal *Boufflers* to attack Baron *Obdam*, and to cut off his retreat, if poſſible.

The Marſhal to conceal his deſign, advanced our troops towards *Dieſt*, while my Lord *Marlborough* advanced on the ſide of *Antwerp*. At the ſame time Marſhal *Boufflers* marched with great diligence at the head of a detachment of thirty companies of grenadeers and thirty ſquadrons, and arrived on the thirtieth of *June* at *Dureſt* near *Antwerp*, where was the general quarter of the Marquis of *Bedmar*, with whom he conferred. Their troops being joined together conſiſted of twenty eight battalions and forty eight

eight fquadrons. Marfhal *Boufflers* had taken
with him the Duke of *Villeroy*, the Marquiffes
of *Gaffion* and of *Bay*, Lieutenant-generals, the
Duke of *Guiche*, the Prince of *Epinoy*, and Count
Horn, Marfhals de Camp. Marfhal *Villeroy* defired to have the Duke of *Berwick* with him.
We began with advancing fome infantry, which
feized fome bridges, dykes, caufeys, and other
paffes whereby the *Dutch* could retire towards
Lillo and *Bergen-op-zom*. We poffeffed feveral
pofts; among the reft, the villages of *Hoenen*, *Orde-*
ren, and *Muyfbroeck*, before the enemy perceived
us. Afterwards we marched by feveral routs to
the enemy, who did not expect fo fudden a vifit;
the Marquis of *Bedmar* attacked them on one
fide, and Marfhal *Boufflers* took them in flank.
The latter not waiting for the infantry, the enemy, after being repulfed, returned to the charge,
and made a terrible fire. The infantry did not
arrive till it was about four of the clock in the evening, after having marched eighteen hours, with
the grenadeers who were commanded by *Mont-*
george, and who had marched thirty four
hours almoft without having halted. Marfhal
Boufflers immediately fent fix battalions to Count
Guifcard and the Duke of *Guiche*, who were on
the right, and he marched with the other twenty
two battalions to the enemy, who were feen
pofted very advantageoufly behind hedges, good
ditches full of water, and watergaans, with
which the country is interfected. The Marquis
of *Thoy*, the Prince of *Epinoy* and Mr. *Labadie*

placed

1703.

1703. placed themselves at the head of our men: fourteen battalions were placed in the first line, and eight in the second: ten pieces of cannon were planted as well in the front as on the left to fire upon them in rear, which succeeded very well, though the enemy did not fail to answer our fire.

We afterwards marched up to them with a very bold countenance: they opposed to us a number of battalions almost equal with ours, and a second line equal to that of Marshal *Boufflers*. When we were near them, we found their front was covered by a brook. Our troops passed it, marched on to the charge, notwithstanding the terrible fire of the enemy, drove them from all the advanced posts which they possessed, and took four pieces of cannon. We pushed them to the village of *Eckeren*, where was their general quarter, from thence we drove two battalions. Here it was that we missed Baron *Obdam*, who retired, being attended by no more than four men. We plundered here, behind the great line which went to *Lillo*, above thirty waggons of baggage and artillery.

As the country was favourable to the enemy, and furnished them at every step with advantageous posts, this success did not produce such a decisive event as might naturally be expected from such a beginning. An engagement ensued which was very brisk and obstinate, and lasted till night, without our ever being able to join with the enemy sword in hand, or to employ our horse,

horfe, by reafon of the difficulties of the ground; 1703.
fo that they ferved only by their bold countenance to ftop the enemy, and to make our infantry the more refolute.

Mean while Count *Guifcard* and the Duke of
Guiche were not idle: for as foon as they received the fix battalions above-mentioned, the
latter attacked the village of *Orderen,* where
there was a ftrong detachment of the enemy,
fupported by two battalions and four pieces of
cannon, and made himfelf mafter of it, notwithftanding the bold refiftance of the enemy.

Our troops having feized a dyke where the
enemy muft neceffarily pafs in their retreat, almoft all the latter muft have perifhed: but General *Schlangenburg* reprefented to them fo well
the danger of giving ground, that they made incredible efforts, and after a moft obftinate engagement, a party of them forced the dyke and
paffed it, and thus gave the reft of their troops
an opportunity of doing the fame: we purfued them till eleven of the clock at night.
The flaughter was terrible; the night alone
put an end to it, and faved the enemy from
a total defeat. The Marquis of *Thoy,* and the
Prince of *Epinoy* paffed almoft the whole night
in the village of *Ekeren;* and the reft continued in the field of battle. As foon as it was
day, our troops joined to return to *Derrea;* and
our artillery with the remainder of our baggage, and the wounded, were brought together,
none of the enemy appearing, the broken re-
mains

1703. mains of their army having retired in great diforder to *Lillo*. The rout was fuch, that Baron
Obdam was twice cut off from his men, and at
laft obliged to pafs unknown through the *French*
army. His misfortune was deemed a crime in
him, and he was even brought to the neceffity
of printing a vindication of his conduct, with an
atteftation of the principal officers of the *Dutch*
army, which was greatly to his honour. But this
did him little fervice; and though his conduct
was approved by fome able Generals, even a-
mong the Allies, yet he was laid afide, and was
not employed again as Commander in Chief.
From his difgrace we may learn, that in the bufinefs of war, the leaft reverfe of fortune blots
out the remembrance of the moft glorious actions, and that there is feldom any diftinction made
between the unfortunate and the criminal. *

Marfhal *Villeroy* decamped, and marched to
Santhoven, and from thence to *Maffenboüen*. He
made this motion, that his army might the more
eafily form into battalia, in cafe the enemy
fhould return towards *Antwerp*. They feemed
to have had fome defign on the maritime towns;

---

* Baron *Obdam*'s thirty years diligent and faithful fervice was
forgot and difregarded upon the abovementioned accident, which
no man could either forfee or prevent. Soon after, Lieutenant-
general *Schlangenburg*, who had received the thanks of the States
for the great conduct, courage and zeal which he had fhewn in
the battle of *Ekeren*, having been too free in cenfuring the Duke
of *Marlborough*'s conduct, whom the States did not at that time
think fit to difoblige, he was laid afide, as well as Mr. *Obdam*,
and loft by the indifcretion of his tongue that reward which he
had deferved by his fword.

but

but thefe had been fecured: forty battalions 1703.
guarded *Oftend*, and twenty battalions were on the
Scheld, within reach of joining Count *La Mothe*,
when occafion required. We were perfuaded
that the enemy intended to fend fome infantry
to join the body commanded by Mr. *Coëhorn*, and
that their defign on *Antwerp* having mifcarried,
they were refolved to make themfelves amends for
that difappointment. But the *English* and *Dutch*
differed in opinion, and the Duke of *Marlborough*
was obliged to fet out for *Breda*, leaving the
command of the army to Mr. *Overkerk*, who
was to confult with Baron *Obdam*, feveral General Officers, and three Deputies of the States.

Mean while General *Coëhorn* being diftreffed
in the country of *Waës*, where he was almoft
befet by Count *Guifcard* and Mr. *La Mothe*,
thought fit to decamp, and fent one part of his
army to *Lillo*, under Baron *Spar*, in order to
embark there, and headed himfelf the reft
which paffed by *St. Jean*. Upon advice of this,
Marfhal *Villeroy* recalled Count *Guifcard* with
fifteen battalions, leaving no more than five to
guard the head of *Flanders*.

The Duke of *Marlborough* being returned to
his army, fent orders to the garrifons of *Breda*,
Boifleduc, *Bergen-op-zom*, *Nimeguen*, *Grave*, and
fome others, to meet under *Lillo*. He fupplied
their room by the militia, and gave out that he
would immediately advance and give us battle.
He was only at the diftance of four leagues from
us. As foon as Marfhal *Villeroy* had notice of
this,

1703. this, he removed every thing that might be a hindrance to an engagement: he fent orders to the Marquis of *Bedmar*, Count *Tferclas*, and the Marquis of *Thoy*, to come and join him, as foon as the body encamped at *Lillo* fhould have joined the Duke of *Marlborough*'s army; and for this purpofe their camp was marked out. The enemy advanced, and encamped their right at *Loenhout*, within carabin-reach of the bridge of *Chebredet*, having in their front the village of *Weyterfet*, and their left at *Hoghftrate*. They had at *Lillo* a bridge of boats, upon which ten men could pafs in front. They made as if they would attack us, and we were prepared to give them a warm reception. But Marfhal *Villeroy* being informed that the Duke of *Marlborough* moved towards *Lillo*, as if he defigned to pafs there the great *Scheld*, he made his army enter the lines, and fent fifty fquadrons under the command of the Duke of *Berwick* between the two *Nethes*, that they might fubfift the more conveniently, and be at hand to join him, in cafe of need. Afterwards, he ordered the camp of *Burcey* to be fortified: this poft was of great importance, and was poffeffed by Count *Guifcard* in the Marquis of *Bedmar*'s abfence. All the horfe of the fecond line, excepting feven fquadrons, marched to *Liere* under the command of the Duke of *Berwick*, where there were meadows, in order to fave the forrage within the lines: befides, this cavalry was not of great fervice in the lines. After having confumed all the forrage about

Liere,

Liere, they went to do the fame at *Waterge*, 1703.
where they lay till the third of *September*, when
they joined the main army. For fome weeks
after this, nothing remarkable happened: each
fide was only intent upon preventing and defeating the defigns of the other. But near the end
of this month, the Duke of *Marlborough* fent a
detachment to befiege *Limburg*. Mr. *Reignac*,
who commanded in it, had been ordered to blow
up the caftle, and abandon the town, if the enemy fhould advance to it; but he was furprifed,
and defended himfelf for fome days, till a confiderable breach was made. On the other fide,
the *Pruffian* troops bombarded the city of *Guelders*: twenty nine mortars and fourteen pieces
of cannon foon reduced this place to great extremity. On the eighth of *October*, Mr. *Bethis*,
who commanded in it, demanded to capitulate;
but they could not agree upon the conditions,
and the bombardment was renewed on the tenth.
Some days after, the enemy were content with
blockading the town: the blockade continued
till the feventeenth of *December*, when the capitulation was figned. The army of the Allies
had feparated by the firft of *November*; and
Marfhal *Villeroy*, after having viewed *Antwerp*
and fort *Santflir*, went to *Verfailles*, and left the
command of our army to Marfhal *Boufflers*,
who continued at *Bruffels* during the whole winter.

As foon as the Duke of *Berwick* returned to
Court, he went to pay his duty to the Duke of
Q   *Burgundy.*

1703. *Burgundy.* He was informed by this Prince, that the King intended to give him the command of the army which was to be sent to *Spain* against the King of *Portugal.* Some days after, he was informed of it by the King himself. This obliged him follicite for Letters of Naturalization, which he obtained on the seventeenth of *December*; for he now saw himself in the way of being soon a Marshal of *France*, and knew that this degree of honour is conferred upon none but the natural or naturalized subjects of the kingdom.

The troops sent from *France* to *Spain*, and those which *Philip* V recalled from *Flanders*, began to march on the first of *December.* They found Commissaries on the frontiers, who were to furnish them with necessaries, and three thousand mules to carry their baggage.

1704. The Duke of *Berwick*, after having received the King's orders, set out near the end of *January.* On the fifteenth of *February* he was received at *Madrid* by the King of *Spain*'s coaches, and above three hundred more, filled with all the nobility who came to compliment him. The next day he conferred with King *Philip* upon the operations of the ensuing campaign; and on the fourth of *March* he set out with his Majesty for the army. They found a numberless throng of people in the streets, who accompanied them a considerable way. The curiosity of the *Spaniards* was attended with such proofs of their affection,

as

1704.

as muft be extremely pleafing to a new King, efpecially to one of *Philip* the fifth's character.

His Catholick Majefty was followed by all the officers of his houfhold, a great number of Grandees and noblemen, by his ordinary guard, the companies of the mufquetcers, the archers, and the *Irifh*, who clofed the march. He arrived about fix of the clock at *Moftolés*, in one of the eftates of Count *Oropefa*. They were obliged to wait at *Placentia* for the *French* troops, whofe march had been delayed by the rains.

The main army was to enter *Portugal* by *Eftramadura*. It confifted of twenty eight thoufand men. Befides, there was in *Andalufia* a body of feven thoufand five hundred men, horfe and foot, commanded by the Marquis of *Villadarias*; another in *Gallicia*, under the command of the Marquis of *Hijar*; and a third under that of the Marquis of *Ronquillo*. The borders of the Kingdom were fo well guarded, that the *Germans*, who were upon the frontiers of *Gallicia*, having attempted to enter it towards the end of *March*, were vigoroufly repulfed by the inhabitants of the country. The enemy had no more than twenty fix thoufand men, including the troops which the Arch-duke had brought with him, from which it was befides neceffary to draw garrifons for the towns. The King of *Spain* had at firft fummoned the nobility of *Eftramadura* and *Andalufia*; but upon the reprefentations which the Duke of *Berwick* made him, who faw that they might be difpenfed

Q 2

with,

 with, his Catholick Majesty suspended their meeting, and only gave orders that they should provide themselves with arms and horses, in case of
need. Being afterwards informed that the Arch-
duke was come from *Lisbon* to *Abora*, where
the *English* and *Dutch* were encamped, he set
out on the first of *May* from *Placentia*. Some
days before, the Duke of *Berwick* had set out
from thence to *Alcantara*, where the *French*
troops were incamped.

His Catholick Majesty, before he left *Placen-*
tia, issued a declaration of war against the King
of *Portugal* and his Allies. He past the night at
Montchermojo, and next day at *Coria*, where the
Bishop of the place, after having complimented
him, made him a present of two thousand pi-
stoles and a great quantity of provisions. On the
fifth, he joined the Duke of *Berwick*, headed
his army, and ordered them to enter *Portugal*;
forbidding at the same time all his men, under
pain of death, to make prisoner or injure any
person whatever, unless he was found in arms.
After this order, he divided the troops into five
bodies, headed himself the first with the Duke
of *Berwick*, and entered on the seventh of *May*
by *Salvaterra* into the province of *Beira*, about
five leagues from *Alcantara*.

On the same day, the four other bodies likewise entred *Portugal*. That which was commanded by Prince *Tserclas* marched towards *Al-*
buquerque. Another, commanded by the Marquis of *Villadarias*, advanced as far as *Serpa* and
Moura,

Moura, upon the *Guadiana:* it confisted of fif- 1704.
teen hundred horse and four thousand men of
the militia of *Andalousia.* The Marquis of *Geoffreville* led one towards *Almeida*, upon the river *Sabugal*, and without attempting to make
conquests, put the country under contribution;
after which they returned, on the eighteenth, to
the army under the King of *Spain* and the Duke
of *Berwick.* The Duke of *Hijar*, who commanded the fifth body, entred by the frontiers
of *Galicia* with a thousand foot, five hundred
horse and four thousand militia.

The first conquest the Duke of *Berwick* made
was the taking of *Salvaterra*, which having been
invested on the seventh of *May*, surrendered the
day following. Don *Diego de Fonseca*, the Governor of this place, was made prisoner of war,
together with his garrison, which consisted of six
hundred men. The Duke of *Berwick* detached
the Marquis of *Risbourg* to take *Segura*, which
surrendered, and the garrison consisting of five
hnndred men were likewise made prisoners of
war, and sent into *Castile.* Count *Aquilar* attacked *Ponha Garzia*, which likewise surrendered: most of the soldiers of this garrison fled
to the mountains, but the Governor was taken
prisoner. On the same day, the enemy abandoned *Ucepedo*, into which place we put a garrison. Another detachment took *Cebreros.*

On the twelfth, the King of *Spain* and the
Duke of *Berwick* went to encamp between *Cebreros* and *Ydanha*, at the *Atalia*, the situation

1704. of which feemed to be advantageous and difficult of accefs. Next day, the Marquis of *Salazar*, Lieutenant-general, was detached with two thoufand foot and three hundred horfe, to attack *Idanha-nova:* the militia who were there in garrifon received him out of the town with their mufquet-fhot; but this coft the place very dear, for we pufhed the enemy fo brifkly, that the *Spaniards* entred it with them, and all who were found in arms were put to the fword. A part of the garrifon retired to the caftle, and were ftrong enough to hold it out for fome time; but they foon after made their efcape by a back-door. The whole town was pillaged, except the churches, and all the effects which were found in them were reftored to the owners.

Prince *Tferclas*, on his fide, took *Aroncher* and *Portalegro*. He was commanded to advance, in order to difcover the army of the enemy, but he could have no account of them.

The Marquis of *Thoy*, Lieutenant-general, and the Marquis of *Leyde*, Marfhal de Camp, were detached on the fifteenth with twelve hundred foot and an hundred and fifty horfe, to attack the town of *Rofmarifios*, the garrifon of which place confifted of *Englifh*, *Dutch*, and *Portuguefe*. After a refiftance of twenty four hours, they all furrendered at difcretion. On the fame day we made our felves mafters of *Santa Margarita, Angelo*, and the town of *Provenfa*, the garrifons of which places were made prifoners of war.

On

On the sixteenth, the Duke of *Berwick* or- 1704.
dered *Monfanto* to be attacked.   This place was
fo advantageoufly fituated, that the engineers
reckoned it as ftrong as *Montmehan* in *Savoy*:
however, on the fame day the town was taken
by affault, and the garrifon was put to the fword.
That of the caftle, which we could not reach
till we had forced three entrenchments, furrendered themfelves prifoners of war; and the town
was delivered over to be pillaged.   This expedition occafioned on the fame day the furrender
· of *Monforte* and *Adveiro*, which demanded the
protection of the King of *Spain*.   On the twenty fecond, the Duke of *Berwick* ordered the Marquis of *Thoy* to attack *Caftel Branco*: next day,
as foon as our battaries appeared, the place furrendered at difcrerion: there were here an hundred *Dutch* and fome militia: the officers were
fuffered to have their baggage.   We found here
great ftore of provifions and ammunition, bombs
and grenadoes, and a large quantity of arms come
from *England*, and the tents of the King of *Portugal* and of the Arch-duke; for which reafon it
was thought that the enemy defigned to make
this town a place of arms.   Upon the approach
of the Marquis of *Thoy*, Mr. *Fagel*, who lay
with four *Dutch* battalions and fome horfe at
Alcareda, three leagues from thence, had retired to the entry of the great mountain at *Sierra
Steilla*, two leagues further off.

On the fame day when the King entred *Caftel Branco*, he had well nigh been killed by his

Q 4

own

1704. own troops. Two *French* soldiers contended for some booty which the *Spaniards* attempted to take from them; whereupon three companies of the regiment of horse of the Queen of *Spain*, without knowing what was the matter, fell upon the *French*, and killed an Aid-major of the regiment of *Barois*, and another officer very near the King's person. The Duke of *Berwick*, to prevent the like contests for the future, desired that those who had raised this disturbance should be punished in an exemplary manner; and as the punishment could only fall upon the *Spaniards* who were the aggressors, the officers of this nation opposed it. However, the Duke was inflexible, and represented to his Catholick Majesty that it was highly necessary to stop in its birth all matter of difference between the soldiers of the two nations, and that this could not be done but by observing an exact discipline, and punishing all those who should break the union.

The King yielded, and only out of form desired that a council of war might be held, where the Duke of *Berwick* presided as General of the army. In this council, consisting of *French* and *Spanish* officers, those who were found guilty were condemned to be hanged. The sentence was immediately put in execution at the head of the camp, and at the same time all quarrels between the two nations were prohibited upon pain of death.

On the twenty fourth, the Duke of *Berwick* detached Mr. *Puissegur* with two regiments of

dragoons

dragoons and one of horfe, to receive at *Villa*
Velba the boats which had been fent down from
Alcantara, to make a bridge over the *Tagus*.
On the twenty fixth he went with *Berry*'s brigade of horfe and *Barrois*'s brigade of foot to
view Mr. *Fagel*'s camp, the fituation of which
appeared to him to be very bad, its flanks being
entirely open, and the country of an eafy accefs.
As we were in fight of the enemy for two
leagues in our march to them, he refolved to
attack them at break of day, there being no
probability that the enemy would continue where
they were, as they had the mountains five hundred paces behind them.   He charged the Marquis of *Thoy* with this expedition, and went to
encamp at *Villa Velha*, where Mr. *Puiffegur* had
begun to build the bridge.   Next day the Marquis of *Thoy* marched to the enemy with a *Spanifh* brigade, the battalions of *Medoc*, *Du Gaft*,
Belle affaire, and *Miromenil*, and a detachment
of horfe.   The enemy, though ill pofted, waited
boldly for him at the head of their camp: he
attacked them both on the right and the left:
after a difcharge of their fire-arms, which killed
but few of his men, the greateft part of their
foot threw down their arms, and we took fix
hundred prifoners, with all the officers.   The
Marquis of *Thoy* purfued with his horfe and
fome grenadeers the horfe of the enemy as far
as a place called *Seburo-de-formofa*, where were
two *Dutch* battalions, which immediately difperfed, and fled beyond the mountains; we took
fome

1704. fome of them, and General *Fagel* narrowly efcaped.

The town of *Niffa* near the *Tagus* in the province of *Alentejo* fent the keys of its gates to the King, and demanded his protection. *Puebla* and *Apalao* furrendered at difcretion on the firft of *June*. At the fame time the Duke of *Hijar* made himfelf mafter of *St. Aleixo*, which is five miles from the *Guadiana*, near *Serpa*; he demolifhed the fortifications of this place, being unwilling to garrifon it, and ordered the artillery, ammunitions and provifions, to be carried off; he likewife took the ifle of *Candelas* in the river *Minho*, where the *Portuguefe* made fome refiftance. The town of *Cratochel*, a grand priory of *Malta*, likewife fubmitted, with twenty villages which depended upon it, and paid contribution.

The Duke of *Berwick* having left five *Spanifh* battalions at *Caftel Branco* under the command of Don *Ronquillo*, marched on the fecond of *June* to inveft *Portalegro*, a ftrong place, with a Bifhoprick, feated between the *Tagus* and the *Guadiana*: It was furrounded with a good wall defended by two baftions and a horn-work, the town being commanded by a citadel very ftrong, by reafon of its fituation and the regularity of its works. It was garrifoned by two *Portuguefe*, and two *Englifh* regiments, and three troops of horfe, befides fome companies of the townfmen whom the Bifhop headed, to encourage them to make a brave defence. The Duke of *Berwick*, after having

having viewed the place, and received a part of 1704.
the artillery, which had been drawn by men over
a mountain about three hundred paces from the
mouth of the *Tagus*, fent Mr. *Goutst*, an engineer, to examine the fortifications with four companies of grenadeers : this examination continued
two days, and it was found that though the
place feemed to be commanded by the mountains which invironed it, its fituation was neverthelefs very advantageous ; thefe mountains being at too great a diftance for the mufqueteers to
annoy the befieged from thence, and being fo
full of flints and fmall ftones that it was impoffible to plant cannon upon them.

As foon as the artillery was in readinefs, that
is, about eight of the clock in the morning, it put
a ftop to that of the befieged, and ruined an advanced work which covered a half-moon, and
afterwards played upon this half-moon with
great fury. A cannon bullet having fet on fire
the powder magazine, the Governor beat the
chamade, and demanded to capitulate. The
Duke of *Berwick* would grant them no other
terms than furrendering at difcretion : The Bifhop was allowed to retire with his family to
Lifbon. Don *Pedro Figuero*, the Governor, and
formerly Envoy of the King of *Portugal* at *Madrid*, his Major and the Commander, were fuffered to go thither upon their parole, with this
condition, that they fhould return in two days.
The townfmen gave fifty thoufand crowns to
redeem the place from being pillaged. Whilft
they

 they difputed upon this, the fuburbs were plundered by the maroders, who made there a very confiderable booty. They had even begun to make fome opening into the town itfelf, but the capitulation being prefently figned, the Duke of *Berwick* took great care to prevent all violence. We found in this place eighteen pieces of cannon. Soon after, Mr. *Geoffreville* returned to the army with a great number of prifoners, after having raifed contributions from a pretty large country.

The Duke of *Berwick* afterwards repaffed the *Tagus* to join the King of *Spain* at the Camp of *Niffa*, and make head againft the enemy's army, which was commanded by the Marquis *Dafminas*, who was encamped under *Pana-mayor* having in its front a fmall river, and a town in its rear. Notwithftanding this, we befieged *Caftel-David*, and on the twentieth fent thither four battalions and a regiment of *Spanifh* horfe under the command of the Marquis *Aytona*, Lieutenant-general. The Chevalier *d'Asfeld* arrived there on the twenty firft with the artillery and the three battalions of *Barois*, *Du Gaft* and *Belle Affaire*; the Marquis of *Thoy* likewife fet out on the fame day to join the troops which lay at *Caftel Branco*, from whence he fent to the King's army Count *Aguilar*, the Marquis of *Bay*, and Meffieurs *Geoffreville* and *Richebourg*. The Marquis of *Villadarias*, who was to command the fiege of *Caftel-David* arrived before the place with eleven battalions and a thoufand horfe,

horfe, which he brought from *Andalufia*, where- 1704.
of he was Captain-general.   We immediately
began to fire upon the place which was only defended by a very bad wall and a weak caftle.
The garrifon confifted of one *Englifh* and two
Portuguefe regiments.   Neverthelefs, the eight
pieces of cannon, which at firft fired above the
parapet, did not batter in breach till the twenty fifth : in fix or feven hours the Governor
was obliged to propofe a capitulation : he fent as
hoftages the Colonel of the *Englifh* regiment *,
and a *Portuguefe* Colonel. The Chevalier *d'Asfeld*,
who was that day upon duty in the trenches, demanded that they fhould furrender at difcretion.
The *Englifh* Colonel would not confent to it;
and feeing that no regard was paid to his refufal, he run to the head of the trench, and called out to his men to ftand to their arms, and
not to furrender.   Whereupon the *Englifh* regiment refufed to admit into the town the *Spanifh*
grenadeers who had been fent to take poffeffion
of it; but not being able to keep them out, becaufe of the *Portuguefe*, who defired to fave the
town from being plundered, they retired into
the caftle, drove all the *Portuguefe* from thence,
except the Governor and fome of the principal
inhabitants, whom they fhut up with themfelves.
They here found themfelves without ammunition, becaufe the *Portuguefe*, as foon as they perceived their defign, had thrown the powder into

* This was Colonel *Stewart*.

a well.

1704. a well. Notwithſtanding, we offered to ſend the *Engliſh* Colonel and his battalion to *England,* if he would promiſe not to ſerve during this war. He refuſed it, and would not ſurrender. At laſt, next day being the ſixth of *July,* the Marquis of *Villadarias* went himſelf to confer with him, and perſuaded him to yield himſelf priſoner of war. In this place we found twenty four pieces of cannon; and the taking of it was ſo much the more important, as it facilitated the communication between *Portalegro* and *Alcantara.*

Immediately the Duke of *Berwick* ſent the Marquis of *Leyde* to attack *Montalva,* where were two companies of foot, which ſurrendered without making any reſiſtance. Another detachment went to attack the town of *Marvan,* the caſtle of which place being very ſtrong by reaſon of its ſituation upon the top of a rock, would have greatly annoyed us on the rode to *Valencia,* from whence we received the greateſt part of the proviſions of the army. We had only the trouble of appearing before the place, the Commander, who had but one company of *Portugueſe,* having immediately ſurrendered at diſcretion.

The great heats not ſuffering us to keep the field any longer, without hazarding the loſs of our cavalry, and the enemy, on their ſide, taking meaſures for retiring into quarters of refreſhment, the King of *Spain* and the Duke of *Berwick* reſolved to do the ſame. His Catholick
Majeſty

Majesty went to *Madrid*, and the Duke retired
to *Valencia*.   In this half year's campaign the
Duke of *Berwick* made himself master of thirty
two of the enemies towns, and took prisoners
eight *English*, two *German*, two *Dutch*, and
four *Portuguese* battalions, and eighteen independent companies. Seldom are conquests made
with so much rapidity. The *Spaniards* were
amazed, and could not help thinking that there
was something miraculous in it.

Let us now consider what the *English* and
Dutch were attempting. Admiral *Rooke* had
brought the Arch-duke into *Portugal*; he was
followed by Vice-admiral *Leake*, who conducted
the rest of the troops which were furnished by
England and *Holland.* After they had landed, they
marched towards the frontiers under the Duke of
Schomberg, and came to *Elvas*, which was the general rendezvous of the *Portuguese* and auxiliary
troops.   This army lay inactive, while the
Duke of *Berwick* penetrated into *Portugal*, as
we have seen above: the reason of it was, that
before they would act, they waited to have an
account of the attempt which the Prince of
Darmstadt was to make upon *Barcelona.*

A conspiracy was formed in this town in favour of the Arch-duke; but the Viceroy discovered and defeated it. The authors of it were
apprehended; they were Don *Emanuel de Toledo,*
Don *Baltasar Gelsen,* and the Viquier of the
town. The Bishop of *Barcelona,* who was at the
head of them, found means to escape to *Avig-*
non.

1704. *non.* As soon as the Marquis *Das minas* was joined by General *Fagel,* he marched to *Pennamacor* with about twenty five battalions and thirty five squadrons, encamped at *Sabugal,* and from thence continued to march towards the frontiers of *Spain.* The Duke of *Berwick* having advice of this, brought together his forces with all possible diligence, and advanced towards *Elbidou,* where he was reinforced by some other troops, to the number of twenty two battalions, and as many squadrons. The enterprize upon *Barcelona* having miscarried, the enemy formed a design to make themselves masters of *Gibraltar,* and these motions of the *Portuguese* were only intended to keep the *French* and *Spanish* troops in awe, in order to favour that design. The affair was of the highest importance to the Allies, who were to send a fleet into the *Mediterranean.* Admiral *Rooke* and the Prince of *Darmstadt,* with the fleet and the land forces, having arrived before the place, summoned the Governor *Don Diego Salinas* to surrender without delay, threatening in case of refusal to put the whole garrison to the sword. *Don Diego* having only a hundred men to defend it, sent hostages and capitulated *. The Prince of *Darmstadt*

entered

---

* The Governor at first answered, that *being intrusted with the town by his natural Lord King* Philip V. *he should make a very bad return for the honour done him, if he gave up the place to his enemies without making any defence.* Whereupon Admiral *Rooke* cannonaded the town, and in less than six hours threw fifteen thousand bullets into it. The besieged being driven from their

guns

entred the town, and took poffeffion of the gates 1704.
and out-works. The garrifon went out with the
ufual honours: they were allowed their baggage
and all their effects, three pieces of cannon, and
twelve charges of powder and ball, provifion for
fix days march, and were furnifhed with the neceffary waggons: it was likewife ftipulated that
their baggage fhould not be fearched, and that
the Governor fhould have three days to evacuate
the place; befides, that the religion and tribunals of the place fhould fuffer no change. The
inhabitants were allowed either to continue in
the town, or to follow the garrifon; and it was

guns and fortifications at the fouth mole head, fome feamen went
afhore, feized this work, drove the *Spaniards* from a fmall redoubt and a caftle, and turned their cannon upon them. Notwithftanding, the latter fprung a mine, blew up the work, and killed
about fixty of our men, and two Lieutenants. Some more feamen coming afhore, the attack was renewed with great brisk-
nefs, and the affair was foon at an end. The capitulation was
figned on the twenty fourth of *June*, and in the evening the *Englifh* took poffeffion of two gates.
  The *Spaniards* have been juftly cenfured for their great neglect,
in trufting fo important a place to fo weak a garrifon; for it
confifted only of between fourfcore and an hundred men. We
found the town well fupplied with ammunition, and extremely
ftrong, with an hundred guns mounted, all facing the fea and
the two narrow paffes to the land; and it was the opinion of feveral officers who have feen the works, that fifty men might have
defended them againft thoufands. But the bravery of the *Britifh*
feamen was beyond example.
  Bifhop *Burnet* gives a different account of this matter. "Some
" bold men, fays he, ventured to go afhore in a place where it
" was thought impoffible to climb the rocks; yet this they did,
" and feized all the women at prayers in a chapel without the
" town, which was the chief occafion that the place furrendered."
So that, according to the Bifhop, the *Spaniards* furrendered *Gibralter*, to recover their wives and daughters.

R   promifed

1704. promifed that thofe who fhould remain in it fhould have the fame privileges which they had enjoyed in the reign of King *Charles* II. But the Prince of *Darmftadt* requiring them to take the oath of allegiance to the Arch-duke as King of *Spain*, they all chofe rather to quit the town than comply. Here the enemy placed a garrifon of two thoufand men, under the command of the Marquis *Valferto*. The *Englifh* and *Dutch* plundered the church of *N. D. d'Europe*, that of *S. Jean de Dieu*, and fome others, under pretence of punifhing the inhabitants for refufing to continue in the town. A Minifter of the King of *Spain*, to whom this lofs was imputed, was greatly blamed; and meafures were immediately taken for repairing it. The King called his Council of State, wherein it was refolved that the Marquis of *Villadarias* fhould approach *Gibralter*, whilft the neceffary preparations were making for befieging it. For this purpofe, he received fome days after, eight thoufand men partly from the Duke of *Berwick*'s army.

At the fame time the King of *Spain* fent a courier to Count *Touloufe*, High Admiral of *France*, who was then before *Barcelona*, to engage him to fecond this enterprize.

The Earl of *Galway*, whom the Queen of *England* had fent to *Portugal* with new reinforcements, arrived at *Lifbon* on the tenth of *Auguft*. From thence he fet out on the fifteenth, with the *Englifh* officers whom he had brought with him, and went to meet the King of *Portugal*

and

and the Arch-duke. The bloody fluxes which 1704.
reigned at that time, and with which the Arch-
duke himſelf was attacked, had obliged them,
for a change of air, to go to *Coimbra* in the province of *Beira*. The *Engliſh* reinforcements burnt
Herrera, after having carried off the corn, and
tranſported it to *Caſtel de Vidé*, the fortifications
of which place had been repaired.

The Duke of *Berwick*'s army was conſidera-
bly leſſened by the detachment of the Marquis
Villadarias, and conſiſted only of fifteen thouſand men; for which reaſon he could make no
further conqueſts, and was obliged to content
himſelf with obſerving the enemy. The King
of *Portugal*, with the Arch-duke, accompanied
by the Admirante of *Caſtile* and the Earl of *Galway*, advanced with about twenty thouſand men
to *Almeida*, a ſmall town in *Portugal*, ſituated
on the river *Sabugal*, where the artillery and a
great quantity of warlike ſtores were prepared.

Mean while Count *Toulouſe*, in purſuance of
the orders he had received from the King of
Spain, ſet out with his fleet from *Barcelona*, and
went in queſt of the enemy, whom he found
off *Malaga*. Though the number of his ſhips
was far leſs than that of the enemy, he nevertheleſs attacked them, and after a very long and
obſtinate engagement, forced them to abandon the place of battle, having deſtroyed two of
their largeſt ſhips, and put many others out of
the engagement. This fight did great honour to
the Marine of *France*, and that Prince gave here

R 2

ſuch

1704. fuch proofs of his valour and intrepidity as were worthy of his birth. Neverthelefs, we did not reap from hence the advantages we had expected; for *Gibraltar* was not recovered *. Count *Touloufe*, before he returned with his fleet into the harbours, fent a fquadron of fhips under Mr. *Pointis*, to affift at the fiege of *Gibralter*.

The King of *Portugal* and the Arch-duke, who were encamped at *Almeida*, after having reviewed their army, which they found twenty one thoufand four hundred and twenty feven men ftrong, held a council of war, wherein it was debated whether they ought to attempt the fiege of fome town, or march to the Duke of *Berwick*, who was then encamped at *Ciudad Rodrigo*. The opinions were divided; but that of

* As for this naval engagement at *Malaga*, both fides claimed the victory; but, to ipeak impartially, neither had a clear title to it. However, as our author here intimates, the *Englifh* and *Dutch* carried their point, which was to difable the *French* from affifting the *Spaniards* in recovering *Gibralter*. —— It mult be obferved, that the *Englifh* fleet having been a confiderable time at fea, having fpent a great deal of ammunition in the taking of *Gibralter*, and furnifhed the garrifon of that place with a valt quantity of powder, was in great want of provifions, both naval and military, and was befides thinly man'd; whereas the *French* fleet was in good cafe, and much fuperior to the other both in number and ftrength: for the *Dutch* had fent home fix of their fhips fome days before, and four *Englifh* fhips of the line were abfent upon convoy. In this action the *French*, according to their own account, loft thirty eight perfons of diftinction, among whom was the Marquis of *Belle-Ifle*, a flag-officer, and Count *Chateau-Renault*. The lofs of men was nearly equal on both fides. After this engagement, the *French* never ventured their fleet at fea, but contented themfelves with fending out fquadrons to difturb the commerce of the confederates, by attacking their convoys.

the

the Admirante of *Caſtile* prevailed : for he aſſur- 1704.
ed them that the Arch-duke ſhould have no
ſooner entred *Spain*, than King *Philip*'s army
would abandon him, and join with them.   He
ſupported his opinion by reading ſeveral letters
written by the principal officers of the *Spaniſh*
cavalry.   Whereupon thirty two battalions and
thirty ſeven ſquadrons marched in order of battle on the firſt of *October*, and encamped between
Gallegao and *Carpio*, three leagues from *Ciudad
Rodrigo*.

The Duke of *Berwick*, who was appriſed of
all this, but eſpecially of what the Admirante of
Caſtile had ſaid, took his meaſures to hinder the
Spaniſh officers from deſerting.   He called them
together, and plainly told them what diſcourſe
was held concerning their pretended diſpoſition
to betray the King.   He awakened their nicety
in point of honour ſo effectually, that they all
proteſted and ſwore that they were ready to ſpill
their blood in the ſervice of King *Philip*.   However, the Duke of *Berwick* did not think fit to
rely wholly upon theſe proteſtations; for the
greater ſecurity, he changed the diſpoſition of his
army, mixing the *Spaniſh* troops with the *French*,
that the latter might watch more narrowly the
ſteps of the former.

As ſoon as the army of the enemy was encamped between *Gallegao* and *Carpio*, as we have
ſaid already, the Admirante of *Caſtile* ſent by
trumpets ſeveral copies of a new declaration of the
Archduke which had been printed at *Liſbon*; but

                              theſe

1704. thefe trumpets were fent back, no body inclining to open the pacquets. Several copies of this declaration were difperfed in the country, but likewife without effect.

Both armies continued in this fituation till the eighth of *October*, when they began to cannonade each other. The Duke of *Berwick* ordered fome troops of horfe to pafs the river, who, being favoured by our cannon, went to attack the advanced guards of the enemy. The King of *Portugal*, who had the ftrongeft army, being provoked that we came to attack him, refolved to give us battle: whereupon he held a council of war, wherein the manner of engaging us was fettled. After this, his army advanced in battalia upon the banks of the river, in order to pafs it at feveral fords. The Duke of *Berwick* prepared to give him a warm reception, and to make him pay dear for his paffage. Accordingly he ordered the fire of the cannon to be doubled, and as the enemy were going to enter the river, he went to a little eminence, in order to obferve their countenance. From thence he perceived among them a certain motion, and I know not what agitation, which feemed to be occafioned by a panick fear and alarm. Soon after, he faw them go back with precipitation, and like people who fled, efpecially the *Portuguefe*; for the *Englifh* and *Dutch* retired in good order. The Duke not knowing what could be the caufe of fo fudden a retreat, endeavoured to make advantage of it. For this purpofe he prefently made his army pafs
the

the river, and purſued the enemy near two 1704.
leagues, though without being able to charge
their rear-guard, becauſe the *Engliſh* troops, of
which it confiſted, retired with great precaution.
The enemy ſtopt at *Affairos*, where they expected the new reinforcements which were to come
from *England.*

The reader will perhaps be curious to know
the reaſon of ſo ſudden and extraordinary a
change of the enemies reſolution. There is
certainly ſomething very ſingular in it: but
in order to underſtand it we muſt begin a
little higher. St. *Anthony* of *Padua* is the Patron
of the kingdom of *Portugal,* and the *Portugueſe*
pay a great devotion to this tutelar Saint, to
whom they think they are indebted for ſeveral
victories. They pretend, that when they ſhook
off the *Spaniſh* yoke to ſubmit to the Houſe of
Braganza, they had infallible proofs that this
Saint favoured and protected them. Whereupon they demanded of their King that St. *Anthony* of *Padua* ſhould be declared perpetual Gene-
ralliſſimo of their armies; and the King was, as
it were, forced to comply with their requeſt.
He accordingly ſummoned his council, to which
all the Grandees of the Kingdom were called;
and the requeſt of the nation was laid before
them. Some repreſented that St. *Anthony* having never ſerved in their armies during his life,
this poſt could not be conferred upon him after
his death; and that it was ſufficient for him to
be the Patron and Protector of *Portugal,* in or-

der

1704. der to be likewise the Patron and Protector of their armies. This reason did not satisfy the nation: they persisted in their request. The King, to please both sides, resolved to make St. *Anthony* pass through all the military degrees, that he might come at last to be Generalissimo.

For this purpose, he made a promotion of General Officers, wherein St. *Anthony* was declared Brigadeer of the armies of the King of *Portugal*. Afterwards he made another, wherein the Saint was declared Marshal de Camp; and a third, wherein he was made Lieutenant-general. After this, he was declared perpetual Generalissimo of the *Portuguese* armies. A houshold and officers were assigned him; and it was ordered that the busto of this Saint should always be carried in the army next to the General, and that the order should always be given in the name of St. *Anthony*. This has been practised by the *Portuguese* ever since.

When therefore the enemy were upon the banks of the river ready to pass it, a cannon bullet carried off the busto of the Saint. Struck with amaze and consternation, the *Portuguese*, like troops who lose a General in whom they repose all their confidence, took the alarm, and now thought of nothing but making their escape. In vain did the King of *Portugal* endeavour to stop them; he was never able to remove their pannic, or to rally them; and was obliged to yield to the torrent: but being chagrined at this

kind

kind of defeat, he quitted the army, with which 1704.
he was highly difpleafed, and returned to *Lifbon*.

The Marquis of *Thoy*, who upon receiving
advice that the enemy advanced to *Ciudad Rodrigo*, had joined the Marquis of *Bay*, and thrown
a regiment into *Valencia*, now retired to *Ciudad
Rodrigo*; and the Duke of *Berwick* fent his
troops into winter quarters.

The greateft part of them were placed along
the *Tagus*, and the reft from the river *Duara* to
the mountains.   The *Portuguefe*, on their fide,
took their quarters at *Almeida* and the neighbouring places; the *Englifh* and *Dutch* at *Por-
to*, *Viana* and the adjacent country.

Mean while the fiege of *Gibraltar* was carrying on; it lafted for a confiderable time.
This enterprife proved unfuccefsful, and made
the *Spaniards* fenfible how important that poft
was, and how dear they were to pay for their
neglect in preferving it.   It was this in particular
which obliged the Duke of *Berwick* to ftand
upon the defenfive, as we have juft feen, and
hindred him from purfuing his conquefts.

This year's campaign was very advantageous
and glorious for *France* in *Italy*, where the
Duke of *Vendôme* took three important places,
namely *Vercelli*, *Ivrea*, and *Verrua*.   The Grand
Prior took *Revero*.   *Robbio* and *Rofafco* furren-
dered to Count *Eftain*, and *Sufa* to the Duke
La Feuillade: but our affairs were far from be-
ing as fuccefsful in *Flanders* and *Germany*.   The
Duke of *Marlborough*, after having bombarded
Namur,

1704. *Namur*, set out with a strong detachment to join the Prince of *Baden* in *Bavaria*. Prince *Eugene*, who was upon the *Rhine*, defeated the vigilance of Marshal *Villeroy*, who commanded there in the room of Marshal *Tallard*. He left a part of his army encamped in such a manner as to make it believed that all his troops were there, and marched with the rest to join the Prince of *Baden*. As soon as the army of the Allies was united, they attacked that of the Elector of *Bavaria* and Marshal *Tallard*. Never was any battle more unfortunate for *France*: this is the famous battle of *Hochstet*. Besides a vast number of prisoners, among whom was Marshal *Tallard*, we lost all *Bavaria*, and all the places which we had conquered in *Germany* *. After

* This battle was fought on the thirteenth of *July*, N. S. The confederate army was commanded by Prince *Eugene* and the Duke of *Marlborough*. Above 13000 *French* and *Bavarians* were here taken prisoners; near 20000 killed, wounded, or drowned in the *Danube*; and the Allies took above 100 pieces of cannon, 24 mortars, 129 colours, 171 standards, 17 pair of kettle-drums, 3600 tents, with their treasure, baggage, ammunition, &c. But the battle of *Hochstet*, or *Blenheim*, is so well known, especially to the *English* readers, that it is unnecessary to mention any farther particulars of it. This memorable victory was preceded by the action at *Schellenberg* near *Donawert*, where the Duke of *Marlborough* and Prince *Lewis* of *Baden* attacked the *Bavarian* intrenchments, and carried them after a very sharp engagement, wherein several thousands were killed and wounded on both sides. Of the Confederates, Lieutenant-general *Goor* and Major-general *Beinheim* in the *Dutch* service were killed, Prince *Lewis* of *Baden*, General *Thungen*, Count *Horn*, Count *Stirum*, the Prince of *Hesse*, Lieutenant-general *Wood*, Major-general *Paland*, and a great many other officers were wounded. On the third of *July*, being the day after this action, the *Bavarian* garrison quitted *Donawert*, and the Allies took possession of it.

having

having retaken *Ulm*, *Landau*, and *Traerbach*, 1704.
the enemy fat down at laft before *Brifac*, of
which they in vain attempted to make themfelves mafters.

Marfhal *Villars* was then in *Languedoc*. This
province had been for fome time the theatre of
a moft cruel inteftine war concerning religion.
We fhall have occafion to fpeak of it in the fequel of thefe Memoirs.

The victory at *Hochftet* enabled the Emperor
to fupport the war in *Hungary* which had begun in the year preceeding. He fent thither
a part of his troops which had been employed
in *Bavaria*. We think it will not be foreign
to the prefent fubject to enter into fome detail
of this affair; efpecially as all the tranfactions
and events which happened at that time in *Europe* are fo linked together, that it is impoffible
to have a juft idea of one without underftanding
all the reft.

As foon as the Emperor *Leopold* afcended the
throne of *Hungary*, he formed a defign of making
himfelf abfolute mafter of that kingdom, and
particularly of rendering the Crown hereditary in
his own family. The firft ftep he took for this
purpofe, was upon the death of Count *Wezel* to
fupprefs the office of *Ban*, or perpetual Governor
of the kingdom. This office, which was conferred by the people, had been eftablifhed for the
fupport of the laws and privileges of the ftate,
and ferved as a counterpoife to the regal authority.

The

1704.
The Emperor, upon suppressing this office, appointed *German* Governors throughout the kingdom, that they might the more readily obey the orders sent them from *Vienna*.

Count *Serini* one of the principal *Hungarian* Lords, and one of those who were most attached to the privileges of his nation, dropped some complaints, which though made in secret, became known to the Emperor. This was enough to ruin him at the Court of *Vienna*, and from thence forward he passed there for an enemy. His brother was assassinated in a wood where he had been hunting, and a report had been spread that he was gored by a wild boar. Loud complaints were made against him under various pretences. At last he was arrested, with the Counts *Tattembach*, *Nadasti*, and *Franchipani*, who were all accused of the same crimes. These four noblemen were brought to a trial and lost their heads upon a scaffold: their effigies were confiscated, and the complaints of the son of Count *Serini*, instead of procuring him any redress, occasioned his being imprisoned at *New-stadt* for the rest of his life. His daughter had been married to Prince *Frederick Ragotzi*, who, after his father *George Ragotzki*, had been named Prince of *Transilvania*, under the protection of the *Ottoman Porte*. This province, which formerly made a part of *Hungary*, after having been for some time tributary to the Grand Signior, was erected into a particular Vaivodship under the Sultan *Soliman*.

Frederick

Frederick died in the flower of his age, and 1704.
left a fon called *Francis Ragotzki*, a Prince moſt
agreeable in his perfon, endowed with great wit
and prudence, and equally accompliſhed for the
field and the cabinet, but eſpecially eſteemed a
man of inviolable honour, both with reſpeᶜt to
his enemies and friends.

The Princeſs his mother being yet very young,
was married to Count *Emeric Tekeli*, who from
the age of fifteen years was ſo famous among
the *Hungarian* Malcontents, and was declared
Sovereign and King of *Hungary* by the *Ottoman
Porte*. After the ſiege of *Vienna* had been raiſed,
and the *Turks* driven out of *Hungary*, the Emperor held two general aſſemblies of the Counts of
the kingdom, one at *Preſburg*, the other at
Odenburg, wherein *Joſeph* of *Auſtria*, the Emperor's eldeſt fon, was acknowledged heir of the
Crown, and it was declared that from thence-
forth it ſhould paſs by right of inheritance to the
male and female iſſue of the Houſe of *Auſtria*.

This declaration paſſed chiefly by the intrigues
of Count *Palfi*; but moſt of the Lords had only
ſigned it, becauſe they imagined that they had
ſufficiently provided againſt it by a ſecret pro-
teſtation, which they had entred into at *Alba re-
galis*.

At this time the Emperor placed *German* garriſons in all the principal fortreſſes of the kingdom, and deprived the *Hungarians* of all publick
offices, which obliged ſeveral of them to retire
from that country. The council of *Vienna* declared

1704. clared the eftates of Count *Tekeli* forfeited; *Charles* Duke of *Lorrain* made himfelf mafter of all *Tranfilvania* in the name of the Emperor, and General *Rabutin* a *Frenchman* by birth, was made Governor of it. Prince *Francis Ragotzki*, had at this time a great correfpondence in *Tranfilvania*; we have already mentioned the grounds of his pretentions. He had married on the twenty fifth of *September* 1644 *Charlotta Emelia*, daughter to the Prince of *Heffe Rhinfels*, by whom he had two fons. To the eldeft of thefe Count *Tekeli* was godfather, and made him a prefent of all his eftates in *Hungary*, which the Court of *Vienna* had confifcated, and which were of great value. This Prince demanded them of the Imperial Court in the moft fubmiffive manner, but receiving no fatisfaction, he made fome complaints to which his enemies gave an odious turn, and this ruined his intereft with the Emperor. He was accufed of acting in concert with the *Hungarian* malcontents, and of labouring to get himfelf elected Vaivod, or Prince of *Tranfilvania*. Upon this accufation he was apprehended at *Newftadt* in the month of *April* 1701. This was the Town where Count *Sereni* had been beheaded, and his fon was kept prifoner. However, Prince *Francis Ragotzki* was not difcouraged upon this misfortune, and refolved to lay hold of the firft opportunity of making his efcape: He fained to believe that he fhould be a prifoner for life; whereupon declaring that his plate and equipage were of no ufe

to

to him, he fold them, and thereby furnifhed 1704.
himfelf with a large fum of money. With part
of this money he gained a Captain of dragoons,
called *Labaman*, whom he trufted with the fecret. This man procured for him the habit of
one of his dragoons, wherein he was to make
his efcape. All things being prepared, the Prince
gave a grand entertainment to his guards and
their officers: having made them all drunk,
he laid hold of this opportunity, and made his
efcape on the feventh of *November* 1701, about
two of the clock in the afternoon. He was not
miffed till two hours after, when three letters
were found upon his table; one addreffed to the
Emperor, another to the Emprefs, and a third
to the King of the *Romans*. In that addreffed
to the Emperor, he informed him that he was
ready to throw himfelf at his feet, in order to
juftify himfelf from the calumnies with which
his enemies had blackened him, if his Imperial
Majefty would grant him a fafe conduct, and
appoint unprejudiced judges, fuch as would try
him by the laws of *Hungary*; that in this difpofition of mind he fhould wait his Majefty's orders, refolving to comply with them like a faithful fubject, though without departing from his
rights, or leaving his eftates to his enemies, who
unjuftly detained them from him. In the two
other letters he only begged the Emprefs and the
King of the *Romans* to intercede for him with
his Imperial Majefty. Thefe letters, far from

producing

1704. producing any good effect, ferved only to irritate the Emperor againft him more than ever.

Prince *Ragotzki* being come to the fuburbs of *Newftadt*, where his friends had provided three horfes, one for a man who was to perfonate an officer, another for a valet-de-chambre, and the third for the Prince in his habit of a dragoon, he took the road to *Raab*, or *Javarin*, fituate at the mouth of the river *Raab*, a branch of the *Danube*; he paffed that river, and after having changed horfes he entered *Poland* by the upper *Hungary*, and went with great diligence to join Count *Berzini*, who had headed the malcontents, and who received him with all poffible proofs of efteem and fubmiffion.

Immediately the Emperor publifhed at *Vienna* a profcription of this Prince, wherein he promifed a hundred thoufand florins to any perfon who fhould bring him his head. He ordered his trial to be made in the month of *May* 1703; they condemned him to be beheaded, and to have his goods confifcated. The Princefs his wife, who had the city of *Vienna* for her prifon, was confined to a convent, and his two children were committed to the keeping of the Bifhop of *Javarin*'s fteward. The Captain of dragoons, who had affifted Prince *Ragotzki* in his efcape, had his hand cut off, and was afterwards beheaded and quartered.

Ragotzki underftanding by this that he could expect no juftice from the Emperor, put himfelf in a condition to recover his country from bondage,

bondage, and to reftore its antient liberty. The 1704.
Hungarians ftood very well affected to him, they
chofe him for their Chief, and he promifed on
his part an inviolable attachment to their interefts,
and to lofe his life rather than lay down his
arms before they were reftored to their privileges.
He forfook the *Lutheran* religion which he had
profeffed, and embraced the *Roman Catholick*.
He was at the fame time proclaimed Prince, or
Vaivod of *Tranfilvania* in a general affembly
which was held for that purpofe.

He took the name of Sovereign of that country in the year 1703, and gave the Court of
Vienna to underftand that they muft never hope
he would make any accommodation with them,
unlefs they yielded to him the abfolute and independent poffeffion of that province, to which he
pretended the Houfe of *Auftria* had no right.
But whatever defire he had of afcending the
throne, to which he was called by the unanimous fuffrages of the *Tranfilvanians*, it was not
an eafy matter to drive out of that country General *Rabutin*, who commanded there for the
Emperor, and to maintain himfelf againft the
power of the Houfe of *Auftria*.

However, he eafily formed a confiderable party
in that country, which in the month of *Auguft*
1704, chofe him Sovereign in a moft numerous affembly that was held by the unanimous confent of the nation, and in which the
chief Lords acknowledged that their Principa-
lity was elective, as having formerly made a

S

part

1704. part of *Hungary*, and was governed by the fame laws.

General *Rabutin* began with ordering the Chancellor to be beheaded as a ſtate criminal, under pretence that he was anſwerable for that election.　This ſeverity ſerved only to exaſperate more and more the people of *Hungary* and and *Tranſilvania*.　The Emperor now attempted to appeaſe theſe diſorders by means of a negotiation: for this purpoſe he ſent Prince *Eugene* to *Preſburg*, but that Prince had no ſucceſs. Whereupon the Emperor reſolved to ſend troops into *Hungary* in order to gain by force what he could not obtain by other means.

Ragotzki, on his ſide, not contented with the militia who offered to ſerve him, brought together under his ſtandard above a hundred thouſand men; but they were undiſciplined.　Beſides, he called into *Hungary* foreign troops, and choſe officers proper to form his whole army, and by degrees to eſtabliſh a good diſcipline.

He at firſt divided his forces into four bodies, and afterwards into ſix; the chief of them were under the command of the Counts *Berzini* and *Caroli*.　Theſe Generals made themſelves maſters of the iſle of *Schut*, which of all the paſſages of the *Danube* is the moſt convenient and the moſt eaſy for paſſing from upper to lower *Hungary*. He commanded them to make incurſions to the very gates of *Vienna*, *Buda* and *Peſth*, which lie below that iſland.　At the ſame time Prince *Eugene* was at *Preſburg*, where he laboured in

vain

vain to bring together an army capable to make 1704.
head againſt the malcontents. *Ragotzki* ſent a
third body under the command of Count *Otſkai*,
and kept for himſelf the ſtrongeſt army on the
ſide of the *Teiſſe* and *Tranſilvania*, that he might
be within reach of penetrating into that country
whenever he pleaſed, and of ſeizing all the places
which were in the neighbourhood, and in his
paſſage.

Toward the end of the year 1703 he made
himſelf maſter of an important poſt upon the
Danube near *Gran*, or *Strigonia*, a place confiderable for its riches, ſituation and archbiſhop-
rick; and thus he commanded both ſides of the
river. In the neighbourhood of this town he
placed his magazines. Whilſt the firſt troops
above-mentioned acted according to their orders
and alarmed *Vienna*, *Peſth*, and *Buda*, by the
ſudden incurſions which they made to the very
gates of theſe cities, *Ragotzki* blocked up on the
ſide of the *Teiſſe*, *Tokay* which ſoon ſurrendered,
as well as *Zatmea* and *Caſcaw*. This laſt town
was reduced by famine. He afterwards took the
fortreſs of *Agria* and the famous caſtle of *Mont-
kars* which nature and art ſeemed to have rendered impregnable.

The Emperor, who was embaraſſed and even
alarmed by this war, being beſides ſollicited by the
Engliſh and *Dutch*, propoſed an accommodation:
he offered paſſports to the Counts *Berzini* and
Caroli, if they would come to *Vienna* in order to
manage this negociation: they refuſed them by

 order

1704. order of Prince *Ragotzki*, who thought there was no trusting to these passports. Whereupon the Emperor being greatly straitned on the side of *Hungary*, and having every thing to fear from the *French* army which was in *Bavaria*, resolved to take the *English* and *Dutch* as mediators, and to send deputies to the malcontents.

This War in *Hungary* made a diversion so favourable to *France*, that it was not doubted but his Most Christian Majesty contributed to it. In this he only returned to the Allies what they had done to his Majesty by fomenting the revolt of his subjects in the *Sevennes*, by the promises they made, and the supplies of money they sent into those parts. Such was the situation of affairs when the battle of *Hochstet* was fought. The Emperor being delivered from the *French* army, changed his design and thought no longer of negociating with Prince *Ragotzki:* He sent, as we have said above, part of the troops which had been employed in *Bavaria* to reduce the *Hungarians* by force of arms.

The King of *France* made new efforts to repair the misfortunes and immense losses which he had sustained in this year's campaign. His Majesty was sensible that it was necessary to employ better Generals: he recalled the Duke of *Berwick* from *Spain*, and sent Marshal *Tessé* in his room. The King of *Spain* was greatly concerned at this change: he was going to lose an experienced General in whom the *Spaniards* had

an

an entire confidence; but his Christian Majesty's 1704.
orders were positive.   As soon as the Duke of
Berwick was informed of Marshal *Tessé*'s arrival
at *Madrid,* he went thither to confer with him,
and to take his leave of the King of *Spain.*   This
Prince said to him at his last audience, *I am very
sorry that you are going from us; but I hope you
will return to us in a short time.*   He arrived at
Versailles in the end of *December,* and met with
a most gracious reception from the King, who
expressed the particular esteem he had for him.
He went afterwards to pay his duty to the Duke
of *Burgundy.*   This Prince told him that he had
contributed to his being recalled, having represented to his Majesty how much a person of the
Duke of *Berwick*'s merit was wanted; and that
after what had happened, he knew no other Generals in *France* but the Duke of *Vendôme,* him,
and Marshal *Villars,* who were able to retrieve
the losses of the last campaign.   It will soon appear that this Prince had great reason to think
thus of the Duke of *Berwick,* since all the enterprizes with which he was entrusted were attended with success.

The enemies of *France,* elated with the victo- 1705.
ry of *Hochstet,* expected to gain mighty advantages in this year's campaign.   As they had a
great many troops in winter quarters upon the
Moselle, they formed a design to besiege *Thionville,* their troops lying near this place, to make
themselves afterwards masters of *Mentz,* to pass
into *Lorrain,* and penetrate into *France.*

S 3

The

1705. The King being apprifed of their defigns, took the proper meafures to defeat them. He recalled Marfhal *Villars* from *Languedoc*, and gave him the command of the army on the *Mofelle*, where the war was to be carried on with great vigour. Marfhal *Marcin* commanded on the *Rhine*; and the Elector of *Bavaria*, who came into *France* after the battle of *Hochftet*, was named Generaliffimo of the army in *Flanders*, having under him Marfhal *Villeroy* and Marfhal *d'Arco*. Thefe three armies were to act in concert, and fend fuccours to each other, in cafe of need.

The care and application of Marfhal *Villars* ought, one would think, to have fuppreffed and put an end to the troubles of the *Sevennes* in *Languedoc* *: but when we have to do with a head-ftrong, obftinate people, who know neither reafon nor duty, we can rely upon nothing. It foon appeared, that they were difpofed to continue their difturbances and revolt. For which

---

* The *Sevennes* is a part of the province of *Languedoc*: Its territory is mountainous, but far from being unfertil; in length about twenty two leagues, and in breadth about twelve or thirteen. It is divided into higher and lower *Sevennes*. *Viviers* is its capital city, feated on a hill, the bottom of which is wafhed by the *Rhone*. In the reign of *Lewis* XIII the *Sevennes* was wholly inhabited by Proteftants. Under his fon *Lewis* XIV they were perfecuted on account of their religion: feveral of them made a fhew of turning Roman Catholicks, and were on that account ftiled New Converts. Yet, as they had been forced to it, they were ready to embrace the firft opportunity of returning to their former religion; and the hardfhips they fuffered both from the Court and the Clergy confirmed them in their averfion to the Romifh Church.

reafon,

reafon, when the King recalled Marfhal *Villars* 1705.
from the *Sevennes*, he thought fit to fend in his
place a General who might put an end to that
inteftine war by force of arms and punifhments,
fince it could not be done by mildnefs and clemency : and feeing no perfon fitter for this purpofe than the Duke of *Berwick*, his Majefty appointed him to command in *Languedoc*.

As this province is indebted to the Duke of
Berwick for the fuppreffing of thefe difturbances,
and for that tranquillity which it has enjoyed ever
fince, we fhall here give a fhort account of the rife
and progrefs of this war, of the misfortunes it produced, and of the fituation of affairs in *Languedoc*, when the Duke of *Berwick* arrived in that
country.

Thefe inteftine divifions began in the year
1702, and were fo much the more cruel, as no
rules were followed in them, nor any law divine
or human obferved. In the beginning of thefe
troubles, the pretence laid hold on was that the
Curés, or country Parfons, purfuant to the orders of the Intendant of the province, had given
in eftimates of the wealth of their refpective pa-
rifhes, according to which they were rated in the
rolls of capitation : they made loud complaints,
becaufe, faid they, the new converts were over-
rated in thefe rolls. Mean while, the Abbé
Chayla carried off two maids, the daughters of a
gentleman of fome rank, becaufe they neglected
to do their duty of new Catholicks; and inftead
of putting them into a convent, as he had been
S 4 ordered

 ordered by the Court, he put them into a caftle of his own; which highly irritated the new converts. Sometime after, that is, in the month of *June* of this year, the receivers of the capitation having ordered fome private perfons who had refufed to pay the tax to be hanged in the villages of the higher *Sevennes*, they were dragged in the night from their houfes, and hanged on trees before their doors, with the capitation rolls about their necks. Thofe who committed this outrageous action had difguifed themfelves by putting fhirts over their clothes, from whence thefe rebels had afterwards the name of *Camifars*.

Count *Broglio*, who commanded in *Languedoc*, having received advice of thefe difturbances, fent the Marfhalfey of *Montpelier* with a body of troops, to punifh thofe who were deemed guilty of this violence; but this remedy encreafed the diftemper. Several bodies of this fort of people began to pillage and fteal in the night, in places where they expected to find any booty; and this at firft was done without bloodfhed: for which reafon it was believed that their miferable poverty was the occafion of fuch robberies. But it was afterwards obferved that they particularly fell upon the Priefts, and religion appeared to be the true motive to thefe outrages.

The Ecclefiafticks called for the fecular arm. A body of troops was fent to them, and took three of thofe villains, who were condemned to be broke alive: the reft, to revenge their deaths, maffacred all the Priefts they could meet, and

pulled

pulled down some churches; after which, they 1705.
assembled together to the number of five hundred, and this company daily encreased: their
retreat lay in the woods, rocks and mountains in
the *Sevennes*.

We now heard of nothing but robberies, mur-
ders, burnings, sacrileges, and the most hideous
crimes, committed over the whole provinces, but
especially in the *Sevennes*, where the inhabitants
were continually alarmed. It was no longer safe
to travel here without an escort. The greatness
of this evil was for sometime concealed from the
King, because they hoped that it would have no
dangerous consequence; but at last when it was
known that the Camisars were secretly encouraged by the *English*, who furnished them with
money and arms, in order to give a diversion to
France, it became necessary to inform his Majesty of these disorders. The King sent thither
Marshal *Montrevel*; but as this revolt was yet
neglected, and only considered as one of those
popular seditions which are presently suppressed
by the punishment of some of the ringleaders,
the Camisars were used with great clemency and
mildness.

However, this was a Hydra whose heads daily
encreased. There came from *Switzerland* and
Savoy several officers and deserters to join the rebels, with false credentials from those who were
engaged in the service of the enemies of *France*.
They were promised a ready supply of troops,
and were assured that neither money, arms, nor

ammu-

1705. ammunition fhould be wanting to them: they were told that armed fleets were coming to land upon their coafts, and frefh pretences were daily invented to excufe the delay of their arrival.

This revolt produced the effect which the enemies of *France* expected from it: for, in confequence of thefe promifes, the rebels increafed to fuch a number, that there were very few towns in that province where the fanaticks did not frequently hold publick meetings.

They had for their firft leader one *Roland*, the fon of a miller, who, to compleat his extravagance and folly, was intituled a Count. Afterwards, as they were obliged to divide into feveral bands, they chofe feveral leaders, the moft famous of whom was *Cavalier* *.

Marfhal *Montrevel* found feveral obftacles which he did not feem to have expected. To reduce the rebels by force of arms was a hazardous attempt in a country where all the inhabitants fecretly favoured them.

The maffacres they made fpread a general terror: even the foldiers who fought againft them were daunted; and as they could hope for no quarter, they did not encounter them with fo much ardour and courage as they would have fhewn againft a lefs cruel and inhuman enemy.

* He is at prefent a Brigadeer-general in the *Britifh* fervice. He was lately appointed Governor of the ifland of *Guernfey*, and had the command of an independent company of foot given him in the faid ifland.

Befides,

Befides the King had occafion for his troops: accordingly fuch refolutions were taken as were agreeable to the conjuncture at that time, and Marfhal *Villars* was fent to put them in execution.

Upon his arrival, he purfued the rebels with great vigour, and without giving them any refpite; but at the fame time he let them know, that the King was inclined to be merciful, and made them hope for a general pardon, if they would lay down their arms, and fubmit. The greateft number of them complied. *Cavalier,* their leader, in a conference he held at *Nifmes* with Marfhal *Villars,* agreed to put an end to the war, and the Camifars had paffports to go out of the kingdom. Marfhal *Villars* fet out from *Montpelier* on the fixth of *January* 1705.

It was thought that this difturbance was now fuppreffed, and *Languedoc* expected to recover its former tranquillity: all appearances were for it; the fanaticks had laid down their arms, they had accepted the amnefty, and their principal leaders had quitted the kingdom: but thefe troubles were revived by the intrigues of Abbot *la Bourlie,* who was gone into *Holland,* and had taken meafures with the *English* and *Dutch* to renew this war *.

This

* This Abbot was brother to Count *Guifcard,* a General in the *French* fervice. Having received fome difgufts from the Court of *France,* he retired into *Switzerland,* and from thence repaired to the Court of *Turin,* where he ftiled himfelf Marquis of *Guifcard.* Being a man of a bold fpirit, great ambition, and
                                                            much

1705. This Abbot engaged *Ravanel* and *Catinat*, leaders of the fanaticks, to return in difguife to *France*, with fome others of his party, one of whom was called *Vallars*, though his true name was *Vila* : He was a native of *St. Hypolite*, and had been a Lieutenant in the regiment of *Languedoc*.

much addicted to revenge, he endeavoured, though a Popifh Clergyman, to foment the difturbances in *France* on account of religion. He was well known to the Grand Penfionary *Heinfius*, and to the Duke of *Marlborough*, who gave him hopes of being employed, in cafe any defcent was attempted upon *France* : He was likewife known to King *Charles* III of *Spain* (the prefent Emperor) and to the Earl of *Peterborough*, by whom he was well recommended to the *Englifh* court. He was imployed as Lieutenant-general in the defcent intended to be made upon *France* in the year 1706, under the command of the Earl of *Rivers*; but this enterprize was laid afide by reafon of the contrary winds. Upon the change of the *Englifh* Miniftry in the year 1710, the Marquis of *Guifcard*, as he had been Colonel of a regiment which was ruined at the battle of *Almanza*, and was never raifed again; and as befides he had been admitted to a confidence and community of pleafures with one of the new Minifters; he expected a fuitable preferment : by the recommendation of that Minifter he received a penfion of five hundred pounds; but that penfion being brought down to four hundred pounds by Mr. *Harley* (afterwards made Earl of *Oxford*) and befides being ill paid, he wrote two letters to one Mr. *Moreau*, a banker at *Paris*, wherein he made fome fatyrical reflections on the Miniftry. Thefe letters being ftopped, and fent to them, *Guifcard* was apprehended for high treafon, and brought before a committee of Council at the *Cock-Pit*. After he was examined, he defired to fpeak a word afide with Mr. Secretary *St. John* (the late Lord Vifcount *Bolingbrook*) the latter told him, *that was impracticable and unufual: that he was before the committee of the Council as a criminal, and if he had any thing to offer, it muft be faid to them all*. Whereupon *Guifcard* ftep'd towards the table, as if he defigned to fay fomething to Mr. *Harley*, drew a penknife which he had found in a room where he had been confined, and faid *J'en veux donc à toy, Then have at thee*; and immediately ftabbed him about the middle of the breaft : but the knife lighting upon a rib, fnapped in two, and gave him but a flight wound.

During

guedoc. Thefe men having affociated themfelves 1705.
with fome deferters, formed a confpiracy to
murder the Governors of *Montpelier* and *Nifmes,*
the Commander and Intendant of the province,
and all the King's officers; afterwards they propofed nothing lefs than to rid themfelves of all
the old and new Catholicks who were not of
their party.   After this, appearing openly, and
taking for their device LIBERTY OF CON-
SCIENCE AND NO TAXES, they were to form
an army, and march to the fea-coaft, in order
to facilitate the landing of the fuccours which
the *Englifh* and *Dutch* had promifed to fend
them.   But their defign was difcovered, as will
appear in the fequel.

Such were the beginnings and the progrefs of
this war, and fuch was the fituation of affairs
in *Languedoc,* when the Duke of *Berwick* arrived
there.   He was received at *Montpelier* on the
twenty fifth of *March* with the greateft expreffions of joy: the whole province had a great
veneration for him: the remembrance of his

During the furprize and confternation which this occafioned,
fome of the committee drew their fwords, and wounded *Guifcard*
in feveral places: others ran out of the room to call for help:
whereupon the meffengers and door-keepers rufhing in, went to
lay hold on him.   *Guifcard* ftruggled for awhile, and overthrew
feveral of his affailants; but was at laft overpowered, after having received feveral bruifes, one of which was mortal.   Being
committed to *Newgate,* he died there on the feventeenth of
March 1710.   It is thought *Guifcard's* firft defign was to ftab
Mr. *St. John,* but that not being able to come at him, he pitched upon Mr. *Harley,* becaufe he never found that Minifter inclined to truft or favour him; refolving to make his ruin fatal
to thofe who occafioned it.

virtues

1705. virtues and great qualities was revived and en-
livened by the manner in which he had begun
the war in *Spain*; and from that time the people of *Languedoc* were accuftomed to look upon
him as the Deliverer whom they had fo long
wifhed for.

After having taken the neceffary precautions,
he made a tour through all the fufpected diftricts,
both to view the country, and to fhew himfelf
to the people whom he was to contain in their
duty; and he gave every where the neceffary
orders for obliging the communities to behave
like good fubjects. From thence he went to
view the maritime coafts, from *Montpelier* to
Narbone; he carefully examined all the places
where the enemy could make a defcent, and
fecured the whole coaft.

Whilft the Duke of *Berwick* was taking thefe
meafures, the troops which were in the higher
Sevennes, and in the plain, were inceffantly employed, by his orders, in detecting and apprehending the rebels who had not yet made their
fubmiffion, and efpecially thofe who were known
to have returned from foreign countries. Some
of them were taken and confined to the prifons
in *Montpelier*: they were not the moft confiderable; yet the taking of them was of great confequence: for one of them whofe name was
Chevalier having faid one day; " that an event
" would foon happen more extraordinary than
" any that had ever yet appeared, and that it
" muft be expected in four or five days;" He

was

was afked what it was: the fanatick anfwered, 1705.
" that Mr. *Bafville* (this was the Intendant
" of the province) had need to take great care
" of himfelf; that there was a defign to kill
" him, and to carry off the Duke of *Berwick*;
" that there were already thirty men arrived in
" the town to put that defign in execution;
" that they waited only for the parties which
" *Ravanel* and *Catinat* were to bring thither,
" confifting of their moft refolute men; that
" the twenty fifth of *April* was the day appoint-
" ed for putting this project in execution; that
" they were to begin by fetting on fire Mr.
" *Bafville*'s hay-loft, which was before his houfe,
" and that people would be pofted in certain
" places to fire upon him, when he fhould come
" out of his houfe, or appear at his windows.

He was preffed to tell where thefe thirty men
lodged who were already in *Montpelier*; he
anfwered " that he well knew it, but that they
" ought to be content with his apprifing them
" of the mifchief which was to happen, fo that
" they might prevent it, without requiring him
" to be the caufe that his brethren fhould be
" put to death, by declaring their abodes; that
" for the reft, it would be in vain to afk him
" any more queftions; for he would give them
" no further fatisfaction.

On the nineteenth of *April*, about eleven of
the clock at night, the Duke of *Berwick* had
notice of all this. He immediately ordered the
guards at the gates of the town to be doubled,
and

1705. and that when next morning they should be opened the guards should suffer no suspected person to go out or enter; and that they should confine at the guard-house all persons of whom they could have the least suspicion. At the same time he sent people to search in all the houses of the town for the fanaticks who were in it. Soon after, the Duke of *Berwick* had notice that three suspected persons were lodged in the house of a packer, whose name was *La Rose*: whereupon he sent the Provost with two archers, accompanied by an officer and six *Irish* soldiers.

The Provost entring the chamber, one of the Camisars pretending to dress himself, took two pistols from under his coat, and fired them upon him. One of the shot burnt his wig, and went through his hat; the other wounded one of the archers in the hand: but the Provost having clapt a pistol to the Camisar's breast, shot him dead upon the spot. Several papers were found about him, which served to discover a great number of his accomplices. The other two were taken, and brought before the Duke of *Berwick*.

One of them was a surgeon in the *Sevennes*, a dragoon and deserter from the regiment of *Firmacon*; the other was a native of *Geneva*, and a deserter from the *Swifs* regiment of *Courten*. This last fell at the Duke of *Berwick*'s feet, begged his life, and promised to discover to him things of the utmost importance. The Duke promised him his life, under the King's good pleasure:

whereupon

whereupon he declared that he knew the houſe 1705.
at *Niſmes* where *Ravanel, Catinat, Villars,* and
Jonquet were concealed. Immediately the Duke
of *Berwick* ſent him to *Niſmes* under the guard
of the Provoſt and the two archers. They arrived there next day towards night, and went to
the houſe he mentioned, which was that of *Aliſon*
a ſilk merchant. Finding the door open, they entred it. The Provoſt hearing ſomebody ſpeak
pretty loud in a chamber which was even with
the court, he liſtned, and heard a hoarſe voice ſay,
*Before God, I will anſwer that in leſs than three
weeks the King ſhall not be maſter of* Languedoc,
nor of Dauphiny : *they ſearch for me every where ;
I am here, and fear nothing.*

It was *Ravanel* who ſpoke. He was in company with *Jonquet* and *Villars*. The Provoſt
and his archers ruſhed into the chamber, and
ſiezed the three villains. The ſilk merchant
who owned the houſe, and another whoſe name
was *Alegre*, who had both ſupped on the nineteenth with *Ravanel* and *Catinat*, were likewiſe
apprehended, with all their families and dome-
ſticks.

As for *Catinat*, he was not ſo ſoon taken : but
the Duke of *Berwick* having arrived at *Niſmes*
in the night, and being informed of what had
paſſed, as he was certain that the fanatick was
in the town, ordered the gates to be kept ſhut,
and at the ſame time publiſhed an ordinance,
wherein he " promiſed to give an hundred louis-
" d'ors to any perſon who ſhould deliver up *Ca-*

T

" tinat,

1705. " *tinat,* or caufe him to be taken ; declaring that
 " he would pardon the perfon who fhould have
 " harboured him, provided he would give no-
 " tice of him before the general perquifition,
 " which was going to be made in all the houfes
 " of the town ; but that afterwards the inhabi-
 " tant of the houfe where he fhould be found,
 " fhould be immediately hanged before his door,
 " his family imprifoned, his goods confifcated,
 " and his houfe razed to the ground, without
 " any other form of procefs."

This ordinance had the defired effect. It was
well known how exact the Duke of *Berwick* was
to his word ; no body would give a retreat to
Catinat. Thus he was driven from the houfe
where he was concealed, and having clad himfelf like a beggar, he mixed with the croud,
waiting for fome opportunity of efcaping out of
the town ; but he was difcovered near one of the
gates, and on the twenty feventh in the morning
the officer of the guard apprehended him.

He was brought before the Duke of *Berwick,*
who afked him why he had returned into this
country after he had left it with a paffport, and
had promifed never to return thither, or carry
arms againft the King? This infolent man had
the boldnefs to anfwer, " that he was come back
 " with the character of Envoy Extraordinary
 " from the Queen of *England* to the Proteftants
 " of *France* ; and that, if he might be permitted
 " to write to *London,* he would venture to af-
 " fure him that her *Britifh* Majefty would con-
                                        " fent

" fent to exchange his perfon with that of
" Marfhal *Tallard*."

The Duke of *Berwick* replied to him, that fuch
idle difcourfe was very confiftent with his fanatick deportment; but that if he had nothing
more pertinent to fay, he might expect in a few
hours the regard which was due to his pretended embaffy. In effect, two hours after thefe
wretches were condemned, namely, *Catinat* and
Ravanel to be burnt alive, *Villars* and *Jonquet* to
be broke upon the wheel; and all four after being put to the torture ordinary and extraordinary, in which *Catinat* owned much more than
the reft.

This fentence however was not put in execution till next day, by reafon of the number of
accomplices, with whom it was neceffary to con-
front them.   The bodies of the two latter, after
having been broken, were thrown yet alive into
the fame fire where the other two were burning.

There was found in a mill a great quantity of
powder, fire-arms, and bayonets; and a great
many of the like arms was feized in the houfes
of the armourers of *Nifmes* and *Montpelier*, moft
of whom were apprehended, as well as many
others, to the number of three hundred and fifty,
among whom were fome bankers, who received
by the way of *Genoa* the remittances which came
from *England* and *Holland*.

The executions continued : *Alifon* and *Alegre*
were broke alive; others were hanged.   The

1705. houfes of the two former were razed.   The mafter of the publick houfe where *Alifon* and *Alegre* met, was likewife broke alive, and his houfe
razed.

Some time after, three mules were feized, led
by three cripples, pretending to be dealers in
fkins; thefe mules were loaded with thirty
thoufand louis d'ors in fpecie.   It appeared by
the laft words of all thefe unhappy people that
the twenty fifth of *May* was the day fixed on
for the breaking out of the revolt; they having
intended firft to murther the Governors and officers, and afterwards to fet on fire the cities of
Montpelier and *Nifmes*.   They were to wear on
that day green ribbands in their hats; and in effect, they had gathered together a great quantity
of thefe ribbands : *Alifon* and *Alegre* had caufed
more than three hundred pieces to be dyed of
this colour.

The *Englifh* and *Dutch* had promifed to the
confpirators to land three or four thoufand men
at the porte of *Cette*, together with arms and
ammunitions.   The Camifars of *Montpelier* were
to join them in the plain of *Frontignan*, and
a lift had been made of thofe who could be armed at *Nifmes*, *Ufez*, *Alais*, *St. Hypolite*, and the
other neighbouring villages and boroughs.

In the month of *May* the Duke of *Berwick* vifited the maritime coafts from the *Rhône* to *Montpelier*.   He afterwards fent fome detachments to
find out other leaders of the malcontents, who,
according to the intelligence he had received,
had

had come back into the kingdom in great num- 1705.
bers, and there difperfed writings proper to raife
a general infurrection. Several of them were
apprehended, and had the fame fate with the
reft. Some of them fled into the *Vivarais*; but
Lieutenant-general *Julien*, whom the Duke of
Berwick fent thither, hanged feveral of them,
and difperfed the reft. Thefe rigorous executions
fufpended for fome time the robberies and difturbances of the fanaticks, and at laft put a ftop to
them.

The tranquillity of *Languedoc* was now reftored; the fairs and markets refumed their ufual
courfe; only the Duke of *Berwick* had the precaution to fend troops thither for their farther fecurity. The feverity which he ufed upon this
occafion was neceffary in order to punifh thofe
criminals, and fhews that when we have to do
with rebels, mildnefs and lenity ferve only to
give them time to form and execute the moft per-
nicious defigns.

It is indeed a great affliction for a Prince to
be obliged to deftroy his fubjects, even when
they revolt: but upon fuch occafions it is un-
neceffary to inflict cruel punifhments on the
multitude; it is enough if the ringleaders of fe-
dition meet with no mercy: Thefe are they who
muft fink under the weight of power and authority; as for the others, who are only guilty of the
weaknefs of fuffering themfelves to be feduced
and mifled, they may be pardoned; though at
the fame time the neceffary meafures muft be

taken

 taken to prevent their ficklenefs and inconftancy.
Thus *Languedoc* was indebted to the Duke of
Berwick for the reftoration of its peace : he was
inflexible againft the *Ravanels, Catinats, &c.* the
moft fpeedy and fevereft punifhment was the
only refource he could find againft their boldnefs
and malice : but he did not deftroy any of the
multitude, except in fuch conjunctures wherein
he found it impoffible to fave them.

The Duke of *Berwick* continued in this province till the beginning of *October*, when he fet out
to command in the county of *Nice*, in the room
of Mr. *Uffon*, who died fome time before at *Mar-
feilles*, whither the diftemper, which reigned in
Italy, had obliged him to retire. The Duke of
Savoy by this time held only the citadel of *Nice*,
the King being mafter of the town and of the
county. The Marquis of *Carail*, Governor of
the citadel having broke the fufpenfion of arms
agreed upon with Mr. *Uffon*, the latter blew up
the fortifications of the town, which he had ordered to be undermined in the night between the
feventeenth and eighteenth of *Auguft*, and retired
to *Villefranche* with fome of his troops.

He fent into *Provence*, according to the orders
he had received from court, five battalions and
fome fquadrons, to reinforce the troops commanded by Count *Touloufe*. A defign was formed to befiege the citadel of *Nice* when the
Duke of *Berwick* arrived at *Toulon*, where he
ftopt for fome time in order to make the neceffary preparations for that purpofe. The conqueft

of

of this place was much more difficult now than 1705.
it was in the time of Marſhal *Catinat*. The Duke
of *Savoy* had cauſed ſubterraneous places to be
dug under it, and the vaults were twenty foot
thick, to the end that this fortreſs might not
again be expoſed to the accident by which it
was formerly loſt.

He had expended near two millions, both in
covering the mountain with fortifications, and in
furniſhing the place with all that was neceſſary
for ſtanding out a long ſiege. The Marquis of
Carail had time to rebuild the rampart of the
town, and had made ſo great diſpatch, that
every thing was in very good caſe, when the
Duke of *Berwick* arrived there. Beſides, the citadel is one of the ſtrongeſt fortreſſes in *Europe* ;
it is ſituated upon a ſteep rock in three parts of
its extent ; it is impoſſible to aſcend thither except on the ſide of the town where the rock
flattens and runs into a ſteep declivity, and is defended by three covered works, built in form of
an amphitheatre, one upon another, and fenced
by good ditches and a double covered way, all
mined, together with retrenchments counter-
mined : above the citadel is a caſtle ſtill more ele-
vated, and a tower, or platform which commands the caſtle. The garriſon conſiſted of
fourteen hundred men, and was defended by
one hundred and ſixteen pieces of cannon.

On the thirty firſt of *October*, the Duke of
Berwick arrived before *Nice* with fifteen battalions : he expected thirty two companies of gre-

T 4

nadeers

1705. nadeers which were ordered to march from the army on the *Rhine*, but they could not arrive before the affaults were made. When occafion required, he could employ the garrifons of *Ville franche*, *St. Aufpice* and *Montalban*.

A great quantity of artillery was appointed for this fiege. Mr. *Vauvray*, Intendant of *Toulon*, was ordered to fhip it off with all fpeed; but the contrary winds having obliged the veffels which carried it to ftop at the ifles of *Hieres*, it could not arrive at *Ville franche* till the tenth of *November*; and becaufe it was taken from the marine, the officers of that body were ordered to ferve it. As foon as the Duke of *Berwick* was in readinefs to begin, he ordered a battery of fix pieces of cannon to be raifed before the town: this battery began to fire on the twelfth. At the fame time he fummoned the Governor to furrender at difcretion: the latter was obliged to comply on the twenty fourth, without being able to obtain any other capitulation, becaufe the inhabitants had taken arms. However, the Duke promifed that no violence fhould be offered to them, till the return of a Courier whom he had difpatched to *Verfailles*, to know the King's intention.

As foon as he was mafter of the town he ordered fome batteries of cannon and mortars to be raifed againft the caftle: after fome bombs were thrown, a truce was made with the Governor for two days; which being expired, hoftilities were renewed, and the trenches opened on the

night

night between the feventeenth and eighteenth, 1705.
by one battalion and five companies of grenadeers. The fame difpofition was continued during the whole fiege. In order to cut off the
communication between the caftle and the town,
on the night between the twentieth and the
twenty firft, a retrenchment was begun on the
fide of the baftions of the *Provifiere :* this engaged the enemy to make a fally on the twenty
fecond about two of the clock in the afternoon,
with pioneers, in order to attempt to fill up that
retrenchment, which till it was finifhed, was too
much expofed for our men to be lodged there in
the day-time; but they were vigoroufly repulfed,
loft feveral of their men, and were obliged to
retire and leave their tools behind them: they demanded a fufpenfion of arms, in order to carry
off their dead and wounded; and the Duke
of *Berwick* complied with this requeft. All
the reft of this month was employed in carrying
on the works, and in raifing batteries; thofe on
the height of *St. Charles* were finifhed by the fecond of *December*, and began to play at ten of
the clock in the morning. Before they could be
raifed, we were put to an immenfe labour; feventy four pieces of cannon and thirteen mortars
were inceffantly fired during all that day. We
were informed by a deferter, that the firft of the
five hundred bombs which were thrown into the
caftle, killed more than a hundred and fifty
men,

On

1705.   On the ninth, at break of day, we fired very fiercely on the castle: four pieces of cannon of the besieged were difmounted, and twenty of their cannoneers were killed or wounded: from this time we began to batter the bottom of the redan of the face of the new baftion and the curtain on the fide of *Montalban*. Befides the cannon which fired upon the batteries of the place, four of our cannon were employed in ruining the redoubt which had been raifed on the fea-fide near the gates of relief; and that no perfon might enter the caftle, we made a boyau, by the favour of which we pofted ourfelves behind the rock upon which this redoubt was raifed.

Our artillery was fo well ferved, that a breach was begun on the fame day in the face of the new baftion, and the redan was very much damaged, as well as the large tower within the new baftion; the batteries of mortars were fo advantagioufly placed, that all the bombs fell into the caftle; at laft we fucceeded in allaying the fire of the enemy, which became very inconfiderable. Mr. *Filley*, chief of the engineers, and Mr. *Charmond*, a Brigadeer, were killed by a cannon-fhot; the fkull and the brain of the former flew into the face of the Duke of *Berwick*, who went every where, and would be witnefs himfelf to the leaft operations.

On the tenth, we continued to batter in breach, and the redoubt was fo much bored and fhattered by the cannon, that the befieged abandoned it.

Thus

1705.

Thus the enemy could no longer defcend from the caftle by the gate of relief, without being ex- pofed to our fire within half mufket-fhot. When the trench was advanced to the foot of the rampe of the caftle (this was on the twelfth of *Decem- ber*) the Duke of *Berwick* ordered a great paral- lel to be drawn from a village which was near that place, as far as the fea. This line was not finifhed till the fixteenth; after which feveral boyaus of communication were made, with a fe- cond parallel, which was drawn along the *Lim- pia*. In this interval, feveral batteries were raifed towards *Montalban*, whither our cannon was brought with great difficulty, being drawn up by men; a battery was raifed with the fame diffi- culties upon a rampart which led to the caftle, and run from the town as far as the fea. We likewife planted ten pieces of cannon of thirty fix pounders, from the bridge of the *Limpia*, or from the garden of *Lafcaret*, to the fea; thefe cannons razed all the new fortifications.

On the eighteenth, the citadel was open on feveral fides, and we began to batter the body of the caftle. From that day the trench fur- rounded it within the diftance of half mufket- fhot. The batteries which were to fire in breach on the horn-work began to play on the twen- tieth; they likewife played upon the new baftion which covered the tower on that fide, and fired with fo much fuccefs that almoft all the artille- ry of the befieged was difmounted, fo that the next and following days they fired only about

thirty

1705. thirty shot. The breach which was made in the body of the castle was greatly widened.

We had now eighty four pieces of cannon, which played all day, and part of the night. We had fired by this time thirty five thousand cannon shot; the bombs had dug up the ground over the whole castle, and very much weakened the garrison, and the besieged were obliged to retire into the subterraneous places which were proof against the bombs. On the twenty third, two miners were employed upon the glacis, in quest of the galleries which the enemy had made under the covered way, and under the new bastion.

Notwithstanding the great fire made by our batteries, the besieged continued to raise a-new some of theirs, which did not fail to annoy those of the besiegers. This inconveniency was presently redressed, and activity made amends for the disorder which is inevitable when the troops on one side make a vigorous attack, and those on the other make a brave defence.

The besieged had the good fortune to receive a supply, which, in the circumstances they were in, was of great importance. It consisted of two engineers, several cannoneers, fifteen barrels of powder, and some money, which the Duke of *Savoy* sent into the town in a small vessel that passed without being seen by our galleys. The new batteries which were raised on the side of the attack were finished by the twenty eighth of *December.* One of them consisted of eight pieces

of

of cannon, and another of fix, which made in the whole ninety cannons on that fide alone. As we continued to fire without interruption, not only the touch-holes of the cannons were very much enlarged, but feveral cannons were dif-abled. By this time we had fired fixty thoufand cannon-fhot and eight thoufand bombs, fo that the whole caftle and citadel were a mere heap of ftones on the fide of the attack. This fiege alone coft feven hundred thoufand pound weight of powder.

The Duke of *Savoy*, who left nothing unef-fayed for the preferving of this citadel, went dif-guifed as far as *Saregio* to vifit the defiles of *Tende*, with a defign to attempt fome enterprize for the relief of the place. He ordered fome militia and fome regular troops to meet; but the Duke of *Berwick* having had notice of it, took care to guard all thefe defiles, and even fent thither fome fmall pieces of cannon. He had already caufed redoubts to be built in the places where he thought they were neceffary. Thus all the at-tempts of the Duke of *Savoy* for the relief of this place proved ineffectual. Mean while, the Marquis of *Carail*, finding himfelf expofed by the great breaches which were made in the cita-del, and fearing leaft it fhould be taken by af-fault, abandoned it on the firft of *January*, and retired into the caftle, having only left there a few troops, with orders to retire in cafe they fhould be attacked. The Duke of *Berwick* hav-ing perceived this, ordered fome troops to march
thither.

1705.

1706.

1706. thither.   The enemy held out for fome time, and afterwards retired: whereupon our men lodged themfelves in the citadel.

On the fecond of this month, preparations were made for ftorming the caftle; and for this purpofe it was refolved that we fhould firft make a great fire of the artillery during fix hours, in order to ruin the new retrenchments which the befieged had made to defend the breaches.

The Marquis of *Carail* was refolved, as foon as the Duke of *Berwick* fhould make himfelf mafter of the caftle, to retire to the tower, or plat-form, and there to defend himfelf to the laft extremity.   He might have held out there for fome time, as he neither wanted ammunition nor provifion; but his garrifon having mutiny'd and threatened to defert, he was obliged to demand a capitulation on the fourth, after having defended the place fifty five days from the opening of the trenches.   About four of the clock in the afternoon, the Duke of *Berwick* being at the batteries, heard the befieged beat the Chamade: whereupon he ordered the firing to be difcontinued.   Hoftages were exchanged, and the articles of capitulation were drawn up.   Thefe articles were very honourable for the Marquis of *Carail* and his garrifon.

The Duke of *Berwick* immediately difpatched Brigadeer *Herouville* to give notice of this to the King; and a few days after he fent my Lord *Bulkley*, his brother-in-law, to carry to his Majefty the articles of capitulation.   On the fixth of

January

January the Marquis of *Carail* went out of *Nice* 1706.
by the breach, at the head of his garrifon, with
arms, baggage, fix pieces of cannon and two
mortars. The garrifon which confifted, as we
have faid above, of fourteen hundred men, was
now reduced to five hundred and fifty men and
eighty officers. It was conducted to *Saorgio*. We
found in the place an hundred and ten pieces of
cannon, of which feventy fix were in very good
cafe, a great many fire engines, and a large quantity of all forts of ammunition. The befieged
left there two hundred men wounded, who were
to be taken care of at the King's expence.

When the garrifon left the place, the Duke
of *Berwick* publifhed an amnefty for all deferters
who fhould return to their regiments: this was
accepted by more than an hundred foldiers. It
was no hard matter to conquer the reft of the
county of *Nice*.

The Duke of *Berwick*, crowned with glory,
after an expedition wherein his valour, vigilance,
activity, and ability had been as confpicuous as
ever, returned to the Court, according to the
King's order. He arrived there towards the
end of *January*, and was received with thofe
fentiments and that confidence which the prefence of a General infpires, who is univerfally
efteemed, and whofe reputation is fupported by
fuccefs. In the prefent conjuncture the advice
of the Duke of *Berwick* was highly neceflary,
and he had a great fhare in forming the projects
for the enfuing campaign.

Never

1706.   Never were juster meafures taken, and every thing feemed to promife the utmoft fuccefs. The Elector of *Bavaria* was to command the army of *Flanders*, having under him Marfhal *Villeroy* and the Duke of *Berwick*; but his Majefty afterwards changed his refolution with refpect to the Duke, and employed him elfewhere, as will appear in the fequel. Marfhal *Villars* was appointed to command on the *Rhine*, where he was to be affifted by Marfhal *Marçin*, who had an army upon the *Mofelle*: thefe two Generals were to act in concert, and had orders to drive the *Germans* from the lines of the *Moutre*, and to relieve *Fort Lewis*, which the latter blocked up: afterwards Marfhal *Marçin*, with the troops which were under his orders, was to march into *Flanders* and join the Elector of *Bavaria* and Marfhal *Villeroy*, in order to give battle to the army of the Allies, commanded by the Duke of *Marlborough*.

The Duke *la Feuillade* was ordered to befiege *Turin*, while the Duke of *Vendôme* was to facilitate the conqueft of that place, by keeping the *Germans* at *Bay* in *Italy*. Marfhal *Teffé*, who commanded in *Spain*, was ordered to lay fiege to *Barcelona*, and was to be fupported in this attempt by our fleet under the command of Count *Touloufe*; while the Duke of *Noailles* in *Rouffillon* was to penetrate into *Catalonia*, which had revolted, and to contain the rebels; and was afterwards to join Marfhal *Teffé*, if it was neceffary, in order to fhorten the fiege of *Barcelona*.

All

All thefe fine hopes vanifhed away, and we had the misfortune to fee thefe well concerted projects defeated. In *Flanders* the lofs of the battle of *Ramillies*, which was hazarded too foon and without neceffity., being fought before the arrival of Marfhal *Marfin*, brought on the lofs of a great number of places in the *Low Countries*. The furprifing defeat and rout of our army before *Turin*, and the raifing of the fiege of that place, · made us lofe all *Italy*. We were not more fuccefsful in *Catalonia*, where we were obliged to abandon the fiege of *Barcelona* : fo that by a concert of misfortunes, which can hardly be credited or comprehended, almoft all the armies which *France* had in the field this campaign received terrible checks. *

1706.

There

* The victory at *Ramillies* was obtained on the twelfth of *May*, O. S. by the Duke of *Marlborough*, over the Elector of *Bavaria* and Marfhal *Villeroy*. Several thoufands of the enemy were killed, and fix thoufand taken, with a great part of their artillery and baggage. The lofs on the part of the Confederates was very inconfiderable. Two days after this victory the Duke of *Marlborough* took poffeffion of *Louvain*; and in lefs than a forthnight *Bruffels*, *Mechlin*, *Ghent*, *Oudenarde*, *Bruges*, *Antwerp*, and feveral other confiderable places in *Flanders* and *Brabant* made their fubmiffion, and acknowledged King *Charles* III for their Sovereign. Befides, in this campaign the Duke of *Marlborough* befieged and took *Oftend*, *Menin*, *Dendermond*, and *Aeth*.

On the feventh of *September*, the Duke of *Savoy* and Prince *Eugene* attacked the *French* in their retrenchments before *Turin*, and obtained a compleat victory. The Duke on the fame day entred his capital city in triumph. It had been reduced to the greateft extremity, having endured a four month's fiege. In this engagement the Duke of *Orleans* and Marfhal *Marfin* were wounded, the latter mortally ; near five thoufand of the *French*

U

were

1706. There were only the armies commanded by Marſhal *Villars*, and by the Duke of *Berwick*, which made conqueſts and gained victories. Theſe two great men, who have been juſtly compared with *Fabius Maximus* and *Paulus Emilius*, who were formerly the reſource of the *Roman* Empire, ſupported the glory and honour of the *French* arms, and were able always to preſerve that ſuperiority and good fortune which eve:y where attended them. *France* can never forget the ſignal ſervices which ſhe has received from theſe Generals, and will tranſmit to lateſt poſterity the memory of her Deliverers.·

The Duke of *Berwick* was preparing to ſet out for the army in *Flanders*, when the Duke of *Alva*, the King of *Spain*'s Embaſſador in *France*, demanded him from the King, in the name of his Maſter, to command the army which was to act in *Portugal*. His Moſt Chriſtian Majeſty conſented to it with pleaſure, and ſaid to the Ambaſſador, *I am very glad that the*

were killed, and above ſeven thouſand taken priſoners. The Allies took an hundred and fifty pieces of cannon, fifty mortars, and all the tents, baggage, ammunition, and proviſion belonging to the *French* army, and that with very little loſs on their ſide.

The preſent King of *Spain* and Marſhal *Teſsé* had laid fiege to *Barcelona* on third of *April*. On the ſeventh of *May* the *French* fleet, which favoured this fiege, having advice of the approach of the *Engliſh* commanded by Sir *John Leake*, thought fit to retire from before the town ; and on the twelfth, the Earl of *Peterborough* raiſed the fiege of it, the *French* and *Spaniards* leaving behind them an hundred and fix braſs cannons, twenty three mortars, and prodigious quantities of ammunition and proviſion.

King

King your master desires to have the Duke of Ber-
wick *to command in* Portugal: *I could not send*
him any person more capable to serve him. Immediately after this audience, he went to the
Duke of *Berwick* to acquaint him that he had
demanded him in the name of the King his master; that his Most Christian Majesty had granted his request; and that he (the Ambassador)
intreated him, in the name of his Catholick Majesty, to set out immediately for *Madrid*.

The next day, being the sixteenth of *February*, the King sent for the Duke of *Berwick*,
and told him that the King of *Spain* having demanded him for the command of the army in
Portugal, he could not refuse sending him thither, how much soever he wanted his service in
other parts: at the same time he ordered the
Duke to prepare for his journey as soon as possible; adding, that before his departure, he would
shew him how well he was satisfied with his
services, by making him Marshal of *France*; and
that his Catholick Majesty would deliver him
the Commission upon his arrival in *Spain*. It
was for this reason that the Duke of *Berwick*
could not take the usual oath upon such a preferment till two years after, when he returned
into *France*. He now recalled his equipage,
which had already set out for *Flanders*, and ordered it to *Spain*. He went afterwards to take
his audience of leave, and received fresh proofs
of his Majesty's esteem. When he went to see
the Duke of *Burgundy*, that Prince charged him

1706. to write to him regularly an account of what paſſed in *Spain*. The Duke of *Berwick* was extremely ſenſible of the honour which was done him on this occaſion, and very exact in obeying that Prince's orders.

He ſet out on the firſt of *March* for *Madrid*, where he arrived on the eleventh. The King of *Spain* expreſſed a great ſatisfaction to ſee him again, and delivered to him the commiſſion of Marſhal of *France*, accompanying that preſent with the greateſt marks of diſtinction. The commiſſion was dated on the ſixteenth of *February*. After having conferred with his Catholick Majeſty, and received his orders, Marſhal *Berwick* ſet out on the eighteenth of *March* from *Madrid* to *Eſtramadura*, where the *Spaniſh* troops met: they conſiſted of twenty ſeven battalions and forty five ſquadrons, including the militia.

Being arrived on the frontier, he was informed that the *Portugueſe* army was encamped two leagues below *Badajox*: whereupon he marched thither with twenty five battalions and forty ſquadrons, and obliged the enemy to retire. The *Engliſh* and *Dutch* auxiliaries, whom the Marquis *Das Minas* expected, joyned his army on the twenty fifth of *March*, the Earl of *Galway* having ſet out the day before from *Elvas*. This army was encamped between the rivers *Caya* and *Cagola*. It having been reſolved in a council of war, which my Lord *Galway* had held with the Marquis *Das Minas*, Count *Atalaya*, and the Marquis *Fonteyra*, that they ought to undertake the

ſiege

fiege of fome town, they pitched upon *Badajox*, 1706. and expeded to fucceed the better in it, as the Spanifh army had been confiderably weakened by the departure of the *French* troops, which had been fent into *Catalonia* to the fiege of *Barcelona*. Marfhal *Berwick*, who knew their defign, not only put that place in a ftate of defence, and threw troops into it, but prevented the enemy's march, and pofted his army before the town : for which reafon they thought fit to remove to *Alcantara*. On the firft of *April* they encamped at *St. Salvador* with fifteen thoufand foot and five thoufand horfe, having left the reft of their troops to guard the frontiers. On the fecond, they came to *Majorgas*, where the artillery joined them. On the third, they went to *St. Vincent* : afterwards, they paffed on the fourth to *Salorima*, of which they made themfelves mafters. They afterwards advanced near *Membira*, which they likewife feized : here they lay on the fifth. From hence they fummoned the Judges and Magiftrates of *Barcos* to come and take the oath of fidelity to the Arch-duke, which they refufed, upon receiving advice that Marfhal *Berwick* was advancing to their relief. In the night the enemy fent a detachment commanded by Don *Juan Manuel*, to fecure a poft upon the river *Salors*, and to guard the fords where they defigned to pafs the next day; for Marfhal *Berwick* had taken the precaution to deftroy the bridge. On the fixth, they paffed without oppofition, and continued their march between

rocks

 rocks and through defiles, being obliged in several places to make a way for their artillery.

Marshal *Berwick*, who followed this army at
some distance, arrived on the fifth of *April* at
Barcos, from whence he sent six battalions to
reinforce the garrison of *Alcantara*, which consisted only of three: he distributed the rest of
his infantry into other posts which might be use-
ful, and kept only with himself his cavalry, consisting of five thousand horse. Whereupon the
Earl of *Galway* formed a design to attack him:
he divided his army into two bodies; the first of
which consisted of a great part of the horse
and foot, headed by the Marquis *Das Minas*,
who marched with it on the seventh to *Barcos*:
he other body of the army remained behind,
under the command of the Earl of *Galway* and
Count *Corsana*, Lieutenant-general, to secure
the artillery, provisions and baggage, which
had not yet passed the river.

As soon as Marshal *Berwick* perceived the
enemy in the plain of *Barcos*, he thought fit to
retire, not having a sufficient number of troops to
make head against them: his men were covered
by a wood which lies between the town and *Caceres*. The Marquis *Das Minas* sent a detachment to *Barcos*, which town being discouraged
by Marshal *Berwick*'s retreat, opened its gates
to the enemy. Their cavalry advanced towards
the wood, and their infantry were ordered to
follow with all possible diligence. They fell upon
the Marshal's rear-guard; whereupon he order-

ed

ed two regiments to wheel about, and with thefe
he engaged the headmoft troops of the enemy:
but the *Englifh* horfe, the *Dutch* dragoons, and
the horfe of *Beira* being arrived to their relief,
and Marfhal *Berwick* keeping his ground, the
action became brifk and bloody. Though the
Marfhal had only five thoufand horfe, and the
enemy above twenty thoufand, yet he pufhed
them fo vigoroufly that he forced them to retire,
after they had loft feveral of their men, who were
either killed or taken prifoners. The Marquis
Das Minas had like to have been in the number
of the latter; but Count *Atayla*, his Nephew,
came very opportunely to his relief, and brought
him off. After this action, which ended very
late, the enemy retired to *Barcos*, and put a
garrifon into the caftle. They continued there on
the eighth, and went on the ninth to encamp in
fight of *Alcantara*, which they immediately invefted. This place furrendered on the fixteenth,
after having made a fhew of defending itfelf for
five or fix days. It might have held out much
longer, confidering the troops with which it was
guarded, and ought to have obtained a more honourable capitulation: but the Governor had
long before held a correfpondence with the Court
of *Lifbon*. Notice of this had been given to
the council of *Madrid*, which believing him in-
capable of fuch treafonable practices, had been
content to communicate to him the information
they had received, that they might the better fecure his fidelity by the confidence they repofed

U 4 in

1706. in him. The traitor, the better to play his game, made the greateſt proteſtations of fidelity, and the council being prejudiced in his favour, relied upon the freſh aſſurances which he had given of his duty and attachment to King *Philip*. It is certain that he could have ſaved the garriſon, whom neverthefs he ſuffered to be made priſoners of war, for want of having cut the arch of a bridge over the *Tagus*. Marſhal *Berwick* had ſent him a truſty perſon to acquaint him that as ſoon as he found himſelf preſſed, he ſhould give the ſignals which that perſon was to acquaint him with, and come out of the town at the place he ſhould point out to him ; becauſe at the ſame time that he ſhould come out, the Marſhal would attack the enemy on that ſide : but this perſon was taken priſoner at the very gates of the town. The Governor had delivered one of the gates to be guarded by ſome *Spaniſh* officers, who were his accomplices : theſe introduced into the town, during the night, ſome *Engliſh* and *Dutch* troops ; whereupon finding himſelf ſupported by theſe forces, he made his garriſon lay down their arms, and ſurrender upon diſhonourable terms. After the *Portugueſe* had made themſelves maſters of this place, they endeavoured to put it in a poſture of defence, and continued in the ſame ſituation till the nineteenth, when the Marquis *Fonteira* began to march with the troops which he commanded, and advanced towards *Coria*. The next day the whole army of the enemy followed him, and

encamped

encamped on the twenty second at *Pedras albas.* 1706.
The day following *Morateio* surrendered, and
the next day *Coria.*

Marshal *Berwick*, who with the inconsiderable body which he commanded could not put a stop to the progress of the enemy, decamped on the twentieth from *Acousar de Caceres.* After three days march, he was informed that the enemy moved to *Pedras albas*, and arrived at *Malpertide de Placentia*, having passed the *Tagus* at the bridge of *Canaveral*, between *Almeras* and *Alcantara.* He had sent before him Mr. *Geoffreville* with twelve squadrons to encamp at *Placentia*, where he joined them on the twenty fourth. Having advice that the enemy marched towards *Placentia*, he retired beyond the brook of *Teisar*, leaving Mr. *Geoffreville* on the side of *Placentia* with his twelve squadrons to observe the enemy. The latter continued to advance, and it was impossible for the Marshal to stop them, or even hinder them from marching to *Madrid.* He sent the Queen notice of the danger to which she would expose herself by continuing in that city. The King was then before *Barcelona*, carrying on the siege of that place. The Queen, upon this advice, summoned together the Grandees who were near her person, and represented to them the danger they run, and how necessary it was for every body to take arms. On the first of *May* she called together the Magistrates, and beseeched them to engage the townsf-men to take arms for
the

1706. the protection of themſelves, as well as of her, in the capital of *Spain:* She told them in a very affecting manner, that whilſt the King expoſed his perſon for their defence, it might be hoped that they would not be wanting in their duty upon ſuch a preſſing occaſion; that it was probable *Catalonia* would ſoon be reduced (in effect our affairs were very ſucceſsful in that country) but that things were not in ſo good a poſture in *Eſtramadura,* where Marſhal *Berwick* had not a ſufficient number of troops to oppoſe the enemy; that it was ſurpriſing that the *Portugueſe,* always ſo weak before the *Caſtilians,* ſhould now offer to attack them: that it was true they were backed by ſtrangers; but that a confidence ſupported by heretick troops did not render them more formidable. In ſhort, ſhe omitted nothing ſhe thought proper to animate them to their duty upon this occaſion: " The fate of the " *Spaniſh* monarchy, ſaid the Queen to them, " depends this day upon you; conſider what " you owe to your King, your country, your " families, and your ſelves: I am the firſt Queen " that ever was obliged to take the courſe which " I am now reduced to; but my affection for " you would not permit me to neglect what I " thought a means of contributing to ſave you, " and to ſave the kingdom.

This ſpeech made a great impreſſion upon the *Spaniards*; and they reſolved upon the moſt effectual means for preventing the misfortune with which they were threatned; but all they

could

could do was to little purpofe, and they were 1706.
obliged to give way to the enemy. It may be
obferved more than once, and few wars furnifh
us with fo many inftances of it as this does, that
fometimes the fineft appearances have vanifhed
away without our knowing how, and fometimes
the moft diftreffing misfortunes have had fuch
an iffue, as could hardly be expected from the
greateft fucceffes. The enemy, after having taken *Ciudad Rodrigo*, had refolved to retire into
fummer quarters, and the Marquis *Das Minas*
had afked the King of *Portugal*'s orders for that
purpofe; but the Earl of *Galway*, and the *Englifh* Envoy at *Lifbon*, being informed of the raifing of the fiege of *Barcelona*, and of the little
refiftance which the Marfhal of *Berwick*'s army
could make, judged that it was the intereft of
the Houfe of *Auftria* to improve this opportunity, by pufhing their conquefts further, and not
giving time to the King of *Spain* to gather together forces capable to ftop their progrefs: whereupon they made their remonftrances to the King
of *Portugal*, who yielded without any difficulty,
and fent them the order which they had afked
to advance to *Madrid*. Immediately their army
decamped from *Ciudad Rodrigo*, arrived next
day, being the third of *June*, at *Sumacnas*, and
marched ftrait to *Salamanca*.

Marfhal *Berwick*, who was then in that place,
left it on the fifth, at the fame time that my
Lord *Galway* approached it. This town, which is
a Bifhop's feat, ftands on the river *Orme*. It was
only

1706. only defended by a plain wall, without citadel, caftle, or any other fortification; fo that the *Portuguefe* army entred it on the feventh, without meeting any refiftance. The enemy found nothing in this place, for Marfhal *Berwick* had the precaution fome few days before to order all the warlike ftores and ammunition to be taken away, and had even caufed a part of the provifions, which had been brought together in that place, and could not be taken away, to be thrown into the river.

After the raifing the fiege of *Barcelona*, the Duke of *Noailles* continued to command in *Rouffillon* with nine battalions and three regiments of dragoons, while Marfhal *Teffé*, with the reft of the army, advanced into *Navarre*, in order to join Marfhal *Berwick*, and ftop the progrefs of the *Portuguefe*. As for the King of *Spain*, he had taken the road to *Pampelona*, where he had arrived on the fecond of *June*, in a poft chaife. His Catholick Majefty declared, as he entered the gate, that he would have no other guards, nor any other efcort than the love and fidelity of his fubjects. He ordered Mr. *Amelot*, Ambaffador from the King of *France*, to fummon together the Grandees of *Spain*.

Mr. *Amelot* in this affembly told them, that he was ordered by the King of *France* to afk of them what were their real fentiments, and whether the two misfortunes which had happened in *Catalonia* and *Flanders* had made any change in their attachment to King *Philip?* That his

Moft

Moſt Chriſtian Majeſty had reaſon to doubt of 1706.
it, and that he could not help complaining of
the little aſſiſtance which he received from them;
that for the reſt, he was commanded to tell
them, that though the King his grandſon was
called by right of blood to the Crown of *Spain*,
yet his Moſt Chriſtian Majeſty did not pretend
to maintain him there againſt the inclination
which ſeveral of them ſeemed to have for the
Arch-duke; a Prince who had no other right,
but what he could uſurp, by coming with an
armed force to diſturb the tranquility of the
Spaniſh monarchy: that it could hardly be believed, that a King of ſo amiable a character as
Philip V, did not find in their nation that
attachment to him which he deſerved; and that
the Catholick kingdom preferred to the Sovereign
whom God had given them, a Prince, whoſe
army conſiſting moſtly of hereticks, contributed
to eſtabliſh him on the *Spaniſh* throne, by plun-
dering Churches, and overturning altars: That
the King of *France* being ever reſolved to ſacrifice all Crowns to the worſhip of God and the
happineſs of the people, he would rather conſent to recall his grandſon, than to be in ſome
reſpect the occaſion of all the ſacrileges which
would be committed; that for theſe reaſons he
conjured them to be ingenuous, and not to conceal from him their ſentiments with regard to
their Prince.

This ſpeech being ended, the Duke of *Medina*
Celi was going into a detail of ſome grievances
which

1706. which the Grandees and chief men of the nation had reason to complain of. Mr. *Amelot* immediately resuming the discourse, assured them that the King his master had given him a power of procuring them all the satisfaction they could desire; that he would immediately remove all occasions of complaint, and would even prevent any disorders which might be apprehended: he intreated them to deliver their opinions with freedom, promising that the greatest regard should be had to their advice.

Upon these assurances, the Duke of *Medina Celi* answered, in the name of the whole assembly, that the King of *Spain* might be assured that they would sacrifice their lives and fortunes to maintain him on the throne; that his Majesty might safely return to *Madrid*, and should know by their dutiful behaviour how much they were attached to him. Afterwards, addressing himself to the whole assembly, he added, that if there were among them any disaffected persons, who persisted in adhering to the Archduke, they might retire, and that their rents should be paid them wherever they were; but that if after this declaration, any of them should betray the King or the nation, his life should pay for his treason, and his estate should be confiscated: that as for himself, if ever he should be known to act against the interest of his Prince, he would consent to be made an example to others. He concluded these protestations with crying out, *Long live King* Philp V.

our

our rightful Sovereign. The whole affembly anfwered with the fame acclamation.

After this, the King went to *Madrid.* Being
arrived there, he again called together the Grandees, the Minifters, and Chiefs of the principal
Courts of Judicature, with whom he held a long
conference. They agreed that the Court was
not fafe at *Madrid,* becaufe the armies were at
a great diftance; and the town being neither fortified nor garrifoned, they were not able to refift
feventeen or eighteen thoufand men whom my
Lord *Galway* had under his command, and with
whom he advanced with great diligence.

This General, after having made himfelf mafter of *Salamanca,* paffed on the feventeenth with
his army over the mountain *Guadarama,* which
lies only half a league from *Efcurial,* and feven
leagues from *Madrid.* The confternation in this
city was fo much the greater, as it was well
known that the King and Queen would be forced to depart from it. In effect, on the eighteenth, the Grandees and Chiefs of all the councils affembled again at the palace, and it was unanimoufly refolved that the Queen fhould leave
the city on the fame day; which fhe did, being
accompanied by the Princefs *Urfini,* the ladies of
her Court, fome Grandees, and the officers of
her houfhold. She was efcorted by two hundred life-guards and an hundred *French* troopers
as far as a country feat, called *Beflanga,* belonging to the Conftable of *Caftile,* about twenty four
leagues from *Madrid.*

It

1706. It was likewife refolved, that all the Grandees, the Councils, and Courts of Judicature fhould leave the town, and that no perfons in employment fhould be left in it, except the Corrigedors, Regidors, and their Officers: fo that no Magiftrate, Notary, or perfon capable of drawing a publick act was left in *Madrid.* As foon as the people were informed of this, they came in crouds to the palace, and the adjacent places: they afked earneftly for arms, and begged that their King would not abandon them. This teftimony of their loyalty very much affected the Council, who could not help promifing to grant them their requeft. On the nineteenth, according to the above mentioned refolution, the King left his capital, and went to *Toraiou*, four leagues from thence, to join Marfhal *Berwick*, who had arrived there with his troops, after having obferved the enemy's army. His Catholick Majefty took with him the jewels and treafure of the Crown.

Mean while, the Earl of *Galway* continued his march to *Madrid*, where he arrived on the twenty fifth. He entred it with the Marquis *Das Minas.* They went through this great city without feeing any of the inhabitants, none of them ftirring out of their houfes. They affembled the Town-council, and would oblige them to cry, *God fave King* Charles *the third.* The Town-council ftood filent; and when they were at laft forced to fpeak, they could only cry out, *God fave King* Philip *the fifth*. It was only fome

days

days after, by threats and force, that the Earl 1706.
of *Galway* caufed the Arch-duke to be proclaimed King of *Spain* in that capital. He was
obliged to conceal his refentment, when at the
time that one part of the people cried very faint-
ly, *Long live King* Charles III; the greateft
number cried with a loud voice, *Long live King*
Philip V. After this fort of proclamation, he
difpatched a courier to the Arch-duke, inviting
him to come to *Madrid:* but the Generals who
were with the Arch-duke, were not of opinion
that he ought to comply with this invitation;
and this Prince was made fenfible, that it was
not fafe for him to be in *Madrid.* Sometime
after, my Lord *Hatton* was himfelf obliged to
leave *Madrid*, and to retire to *Guadalaxara*,
where the Arch-duke joined him with fix batta-
loins and fix hundred horfe.

When the King of *Spain* was informed that
the enemy's army had quitted *Madrid*, he wrote
a letter to the town council, dated the third of
Auguft, and ordered the Marquis of *Majorada* to
deliver it. He accordingly went thither with four
hundred horfe. Upon his entry into the town,
fome Miquelets, and fome of the militia of *Valencia*, commanded by Count *Las Amajuclas*, intrenched themfelves at the arch of the palace,
and afterwards at the treafury; but their leader
being mortally wounded, they quitted it on the
fifth, to the number of three hundred and
feventy men, without making any capitulation,
and were all taken prifoners. The town coun-

X

cil

 cil and the people received the King's troops with the greatest demonſtrations of joy: nothing was heard on all ſides, but *Long live King* Philip *our rightful Sovereign.* They ſet on fire ſeven or eight houſes belonging to thoſe who had acknowledged the Arch-duke; they publickly burnt that Prince's ſtandard and picture, as well as all the publick acts which had been made in his name. Thus the capital city of *Spain* was again brought under the power of its lawful ſovereign, whilſt his army was daily increaſing by the troops which all the provinces ſent thither, emulating one with another in loyalty to King *Philip* V.

On the twenty eighth, Marſhal *Berwick*, who knew that the enemy poſſeſſed ſeveral mills upon the *Tagus*, and among the reſt, one oppoſite to their left, where they had two hundred and fifty men pretty well retrenched by the ſituation of the place, ordered two companies of grenadeers of the regiment of *Mayne* to march in the night to attack this mill on one ſide, whilſt he ſent two companies of grenadeers of the crown, to attack it on the other. Theſe two detachments were to arrive before day-light at the place appointed, and to fall upon the enemy at the ſignal agreed upon. Theſe grenadeers were ſupported by ſome horſe and dragoons, that if the enemy were forced, none of them might eſcape.

The ſignal being given, the two companies of the crown, after having born two diſcharges of

the

the enemies fmall arms, poured in upon them: 1706.
the latter were not able to bear the fhock, and
the foremoft of our men fell upon the main body
of their troops, who, during this firft fire, had
formed into battalia in the place of arms of their
retrenchments. From thence they fired very
brifkly upon our grenadeers, who were covered
for a while by an eminence, not expecting to be
attacked on the other fide. As it was not yet
day-light, the enemy endeavoured to difcover on
what fide they were attacked; but they were
greatly furprized, when they found themfelves
attacked on the other fide by the two companies
of the regiment of *Mayne*, which falling upon
them with their ufual fhouts, put them into fo
great diforder, that they either afked quarter, or
betook themfelves to flight: but the horfe which
were placed in their paffage fuffered none of them
to efcape, and moft of them were flain. The
Spaniards were not difpofed to make them prifoners, becaufe they were all *Portuguefe*. The
grenadeers fearched all the reeds of the morafs,
where fome of them had concealed themfelves,
and killed them with their bayonets. After this
expedition, the peafants, as they were commanded, broke to pieces with their mallets the
mill-ftones, and the other parts of the mill.

Next day, Marfhal *Berwick* was informed that
the enemy made a forrage on their left: whereupon he put himfelf at the head of a detachment, and went to attack them; which he did
with fo much vigour, that he repulfed the ef-

X 2

cort,

1706. cort, confifting of fix hundred horfe, befides infantry, and took from them fix hundred horfes,
or mules, killed or wounded fix hundred of their
men, and took three hundred and fifty prifoners. At the fame time he detached Mr. *Cariffo*,
a *Spanifh* Colonel, with fix hundred horfe to
fcour the country. This officer deftroyed the
mills of the enemy, though they were guarded
by eight hundred men, of whom he flew a
hundred upon the fpot, and brought back thirty
three *Englifh*, one Captain, and one Lieutenant,
prifoners. The *Spaniards* had taken or killed of
the enemy, before the firft of *September*, above
fix thoufand men; and their lofs was ftill greater,
by reafon of the deferters. Thus Marfhal *Berwick*, knowing that they would foon be obliged
to decamp, ordered a bridge to be made over
the *Tagus* before *Aranjuez*, in order to follow
them, being refolved to engage them, and to
drive them out of *Caftile*.

The King of *Spain* had ordered the Viceroy of
Pampelona to fend him two *French* battalions
which were in *Navarre*. Thefe troops fet out
from thence on the firft of *September*; and as
we were informed that the *Portuguefe* had affembled fome forces at *Ciudad Rodrigo*, a detachment of regular troops was fent to cover old
Caftile, and join the militia which were there in
arms.

At laft the want of provifions obliged the enemy fecretly to quit their camp on the night of
the eighth of *September*. They had been fo
hemmed

hemmed in, and fo much harraffed by the parties which Marfhal *Berwick* had fent out, and
by the peafants of that country, that they were
obliged to kill the oxen which drew their artillery
and their baggage, in order to feed their foldiers. As foon as the King was informed that
they had decamped, and were paffing the *Tagus* upon rafters, which they had made of the
timber of the houfes they had pulled down, his
Catholick Majefty paffed the fame river upon the
bridge which Marfhal *Berwick* had caufed to be
made near *Aranjuez*, to cut off the paffage of
the *Portuguefe*, who now only thought of retiring into their country by *Eftramadura*.

At the fame time, Marfhal *Berwick* advanced
with a detachment of horfe, with which he attacked the rear-guard of the Arch-duke, killed
about five hundred of his men, and made as
many prifoners. The King purfued the Arch-
duke no farther than *Velez*. On the fixteenth,
he held a council of war, wherein it was refolved, that fince the enemy avoided coming to an
engagement, it was proper that his Catholick
Majefty fhould return to *Madrid*, and leave the
command of his army to Marfhal *Berwick*. Accordingly that Prince left the army, and arrived
in his capital on the twenty fecond, being efcorted
only by two battalions and four fquadrons of his
guards. He was received with the joyful accla-
mations of all his people, who for feveral days
made extraordinary rejoycings. The foreign Minifters, the Grandees, all the Bodies and Heads

of

1706. of the communities complimented his Majesty upon his return, and congratulated him upon having driven out of *Castile* the enemies of the state and of the Catholick Religion. The Courts of Judicature, which had been stopped or removed to *Burgos*, renewed their functions; but those members of the councils who had continued in *Madrid*, and had been wanting in their fidelity by acknowledging the Arch-duke, or favouring his party, were banished three leagues from thence, and ordered to come and give an account of their behaviour, as often as it should be required, before the juncto, or extraordinary Council of State, appointed to examine those who were accused of treason.

After the King of *Spain*'s departure, Marshal *Berwick* followed the enemy as far as *St. Clemente* and *Poso Laurente*. He marched on the twenty fifth and twenty sixth, in order to come up with and attack them. The enemy stopped at the village of *Ouniesta*, where they found a very advantageous post. The Marshal of *Berwick* went to reconnoitre them; of which being informed, they planted a cannon opposite to a gorge where the Marshal was to pass in his return. The danger was exceeding great; but by good fortune only a *Spanish* officer and an Aid de Camp were wounded, and had their horses killed about two paces from the Marshal, who likewise bore several carabin-shots, which wounded his horse.

The enemy had fifty battallions, and as many squadrons, the whole being in a very weak condition.

dition. Marſhal *Berwick* reſolved to advance 1706.
and attack them : for this purpoſe he called together the General Officers : theſe were of opinion, that the enemy could not be forced in
their poſt, and that it was better to make ſome
attempt upon their left flank. In compliance
with their opinion, the Marſhal immediately ordered his army to make a motion that way : but
he was obliged to make ſo large a circuit, that
when they arrived at the brook near the enemy,
they had only about an hour of ſun-ſet, and it
was too late to undertake any thing. Marſhal
Berwick now reſumed his former reſolution,
formed his army into battalia upon two lines,
and thus they paſſed the night, in order to advance to the enemy at day-break. But towards
the evening, the latter retired to the bridge of
Val-Deſcana upon the river *Cubriel,* and went
into the mountains.

Immediately the Marſhal detached Mr. *Me-
dinilla* with nine ſquadrons and four battalions
to follow them in the road to *Alicant* ; while
Mr. *Geoffreville* with ten battalions and eighteen
ſquadrons marched on the ſide of *Villena,* in the
kingdom of *Murcia,* on the frontiers of new
Caſtile, and of the kingdom of *Valencia.* The
Marſhal had kept with him fifteen battalions
and thirty three ſquadrons, with whom he returned to the camp he had quitted, where
he had left his baggage. He continued there
two days, and then followed his detachments,
which ſtill purſued the enemy. On the thirtieth,

X 4

he

1706. he detached Lieutenant-general *Heſſy* with twenty five companies of grenadeers, two regiments
of dragoons, two hundred horſe, and three
pieces of cannon, to make himſelf maſter of
Cuença.

Upon the approach of Mr. *Heſſy*, the troops
of the Arch-duke abandoned the ſuburbs. As
ſoon as he had made himſelf maſter of an eminence which commanded the town, the garriſon
demanded to capitulate; but he anſwered, that
they muſt expect no other terms but thoſe of
being made priſoners of war: whereupon Mr.
Amanda, who commanded in that place, and ſeveral officers who had deſerted, fearing that if
they made any reſiſtance they ſhould meet with
no quarter, ſurrendred priſoners, on condition
that they ſhould undergo no puniſhment, and
ſhould be exchanged: this garriſon quitted the
town on the tenth of *October:* it conſiſted of
two thouſand three hundred men.

In this interval, Mr. *Geoffreville* and Mr. *Me-
dinilla* penetrated into the kingdom of *Valencia*;
the latter having joined the Biſhop of *Murcia*,
took *Orihuella* ſword in hand, delivered that
town to be pillaged for twenty four hours.
The plunder of it was valued at near a hundred
thouſand crowns. The Biſhop of *Murcia* diſ-
armed the inhabitants, and deprived them of
their original charters, as well as all the adjacent
places which had joined in the revolt.

On the fifteenth, Marſhal *Berwick* went
to *Valencia*, to view a body of troops which
were

were ordered to meet in the neighbourhood of 1706,
that town. He expected some more troops which
were upon their march, and with which he designed to penetrate into the kingdom of *Valencia.*
As soon as they arrived, he took the road to
Elehc, two leagues from *Alicant,* where he arrived on the twenty first. Three days before,
Mr. *Geoffreville* had invested this place with four
brigades, twenty squadrons, and some troops of
the Bishop of *Murcia.*

This place was garrisoned by nine hundred
foot and four hundred horse, who were greatly
surprized at the arrival of Mr. *Geoffreville,* by
whom they were so straitly blocked up, that
none of them could escape. However, the garrison refused to surrender. But Marshal *Berwick* being arrived, summoned them again, and
sent them word that if they fired one single piece,
they must expect no quarter. At the same time,
the infantry, which arrived on one side, was ordered to file off in their sight, while the horse
and the baggage arrived on the other by the
high-way, this country being all intersected by
valleys and mountains; so that the garrison
thought it most advisable for them to surrender
at discretion. The soldiers of Marshal *Berwick*'s
army seeing that the enemy had given over firing, continued to draw nearer, in order to be
within reach of pillaging the town, if they found
an opportunity, which could hardly escape their
vigilance. Accordingly, having searched in several parts, they found means to enter the town,
and

1706. and in an inftant it was plundered, there being
no poffibility of preventing it. This town, which
is very large, was filled with vines and corn; and
we found in it two thoufand five hundred mules.
All was carried off in lefs than three or four hours,
excepting the barley, of which there were above
an hundred thoufand facks, which were put into
the magazines for the ufe of the army.

Marfhal *Berwick* marched afterwards to *Elda*;
from whence he went, on the twenty feventh,
to *Murcia*, to order the neceffary preparations
for the fiege of *Cartagena*. He detached the
Chevalier *d'Asfeld* and Mr. *Mahoni* to reconnoitre the place, whilft he went to *Orihuilla* to
caufe that town to be fortified, and to place in
it a ftrong garrifon, which might protect it from
any infult during the winter. From the time
that he entred the kingdom of *Valencia*, above
two hundred towns, burghs, or villages, were
recovered to the King of *Spain*.

The Chevalier *d'Asfeld* being arrived before
Cartagena, fent a trumpet to fummon the town
to furrender, offering the inhabitants an amnefty,
and all manner of good treatment; threatning
at the fame time, if they refufed to furrender,
to treat them like the inhabitants of *Orihuella*.
They anfwered, that they had never been wanting in their fidelity to their lawful Prince; that
though they had been forced to acknowledge the
Arch-duke, they ftill continued faithful fubjects
to King *Philip* V. but that they had not been
mafters of their fort from the time that a garrison

son of foreigners and hereticks were in posses-
sion of their town.   Upon this answer, the place
was invested, while we expected the infantry
and artillery which were to be sent thither by
Marshal *Berwick*, who, as we have said above,
was at *Orihuella*.

Cartagena was then garrisoned by one *English*
battalion, one *English* regiment of horse, who were
all dismounted except two hundred troopers,
and about three thousand militia.   The Chevalier *d'Asfeld* made the necessary dispositions for
opening the trenches, expecting Marshal *Berwick*, who arrived before the place on the eleventh of *November*.

Whereupon he again summoned *Cartagena*,
and sent word to the Governor that if he did not
surrender before the attack began, he must expect no favour.   The Governor answered, that
he esteemed it a particular honour to be besieged
by so great a General, and was resolved, as well
as the garrison, to defend himself to the last extremity.

By this time, four *French* brigades were arrived.   They were posted behind a little mountain, which was the nearest to those that surrounded and defended the town on the side of
the plain.   A castle commands the whole, and
takes in that part of the town which is next the
sea, where there is a very good bastion defended
in the entry by mountains on its right and left,
advancing into the sea at equal heights and di-
stances.

The

1706.
The enemy had a numerous artillery, wherein their principal ftrength confifted: the walls, which reached from mountain to mountain, and ftopt the opening of the rocks, were only built of earth; and likewife within, walls of earth formed a double and triple inclofure. Marfhal *Berwick*, waiting for his great cannon, raifed a battery of field-pieces againft the befieged. They anfwered by a general difcharge of all their artillery. On the night between the fourteenth and fifteenth the trenches were opened and carried foreward a confiderable way; and the great cannon being arrived, was planted in battery. On the fixteenth, we began to fire, though with little effect, becaufe the wall of the town was very high. Mean while, the Governor finding that his garrifon was not ftrong enough to defend both the town and the fortrefs, and befides that the inhabitants were not well affected to the Arch-duke, demanded to capitulate.

Marfhal *Berwick* would liften to no other propofals but of his furrendering himfelf and his garrifon at difcretion; which he was obliged to do on the eighteenth, three days after the opening of the trenches. We found in this place feventy five pieces of cannon, thirty fix of which were brafs, three mortars, and a great quantity of provifions and warlike ftores. Count *Santa-Crux*, formerly Admiral of *Spain*, who had quitted the King's party, was at that time in the harbour with two gallies; but fearing left he fhould be killed, or delivered up by the inhabi-

tants,

tants, he ftood to fea on the feventeenth, and 1706.
fteered to *Alicant*.

After this expedition, Marfhal *Berwick* gave
the command of *Cartagena* to Mr. *Mahoni*, and
fent his troops into winter quarters in the kingdoms of *Murcia* and *Valencia*. He afterwards
fet out for *Madrid*, where he arrived on the
fifth of *December*. It was there he received a
letter from the Duke of *Burgundy*, to whom he
had given an exact account of all that had happened in this campaign. That Prince expreffed
to him the fatisfaction he had upon being informed of the taking of *Cartagena*, and the other advantages the Marfhal had lately gained. At the end
of his letter, he wrote to him, *I was much furprized to know that your army was weakned by the detachments taken from it in the beginning of the campaign, and from that time I feared that the confequences would be worfe than they have proved to
be. The Marquis* Das Minas *and my Lord* Galway *have acquired no glory by the fruitlefs excur-
fion they made as far as* Madrid; *but I faw with
pleafure that they never could nor durft attack you,
though you had then only five thoufand men, and
they near thirty thoufand, and though you always obferved them very nearly in their march.
Thefe are proofs of your prudence and ability,* &c.

The King of *Spain* had ordered Marfhal *Berwick* to come to *Madrid*, in order to communicate
to him the defign he had formed of undertaking
once more the fiege of *Barcelona*. The Marfhal
reprefented to his Catholick Majefty, that the
enterprize

1706. enterprize was then impracticable; that it would coft him a great part of his army, which was already much fatigued; and that it was more advifable to allow them to refrefh themfelves, that they might be in a better condition for the enfuing campaign: he added, that it was neceffary to provide for the fecurity of his towns, moft of which had neither provifions, troops nor ammunition; upon which account the enemy had eafily made themfelves mafters of feveral of them.

The King approved this advice, and took the neceffary meafures for putting it in execution. They had feveral conferences together upon this fubject; after which, his Catholick Majefty defired Marfhal *Berwick* to vifit the towns in the kingdoms of *Valencia* and *Arragon*, and to provide for their fecurity as he fhould think proper. Accordingly, the Marfhal fet out upon this journey on the fecond of *January* 1707.

1707. Whilft they were taking thefe meafures at the Court of *Madrid*, that of *France* prepared, on their fide, for the enfuing campaign. The King named the Generals who were to command his armies. The command of the army in *Flanders* was given to the Elector of *Bavaria*, and under him to the Duke of *Vendôme*; that of *Germany* to Marfhal *Villars*; that of *Dauphiny* to Marfhal *Teffé*; and that of *Catalonia* to the Duke of *Noailles*.

To prevent the defcent which the *Englifh* and *Dutch* might attempt on the coafts of *France*, it was thought fit to provide them with troops

and

and Generals to defend them. The King nam- 1707.
ed for this purpofe Marfhal *Chateau-Renault* to
command in *Britany*, Count *Matignon* in *Normandy*, Marfhal *Chamilly* in *Poitou*, Marfhal *Montrevel* in *Guienne*, and the Duke of *Roquelaure*
in *Languedoc*, where he was fince laft year. The
Marfhal of *Berwick* returned to *Madrid* on the
fifteenth of *Frebruary*, and gave the King an account of the pofture of his towns and garrifons,
and what it was neceffary to do for their further
fecurity. Upon his arrival, he was informed
that Mr. *Mahoni* had fet out on the fixteenth of
this month for the frontiers of *Valencia*; that he
there affembled troops, waiting for the Marfhal's
arrival: for which reafon he entreated his Catholick Majefty to give him leave to fet out immediately for the army; to which the King
confented with pleafure, being highly pleafed
with the zeal and forwardnefs which this General expreffed for his fervice.

Marfhal *Berwick* fet out by poft for *Madrid*
on the fame day, being the fifteenth of *February*,
with the Duke of *Popoli*, the Marquis of *Aytona*, Count *Aguilar*, Don *Antonio del Vallé*, and
Don *Carlos de Songit*, Lieutenant-generals. The
troops which were in the *Mancha* fet out from
thence on the fixteenth for *Orihuella*, where, after having formed a fmall body (for the reft were
left in their quarters) he marched to *Elehc*, and
drove the enemy both from *Elda* and *Novelda*.

On the fame day, being the eighth of *March*,
there happened an encounter between a party of
the

1707. the enemy who retired with their baggage, and a detachment commanded by Don *Joseph Vallexos:* the latter attacked them so briskly, that after having killed a hundred and twenty men, he forced the rest to betake themselves to flight, and took from them nineteen mules laden with cloaths for the officers, and a great deal of silver plate. The enemy likewise abandoned *Denia,* and several other posts upon the frontiers: they caused the troops which possessed these posts to advance on the side of *Valencia.* The town of *Alcoy* surrendered as soon as Marshal *Berwick* appeared before it, without waiting for an attack. In all the places we seized, we found great stores of ammunition, and left troops to secure them.

My Lord *Galway,* and the Marquis *Das Minas,* were very diligent in putting their troops in a condition to take the field betimes. On the last of *March* they came to *Xativa,* where they ordered their artillery to be brought, being the place of their rendezvous. When they saw that Marshal *Berwick*'s army was not yet assembled on the ninth of *April,* they marched with all their forces to *Villena,* four leagues from *Yescala,* where the Marshal lay. As soon as he was informed of this, he sent out of *Villena* all the troops he had in that place, leaving only a hundred men to guard the castle. The next day he abandoned *Yescala,* and sent the troops which were there to *Montalegro,* under the command of the Duke of *Popoli.* He went to *Pretora,* three leagues from thence,

thence, where he compleated the forming of his 1707.
army. He continued three days in this situation,
the enemy always following him, and encamping in the places which his army left. At last
he waited for them at *Chinchilla*, where he had
arrived on the sixteenth, and expected that there
would happen an engagement; but the enemy
found him so well prepared to receive them,
that they returned, and went to besiege the
castle of *Villena*: he then decamped and moved
to *Almanza*, which is six leagues from *Villena*.

My Lord *Galway* had sent a detachment to
attack that place, and encamped with the rest of
his army, his right at *Fuenta*, and his left at *Al-
forine*, to cover the siege. He there held a
council of war on the twenty first, wherein he
represented that the Marshal of *Berwick* having
a design either to relieve *Villena*, or to cut off
their communication with *Valencia*, from whence
they drew their subsistence, he thought it proper to advance and give him battle before he
was joined by the new troops he expected; that
otherwise they would be obliged to abandon that
kingdom, especially as the magazines they had
on that frontier were exhausted. His advice was
followed.

Before the Marshal of *Berwick* had arrived
at *Almanza*, he had acquainted the Court of
Madrid of the situation of affairs, and how important it was to relieve the castle of *Villena*.
At the same time he gave notice that without
waiting for the rest of his troops he was resolved

Y

to

 to save the enemy half their journey, having marched to *Almanza* only that he might be nearer them.

During all these motions, and while each side was preparing for the great battle, of which we are going to give a particular account, the Duke of *Orleans*, who had desired the King of *France* to give him the command of the army in *Spain*, and had obtained the consent of the two Kings, set out from *Paris* on the second of *April*. His Royal Highness travelled so fast, that he arrived on the eighth at *Bayonne*, and on the eighteenth at *Madrid*. The King of *Spain* sent Don *Gaspard Giron*, his Major-Domo, to meet him, and to complement him in his Majesty's name. He likewise sent to him the Marquis of *Solera* with fifty horse guards. The same honours were payed to him as to the Infants of *Spain*.

In the mean time, Marshal *Berwick* detached on the twenty fourth in the morning Count *Pinto*, and Mr. *Courville*, Brigadeer and Colonel of the regiment of *Mayne*, with fifty men out of each battalion, to make himself master of the castle of *Ajora*, a post occupied by some Miquelets of the kingdom of *Valencia*, who disturbed his army in their forrages. After some resistance, the garrison demanded to capitulate: whilst they were agreeing upon the articles, some soldiers of our troops having plundered the houses in the village, the garrison retook their arms, and Mr. *Courville*, being quite exposed, received a musquet-shot, which broke his arm:

being

being carried to the caftle of *Almanza*, he there 1707.
died of this wound.

The enemy now quitted the fiege of *Villena*, and advanced to Marfhal *Berwick*, expecting he would not ftay for them : they encamped a league from his army in a place called *Candete*. The Marfhal being informed of this, no longer doubted but that he would be attacked next morning. He fent word to Count *Pinto* to return with his detachment, which he could not do till fome hours before the battle. Next day, being the twenty fifth, the enemy advanced in four columns towards *Almanza*.

The Marfhal went himfelf to reconnoitre them at a very little diftance, and afterwards returned to mark out the ground where he was to draw up his army in battallia : after having made fome alterations in the difpofition of his left wing, he ordered a cannon to be fired, to call in the forragers who were not yet returned to the camp. About eight of the clock in the morning, he difcovered on the heights, about two miles from his army, fome battalions of the enemy; and as he was informed from time to time that the reft of their troops were forming behind thefe heights, he fired another cannon, fent all his baggage to *Almanza*, and formed his army into battalia; the *Spaniards* in the right, and the *French* in the left. This army confifted of fifty two battalions and fixty two fquadrons. His right extended as far as an eminence near *Montalegro*, and his left was covered by an emi-

Y 2

nence

1707. nence facing the road to *Valencia*. A ravine, which covered the infantry of his right wing, diminished infenfibly, reafcending towards the eminence which was upon its flank.

Having thus formed his army, the Marfhal of *Berwick*, as foon as he faw the heads of the enemy's columns, rode to the right, and faluted the line, faying in *Spanifh*, *I depend, Gentlemen, upon your Loyalty*; and then advancing to the left, he faid, *I rely upon your Valour*. After this, he delivered to every General Officer his directions in writing, which were very fhort and clear. In this interval, fome pieces of cannon were planted on the heights, and the reft of the artillery at the head of the troops.

When it was noon we perceived the enemy, who entred the plain upon four columns in very good order and very clofe. They continued their march till they came within a mile of the *Spanifh* army, and then halted, that they might the more eafily form into battalia. My Lord *Galway*, to fupply the deficiency of his cavalry, which was weaker than that of Marfhal *Berwick*, interlined his horfe and his foot, placing in his right five battalions, and next to them five fquadrons, and continuing the fame difpofition throughout his two lines. This army confifted of fifty one battalions, amounting to twenty fix thoufand foot, and of feventy fquadrons, making feven thoufand horfe; and the whole making thirty three thoufand men. As foon as they were in readinefs, they offered to pafs the ravine

above

above mentioned, which they did without opposition, the Marſhal having forbid his troops to diſpute their paſſage, that the enemy might fight between that ground and the front of his army. They were formed into battalia by half an hour after two of the clock, and within cannon reach of the army of the two Crowns, which then began to fire upon them.

Though the order of battle of Marſhal *Berwick* was different from that of my Lord *Galway*, yet he made no change in his diſpoſitions: he continued his infantry in the centre, and his horſe in the two wings; and only drew ſome ſquadrons from his left wing, in order to give the enemy the better reception in his right. Lord *Tyrawley*, who commanded the enemy's left wing, perceiving this, ordered part of his horſe of the ſecond line, which was under the command of Count *Atalaya*, to double upon the firſt, that they might make a front equal to that of the *Spaniſh* army.

About three of the clock in the afternoon, Lord *Galway* putting himſelf at the head of the *Engliſh* dragoons, advanced againſt the *Spaniards*. Immediately Marſhal *Berwick* ordered a battery of nine pieces of cannon, which had been raiſed upon a neighbouring eminence, to play upon them. Whereupon Lord *Galway* detached Colonel *Dormer* with ſome dragoons, to make himſelf maſter of theſe cannon: but in this he was prevented; for after three diſcharges the engineers had directions to withdraw them; and

Y 3

they

1707. they were accordingly withdrawn before this detachment arrived. The artillery was of no great
ufe in this action on either fide, for both armies
came to a clofe engagement as foon as poffible.

When the left wing of the enemy was within
an hundred paces of the right wing of the *Spanifh*
army, the latter moved, and the engagement
began on that fide with great vigour; but after
fome refiftance on the fide of the enemy, the
Spanifh horfe led by the Duke of *Popoli* and
Mr. *Silly* broke them, and obliged them to retire
above an hundred paces. The regiments of foot
of *Southwell* and *Wade*, which were interlined
with the horfe, made fo great a fire on the *Spanifh* cavalry, that the latter were forced, in their
turn, to retire in diforder; which gave the enemy
time to rally. Whereupon they advanced five
Englifh battalions, which defiled by their left, in
order to take in flank the infantry of the two
Crowns, which was now left naked.

Marfhal *Berwick*, who now advanced his left
wing of the fecond line, to give time to the cavalry of the firft line to rally behind them, perceiving the motion of thefe five battalions, ordered the brigade of *Mayne*, which made the
right of the infantry of the fecond line, to advance at the fame time with thefe battalions.
They continued to defile by the left; and *Mayne's*
brigade was obliged to make nearly the fame
motion by the right. At laft, being come within thirty paces of each other, the enemy wheeled

to

to the right, *Mayne*'s brigade to the left, and the 1707. former fired. Immediately the brigade poured headlong upon them, fired with the mouths of their pieces at the enemy's breasts, broke them with their screwed bayonets, and put them into such disorder, that they fled without being able to rally: and as they were obliged to repass the ravine above mentioned, a dreadful slaughter ensued.

By this time our cavalry had rallied: whereupon the Marshal, seeing the success of *Mayne*'s brigade, led himself the cavalry against the rest of the enemy's battalions, and utterly routed them, as well as the horse who had advanced to support them.

Whilst things passed thus successfully on the right, the brigades of the Crown and of *Orleans*, marched to the enemy in the center, and attacked them: after having bore with great intrepidity the enemy's fire within pistol-reach, they drove them upon their second line with their screwed bayonets. Mean while a brigade of *Dutch* troops charged a *Spanish* brigade of recruits, broke, and put them to flight. Whereupon the enemy's right wing, their foot being interlined with horse, took both in flank and in front the brigades of *Orleans* and of the Crown, which had acted with too much precipitation, and obliged them to retire.

The brigade of the Crown rallied about forty paces from thence, by the favour of a little ditch, and then fired upon the two squadrons

Y 4

of

1707. of the enemy who purfued them, and who fuffered very much from this fire. The brigade
of *Orleans* was driven as far as *Almanza*, as well
as the *Spanifh* brigade above mentioned. The
Chevalier *d'Asfeld* obferving that this made a
great impreffion on the infantry, fent his Aids de
Camps along the line to tell them that it was
done by Marfhal *Berwick*'s order, and that they
would fee the reafon of it prefently.

In effect, the Marfhal, who had an eye every
where, fent to the relief of thefe two brigades,
four fquadrons of the right of his fecond line;
whereupon the brigades rallied, and charged the
Dutch battalions, and at the fame time the four
fquadrons took them in flank, and cut them to
pieces. The regiments of *Hill* and Lord *Mark Ker*,
which had been placed amongft the cavalry of
the fecond line, advanced to fuccour them, and
affifted them in making their retreat.

The Marfhal perceiving that the right wing of
the enemy did not advance fo faft as their left,
detached fome fquadrons to attack them, and
fupported them by his left wing, which followed
at a flow pace. The detached fquadrons, at their
fecond firing, broke thofe of the enemy which
confifted of *Portuguefe*, who foon abandoned the
battalions with which they were interlined *.

* This proved as fatal to the *Portuguefe* fquadrons, as to the
battalions they abandoned: for two battalions of *Portuguefe*, being pofted at fome diftance, and obferving a body of horfe advancing towards them with great fpeed, made no doubt but that
it was the cavalry of the two Crowns, and fired upon them fo
briskly, that a great number of them were killed and wounded.

The

The main of the infantry of the enemy's right
wing remained yet firm, and could not be broken
by the left wing of the army of the two Crowns,
though the latter had charged them several times.

The Marshal, in order to end the battle before night, sent two brigades to take them in
flank; which they perceiving, retired in good order towards the mountains: they were followed
very close by the horse of our right wing, which
cut to pieces several *Portuguese* battalions in this
retreat. At this time, the Marshal perceiving
that a *Portuguese* regiment had formed itself into
a square battalion, in order to retreat, caused it
to be attacked on the right by the *Spanish* horse,
and on the left by the *French* foot, while he
himself charged it in rear. This regiment, which
deserved a better fate, made a wonderful defence,
though abandoned by the horse; they suffered
themselves to be cut to pieces rather than break,
and all the soldiers of this regiment were hewn
down in their ranks.

The left wing of the enemy, consisting most-
ly of *English* troops, still maintained themselves:
they had even charged and repulsed fifteen or
sixteen squadrons from the right wing of the army of the two Crowns, and being sustained by
the regiments of *Southwell, Blood, Wade, Mont-
joy,* and *Stewart,* they made a very brave stand.
Whereupon the Marshal caused nine battalions
to fall upon the right wing, which at last broke
it.

By

1707.   By this time the whole army of the enemy was routed every where. The brigade of *Spanish* guards, and that of *Mayne*, ftill improved the advantage they had gained, and purfued the enemy as far as the mountains. Some of the enemy's officers * having gathered together fome foldiers who were fcattered, formed a body of above four thoufand men. They were followed two leagues, but no further. The night was almoft come on, and the victorious army returned to the field of battle.

Marfhal *Berwick* had fent fome horfe to fecure the paffes in the mountains. And now the remainder of the enemy's left wing, confifting of thirteen battalions, finding thefe paffes fecured, thought fit to furrender. Count *Dhona*, who commanded it, fent a Major to the Marfhal, to tell him that he was his prifoner; and the Chevalier *d'Asfeld* was ordered to bring them next day to the camp †. Six battalions had already been taken in the action.

* They were Major-general *Shrimpton*, Brigadeer *Mackartney*, Colonel *Hill*, and fome other *Englifh* officers, who, together with Count *Dhona*, and Don *Emanuel*, brother to Count *Atalaya*, a Major of horfe, affembled a mixed body of *Englifh*, *Dutch* and *Portuguefe*, and carried them off from the field of battle, in the beft order poffible.

† It is generally agreed, that this mixed body of troops might have fafely marched off in the night. But Count *Dhona* and Major-general *Shrimpton*, upon a falfe report that the *Spaniards* and *French* were furrounding them, thought fit to fend a Major to the enemy's camp with a propofal to furrender prifoners at difcretion; which Marfhal *Berwick* readily accepted. Don *Emanuel* would have no fhare in fo difhonourable a capitulation; and to fhew how eafily it might have been avoided, they fafely retired with a few *Portuguefe* horfe, as did alfo a Serjeant with about eighty men.

The

1707.

The enemy left five thousand men killed upon the spot. Six Major-generals, six Brigadeers, twenty Colonels, eight hundred Subalterns, nine hundred men, and the thirteen battalions above mentioned, were all made prisoners. They lost all their artillery, consisting of twenty four pieces of cannon, almost all their baggage, and an hundred and twenty colours and standards. A great number of them were wounded: among these was the Earl of *Galway*, who received two deep cuts in the face near his right eye, which disabled him for acting for some time. The Marquis *Das Minas*, General of the *Portuguese*, lost all his equipage, and likewise his papers, where were found several letters of his correspondents at the Court of *Madrid*. His mistress, clad in the habit of an *Amazon*, was killed by his side. This signal victory, which secured the Crown of *Spain* to King *Philip*, cost his army no more than two thousand men killed or wounded *.

My

---

* The writers on the side of the Allies affirm, that this was not a bloodless victory, the army of the two Crowns having lost at least three thousand men, among whom were several General Officers and a great number of Subalterns. It is owned that the Earl of *Galway* behaved with the greatest courage in that action. The Marquis *das Minas* did all that could be expected from him. Colonel *Hill*, General *Kirk*, and many other *English* officers greatly distinguished themselves on that unfortunate day. The battle of *Almanza* may be said to have been as fatal in itself and its consequences to the Allies in *Spain*, as the battle of *Blenheim*, or that of *Turin*, was to the *French* in *Germany* and *Italy*. The loss of it was imputed to the superior strength of the

enemy's

1707.   My Lord *Galway* with the remainder of his
cavalry, amounting to about three thousand five
hundred horse, retired to *Alcira*, where he put a
garrison of foot as well as in *Xerica*, and afterwards
went to the head of the *Ebor*, near *Tortosa*, with
a design to join the troops of the Arch-duke, for
the defence of *Catalonia*. He left a strong garrison in *Alicant*, which was well provided with all
the necessary ammunitions and stores.

The Marshal of *Berwick*'s valour, conduct,
and presence of mind were admired throughout
the whole course of this action. He himself
charged the enemy several times, and rode along
all their ranks with as much composure and
coolness, as if he had been at a review. He redressed so seasonably the disadvantages which his
troops received, that these checks seemed only
to have happened in order to encrease his glory.

There was great plenty in the camp after this
battle. Horses were sold for a crown, cloaths
for fifteen pence, musquets for a groat, and mules
were given for nothing. The loss which the
army of the two Crowns sustained in this action
was almost entirely repaired by the *French* who
had been taken prisoners at the battle of *Hochstet*
and *Ramillies*, whom the enemy had forced to
take arms on their side.

enemy's cavalry, the great fatigue which the troops of the Allies
had undergone, and their having been weakened by the want
of provisions : but the chief cause of it was the superior skill
and experience of the enemy's General.

The

The Duke of *Orleans,* who, as we have said above, was arrived at *Madrid,* had set out from thence as soon as he was informed that the two armies drew near; but he did not arrive till the action was over. His joy was somewhat lessened by the vexation he had, not to have arrived betimes. Marshal *Berwick* went to meet him, and told him that he had done his utmost to defer the the engagement till the arrival of his Royal Highness; but that he had found it impossible, having been first attacked: he added, that he was well persuaded that the report of his coming had made the enemy hasten the action, and that he doubted not but his name alone had greatly contributed to the victory. That Prince answered the Marshal, that he ought not to endeavour to diminish the glory which he had acquired upon this occasion, and that the honour of this victory was justly due to him.

A council of war was held, upon the measures which were now to be taken to improve this victory. Marshal *Berwick* was of opinion, that the horse ought to be sent in pursuit of the enemy, with orders not to separate. This advice was followed. The horse immediately set out, and after marching three leagues, came up with the rest of the enemy's baggage, with waggons, coaches and chaises, the number of which exceeded four hundred, and they made besides fifteen hundred prisoners. After this, the army was allowed to rest till the thirtieth, when they marched to *Albora*; next day they passed the

river

1707. river *Cabriel*, and went to *la Rambla de Bagolo*, and on the fecond of *May* to *Requena*, which furrendered: on the fourth we received from feveral parts of the kingdom of *Valencia* deputies, who came to take an oath of allegiance to King *Philip*; but Marſhal *Berwick* having reprefented to his Royal Highnefs, that we never could be fully maſters of that kingdom, whilſt its capital was in the enemy's hands, it was refolved to befiege *Valencia*, and afterwards march into *Arragon*.

On the fixth, the army advanced near *Valencia*. The Commander and his troops had left the place the night preceeding, and the inhabitants made as if they would defend it: but his Royal Highnefs having fent a trumpet to fummon them to fubmit, they came to implore the King's clemency, and furrendered at difcretion. A ſtrong garrifon was put in this place; and afterwards the Duke of *Orleans*, having given his orders to Marſhal *Berwick*, fet out on the ninth by poſt for *Madrid*, from whence he went on the fifteenth to head the troops which were ready to enter *Arragon*. The day after the Prince's departure, Marſhal *Berwick* having gone to the Cathedral Church of *Valencia*, the Clergy and the Magiſtrates received him with the fame honours which are paid to Princes. However, he caufed the walls of the town to be demoliſhed, and a citadel to be built, in order to curb the rebels: he difarmed the inhabitants, feized their archives, and demanded forty thoufand piſtoles, over and

above

above the fums to which they fhould be taxed by
the King of *Spain.* He treated in the fame pro-
portion the other rebellious towns. In a harbour
near *Valencia* he found three fmall fhips, which
had been driven thither by ftrefs of weather. They
were laden with five thoufand mufkets, ten thoufand pair of fhoes, twelve thoufand fhirts, fix
thoufand pair of ftockings, eight thoufand fuits
of cloaths, and two thoufand facks of corn, all
which they carried to the enemy. On the eleventh, the army went to encamp at *Morvedro*,
four leagues from *Valencia.* It confifted of twenty four battalions and forty four fquadrons. The
enemy were then encamped at *Cabagna.* Marfhal *Berwick* having fecured the places of which
he had made himfelf mafter in this kingdom, fet
out with part of his troops for *St. Matheo*, which
is feven leagues from *Tortofa :* he arrived there on
the feventeenth of *May.*

The enemy, to the number of four thoufand
horfe, and very few infantry, (for moft of the
latter had been killed or taken prifoners in the
battle of *Almanza)* were within two days march
of the Marfhal's army. They paffed the *Ebor* at
Tortofa; the Marfhal followed them, incamping
in the places which they quitted. On the twenty
third he arrived before *Tortofa*, and next day
feized the fuburbs which were on the other fide
of the river. He caufed the bridge to be broke,
to hinder the enemy from making incurfions into
the kingdom of *Valencia.* After which he left
the Chevalier *Croy* with a detachment, and fet

out

1707. out with eighteen battalions and twenty four squadrons to join the Duke of *Orleans*, who was making all the neceſſary preparations for the ſiege of *Lerida*. On the ſixth of *June* he met the Prince at *Saragoſſa*, where, after they had held a council of war, he returned to his troops on the eighth.

On the fifteenth his Royal Highneſs made a long and painful march to *Bajaloras:* he left the army, and came only with his guards to Marſhal *Berwick*'s camp, which was then three leagues farther off. Next day the army ſet out for *Cudanos*, where were the Duke of *Orleans* and Marſhal *Berwick:* the army continued there two days, and afterwards marched to *Ballevar*. After the junction of the troops of Marſhal *Berwick*, this army conſiſted of thirty ſix battalions.

His Royal Highneſs ordered fourteen battalions to paſs the *Segne*. On the eighteenth Marſhal *Berwick* paſſed the ſame river below *Lerida*, and ſeized *Balaguer*, where the Duke of *Orleans* took his quarters. The troops had aſſigned to them quarters of refreſhment, the heats of the months of *July* and *Auguſt* not permitting the army to keep the field in that country: however, theſe quarters were diſpoſed in ſuch a manner, that *Lerida* was, as it were, blocked up.

At this time the Court of *France* being informed by Marſhal *Teſſé*, who commanded in *Dauphiny* and *Provence*, of the Duke of *Savoy*'s enterpriſe upon *Toulon;* that being ſupported by
the

the *English* fleet, he was preparing to befiege that town; the King yielded to the earneft in- treaty of the Duke of *Burgundy*, and confented that he fhould go thither, in order that his pre- fence might revive the ardor and zeal of his fub- jects, and contribute to drive the enemy from *Provence*, which they had already entred. The Duke of *Burgundy* demanded of the King the Marfhal *Berwick*. Immediately his Moft Chriftian Majefty ordered a courier to be difpatched into *Spain*, to defire the Marfhal to fet out forth- with for *Provence*, in order to join that Prince. At the fame time he was ordered to fend four thoufand horfe of the *French* troops which ferved in *Spain*, to join with all poffible diligence the army under Marfhal *Teffé*.   The Duke of *Bur- gundy* wrote to him by the courier, and ac- quainted him, that as he was going into *Pro- vence* to drive the enemy out of that country, the confidence which he had in the Marfhal had obliged him to demand him of the King; and that he intreated him to take his meafures fo, as that both of them might arrive there at the fame time.

Marfhal *Berwick* communicated thefe orders to the Duke of *Orleans*, who immediately fent out the four thoufand horfe under the com- mand of Mr. *Arrenes* Lieutenant-general. Next day the Marfhal fet out by poft, taking the road by *Navarre*: arriving at *Befiers* in *Languedoc*, he was informed that the fiege of *Toulon* had been raifed, and that the enemy had retired from

Z

Provence,

1707. *Provence*, fo that the Duke of *Burgundy* was not to go into that country. Upon this intelligence he ftopped at *Befiers*, forefeeing that if it was true, he would foon receive a counter order, both for himfelf and for the troops which came from *Spain*.

In effect, he received a courier next day, with an order to return, and bring back to *Spain* the four thoufand horfe which had fet out with him. The Duke of *Burgundy* wrote to him, that the fudden retreat of the Duke of *Savoy* had prevented his going into *Provence*, and deprived him of the pleafure of having the Marfhal near him. He concluded his letter thus: " You re-
" turn to *Spain*, but you will not be there for
" a long time, for I hope you will come and
" fee us next year, at leaft I wifh it, and will
" endeavour it fhall be fo." The Marfhal immediately fet out from *Befiers*. At *Touloufe* he met Mr. *Arennes* with the four thoufand horfe, who were coming with all fpeed, and ordered them to return to *Spain*. He joined the Duke of *Orleans* before *Lerida*, which they were ready to befiege. The lines of circumvallation were finifhed, and on the night, between the fecond and third of *October*, the trenches were opened.

The Prince of *Darmflat*, who commanded in the place, prepared to make a vigorous defence; and fuch it was in the beginning: but on the thirteenth, when a fufficient breach was made to give the affault, and we were ready to mount it, the Governor retired with his troops

into

into the caſtle; whereupon we ſeized the town. 1707.
His Royal Highneſs left it ſoon after, and ſaid to
the Duke of *Berwick* as he went out of it, *You
may ſuffer the ſoldiers to plunder the town.* The
whole army was enriched by this plunder: the
little towns and villages in the neighbourhood
had brought to this place their moſt valuable
effects. The pillage continued for eight hours.

The trenches were opened before the caſtle on
the ſixteenth. My Lord *Galway* having brought
together his troops upon the upper and lower *Seigres*, in order to attempt to throw ſuccours into the place, or at leaſt to annoy our
army; Marſhal *Berwick* took twenty eight battalions, and ſixty ſquadrons, which he formed
into an army of obſervation, and headed them, in
order to keep the enemy in awe; till at laſt the
Prince of *Darmſtat* loſing all hopes of being relieved, beat the chamade on the eighth of *November*, capitulated, and ſurrendered the caſtle.
As ſoon as *Lerida* was taken, moſt of the inhabitants of the mountains acknowledged King
Philip V as their lawful Sovereign. Afterwards,
the troops were put into winter quarters, and his
Royal Highneſs went to *Madrid.* Marſhal *Berwick* went thither likewiſe: he there received a
proof how well the King of *France* was ſatisfied
with his ſervices, his Majeſty having made him
Governor of *Limoſin:* The King of *Spain*, being likewiſe deſirous to acknowledge the important ſervices which the Marſhal had rendred to
him, made him Duke of *Liria* and *Xerica*,

Z 2

Grandee

1707. Grandee of *Spain* of the firſt claſs, himſelf and one of his ſons at his choice, and likewiſe inveſted him with the collar of the Order of the *Golden Fleece*.

1708.   In the beginning of the year 1708 he was ordered to return to *France*. Before his departure the King of *Spain* deſired him to be preſent at a Grand Council which he held with all his Miniſters and ſeveral Grandees of the kingdom, in order to regulate the operations of the enſuing campaign.

Upon his arrival, he met with a moſt gracious reception from the King of *France*, who expreſſed a great ſenſe of his merit. When he went to pay his duty to the Duke of *Burgundy*, that Prince ſaid to him, *My Lord Duke, after having done ſuch important ſervices in* Spain, *it is but juſt that you ſhould come and do the ſame here, and ſatisfy the impatience I had to ſee you.* It was at this time he took the oath of fidelity to his Majeſty for the eſtate and office of Marſhal of *France* and Governor of the upper and lower *Limoſin*.

The King appointed betimes the Generals of his armies. The Duke of *Burgundy* had deſired to command in perſon the army of *Flanders*. His equipage was prepared, as well as that of the Duke of *Berry*, who was going to make his firſt campaign, and that of the King of *England*, who deſired to accompany theſe two Princes in the quality of Volunteer, under the name of the Chevalier *St. George*. The Duke of *Burgundy*

was

was to have under his command the Duke of *Vendôme* and Marſhal *Matignon.*

The Elector of *Bavaria* commanded the army on the *Rhine,* having under him the Marſhal of *Berwick.*   Marſhal *Villars* was appointed to command the army in *Dauphiny.*   The Duke of *Orleans* returned to *Spain,* with Count *Bezons,* whom the King named Marſhal of *France.* The Duke of *Noailles* had the command of the army in *Catalonia :* and the ſame General Officers were continued upon the coaſts, and in ſome provinces, who had commanded in the year preceeding.

Marſhal *Berwick* was appointed, as we have ſaid above, to command on the *Rhine* under the Elector of *Bavaria ;* but he was firſt obliged to accompany King *James* III in an enterprize made at that time upon *England,* of which we ſhall here give a particular account.

The people of *Scotland,* naturally attached to the Houſe of *Stuart,* which deſcends from their Kings, and had given Sovereigns to *Great Britain* for more than a century, were highly diſcontented with the treaty of union which Queen *Anne* had lately concluded between that kingdom and *England.*   They who were formerly independent were by this treaty ſubjected to the *Engliſh,* for whom they have a natural antipathy.   They wanted to ſhake off their yoke ; and ſeeing that there were but a few land forces and ſhips in *England* at this time, they endeavoured to improve ſo favourable an opportunity, and to re-

call

 call to the throne of their ancient Kings the only remaining Prince of the Houfe of *Stuart*, who was then in *France*, under the name of *James* III.

Several *Scots* Lords came over fecretly to this Prince, and affured him that a very confiderable party in *Scotland* would declare for him, as foon as there fhould be any appearance of their being fupported. They preffed him in the name of the whole nation to come and head them; in a word, they made fuch reprefentations as prevailed with the Court of *St. Germains*.

Whilft an armament was preparing at *Dunkirk*, the Chevalier *Nangis*, Captain of a fhip, was fecretly fent to *Edinburgh* in a frigate, with credentials, and inftructions for his endeavouring to know the difpofitions of the nobles and people. He was there received with great marks of joy and diftinction; and all that had been faid in *France* concerning the zeal of the *Scots* for that Prince was there confirmed to him. He put into the hands of the principal Lords a great many arms, and feveral warlike ftores which he had on board the frigate. The Lords with whom he conferred told him that *England* was not then in a condition to undertake any thing, or to oppofe their defign, and that as foon as King *James* III fhould land, he might rely upon thirty thoufand *Scots* who would take arms for him; and they fent with him new deputies to compliment his *Britifh* Majefty in the name of the nation, as foon as he fhould arrive at *Dunkirk*.

The

The intended armament was made, and the 1708.
neceſſary preparations for this expedition were
carried on, with ſuch ſecrecy, though within
ſight of the troops of the Allies which were in
Flanders, that the *Engliſh* and *Dutch* were not
informed of this deſign, till the fleet was ready
to put to ſail. It conſiſted of eight large ſhips,
twenty four frigates, ſeventy tranſports, and a
great number of ſmall craft, the whole commanded by the Chevalier *Forbin*. The land
forces which were to embark amounted to twelve
battalions, and were commanded by Count *Gacé*,
who was afterwards made a Marſhal of *France*,
with the title of Marſhal *Matignon*. The ſhips
carried three thouſand muſkets, ten thouſand
ſadles, the ſame number of bridles and pairs of
piſtols, cloaths for a company of the King of
England's life-guards, a conſiderable number of
colours and ſtandards, and, in ſhort, every thing
that was thought neceſſary, in abundance.

When all things were ready, that is, on the
ſeventh of *March*, the King of *England* ſet out
from *St. Germains* in a poſt-chaiſe, being accompanied only by my Lord *Middleton*, two
Gentlemen of his houſhold, and two Valets de
Chambre. Marſhal *Berwick* had ſet out before
him. He went upon this enterprize without
having any command over the *French* troops,
and only with a deſign to accompany the King
of *England*, and to ſerve him in *Scotland*.

The day before the departure of that prince,
the King of *France* went to *St. Germains* to

wiſh

1708. wifh him fuccefs in his expedition; and his
Moft Chriftian Majefty embracing him, affured
him that he would never abandon him. He
prefented him with a cafket, in which were
one hundred thoufand louis-d'ors, befides a
fine fet of gold and filver plate, a great number of magnificent cloaths, and a confiderable
quantity of linen which the King had fent to
Dunkirk. That young Prince expreffed how
grateful he was for fuch generofity, and affured
his Moft Chriftian Majefty that he would never
forget the obligations he was under to him and
all his kingdom. The Queen Dowager, his
mother, prefented him with forty thoufand louis-
d'ors, and with jewels to the value of two hundred and eighty thoufand livres. He arrived at
Dunkirk on the ninth, when he declared to
the Lords who followed him, that during his
voyage he would only be called the Chevalier
St. George.

As foon as the enemy had notice of the armament at *Dunkirk,* Major-general *Cadogan* provided ten battalions to be tranfported from *Oftend*
to *Great Britain;* the *Britifh* admiralty provided
a fleet of above forty fail with incredible diligence.
The forces in *England* were ordered to march towards *Scotland;* the Earl of *Leven,* Commander
in chief of the forces in that kingdom, was fent
to *Edinburgh,* and all the neceffary difpofitions
were made to baffle this defign.

The King of *England,* upon his arrival at
Dunkirk, found that the *Englifh* fleet was within

1708.

in view of fort *Mardick*, and made as if they blocked up that port. The embarkment which was to be on the tenth, was deferred till the thirteenth, by reason of an indisposition that happened to the King. This indisposition delaying his departure, made them lose the favourable wind; and when they were ready to put to sea, the winds were contrary. The Chevalier *Forbin* in vain represented this to the Prince, who insisted upon their sailing: but the bad weather, and the *English* fleet which cruised in the Channel, obliged that of *France* to return to our harbours. The Chevalier *St. George* landed at *St. Omer*, where he stopped for some time; afterwards he set out for the army in *Flanders*, in order to serve in the quality of a Volunteer under the Duke of *Burgundy*, as we have said above *.

The Marshal of *Berwick* came from *St. Omer* to *Versailles*, where he continued till the month

* The *French* fleet sailed as far as *Edinburgh* Firth, where they were seen on the eleventh of *March*. But the next day Sir *George Byng* arriving there with the *English* fleet, the *French* put to sea, and Admiral *Byng* gave them chace. He took one of their men of war, on board of which were Lord *Griffin*, the Earl of *Clermont*, his brother Mr. *Middleton*, Colonel *Wachop*, the Marquis *de Levi*, a *French* Lieutenant-general, and several other *French* and *Irish* officers, with five companies of *French* soldiers. He chased the rest of the fleet northward, till he lost sight of them. This intended invasion occasioned a prodigious run upon the Bank of *England*. The Queen, in order to keep up the publick credit, allowed, for six months, an interest of six *per cent.* upon Bank bills, which before paid only three *per cent.* At the same time the Lord Treasurer *Godolphin*, the Dukes of *Marlborough*, *Newcastle*, and *Somerset*, and several other Peers, offered the Bank considerable sums of money.

of

1708. of *May*, when he set out for *Strasburg*, there to assemble the army which he was to command under the Elector of *Bavaria*. Prince *Eugene* commanded the army of the Allies upon the *Rhine*. Nothing considerable happened on this side, both armies being content with observing each other. In the beginning of *July*, Prince *Eugene* set out with part of his troops to joyn the Duke of *Marlborough* in *Flanders*.

As soon as the Elector of *Bavaria* had certain intelligence of this, he detached Marshal *Berwick*, according to the orders he had received from the *French* Court, with a body of troops to join the Duke of *Burgundy* in *Flanders*. The Marshal arrived there, between *Lisle* and *Tournay*, on the twelfth of *July*, some time after the affair of *Oudenarde* * ; he was there joined by a part of the troops of the Duke of *Burgundy*'s army, which had been intercepted in their retreat. On the fourteenth, he went with thirty squadrons

* On the eleventh of *June*, the *French* army under the Duke of *Burgundy* and the Duke of *Vendôme* having laid siege to *Oudenarde*, was attacked and totally defeated near that place by the Duke of *Marlborough* and Prince *Eugene*. Above six thousand of their troops were taken prisoners, and a great slaughter made among their foot. In this action his present Majesty, then Electoral Prince of *Hanover*, exposed himself as much as any private man, had a horse shot under him, and at the head of a squadron of *Hanoverian* dragoons charged and broke a squadron of the Houshold troops of *France*. Prince *Eugene*, who had the care of the right wing, fought at the head of the *English* troops ; and the present Duke of *Argyle*, and several officers of the Allies, greatly distinguished themselves in this battle ; which, had not the Duke of *Vendôme* made a very good retreat, wherein he was favoured by the night, would have proved much more fatal to the *French* than the battle of *Ramillies*.

very

very near *Lisle*, and threw a part of his infantry into that place, and into *Tournay*.

On the sixteenth, the troops detached from the Duke of *Burgundy*'s army arrived there likewise, having taken the road along the sea by *Plassendal* and *Dixmude*. Marshal *Berwick* put three thousand of his troops into *Ypres*, *la Kenoque*, *Lisle*, *Furnes*, *Dixmude* and *Tournay*, and went afterwards to *Lovendeyghem*, to confer with the Duke of *Burgundy*. He left his flying camp at *Haut Bourdin*, about half a league from *Lisle*, under the command of the Marquis of *Hautefort*; he returned to it two days after, in order to observe the motions of the enemy, and to cover the country as much as possible.

On the fourteenth of *July* the enemy held a council of war, in which it was debated, whether they should march to the Duke of *Burgundy*, and attack him in the post which he possessed, and which greatly annoyed them, or whether they should besiege some town: it was resolved to take the latter course, the former being too dangerous. Whereupon they formed a project of besieging *Lisle*; for which purpose they made all the necessary preparations, and it was not long before we knew their design upon this place. Marshal *Berwick* was still in the same camp, near *Doway*, five leagues from *Lisle*, watching their motions, and endeavouring to find out their real design.

Lisle is one of the strongest towns in the *Low Countries*. Marshal *Vauban* had fortified it, and

had

1708. had there built a very strong and regular citadel. He had drawn a plan of defence for this place, which was in the hands of Mr. *du Puy-Vauban*, his nephew, chief engineer and Lieutenant-general in his Majesty's armies, who threw himself into this town as soon as it was threatened. Marshal *Boufflers*, Governor of *Flanders*, who had an unbounded zeal for the service of the King, and that of the State, asked his Majesty's leave to defend it in person: this was granted, and he accordingly entred *Lisle* on the twenty ninth of *July*.

The enemy hoped to hinder the junction of the Marshal of *Berwick*'s army with that of the Duke of *Burgundy*, one of which was at *Ghent*, and the other near *Mons*. The Marquis of *Hautefort*, Lieutenant-general, arrived at *Valenciennes* with the troops which were on the seaside, to join Marshal *Berwick*. All our troops were then in motion, in order to increase the army. The militia of the *Boulonnois* supplied the place of the troops which were on the sea-side and at *Ypres*; as well as the garrisons of *Thionville* and of *Sar-Louis*, which marched to *Luxembourg*, while the garrisons of that place and of *Namur* joined Marshal *Berwick*. Besides this, Mr. *la Croix* drew some thousands of men from the troops which were under his command, and brought them to the Marshal. The trenches were opened before *Lisle* on the twenty second of *August*. The Duke of *Burgundy*, who waited in the camp at *Louvenghen* to see what course

the

the enemy would take, in order to oppofe their enterprizes, was no fooner informed that they had fixed upon *Lifle*, then he prepared to joyn his army with that of Marfhal *Berwick*, to attempt the more effectually the raifing of the fiege of *Lifle*. With this view he fent orders to the Marfhal to advance towards him, and commanded his troops to be ready to march upon the firft notice, in order to meet Marfhal *Berwick*'s army.

The following days were imployed in making ready provifions, in working at the fortifications of *Ghent*, and in taking meafures for fecuring the camp of *Louvenghen*, where that Prince left Count *la Mothe* with nineteen battalions, advancing with the reft of his army to *Melle*, which is two leagues from *Ghent*. Marfhal *Berwick*, on his fide, reaffembled his troops about *Mons*; they confifted of twenty feven battalions, and ninety two fquadrons; with thefe he marched on the twenty fifth of *Auguft* to the caftle of *Baye*; on the twenty fixth to *St. Guillain*; on the twenty feventh near *Mons*; on the twenty eighth to *Enghien*, and on the twenty ninth to *Leffines*.

The Duke of *Marlborough*, being informed of the Duke of *Burgundy*'s defign, made a motion on the twenty fecond towards the *Scheld*, and paffed it at *Elchin*, upon the four bridges which he had ordered to be made over that river. Prince *Eugene* had joined him with a part of his infantry, and more than the half of his horfe; and

1708. and they encamped, their right at *Efcanaffe*, and their left at *Aimiere*. My Lord *Marlborough* took his quarters at *Moufter*, and Mr. *d'Auver-querque* at *Waudripont*, having before him the little river which is in that place.

His firſt deſign was, as we have ſaid above, to hinder the junction of the two armies; and he might have eaſily prevented it: but he did not afterwards think it proper, conſidering the precautions which the Duke of *Burgundy* had taken, as well as Marſhal *Berwick*; ſo that the enemy continued five days in this camp without unlading their baggage, being ready to march at the firſt order. The Duke of *Burgundy* encamped on the twenty eighth at *Ninoven*, which is about four leagues from *Melle*. Marſhal *Ber-wick* went thither to confer with him. This Prince continued there next day. On the thirtieth, the two armies having begun to march, joined in the plain which lies between *Grand-mont* and *Leſſines*, and encamped next day in the plain of *Leuſe*, about three leagues from *Tournay*.

On the firſt of *September* they drew near this city, and paſſed the *Scheld* in three different places, above, below, and at the town; on the ſecond, the whole army had paſſed that river, and formed into battalia in a plain which leads to *Liſle*. They had here two hundred pieces of cannon all in good caſe. A battle was expected; for it could not be imagined that two Generals ſo renowned as Prince *Eugene* and the Duke of *Marlborough*, would ſuffer an army to paſs quietly

by

by them, which had been fatigued by a march 1708.
of fix or feven days. However, they fuffered it;
and repaffing the *Scheld*, they went to encamp
at *Elchin*.

The Duke of *Burgundy*, who was encamped
between *Tournay* and *Lifle*, at *Croix Notre Dame*,
found himfelf obliged to feek a paffage elfewhere.
His army began to march on the third of *September*, and encamped at *Orchies*; on the fifth
at *Mons en Peule*, three leagues from *Douay*, and
four above *Lifle*, a place remarkable in hiftory
for a battle fought there between the *French* and
the *Flemifh* in the year 1302. in the reign of
Philip the fair.

The artillery could not arrive till the fifth.
The Prince formed his army into four lines, the
right near *Blocus*, the left near *Tumiers*, and the
referve with the dragoons at *Affigney* upon the
Marque. As we could not march out of the
plain of *Lifle*, between the *Marque* and the
Deule, by reafon of the moraffes and the woods
which are near *Epinay*, Marfhal *Berwick* ordered
two thoufand pioneers to level the ground as much
as poffible, in order that three battalions and fix
fquadrons might march in front. This was undertaken, notwithftanding the difficulty of the
work. It delayed for fome days the march of
the army, and gave the enemy time to fortify
themfelves in the poft which they had chofen;
but that could not be avoided.

The Generals of the *French* army differed in
their opinions concerning the meafures which
ought

1708. ought to be taken, and there happened a great mifunderftanding between them.   The Duke of *Burgundy* gave notice of this to the King, and fent to his Majefty a courier to inform him of the prefent fituation of affairs.   The King, who had refolved in a council to put every thing to hazard in order to raife the fiege of fo important a place as *Lifle*, fent Mr. *Chamillard*, Secretary at war, to know himfelf what could be done upon that occafion, and to reconcile the Generals.

Mr. *Chamillard* arrived in the army on the eighth of *September*.   He had a conference with the Duke of *Burgundy*, the Duke of *Vendôme*, and Marfhal *Berwick*.   They continued this day to prepare the roads for the march of the army, as well as the days following.   The Duke of *Burgundy* paffed the *Marque* on the tenth, and when he was within reach of the enemy, he formed his army into battalia, his right behind *Ennevelin* near the *Marque*, his center at *Entralle* and at *Avellin*, and his left covered by a brook which throws itfelf into *Phalempim*, drawing a line on the fide of the village *Seclin*, which the enemy poffeffed.

Marfhal *Berwick*, upon his arrival, drove away fome troops of the enemy which retired under the fire of the village of *Entieres*, from whence they difcharged fome cannon : but the Marfhal having caufed fix pieces of cannon to advance to the right of the caufeway, and batter this village, with the retrenchments which furrounded it, they quickly filenced the cannon of the enemy.

We

We continued to cannonade them till night. 1708.
During that time Marſhal *Berwick* ordered four
thouſand men to make a line from the hedges
of *Seclin* to thoſe which were beyond the cauſe-
way. He cauſed a great battery to be raiſed on
the right of the infantry near *Herines*, where he
placed large cannons, which were to be fired at
break of day upon the village of *Entieres*, from
whence it was impoſſible to drive the enemy by
other means, as they had there ſeven battalions,
and ſeveral pieces of artillery.

On the eleventh, the Duke of *Burgundy* ordered the village of *Seclin* to be attacked; and
after having driven from thence the enemy who
did not fire, he there lodged the left wing of his
army. About three of the clock in the morning,
Marſhal *Berwick* attacked an advanced poſt near
Seclin, guarded by ſix hundred men, whom the
Duke of *Marlborough* had left there only to obſerve us; the Commander had been ordered to
retire at the approach of our troops, and to burn
that poſt; which he accordingly put in execution.

We were inceſſantly examining how we could
ſurpriſe the enemy. The Duke of *Burgundy*,
with the Duke of *Vendôme* and Marſhal *Berwick*,
advanced very near their intrenchments in different places. An officer had a horſe killed under him very near this Prince: he went up to
the ſteeple of *Seclin* with Mr. *Chamillard* and
the Marſhal to view the enemy: he went again
to view their retrenchments, againſt which our
batteries continually fired.

A a

But

 But it was impoffible to force them in fo advantageous a poft.   As we were then informed that they wanted ammunition, a council of war was held, in which it was refolved to put every thing in practice in order to cut off their convoys; and after having caufed the cannon of the batteries to be withdrawn, and the batteries to be levelled, we decamped the next day, being the fifteenth.

The whole army began to march at break of day in four columns, repaffed the *Marque*, and encamped between *Orchies* and *Mons en Peule*, from whence the Duke of *Burgundy* detached forty fquadrons and fome battalions which were fent to *Doway*, two battalions and feven fquadrons to *Arras*, and a like number to *Bethune*, to hem in the enemy, and ftop their incurfions. To hinder them from drawing any thing from *Bruffels*, feveral pofts upon the heights of *Oudenard*, at *Berg*, *Poftes*, and *Herines*, were ordered to be poffeffed.   The head quarters, where the Duke of *Burgundy* and the Princes lodged, were at *Saulfey*, an abby of nuns; all thefe troops could join together in fix hours.

The Marquis of *Conflans*, Marfhal de Camp, had been fent towards *Doway* with thirty five fquadrons, to hinder the enemy from fending any thing between that place and *Bethune*.   Retrenchments were made before *Oudenarde* to hinder the convoys from coming out of that place: by this difpofition the enemy could receive no fupplies of provifions and ammunitions from

Bruffels,

Bruſſels, where were their great magazines. But
they had taken meaſures to prevent this, whilſt
the Duke of *Burgundy*'s army was employed in
ſeeking an opportunity of engaging them; and
they had the precaution of tranſporting all the
proviſions they could to *Oudenarde* and *Menin*.
They had ſo well expected that the Duke of
Burgundy would take the courſe which he actually took, that they had cauſed all the neceſſa-
ries for compleating their enterprize to be brought
by ſea to *Oſtend*, not doubting but that they
might tranſport them in waggons to their
camp, being favoured by the Duke of *Marlborough*'s army.

The Duke of *Burgundy* reſolved to oppoſe it;
and for this purpoſe he ſent an order to Count
la Mothe, who was at *Enghien*, to march towards *Bruges*, for fear that the enemy ſhould
make themſelves maſters of this town and of
fort *Plaſſendal*, by which they might receive all
their ſuccours from *Oſtend :* and knowing that
the enemy were preparing to come this way, he
ordered Marſhal *Berwick*, and Mr. *Bergelk*, Secretary of State to the King of *Spain* in the *Low
Countries*, to march to *Bruges* and join Count *la
Mothe*.

It was a matter of the greateſt importance
that the convoy, which the enemy expected
from *Oſtend*, ſhould not arrive at the ſiege: and
it was for this reaſon that ſo much care was taken for intercepting it. The Duke of *Burgundy*
thought that he could not truſt an affair of that

A a 2

conſequence

1708. confequence to any fitter perfon than Marfhal *Berwick*, whofe prudence and capacity were fo well known; but the Marfhal received his orders too late.   Count *la Mothe*, without waiting for him, began his march, in order to intercept the convoy: he met with it near *Winendale*, guarded by a ftrong efcort, which he attacked; the engagement was very brifk, the enemy had all the advantage, the convoy paffed on, and our troops were obliged to retire in diforder *.   The Marfhal of *Berwick* could not arrive there till the action was over.   The Duke of *Vendôme* went afterwards to *Bruges* with a confiderable body of troops, to cut off the enemy's communication with *Oftend*; he broke all their dikes in the neighbourhood of that place, and advanced as far as *Odemburg*.   But the enemy, who could no longer bring their convoys by thefe ways, had

* This convoy was commanded by Major-general *Webb*, who gained immortal honour by the victory at *Winendale*; the enemy's army confifting of twenty four thoufand men, whereas he had not above fix thoufand, and wanted a train of artillery, which they had.   Mr. *Feuquieres* imputes this defeat to the incapacity of Count *la Mothe*, " who was ordered to intercept this " convoy in its march; which, fays that writer, he not only " failed to do, with a body of troops infinitely fuperior to its " efcort, but alfo found a way to have his troops beaten by that " feeble efcort.   A moft extraordinary event furely! for though " we have heard of convoys that have paffed fafe with a fmall " guard, by reafon of the diligence and fecrecy of their march; " yet it was never before feen, that a convoy attacked by a body " of troops infinitely fuperior to its efcort, not only got fafe off, " but that its feeble efcort beat the fuperior body of troops which " attacked it."   For this victory Major-general *Webb* received the thanks of the Houfe of Commons; and the King of *Pruffia*, as an extraordinary mark of his efteem and favour, fent him *the Order of Generofity.*

recourfe

recourfe to others, in which they fucceeded. They 1708.
made ufe of feveral fmall flat boats, in which
they placed a great number of leathern facks,
filled with powder, and fent them from *Oftend*
to *Leffinghem*, over the inundations which were
favourable to them. Afterwards, by means of
feveral waggons raifed upon wheels higher than
ordinary, they went to *Leffinghem* and brought
their facks, and all their other ammunitions to
the camp before *Lifle*. However, they could
not bring to their camp after this manner more
than a part of their ammunitions, and were
obliged to leave the reft at the village of *Leffinghem*, becaufe they had not a fufficient number
of waggons to tranfport the whole. Whereupon
the Duke of *Vendôme* refolved to make himfelf
mafter of *Leffinghem*; and in this he fucceeded.

Notwithftanding all this, the enemy ftill found
means to receive their convoys; which put them
in a condition to profecute the fiege of *Lifle* with
vigour. Marfhal *Boufflers*, who defended that
place, feeing that it could not be relieved, and
finding himfelf open, and ready to undergo an
affault, thought fit to fave his troops for the defence of the citadel. Accordingly, after having
made a long and vigorous defence, he capitulated for the town, and retired to the citadel,
which he held out for a confiderable time, and
would have defended to the laft extremity, had
it not been for a letter from the King, which
was remitted to him by the Duke of *Burgundy*:
in this letter his Majefty commanded him to

 furrender

1708. furrender the citadel, without expofing to further danger either himfelf, for whom the King
had a great value, or his garrifon, which had
already made fo brave a defence.

After the taking of *Lifle*, the enemy put their
troops into winter quarters. The Duke of *Burgundy* having done the fame, fet out for *Verfailles*
with the Duke of *Berry* and the Chevalier *St.
George*. The Duke of *Vendôme* followed them
foon after. As for Marfhal *Berwick* he returned
to *Germany*, according to the orders which he
had received from the Court. Towards the end
of *November* he arrived upon the *Rhine*, and
took upon him the command of the army; he
immediately viewed the banks of the river, and
the lines, which he fecured by new works.

He went afterwards to *Strafburg*, where he
ordered twenty pieces of cannon to be fent to
fort *Lewis*, that they might foon be brought
into the lines in cafe of need; and he fent back
the reft of the artillery. Being informed that
the army of the enemy was feparated, he difmiffed the General Officers, fent the troops into
winter-quarters, and after all things were fecured,
he returned himfelf to Court.

1709. In the year 1709 fome overtures were made
for a general peace; but the enemy being flufhed
with their victories, their demands were fo bur-
denfome and fhameful to *France* and *Spain*,
that it was utterly impoffible to liften to them.
The King who had fufficiently fhewn how much
he had at heart the peace of *Europe*, and of his
kingdom,

kingdom, by the steps and advances which he 1709.
had made for that end, finding the enemy so
little disposed to concur with him, prepared to
make his utmost efforts for continuing the war,
and retrieving his former losses. His Majesty
knowing the affection which the *French* bear to
their Kings and the Princes of the blood, resolved to put them this campaign at the head of his
armies, as being the surest way of reviving the
ardor and courage of his troops. He declared
that the Dauphin should command in person the
army in *Flanders*, that he should be accompanied
by the Dukes of *Berry* and *Bourbon*, and that
Marshal *Villars* should serve under him : that the
Duke of *Burgundy* should command the army
upon the *Rhine*, having under him Marshal
Harcourt : that the Duke of *Orleans* should
command in *Spain*, as he had done in the two
preceeding years, and should have under him
Marshal *Besons* ; and that Marshal *Berwick*
should command the army in *Dauphiny*. But
these dispositions were not followed, both by
reason of the disorder of the finances, and of the
calamities occasioned by the severe winter, which
obliged the King to remit in several places a part
of the taxes.

Marshal *Boufflers* having refused to command
in *Flanders*, the King sent thither Marshal *Villars*.
The King of *England* was to serve there as a
volunteer under the name of the Chevalier *St.
George*. Marshal *Harcourt* went to command
upon the *Rhine*, Marshal *Berwick* in *Dauphiny*,

A a 4

and

1709. and the Duke of *Noailles* in *Rouſſillon*. There were to be two armies in *Spain*: the moſt conſiderable, conſiſting of *Spaniards* and *French*, was to be commanded by Marſhal *Beſons*, and to act in *Catalonia* againſt General *Staremberg*; the other, conſiſting only of *Spaniards*, and commanded by the Marquis of *Bay*, was to act in *Eſtramadura* againſt the *Portugueſe*.

In the beginning of this year Marſhal *Berwick* had the ſatisfaction to ſee his family augmented by a ſon, of whom his conſort was delivered on the ninth of *January*. We were unwilling to interrupt the narration above, by mentioning that he had a daughter, who was born at the time when he went to beſiege *Nice*. This ſon was named *Francis Fitz-James*: but his joy upon this occaſion was diſturbed by the affliction he had at the death of a Prince who honoured him with his friendſhip and eſteem. I ſpeak of the Prince of *Conti*, who died this year at *Paris* on the twenty ſecond of *February*, in the forty fifth year of his age. Marſhal *Berwick* was deeply and moſt juſtly afflicted at the death of this excellent Prince, to whom he lay under ſo many obligations. He was greatly and univerſally lamented. In ſeveral actions he had ſhewn a diſtinguiſhed valour, and a great genius for war, eſpecially in the battle of *Gran* in *Hungary*, and thoſe of *Steenkerk* and *Landen* in *Flanders*. The ſucceſs of the *French* army in the battle of *Steenkerk* was partly owing to him; for this Prince having put

himſelf

himself at the head of a body of foot, charged 1709.
the enemy, made them lose their first advantage, and thus occasioned the victory. His
great qualities, known to all *Europe*, had engaged
the *Poles* in a general Diet to choose him unani-
mously for their King. His merit alone called
him to that Crown, without his having sought
it; but the intrigues of the Elector of *Saxony*
prevailed over the merit of this Prince.

On the twentieth of *March* the King made a
promotion of twenty Marshals de Camp, and
was wholly employed in preparing for the ensuing campaign. They who were ordered to provide for the army in *Dauphiny* arrived there this
month: they sent forrage to *Sablons* for the
horse which were to arrive there from *Franche-
Comte*; and filled the magazines with all sorts of
ammunition. Marshal *Berwick* having received
the King's orders, set out for the army in *Dauphiny*. As soon as he arrived there, he viewed
all the posts of the country, and assembled
the troops which were to compose his army.
He afterwards disposed them into the places
which he thought most proper for securing this
province and the adjacent countries, and for
defeating the measures which the Duke of *Savoy* had taken for invading it; he placed fifteen
battalions to guard the pass of *Galibier*; he
placed another body at *St. Jean de Morienne*,
and a third at *St. Michel*, and continued with
the main of his army at *Briançon*.

Count

1709. ..... Count *Thaun* commanded the army of *Pied-*
mont in the Duke of *Savoy*'s abfence. This Duke
deferred going into the field, under pretence of
fome difcontent which he had received from the
Emperor. He did not fet out from *Turin* till
the beginning of *July*, when he went to *Suza*.
Two days after he marched towards mount *Ce-*
nis, and left a detachment of horfe and foot
under the command of Count *Rebender*, to obferve the *French* on the fide of *Briançon*. At
the fame time he fent another detachment to
the valley of *Aofta*, to reinforce General *Schu-*
lemberg. A few days after, he fent thither fome
more troops, which made on that fide an army
of near fix thoufand men, horfe and foot.

Count *Thaun* made fome motions on the fide
of mount *Cenis* and *la Morienne*; but durft not
attack any poft of the Marfhal of *Berwick*; he
encamped at *Arfoire* in the upper *Morienne*, and
General *Rebender* at *Salbertron*, with twelve battalions. Afterwards, a ftrong detachment was
fent into the *Tarantefe*, under the command of
Count *la Roque* and Baron *Regal.*

The Marfhal of *Berwick* fortified two defiles
upon mount *Genevre*, and planted fome pieces
of cannon upon thefe paffes. He abandoned the
valley of *Barcellonnette*, and brought back his
troops, which were there, to mount *Dauphin*,
which feparates that valley from *Dauphiny*.
Whereupon Count *Thaun* came to encamp at
St. André, where he waited for the fuccefs of
the detachment under Count *la Roque*, who at
the

the head of ten thoufand men had paffed through 1709.
the *Tarantefe*, in order to go to *Moutieres*, while
Count *Schulemberg* paffed the little *St. Bernard*,
with three thoufand men, to come down to the
town of *St. Maurice :* this happened in the middle of *July*.

As foon as this was known, the Marquis of
Thoy, according to the orders he had received,
abandoned the retrenchments with his eight battalions, and retired to *Moutieres*. He blew up
the two ftone bridges upon the *Ifer*, but could
only poffefs one part of the town, Count *la
Roque* having made himfelf mafter of the other.
After fome fkirmifhes between thefe two detachments, the river running between them, the
Marquis of *Thoy* retired to *Feffons*, and afterwards
to *Conflans*, where he was joined on the twentieth by Count *Medavi*, with fifteen battalions
which were at *St. Jean de Morienne*, and were
reimplaced by the Marquis of *Silly*. By the
nineteenth, Count *la Roque* was returned by the
way he came, and joined Count *Thaun*, who
had advanced as far as *St. André*, while Count
Schulemberg retired on his fide.

The enemy had other detachments on the fide
of *Exilles* and *Feneftrelles*; but Marfhal *Berwick*, who encamped with the main of his army
at *Briançon*, obferved them narrowly, and hindred them from undertaking any thing. He
had caufed twelve pieces of cannon to be tranfported from fort *Barraux* to *Conflans*; but not
believing them fafe in that place, he caufed them

1709. to be brought to the bridge of *Heberiac*, where two battalions were entrenched to guard them.

Count *Thaun* posted his troops from *Conflans* as far as *St. Pierre d'Albigny*. He ordered a detachment to possess *Taloix* and the castle of *Doja*, upon the banks of the lake of *Anneci*. He secured the communication with *Piedmont* by the little *St. André* and by *Val-d'Aosta*, and continued in this situation, waiting for eight thousand horse with some heavy artillery, which was to pass by mount *Cenis*, and to enter the *Tarantese* by the pass of the *Colombe*.

Count *Rebender* was then in the valley of *Oulx* with ten thousand foot and some horse, extending from *Exilles* as far as mount *Genevre*, in order to fall upon *Briançon*, in case the *French* troops should remove from thence. Marshal *Berwick* had then encamped his infantry upon two lines near *Montmelian*. His horse lay behind at *Françin*, where were the head quarters. He kept a communication with *La Morienne* by *Aiguebelle*, by means of the bridge which was over the *Iser*. He placed some troops as far as *St. Jean* and *La Valoire*, to maintain his communication with *Briançon* by the pass of *Galibier*, the preservation of which he looked upon as his principal point. He posted two regiments of dragoons above the castle of *Challes*, in order to have notice when the army of the enemy should advance; for he feared that Count *Thaun* would march on the side of the *Batie*, and attack him in rear. On the fifteenth of *August*

all

all the Duke of *Savoy*'s cavalry joined that General.

In this interval, the Duke of *Savoy*, who was returned to *Turin*, ſtill continued there, in order oblige the Court of *Vienna* to yield to him the country of *Vigevano* dependent on the duchy of *Milan*, as well as the fiefs of *Langues* which had been promiſed to him when he was brought into the Grand Alliance. As the Emperor always deferred yielding to him theſe poſſeſſions, the Duke of *Savoy* had ordered to *Milan* the Marquis of *Graneri* to ſolicite that affair; and Mr. *Palmes*, the *Engliſh* Envoy, ſupported theſe demands. His Imperial Majeſty had named the Biſhop of *Five Churches* to terminate that difference; and it was to haſten the deciſion of that affair, that the Duke of *Savoy* refuſed to head the army of *Piedmont*, though the Queen of *England* had written to him a letter to engage him go into the field, and take advantage of the great diverſion which the Allies made in *Flanders*. That Princeſs repreſented to him, that the conqueſts he might make would partly make amends for what the Court of *Vienna* refuſed to grant him; and beſides, ſhe engaged her Royal word, that after the campaign, ſhe would procure him all manner of ſatisfaction from the Houſe of *Auſtria*. All this was not capable to make him quit *Turin*: that Prince wanted to have things in poſſeſſion, and relied more upon facts than upon words.

Count

Count *Thaun* detached about six thousand men, whom he sent to take possession of the little town of *Annecy*, which was guarded only by an old castle and plain walls. On the nineteenth this detachment seized the town, and made the garrison, consisting of forty five men, prisoners of war. The design of the enemy by seizing this post, was to pass the *Rhone*, and afterwards to penetrate into *Bugey* and *Bresse*, while the *Imperialists* advanced into *Franche-Comte:* but the ill success of Count *Mercy* in passing the *Rhine* rendred this project useless; and the taking of *Annecy* was of no service to Count *Thaun*. It only served to hinder the project of Marshal *Berwick*, who intended to make a line from that town to *Briançon*. At the same time, Count *Thaun* detached General *Rebender* with three thousand foot and two thousand horse, to advance towards the bridge of *La Vachette*, near *Briançon*, in order to disturb our retrenchments, or take the advanced posts.

Lieutenant-general *Dillon*, who possessed *La Vachette*, a village which is very defenceless, sent for a detachment of three hundred foot and two hundred horse, and gave Marshal *Berwick* advice of the enemy's design. He left but a few men in the post, and ordered them to fire but weakly upon the enemy when they should approach. He retired to some distance with the main body of his troops; they were soon after joined by the piquet of the army which Marshal *Berwick* sent him: whereupon he returned silently

lently

lently to the village. On a sudden he fired upon Count *Rebender*'s troops, which had drawn very near, took them in flank, and put them into such diforder, that they fled by different ways; after having left four hundred men upon the place, among whom we found fixty wounded, who were fent to the hofpital of *Briançon.*

Marfhal *Berwick* being informed that one named *Marou*, a Notary at *Exilles*, ferved as a fpy to the enemy, ordered Captain *Bourcet* to apprehend him. This officer having advanced with fixty boors within a quarter of a league of *Exilles*, ftopt at *l'Eclufe*, from whence he fent two peafants to *Marou*, as if it was to engage him to come and draw up the laft will and te-ftament of a man who was dying. He came accordingly, and was feized. The boors, as they brought him away, carried off from the plain feveral of the enemy's horfes. The Gover-nor of *Exilles* being informed of the boldnefs of Captain *Bourcet*, ordered two hundred and fifty chofen men to march after him with all fpeed, and feize the bridge of *Sezannes*, which *Bourcet* was obliged to pafs in his way to *Briançon*, with his fmall party, his prifoner and his booty. *Bour-cet* being overtaken, made as if he would retire. He came up the mountain from whence he had juft defcended, as if with a defign to throw himfelf into the *Pragelas.* The enemy, in order to follow him clofer, and to intercept him, gained the other fide of the river, leaving only thirty grenadeers to guard the bridge. Where-

upon

1709. upon Captain *Bourcet*, who had forefeen this, returned, fell upon this guard, flew ten of the
grenadeers, made as many prifoners, and paffed
the bridge without much lofs or refiftance.

The Governour of *Exilles*, being vexed at the
affront he had received, came next day to that
mountain at the head of three thoufand men;
from thence he faw the troops which guarded
Briançon: he came down and went up two feveral times in order to draw the *French* to him.
Mr. *Dillon* expecting he would return a third
time, fent the boors, who having retrenched
themfelves without noife, and being fupported
by fome infantry in ambufcade behind the fame
mountain, fell fo opportunely upon the enemy,
that they killed three hundred of them, made
feventy prifoners, and put the reft to flight.

Count *Thaun* having fortified the caftle of
Faverges, and received his artillery and his
horfe, thought of attempting fome enterprife.
Marfhal *Berwick* had left five battalions and three
fquadrons near *Chamberi*, and had fent Mr. *Pra-
des* towards *Seiffel*, with five regiments of dragoons, to fecure the paffes of the *Rhone* and of
Bugey, as well as twelve hundred foot to join
the militia of that country, and the militia of
Breffe. So that Count *Thaun*, feeing the Marfhal's army was greatly weakened, made all his
efforts to attack him in his camp at *Franchin*;
but not being able to fucceed, by reafon of the
manner in which the Marfhal was pofted, he
refolved to repafs the mountains with his army,

before

before the snow, which began to fall, had intirely *1709.* shut up his passage.

He accordingly ordered all the avenues to be occupied for that purpose, in order to secure his retreat; and on the twenty second of *September* he ordered the Counts *Prela* and *Mattigny* to march with their detachments, the former to the camp of *Faverges,* and the latter to that of *Conflans.* On the same day, Count *Prela* set out from *Annecy.* On the twenty third his army decamped from *Faverges*; Count *Prela* at the head of the cavalry, and Count *St. Remy,* who commanded the infantry, making the rear-guard. Count *Thaun,* who had gone to the camp of *Conflans,* sent from thence Count *Vermont* to pass mount *Cenis* with a strong detachment, and join the body of troops commanded by Count *Rebender.* At the same time he sent Baron *Klippel* at the head of a hundred horse and a hundred and fifty foot to reconnoitre Marshal *Berwick.* In his march he met a party of gre- nadeers, whom he defeated, but he could make none of them prisoners.

On the twenty fourth, the whole army be- gan to march, and passed safely, though not without fatigue, the mountain of the little *St. Bernard*; from whence they moved to *Aosta.* The *Piedmontese* troops entered *Piedmont*; the infantry was lodged at *Turin, Alexandria, Va- lencia* and *Coni.* The infantry belonging to the Emperor and the King of *Prussia* encamped at *St. Balin,* and the horse at *Trin*; the Duke of

Savoy

1709. *Savoy* sent some troops to *Suza*, and all the frontier places, till the winter quarters were assigned.

General *Thaun* having continued some time at the Court of *Savoy*, and visited the towns of *Piedmont*, set out for *Milan*, where he arrived on the sixth of *November:* and from thence he sent orders for putting the *Imperial* troops into winter quarters.

Thus ended the mighty projects which the Allies had designed to put in execution in *Dauphiny* and the neighbouring provinces. Count *Thaun* durst never attack any post ; so just were the measures which Marshal *Berwick* had taken. He did not so much as attempt to retake *Chambery*, though that town was defenceless. It is true, he put in practice all imaginable stratagems of war, in order to deceive Marshal *Berwick*; but the latter was never at a loss what course to take, and made it his chief point to cover *Briançon*. Thus the enemy's army, so superior to that of *France*, and which threatned to carry every thing before it, was obliged to return to *Piedmont*, after having abandoned *Annecy*, and the other posts which they had possessed during that summer.

This is one of the most glorious campaigns of Marshal *Berwick*, and would alone procure him the reputation of a great General. By the like exploits Marshal *Turenne* attained so high a reputation ; and that which Marshal *Berwick* acquired on this occasion, secured to him the esteem

and

and veneration of all *Europe*.   The Plan he fol- 1709.
lowed for covering *France* on that side has always
been accounted a master-piece; and his conduct
in this campaign was not only highly applauded,
but became a rule to subsequent Generals in that
province.

The enemy having retired, he sent back the
militia of *Bugey*, and put the regular troops into
winter quarters; except some regiments which
were ordered for *Germany* to reimplace the
troops sent by Marshal *Harcourt* to the *Sarre*.
He left in *Savoy* during the winter twelve squadrons and twenty battalions, and in *Dauphiny*
eight squadrons and forty battalions.   He afterwards set out for *Versailles*, leaving the command
of the army to Count *Medavi*.

Soon after he arrived at Court, the King sent
him to *Flanders* to assist Marshal *Boufflers*, who
commanded there since the battle of *Malplaquet*,
where Marshal *Villars* had been wounded. *

He

* The Battle of *Malplaquet*, or *Blaregnies*, was fought on the
eleventh of *September*.   The Allies were commanded by Prince
Eugene and the Duke of *Marlborough*; and the *French* by the
Marshals *Villars* and *Boufflers*.   Each army consisted of about
one hundred thousand men, the finest troops that ever were seen.
The *French* were posted most advantagiously in two woods, where
they had cut down the trees, and rendered the attack extremely
difficult: in several places they were covered by a triple intrenchment, and all the intervals were planted with artillery.   However, after an attack which lasted six hours, the Confederates
forced their strong intrenchments, beat them out of the field of
battle, and won a very remarkable and glorious victory; but at
the expence of the lives of a great many brave men.   It is
thought that the *French* lost here about fifteen thousand men,

                    killed,

1709. He arrived in the army while the enemy were befieging *Mons*. He viewed the banks of the *Sambre* with Marfhal *Boufflers*, from *Maubeuge* as far as *Charleroy*, where Marfhal *Boufflers* left him, and fent him on the twentieth of *October* nineteen battalions and twenty fquadrons to form an intrenched camp.

After the reducing of *Mons*, the enemy's army feparated and went into winter quarters: whereupon Marfhal *Berwick*, to whom Marfhal *Boufflers* had left the command of the army when he returned to Court, received the diftribution of the winter quarters, difmiffed the General Officers, and fent the troops to the places affigned. He only referved a body of foot, whom he left in the camp at *Maubeuge*, to finifh an intrenched camp which he had begun to make in the neighbourhood of that place, upon an eminence which commanded it. He afterwards returned to the Court, which he found wholly occupied with negociations of peace that had been brought again upon the carpet. He had left the command in *Flanders*, during the winter, to Count *Artagnan*, whom the King had lately made Marfhal of *France*, and who took the name of his family, which is *Montefquiou*.

killed, wounded, or taken prifoners; and the Allies have owned that this victory coft them eighteen thoufand men, killed, or wounded. Among the latter was Prince *Eugene*, who was wounded flightly on the head: the prefent Duke of *Argyle* received feveral mufquet-fhots through his cloaths and perriwig: the late Prince of *Orange* had two horfes killed under him; and among the flain were many officers of diftinction.

In

In the beginning of the year 1710 the King 1710. had named for his Plenipotentiaries, Mr. *Huxelles* and the Abbot *Polignac*; but they could not set out till the fifth of *March* for *Gertruydenberg*, near *Breda*, the place agreed upon for the preliminary conferences. We were soon convinced that the Allies did not desire a peace, that their intention was to continue the war, and that the time of seeing an end put to it was not yet come.

In the mean while, though the King had named Plenipotentiaries for treating of a peace with the Allies, his Majesty made all the necessary preparations for sending his armies betimes into the field, and appointed their Generals. As the King wanted all his troops to oppose the Allies, and stop the progress they had too much reason to expect, he was obliged to recall the *French* troops which were in *Spain*. His Majesty likewise left no *French* General in that Kingdom; for it was only towards the end of the campaign that he sent thither the Duke of *Vendôme* to retrieve the affairs of King *Philip*, who, by the battle of *Saragossa*, had lost *Castile*, and was obliged to fly before the Arch-duke, who once more being master of the Capital, had went thither, and caused himself to be proclaimed King of *Spain*.

The Duke of *Vendôme* was no sooner arrived, than with the same troops which had been defeated, and were much disabled, he obliged the Arch-duke to quit *Madrid*, where he settled

the

1710. the King of *Spain*, recovered the kingdom of *Caſtile*, and by the victory of *Villa Vitioſa*, one of the moſt compleat which he ever obtained, forced the Arch-duke to retire with all ſpeed to *Barcelona*. A ſingle man occaſioned this ſurprizing ſucceſs: ſo important it is to have Generals who not only deſerve by their ability and valour the confidence of the officers and ſoldiers, but likewiſe know how to gain it by their winning behaviour.

Marſhal *Villars* being cured of his wound, and able to act, the King gave him the command of the army in *Flanders*, having under him Marſhal *Monteſquiou*. Marſhal *Harcourt* was ſent to the *Rhine*, and with him Marſhal *Beſons*. The Duke of *Noailles* went into *Rouſſillon*, and Marſhal *Berwick* was at firſt deſigned for *Dauphiny*: but as he was preparing to ſet out, the King ſent for him to acquaint him, that being informed the enemy beſieged *Doway*, he was reſolved to make them abandon that enterprize; for which purpoſe, he had ordered Marſhal *Villars* to force their retrenchments, and to relieve the place; but that being unwilling to neglect any thing in ſo important an occaſion, the confidence he put in him did not permit him to chooſe any other perſon for aſſiſting Marſhal *Villars* in that expedition, and for hindering him to put any thing to hazard, if there was any impoſſibility, or if too many obſtacles muſt be ſurmounted to ſucceed in it: that as Marſhal *Villars* was already ſet out, he muſt follow him immediately,

mediately, that they might concert together what could or could not be undertaken: however, that before his departure, he would acknowledge the real fervices which he daily rendered to the kingdom, and tranfmit the proofs of it to pofterity. Whereupon his Majefty ordered Letters Patents to be drawn, which were afterwards regiftred in the Parliament of *Paris* on the twenty third of this month of *May*, by which the King erected in his favour, and after him in favour of his eldeft fon, whom he had by a fecond marriage, and of his defcendants, or failing them, in favour of his other male iffue, the eftate of *Warty*, near *Clermont* in the *Beauvoifis*, into a Duchy and Peerdom, under the name of *Fitz-James*.

Marfhal *Berwick* accordingly fet out for *Flanders*; and this was the fituation in which he found the affairs of that country: The Allies were employed in befieging *Doway*. Marfhal *Montefquiou*, who had been all winter in *Flanders*, brought together the troops of *France*, which came from the *Mofelle*, *Franche-Comte*, and *Dauphiny*. Marfhal *Villars* being arrived at *Peronne* on the fourteenth, where Marfhal *Montefquiou* had joined him, they had fet out on the nineteenth for *Cambray* with the King of *England*, who made likewife this campaign under the name of the Chevalier *St. George*, and with the Duke of *Bourbon*. Marfhal *Berwick* arrived there on the twenty firft. The fame day, and the day following, fixty fix battalions

and

1710. and eighty five squadrons, which had met at *Peronne*, set out for *Cambray*.

Thefe troops were followed by thofe which had been in winter quarters upon the frontier, and thofe which came from the remote provinces; fo that by the twenty third, the army confifted of a hundred and fifty three battalions, and two hundred and fixty two fquadrons. Marfhal *Villars* advanced the left wing of that army towards *Arleux*, and having feized the caftle of *Oify*, which was about half a mile from Count *Tilly*'s quarters, being feparated by the river of *Sanffe*, feveral cannons were fired on both fides. At the fame time, he ordered fome bridges to be laid over the *Scheld* below *Bouchain*, as if he had a defign to encamp between that river and the *Scarpe*, upon the road from *Doway* to *Valenciennes*: but this was only a feint; for the enemy were not only covered by a brook and moraffes, but had likewife fortified all the avenues of that fide with good retrenchments.

As foon as the Generals of the enemy had notice that the troops of *France* were upon their march, they endeavoured to prevent our relieving the place they attacked. For this purpofe, they marked out two camps, one in the plain, upon the road to *Valenciennes*, on the right of the *Scarpe*, and the other on the right of the fame river, in the plain between *Vitry* and *Lens*. They ufed all poffible diligence in fortifying thefe two camps by ftrong lines, broad and deep, flanked by redans, and by crofs batteries.

Prince

Prince *Eugene* and the Duke of *Marlborough* 1710. advanced with a ftrong body of horfe towards *Arras*, both to view the ground by which Marfhal *Villars* might come on the fide of *Lens*, and to furprize fome fquadrons which encamped under that place; but thefe fquadrons having had notice of their approach by the fire of fome cannon, had time to retire. Two days after, another detachment of twenty five fquadrons, commanded by the Prince of *Auvergne*, advanced again towards *Arras*: this was to favour the efcape of Cardinal *Bouillon*, that Prince's uncle, who being wearied with his difgrace, retired into *Holland*, from whence he went afterwards to *Rome*.

On the fame day, nine thoufand men of the Prince of *Heffe Caffel* arrived in the enemy's army, and brought with them dry forage from *Lifle* and *Tournay*. The Allies employed fix thoufand pioneers in their retrenchment, from *Vitry* on the *Scarpe*, as far as *Montigny* near *Henen-Lietard*, which took up a ground near two leagues in extent; they made there, befides the ordinary redans, feveral redoubts furnifhed with cannon. Thofe of their troops which encamped between *Tournay* and *Lifle*, under the command of General *Dorpt*, for the fecurity of their convoys, had orders, on the twenty·fifth of *May*, to joyn the great army, as well as the garrifons in *Ghent*, *Deynfe*, *Aeth*, *Courtray*, *Menin*, *Lifle*, and *Tournay*.

The

1710. The Duke of *Marlborough*, who had taken his quarters at *Flines*, upon the left of the lower *Scarpe*, removed to *Geuvelin*, between *Arleux* and *Doway*. Count *Tilly*, who had his at *Lalain*, above *Doway*, went to *Arleux*. Prince *Eugene* went to *Vitry*, and General *Fagel* kept his poſt between *Serin* and *Lalain*, in the circumvallation; he was ordered to obſerve the *French* troops, which had continued on the ſide of *Bouchain*.

After this new diſpoſition of the enemy, they held a council of war, wherein it was reſolved, that in caſe a battle ſhould happen, Prince *Eugene* ſhould command the right, conſiſting of the *Imperial* troops; the Duke of *Marlborough* the left, with the *Engliſh*; and Count *Tilly* ſhould remain in the center, with the troops which were in the pay of *Holland*. Orders were given for making the neceſſary bridges over the *Scarpe*, from *Vitry* as far as the circumvallation, to bring over the troops more eaſily, wherever they ſhould be wanted.

Whilſt the enemy took all theſe precautions to prevent the relief of *Doway*, Marſhal *Villars*, after the feint above mentioned, began to march on the twenty fifth with his whole army, and advanced on the twenty ſixth and twenty ſeventh on the ſide of *Arras*. He ordered eight bridges to be laid over the *Scarp* between *Athies* and the abby of *Avenes*. On the twenty eighth and twenty ninth, he paſſed that river without meeting any diſturbance, except from a detachment

of

of *Huſſars*, who having made an attempt upon 1710.
his rear-guard, were cut in pieces, and left forty
priſoners. After the army had paſſed, the Marſhal diſtributed amongſt his troops powder and
ball, with bread for four days. As ſoon as the
enemy had notice of this march, Prince *Eugene*
ordered their right wing to file off to the moraſs
of *Montigny*, near *Henin-Lietard*; and as he
moved from *Vitry*, the Duke of *Marlborough*
advanced with his army, whoſe right joined the
left of that of Prince *Eugene*. The *Dutch* army,
which had lain on the right of the *Scarp*, likewiſe paſſed that river, and went to take poſſeſſion of the poſt aſſigned them between the *Impe-
rialiſts* and the *Engliſh*.

On the ſame day, being the thirtieth of *May*,
ten *Palatine* regiments arrived in the enemy's
camp from the country of *Juliers*, and were
placed to guard *Pont-a-Vendin*. Brigadeer *Cham-
brier* was ordered to abandon the poſts of *Com-
mines* and *Warwick*, and to ſend the two battalions which were there to *Liſle* and *Menin*.
Next day, the enemy had joined by a retrenched line all the advanced redoubts they had already
made; and they planted cannon from *Vitry* as
far as *Montigny*.

The enemy's army now conſiſted of an hundred and twenty thouſand men, excluſive of the
troops employed in the ſiege, of thoſe which
guarded *Pon-a-Vendin*, and the garriſons of towns.
The whole infantry was in one line, and extended from *Vitry* to *Montigny*: the horſe were in

two

 two lines, seven hundred paces behind their in-fantry.

The army of *France* marched in two co-lumns, Marſhal *Villars* and Marſhal *Monteſquiou* being in the center, Marſhal *Berwick* in the right, and Marſhal *d'Arco*, a *Bavarian*, in the left. This army advanced into the plain of *Lens* in order of battle, within cannon-reach of the enemy's retrenchments, having their right at *Fampoux* and their left at *Noyelles*. Marſhal *Villars*, with Marſhal *Berwick*, went immedi-ately to view the enemy's camp, which they found in the order we have deſcribed. Marſhal *Berwick* judged that their ſituation was ſo advan-tageous, that he told Marſhal *Villars* it would be hazarding too much to attack them: that how-ever, without relying upon his opinion, it would be prudent to conſult the General Officers upon ſo delicate a conjuncture, wherein the leaſt falſe ſtep might be attended with fatal conſequences. Whereupon a council of war was held, and all the General Officers were of Marſhal *Berwick*'s opinion, and agreed that it was impoſſible to force an army ſo ſuperior, and ſo well retrench-ed; and that by attempting it, they would evi-dently hazard the loſs of the King's army.

This Council was held on the fourth of *June:* after which Marſhal *Villars* ordered the general to be beat at noon, and after having been four hours in the enemy's preſence, he marched to-wards *Arras*, in the ſame order in which his army was then formed. He only removed
about

about half a league from the enemy; his right 1710.
was on the *Scarpe*, near *Garverelle*; his left towards *Auney*, near *Lens*; and his centre in *Fela-
che*. He had expected that the enemy would
have sent out some detachments to charge his
rear-guard, and was prepared to receive them;
but as their sole design was to make themselves
masters of *Doway*, they would not engage in an
action which they saw the *French* army wished
for.

. Marshal *Berwick*'s commission ended as soon
as it appeared that there would be no action; he
accordingly set out for *Verfailles*, and informed
the King of the situation of the armies in *Flanders*, and of the impossibility of relieving *Doway*.
He gave his Majesty a particular account of all
the stratagems which Marshal *Villars* had employed to make the enemy quit their retrenchments, and to bring them to an engagement,
without having been able to succeed in them.
The King sent him afterwards to head his army
in *Dauphiny*.

He was to oppose the Duke of *Savoy*; but as
that Prince had been indisposed, and besides continued to be dissatisfied with the Court of *Vienna*,
his troops and those of the Allies under the command of General *Thaun*, after having advanced
in the month of *July* towards the heights of
Oulx, *Queyras*, and *Barcelonnette*, did not attempt
to descend into the Country; and doubtless the
just measures taken by Marshal *Berwick*, in
order to render all their attempts upon *Dauphi-*

ny

1710. *ny* ineffectual, greatly contributed to keep the enemy inactive.

He had under his command sixty battalions and thirty six squadrons. The greatest part of his horse lay at first in the *Tarentese* and the *Genoese*; and his infantry extended from the *Morienne* by the *Valonne* and the *Galibier*, as far as *Briançon*, from whence it run into the valleys of *Queyras* and *Barcelonnette*. It formed besides a line from *Briançon* as far as *Guilleftre*, and from thence towards *Provence* as far as the *Var*.

The enemy spread a report that they designed to make a second attempt upon *Provence*, being favoured by the *English* and *Dutch* fleet which was in the *Mediterranean*, and had lately made an attempt upon the Port of *Cette* in *Languedoc*, of which we shall speak hereafter. To prevent this, Marshal *Berwick* posted nine battalions, with the regiments of dragoons of the Dauphin and of *Firmacon*, to dispute with them the passage of the *Var* below *St. Laurens*, and disposed every thing in such a manner that upon the first motion the enemy should make on that side, he could march thither by the roads of *Guilleftre, Tournon, Colmars, Eftremos* and *Grace*, where he had magazines prepared for the subsiftance of his troops. Those which were in *Savoy* were to march thither by another road, except the seven battalions which were to be posted in the *Tarantese* and in the *Morienne*, and

fix

fix other battalions which were appointed to guard the retrenchments near *Briançon.*

Mean while, Count *Thaun* feized on the twenty fifth of *July* the poft of *Arche*, and made thofe who defended it prifoners; the *French* abandoned the pafs of *Var* on the twenty feventh, at the approach of the enemy, who pofted themfelves at *Figliofa.* Afterwards fourteen of their battalions advanced to the heights of the *Vachete*, to alarm that town, whilft the main body of their army, which was faid to amount to twenty thoufand men, went to befiege *Caftellet*, a fmall Caftle, fituate upon a very fteep rock, at the entrance of the valley of *Barcelonnette*; as if they had intended to open their way on that fide into *Provence.*

But in this attempt they did not fucceed, and notwithftanding the fuperiority of their troops over thofe of *France*, they could effect nothing: they found that Marfhal *Berwick* oppofed them on all fides. Towards the end of *July* the Marfhal was informed by a Courier difpatched to him from the Duke of *Roquelaure*, who commanded in *Languedoc*, and Mr. *Bafville*, Intendant of that province, that the enemy had landed fome troops at the Port of *Cette*, of which they had already made themfelves mafters, that they threatned to penetrate farther, and to advance into the *Sevennes*, in order to encourage the fanaticks, and renew the former difturbances; that as there were no troops in that province to oppofe them, they intreated the Marfhal of

Berwick

1710. *Berwick* to come with all speed to their af-fiftance.

This defcent, upon which the enemy had founded great hopes, and which made fo much noife in *Europe*, was managed by the Sieur *de Saiffan*, a *French* gentleman, who had under-taken to put it in execution, and actually com-manded the troops which had landed.

The Duke of *Roquelaure* had likewife fent into *Rouffillon* to demand fuccours of the Duke of *Noailles*. But Marfhal *Berwick*, who faw into the enemy's defign in this enterprize, and knew that it was of much more confequence to pre-vent their entering *Dauphiny* and *Provence*, was unwilling to weaken his army, which was al-ready inferior in number to that of the enemy: he accordingly wrote to the Duke of *Roquelaure*, that the fituation of affairs did not permit him to fend any detachment from his army, with-out expofing the provinces of *Dauphiny* and *Pro-vence* to a much greater danger than that which threatened *Languedoc*; efpecially as the Duke of *Noailles*, who was in *Rouffillon*, and nearer to him, not having the fame reafons, might more eafily and fooner fend him affiftance.

In effect, the Duke of *Noailles* brought thither fome troops and heavy cannon with unparallel-ed diligence. The Sieur *Seiffan* was forced to retire, and to reimbark with all fpeed.

The reft of the campaign in *Dauphiny* was very inconfiderable, nothing remarkable having happened. The troops on both fides were fent

to

to their winter quarters, except a detachment of 1710. thirty fix battalions and twenty eight fquadrons of *French* troops, which were fent to *Spain*.

As foon as the march of thefe troops was known in *Turin*, it was believed that Marfhal *Berwick* had countermanded them. And as it was added, that the *French* caufed a great quantity of bifket to be baked at *Grenoble* and fort *Barreaux*, the Duke of *Savoy* apprehended that we had a defign upon fort *Exilles*. For this reafon he ordered that the troops which came to be put in garrifon in *Turin*, and the neighbouring places, fhould immediately return to their pofts: but being afterwards informed that the detachments of the *French* army did actually march towards *Rouffillon* or *Navarre*, he ordered each garrifon to return to the place which had been allotted to it. The *French* had only nine battalions in *Savoy*, but feven more were expected, with twelve fquadrons from the upper *Rhine*. Marfhal *Berwick* affigned them their quarters; after which, giving the command to Count *Medavi*, he fet out towards the end of *October*. Upon his journey he met the Duke of *Noailles*, with whom he had fome conferences in the houfe Mr. *Angervilliers*, Intendant of *Dauphiny*, concerning a project which had been formed for fubduing *Catalonia*.

He arrived at Court in the beginning of *November*, and gave the King an account of what had paffed in *Dauphiny*. His Majefty was highly pleafed with his conduct. In effect, ever

C c

fince

1710. since Marſhal *Berwick* commanded in that country, all the projects of the enemy for invading it were rendered abortive, though their forces were much ſuperior to his.   During three campaigns they did not gain one inch of ground; the manner in which he diſpoſed his troops, the poſts he occupied, his great ſagacity in diſcovering the ſtratagems which were employed to deceive him, the activity with which he moved every where, the good order he always maintained by a ſtrict diſcipline, his extraordinary vigilance, which protected him from being at any time ſurprized, did him as much real honour as the gaining of victories.   There have been few Generals under whom the officers have learned the art of war, ſo well as under Marſhal *Berwick*; all his ſteps, all his orders, were ſo many inſtructive leſſons, both for officers and ſoldiers.

We have ſaid above, that in the beginning of this year his Majeſty had created him a Duke and Peer.   On the eleventh of *December* he was ſworn in that quality; and afterwards he took his ſeat in Parliament as Peer of *France.*

1711. In the month of *January* the King appointed Marſhal *Villars* to command the army in *Flanders,* and under him Marſhal *Monteſquiou*; Marſhal *Harcourt* to command in *Germany,* having under him Marſhal *Beſons*; and the Duke of *Noailles* to command in *Rouſſillon,* where he beſieged and took *Gironne,* notwithſtanding the rains and the ſevereſt weather.   After the reduction of this place, his Catholick Majeſty

made

made him Grandee of *Spain* of the firſt claſs. 1711.
Marſhal *Berwick* was again appointed to command the army in *Dauphiny*.

In the beginning of this year died Marſhal
Choiſeüil, whoſe valour, wiſe conduct, and ſenſe
of honour, had made him juſtly eſteemed. He
died on the fifteenth of *March*, aged ſeventy
eight years. He was Dean (or the ancienteſt)
of the Marſhals of *France*.

This death was followed by another much
more conſiderable, which put the whole kingdom under the greateſt conſternation. The heir
of the Crown, the Dauphin, died of the ſmall
pox at *Meudon*, on the fourteenth of *April*, aged
forty nine years five months and four days, being born at *Fontainebleau* on the firſt of *November* 1661. This Prince was endowed with many
great qualities, and gave proofs of his valour upon
all occaſions when he commanded armies; but
good-nature, ſweetneſs of temper, and a bene-
volent diſpoſition, conſtituted his diſtinguiſhing
character, and had endeared him to the whole
nation. His reſpect and attachment to the King
were boundleſs. He is perhaps the only inſtance
of a Prince, who, when far advanced in life,
has been content to live like a private man. He
renounced the Crown of *Spain* in favour of the
Duke of *Anjou*, his ſecond ſon; being as indul-
gent a father, as he was a dutiful ſon. He
choſe rather to ſee his father and his ſon reign,
than to reign himſelf.

 The

1711. The Emperor *Joseph* I. died in the same month, on the night between the sixteenth and seventeenth, and of the same disease, aged only thirty three years. This Prince was much more active and interprising than his father *Leopold*, or the Emperor *Charles* VI, his brother, who succeeded him. The Electors 'of *Cologne* and *Bavaria*, the Pope himself, and the other Princes of *Italy* felt the most violent effects of his imperious and overbearing temper.

It was at first believed that the Death of the Emperor would occasion some change of affairs in *Europe*; but on the twelfth of *October* the Archduke *Charles* of *Austria*, who was in the twenty seventh year of his age, being chosen Emperor, *Europe* continued in the same posture. This new Emperor gave great hopes: he was of a sweet and peaceful temper, full of equity and justice in the minutest affairs; but he suffered himself for some time to be guided by his Council, which was violent and haughty. In this election no regard was had to the laws of the Empire, and the rules prescribed by the golden bull, which require that all the Electors be summoned upon such an occasion; but those of *Cologne* and *Bavaria*, having joined with *France*, were not summoned to this election, and had therefore protested against the validity of it, as well as because the Duke of *Hanover* was admitted to give his vote; for the raising of a new Electorate by the Emperor *Leopold* in favour of that Prince, was still contested by some of the Electors. All that

passed

paſſed upon this occaſion, ſhews that Princes 1711.
only ſubject themſelves to laws and regulations,
ſo far as it ſerves their intereſt, or when they are
not in a condition to break through them.

Notwithſtanding this violation of the rules of
the golden bull, the Empire applauded the
choice which the Electors had made. That
Prince merited the Imperial Crown both by his
virtues and illuſtrious birth; and beſides his perſonal qualities, all the rules of policy required
that the Electoral College ſhould prefer him to
other competitors.

We have ſeen that in the preceeding years the
Duke of *Savoy*, being diſcontent with the Emperor, had alledged ſeveral pretences for not taking
the field. During the winter the Allies uſed
their utmoſt endeavours to appeaſe him, and induce him to head his army this year. For this
purpoſe the Queen of *England* ſent the Earl of
Peterborough to *Turin*, where he arrived in the
month of *May* : being admitted to an audience
of this Prince, he gave him all ſort of aſſurances
in the name of the Court of *Vienna*, that he
ſhould have the command in chief of the Imperial and auxiliary troops in *Italy*; that the confirmation and ratification of the ceſſion of lands,
which had been made to him in that country,
ſhould be granted to him; and that the diſtrict
of *Vigevano* ſhould likewiſe be yielded to him at
the peace, agreeably to the deſign of the Emperor *Leopold.*

C c 3

After-

1711. The Earl of *Peterborough* affifted afterwards at a great council which was held at *La Venerie* in the prefence of the Duke of *Savoy*, with the Minifters of the Emperor, *England, Portugal,* and *Holland,* where meafures were taken for the enfuing campaign. Afterwards, the Duke of *Savoy* declared that he would command his army in perfon, and prefently gave orders for preparing his equipage, and affembling his troops: they were to be much more numerous than thofe of the year preceeding, and confequently far fuperior to thofe which the King of *France* could fend to oppofe him.

Marfhal *Berwick* fet out from *Verfailles* on the twenty fecond of *May*, paffed through *Lyons* on the thirtieth, and arrived next day at *Grenoble*. Count *Medavi* had begun to fortify fome paffes on the fide of *Piedmont*, and had taken particular care to put thofe of *Tornus* in a good condition. Of the troops which had been appointed to march into *Alface*, the King had countermanded twelve battalions, and ordered them to march towards *Piedmont*, as foon as it was known that the Duke of *Savoy* brought a numerous army to *Dauphiny*. We had in thofe parts fixty five battalions.

The great quantities of fnow which yet covered the mountains retarded the Duke of *Savoy*'s army. On the eighth of *June* the regiment of *Auftray* arrived at *Villeftenon*, and marched on the ninth to *Airafeo*, where the Imperial cavalry had their rendezvous. The Imperial foot to the number of fourteen

fourteen thousand two hundred men, arrived on 1711.
the twentieth and twenty first at *St. Benigno,*
near *Chivas:* Velt-marshal Count *Harach,* who
commanded it, set out for *Turin* on the twelfth,
after having received the Duke of *Savoy*'s orders.
The cavalry of his Royal Highness encamped on
the fifteenth at *Vigon:* Count *Pressa,* who had
the command of it, set out likewise from *Turin*
for the camp, where the regiment of the Duke
of *Savoy*'s guards had arrived the day before.

Whilst these troops arrived, Marshal *Berwick* began to advance his towards the frontiers.
He sent some of the battalions which were in
Savoy towards *Briançon,* and took his quarters
at *Guilleſtre.* Count *Daun* came on the twentieth from *Milan* to *Turin,* from whence Mr.
Rebender set out to command in *Suſa.*

When the troops which were to be commanded by his Royal Highness, had arrived in
the places assigned them, the Barons *Schulemberg* and *Wachtendonck,* and Count *Hautois,*
marched towards *Val d'Aoſta,* with some detachments of horse and foot, being followed by
some field artillery, and by the Marquis *Viſconti*
at the head of the horse. The whole infantry
began likewise to march on the same day. Baron
Schulemberg was ordered to ſtop at the town of
Aoſta, and the Marquis *Viſconti* to continue at
Panquette.

The Duke of *Savoy,* accompanied by the
Prince of *Piedmont* his eldeſt son, who made his
firſt campaign, though he was yet only thirteen

 years

1711. years of age, arrived at *Suza* with Count *Daun*, who commanded the Imperial troops. The main of his army continued in that place. The Imperial troops confifted of thofe of *Brandenburgh, Anhalt-Deffau, Saxe-Gotha,* and of fome other *German* Princes in the pay of *England* and *Holland.* The Duke of *Savoy,* upon reviewing his army, found it confifted of thirty five thoufand men; his horfe efpecially were far fuperior to that of Marfhal *Berwick:* the latter, who was obliged to defend a country above thirty leagues in extent, endeavoured only to preferve the moft important places, as *Briançon, Grenoble,* fort *Barreaux,* and all the paffes of *Dauphiny,* leaving *Savoy* much lefs defended, becaufe the ravages which the Duke of *Savoy*'s troops might commit there, would be at the expence of his own country.

On the fixth, at midnight, the fon of Count *Daun,* and Baron *Regal,* Majors-general, fet out from *Suza* with a ftrong detachment of foot, in order to feize the advanced pofts; and as the principal defign of the Duke of *Savoy* was to make himfelf mafter of the camp of *Briançon,* upon his departure from *Suza,* he left there the Counts *la Roux, Prafla,* and *Caunitz,* with a body of troops, under pretence of guarding the lines, and the towns of *Exilles, Suza,* and *Fene-ftrelles;* but in effect to feize that poft, if Marfhal *Berwick* fhould take away the garrifon. On the fame day he encamped at the great Crofs, under mount *Cenis,* with Count *Daun,* having

left

left Count *Velmerode* in the plain of *Piedmont*, 1711.
with a detachment of horfe, and part of the
field artillery. On the feventh, he marched to
Termignon, where he continued for fome time,
and was informed that Marfhal *Berwick*, who
had advanced to *Guilleftre* with part of his army, had left that place on the firft of *July*, and
had marched towards *Briançon*, without having
ungarrifoned that place, as the Prince had expected.

Whereupon the Duke of *Savoy* decamped
from *Termignon*, and pofted himfelf at *Ignes*.
He ordered the grenadeers of his army to advance to *Pralonga*, while Baron *Regal* continued his march to *Poffel*.

In this interval General *Schulemberg*, who was
gone, as has been faid above, by *Val d'Aofta*,
paffed over the little *St. Bernard*. Two *French*
battalions, a regiment of horfe, and one of dragoons, which were at *St. Maurice*, retired towards *Montieres* as foon as they perceived them,
according to the orders they had received from
Marfhal *Berwick*.

When General *Schulemberg* was informed
that the *French* troops had abandoned *Montieres*,
he moved to that fide, and was there joined by
Count *Regal*. The Duke of *Savoy* and Count
Daun arrived there, whilft his army paffed the
heights of *Venois*, with incredible fatigue, and
went to encamp at *Pralonga*. They were obliged to make the peafants open the paffages
through the fnow: their troops fuffered greatly
by

1711. by the winds and the cold, and the Prince loft there part of his equipage.

The detachments of the Barons *Schulemberg* and *Regal*, which were ordered to march towards *Conflans*, pofted themfelves between *Roche Sevin* and *la Baftie*. The Duke of *Savoy* and Count *Daun* advanced with an efcort of grenadeers and horfe. At their approach, three regiments of horfe and dragoons, and fome *French* infantry, abandoned *Conflans*, paffed the river *Arli*, and broke the bridge. The *Huffars* of the enemy, and a ftrong body of their horfe having likewife paffed that river, in order to charge the rear-guard of the *French*, there happened a very brifk fkirmifh, wherein the latter made it appear, that the ftrength of a body of troops confifts not fo much in the number, as the valour of the foldiers.

The Duke of *Savoy* afterwards caufed this detachment to encamp at *Conflans*, and fent orders to the Marquis *Vifconti* and Baron *Schulemberg* to come to that place: the main body of his army moved to *Portes*, and next day *Montieres*. On the fame day, the Duke of *Savoy* and Count *Daun* arrived at *Conflans*, where were Count *Daun* the fon, and Count *Hautois*. Sometime after, they were followed by all the grenadeers of the army, and a thoufand horfe. The body of troops which had fet out from *Montieres*, ftopt between *Roche-Sevin* and *la Baftie*. At this time Marfhal *Berwick* was affembling about *Montmelian* the greateft part of his troops which

were

were in *Savoy*. He afterwards posted them from that place as far as *Aiguebelle*, so that they could be brought together in a few hours, if it should be necessary.

Whilst the enemy's army went to encamp at *Petit-cœur*, near *Montieres*, the Duke of *Savoy* was informed that the troops of *France* had abandoned *Faverges* and *Annecy*; whereupon he detached the Marquis *Andorno* with a body of horse and foot, to take possession of these two posts. As soon as he appeared, the *French* who were in *Annecy* retired to *Seiffel*, the enemy's *Hussars* being unable to disturb their rear-guard. The enemy, after having made a most fatiguing march, continued at *Petit-cœur*, and went afterwards to encamp beyond *Carli*. The Duke of *Savoy* immediately posted in the pass of *Samia* a detachment of foot, to preserve the communication of his army with *Faverges*.

On the sixteenth, he sent out in the evening two strong detachments, one under the command of Baron *Zumjungen*, and the other under that of Mr. *Arnheim*.

The Marquis *Visconti* arrived next day at *Bastia*, with the horse, and the day after at *Conflans*, where the Marquis *Ourabia*, Minister of the Arch-duke, and Messieurs *Chetwynd* and *Vandermeer*, the *English* and *Dutch* Ministers, had arrived the day before. General *Zumjungen* seized the charter-house of *Aillac*, and pursued the troops which were there as far as the heights of the *Thuize*. The latter attempted to gain

another

1711. another height; but having perceived that General *Zumjungen* and the Marquis *Montmelian* lay in their way, they abandoned that road, as well as that of *Chambery*, and marched to *Barreaux*.

Marshal *Berwick* ordered all the troops which were encamped at *Montmelian*, except a small body which he left there, to retire likewise towards fort *Barreaux*. The Duke of *Savoy* sent a reinforcement to General *Zumjungen*, and on the same day set out with Velt-marshal *Daun* to join General *Arnheim*, to be within reach of giving his orders every where. At this time the castle of *Miolans*, which is built upon a rock about a league from *Montmelian*, and was garrisoned by eighty men, surrendred to the enemy.

The Duke of *Savoy* being gone to *St. Peter d'Albigni*, there fell sick; but he soon recovered, and came to *Chambery*, whither he had sent before him six regiments of horse. From thence he went to *Marches*, where his whole army was encamped. In the mean time, Marshal *Berwick* had extended his troops from fort *Barreaux*, as far as *Champarillan*, along the *Iser*, having broken the bridge over that river, and thus rendred it impossible to insult this post. He had posted Mr. *Silly*, a Lieutenant-general, near *la Croix* and *Echelles*, where the latter was intrenched, so that these two passes were secured, and a communication maintained with *Briançon*.

There was another passage more open, and less guarded, on the side of *St. Genis*, where Marshal

Marſhal *Berwick* could only place militia, till 1711.
the arrival of thoſe troops which were to be ſent
to him from ſeveral parts.   Mr. *Dillon* was encamped in the *Maurienne*, on the banks of the
Arc and the *Iſer :* he had planted ſome pieces of
cannon in thoſe places which were fordable ;
and Count *Medavi* continued undiſturbed in his
camp at *Barreaux*.

The Duke of *Savoy* extended his camp on the
fifth of *Auguſt*, from *St. Peter d'Albigny*, as far
as the plain of *Montmelian*.   He took his quarters at the caſtle of *Marches*, from whence he
obſerved Marſhal *Berwick*'s army.   It was believed that this Prince would be obliged at laſt
to retire, becauſe he ſubſiſted his camp with great
difficulty, and at an infinite expence.   His convoys could only arrive by the way of little *St.
Bernard*, where the roads were very much broken
by the rains, which had continued for fifteen
days ; his horſe met with great difficulty in finding forrage in *Savoy :* notwithſtanding, he continued there for a long time, without being diſ-
couraged.

The motions of the enemy greatly alarmed
the *Breſſe* and the *Lioneſe*.   The militia of theſe
provinces were raiſed to line the *Rhone*, and
hinder the enemy's parties from paſſing that river.   Some retrenchments guarded with palli-
ſadoes were made in the avenues of the ſuburb
la Guillotiere, near *Lyons*.

One of the enemy's engineers was taken drawing a plan of the camp of *Barreaux*, and Marſhal

1711. fhal *Berwick* immediately ordered him to be hanged. Their *Huffars* gave fome alarm on the fide of *St. Genis* and *Pont Beauvoifin*, but durft not pafs the river *Quiers*, which feparates *Savoy* from *Dauphiny*. Mr. *Cadrieux* was then encamped at the entry of a pafs, where the enemy might come on the fide of the charter-houfe and fall upon *Mont Fleury*. Marfhal *Berwick* caufed the paffages to be repaired which led from his camp to *Briançon*, that he might be able to march fpeedily from thence in cafe of need. On the fame day, being the fifth of *Auguft*, he received a reinforcement of eight battalions and four fquadrons.

The horfe which the Duke of *Savoy* expected from *Piedmont* arrived at *Conflans* on the ninth of *Auguft*, and on the thirteenth at *Annecy*, from whence they marched next day to *Aix*, two leagues from *Chambery*. Whereupon the Prince held a council of war with his General Officers, and thofe of the Allies, in which were prefent Mr. *Doutabia*, the Emperor's Minifter, and the *Englifh* and *Dutch* Minifters, who had orders from their mafters to follow that Prince, that they might be witneffes of his conduct, and acquaint the Allies with the execution of the projects which they had formed, as well againft *Dauphiny*, as the countries of *Lyons* and *Breffe*.

In this council it was propofed, that fince the feveral detachments which had been fent to penetrate into *Dauphiny* had found all the paffes well-guarded, it was neceffary to attack Marfhal
Berwick

Berwick in his camp at *Barreaux*, before he fhould receive the reinforcements he expected from *Al-face* and *Languedoc*. General *Daun* infifted much upon this propofal, alledging that the Marfhal having difperfed his army into feveral pofts, remote from each other, he could not have above a thoufand or twelve hundred men in his camp; and that if he was attacked by the whole army of the Allies, he muft infallibly be defeated. The Duke of *Savoy* confented to this propofal, on condition that the *German* troops would pave the way and begin the attack; and as thefe troops were moft of them in the pay of *England* and *Holland*, the Minifters of thefe two powers 'confented that they fhould make the vanguard.

The Generals of the troops of *Brandenburg, Anhalt-Deffau, Saxe-Gotha,* and others, affirmed, that upon fuch occafions detachments ought to be drawn out of all the regiments of the feveral nations, that each might fhare in the fatigue and the danger; and propofed that this van-guard fhould be compofed of an hundred men taken from each battalion of the army, fupported by a like number, formed in the fame manner, and that the reft fhould follow as a body of referve.

This opinion not being relifhed by the Duke of *Savoy*, who had at heart the prefervation of his own troops, to guard his country in cafe of any bad fuccefs, they bethought themfelves of fome other enterprize; and for this purpofe the

Duke

1711. Duke decamped on the fifth of *September*, to join a body of horfe and grenadeers who had made themfelves maflers of the defiles in the pafs of *Lauterrel* and *Galibier*, in the road to *Briançon*, with a defign to feize that place: but Marfhal *Berwick* being informed of this, immediately fent a detachment of troops thither, which prevented the Duke of *Savoy* from having any further defign to attack him, and faved *Briançon*.

The officers and engineers, whom that Prince had ordered to view the paffes through which they could make incurfions near *Lyons*, having reported to him that the horfe could attempt nothing on that fide, without being fupported by a confiderable body of the infantry, this enterprize was thought to be dangerous; efpecially as the camp of *Marches* not being very advantageous, and the *French* army being daily reinforced, that infantry could not be fent away without great danger.

In the mean time, the forrage becoming very fcarce in the army of the Allies, they were obliged to bring their provifions from *Piedmont* upon mules: befides, the rains had broke the roads and fwelled the rivers in fuch a manner, that it was impoffible for them to advance; efpecially as they faw that which ever way they turned, they muft have encountered Marfhal *Berwick*. Thus they abandoned their projects. The Duke of *Savoy* quitted the army on the eighteenth of *September*, and repaired to *Turin*,

where,

where, having fome fits of a fever, he took the 1711.
waters of *St. Maurice*.   Perhaps he was informed at the fame time, that the feventeen *French*
fquadrons which came from *Germany* were arrived, and that the eight battalions, which followed them, and had been detained in their
march by the badnefs of the roads, would likewife foon arrive.

However that may be, the two armies remained in the fame fituation, till at laft the enemy thought fit to decamp.   They at firft had a
defign to take their winter quarters in *Savoy*;
but having confidered how fcarce the provifions
were in that country, and how impoffible it
would be to fend any thither, when the little
St. Bernard fhould be covered with fnow, they
changed their defign, and refolved to regain by
degrees the mountains, in order to return to
Piedmont. They fent their horfe towards *Annecy*,
to be refrefhed there for fome days; and their
infantry marched on the eighth of *October*, taking the road to *Conflans*.   At the fame time,
Marfhal *Berwick* decamped to follow the enemy. He marched firft to *St. Jean de Maurienne*,
and afterwards reafcended towards *Galibier*. He
fent orders to Mr. *Silly* to quit his camp at
Echelles, and to occupy that of *Barreaux*,
and upon his departure to difmifs the militia.
The whole cavalry encamped on the eleventh
near *Grenoble*, in order to return to *Savoy*; and
the troops which had come out of *Chambery*
were commanded to return thither. Marfhal

D d

Berwick

1711. *Berwick* ordered likewife the artillery of the camp at *Barreaux* to move towards *Briançon*; and four hundred oxen were brought together for that purpofe.

The enemy's army, in the mean time continuing their march, arrived at *Conflans*; and the Duke of *Savoy* returned to it. The Minifters of the Allies, who had accompanied him, fet out on the fame day from *Conflans*, and arrived on the feventeenth at *Aofta*. His Royal Highnefs began to march on the thirteenth with a detachment of feven battalions and a thoufand men, towards *Suza* by *Mont Iféran*, in order to reinforce a body commanded by Count *La Roque*. This officer, knowing that Marfhal *Berwick* had caufed mount *Cenis* to be occupied by fixteen battalions, and that he had fent another body of troops to *Termignon*, had immediately given notice of this to the Duke of *Savoy*, who ordered him to continue his march by the valley of *Lens*, if he could not pafs by mount *Cenis*. Almoft at the fame time the latter fent word to that Prince, that the *French* had occupied in the *Alps* the pofts called *the four teeth*, that they feemed to have a defign of attacking the retrenchment of *St. Colomban*, and afterwards *Exilles*: whereupon the Duke ordered the reft of his army, under the command of Count *Daun*, to advance towards *Suza*.

General *Schulemberg* continued his march, and afcended the great mount *Cenis*. He gave notice of this to the Duke of *Savoy* by the Chevalier

1711.

lier *St. Julien*, who was informed by the Marquis *Andorno*, whom General *Daun* had dispatched to him, that Count *Zumjungen* with ten battalions followed General *Schulemberg*. At laſt the enemy's horſe decamped on the eighteenth, and returned to *Piedmont* by *Aoſta*. General *Daun* followed them three days after with the reſt of the army. The Duke of *Savoy* ſent the Marquis *Andorno* to *Feneſtrelles*, to order the *Vaudois* to occupy the heights of that place, and ſet out for *Turin*, where he prepared to receive the Arch-duke, who had embarked at *Barcelona* on the twenty ſeventh of *September*. He was there informed that Marſhal *Berwick* had attacked the retrenchments of *St. Colomban*; that his troops had at firſt been repulſed, but that the Marſhal having gone thither himſelf, had made them return to the charge, and had forced Count *La Roque* to abandon the retrenchments, and retire with his troops to the heights of *Jaillon*. Immediately the Duke of *Savoy* ſent orders to Count *Daun* to blow up the fort of *Exilles*, and to cauſe his troops to paſs immediately over the mountains; this he obeyed, after having withdrawn the artillery and the ammunitions, which were conducted to *Suza*. Marſhal *Berwick* ſent out ſeveral detachments to harraſs them in their retreat. Four of their battalions ſuffered very much; and they loſt a great quantity of meal. They had poſted ſome detachments at *Jaillon*, and above *Feneſtrelles*, to favour the troops which filed off by *Val-d'Aoſta* and the little *St. Bernard*.

D d 2

On

          On the twenty fifth of *October* Marſhal *Ber-wick* arrived with part of his army at the camp of *Jouvenceau*, in the valley of *Oulx*. He extended his right as far as *Villars d'Amont*, in the valley of *Pragelas*, where there were abundance of forrage; and after it was conſumed, he brought back his troops into the valley of *Maurienne*, from whence he diſtributed them into winter quarters.

The troops of *Savoy*, having repaſſed the mountains, took their winter quarters in *Piedmont*, and the *Germans* in *Lombardy*. His Royal Highneſs, inſtead of making conſiderable conqueſts, which had been expected from an army much ſtronger than thoſe in the preceeding campaigns, was again obliged to abandon his Duchy of *Savoy*. Marſhal *Berwick* retook *Chambery*, *Annecy*, *Montmelian*, the caſtle of *Miolans*, and other poſts.

This campaign greatly mortified the Allies, and they could hardly refrain from laying the blame on the Duke of *Savoy*. The Emperor had ſatisfied him with reſpect to ſome of his pretentions, in hopes to engage him to penetrate as far as *Lyons*, with a deſign to draw the principal forces of *France* on that ſide, whilſt *Prince Eugene* and the Duke of *Marlborough* ſhould advance through *Alſace* and *Champagne* as far as *Paris*. They had given him an army much more numerous than that under Marſhal *Berwick*, and could not conceive how this General had been able to guard ſo many diſtant paſſes

with.

with fo few troops; and how all the fine pro- 1711.
mifes which the Duke of *Savoy* had made to the
Allies could end in nothing but giving fome flight
alarms to the *Lionefe*, making himfelf mafter of
Chambery, and a part of *Savoy*, confuming the
forrage and provifions of his own country, and
at laft abandoning it for want of fubfiftence, and
fuffering it to be retaken by the *French*.

The Duke of *Berwick*'s prefence being no
longer neceffary in thefe provinces, he returned
to Court, where he was feveral times highly
commended by the King himfelf. No body
was better pleafed to do juftice to merit than
that Prince.

His Majefty gave proofs of this at the death
of Marfhal *Boufflers*; his good nature and generous mind did not fuffer him to conceal his concern and affliction. That illuftrious General deferved thefe proofs of his mafter's kindnefs. He
was active, exact, exceedingly affectionate to
the King's perfon, and zealous for him and the
good of his kingdom. Of this he often gave remarkable proofs: the reader may have obferved
it in thefe Memoirs, where we fpoke of the
fiege of *Lifle* which the Allies undertook in the
year 1708: Marfhal *Boufflers* threw himfelf into that place, there facrificed his health, expofed
his life, and notwithftanding, his little ftrength,
defended the place with fo great courage and
ability, that he held it out near four months
from the opening of the trenches, and made the
enemy purchafe the conqueft of it by the lofs

D d 3

of

1711. of a great part of their army. The fine retreat he made at *Malplaquet*, after Marſhal *Villars* was wounded, did him as much real honour as a victory; and the zeal he expreſſed
for his country upon that occaſion, by ſubmitting
to the orders of Marſhal *Villars*, who was a
younger officer than he, deſerves alone the higheſt
encomiums.

Beſides the glory which Marſhal *Berwick* had
acquired, and which we may ſay he peaceably
enjoyed in the midſt of the Court, he had the
ſatisfaction to ſee his family increaſe by the birth
of a ſon, of whom his conſort was delivered on
the eighth of *September*. He was chriſtened
Henry.

1712. We are now entering upon the year 1712,
which will ever be memorable in the hiſtory of
France, for the ſucceſs of our campaigns, for
the treaty of peace concluded at *Utrecht*, the
death of the Dauphin and Dauphineſs, and of
their eldeſt ſon, and of thoſe two able and experienced Commanders, the Duke of *Vendôme*
and Marſhal *Catinat*. Both theſe Generals had
a particular eſteem and friendſhip for Marſhal
Berwick; the latter eſpecially commended him
for his prudence and ſtrict diſcipline. This encomium does the more honour to the Duke of
Berwick, as it is well known that Marſhal *Catinat* praiſed but ſeldom, and always with great
diſcernment, and without flattery.

The negociations for peace, which were begun long before, were now renewed. Thoſe in
particular

particular with Queen *Anne* were carried on with 1712.
fucceſs; the *Dutch* and all the other Allies, except the Emperor, were forced to come in to
them. The Plenipotentiaries were named, the
place of congreſs appointed; and they were to
meet by the month of *December* in the year
preceeding. It was hoped there would be no
campaign this year, and that the general peace
would be concluded before the feaſon proper for
taking the field.

It is true, theſe hopes had not been vain, if all
the Powers concerned in this treaty had joined in
concluding it with as much fincerity and diligence as the King of *France* and the Queen of
England: but their particular intereſts prevailed
upon this occaſion over the general good; and this
brought on a moſt bloody campaign in *Flanders,*
but one much different from the former campaigns, fince all the advantage and glory was on
the ſide of *France.*

Prince *Eugene* for the Emperor, Penfionary
Heinfius for the *Dutch,* and the Duke of *Marlborough* fupported by the Whigs in *England,* left
nothing unattempted to baffle the meaſures
which were taken for giving peace to *Europe.*

They did not indeed fucceed in this defign;
but by their intrigues they fufpended the conclu-
fion of the peace, and procured to *France,* certainly without intending it, the glory of forcing
all its enemies, except the Emperor, to accept of
a peace; which ought to be accounted a wonderful event, efpecially if we confider the con-

D d 4

dition.

 dition to which *France* was then reduced, and the nature of thofe events which were its re-fource, and faved it.

The Queen of *England* knowing how averfe the Duke of *Marlborough* was to a peace, and the particular intimacy he had with Prince *Eugene*, Penfionary *Heinfius*, and the Whigs, took from him the command of her troops, and gave it to the Duke of *Ormond*. The Duke of *Marlbo-rough* being difcontented, redoubled his intrigues in the Parliament of *England*, employed all his friends to difturb the negociations, and even en-gaged Prince *Eugene* to come to *London*, in or-der to fupport his oppofition, in the name of the Emperor, and endeavour to withdraw the Queen from the meafures fhe purfued. Not-withftanding all the fine promifes made her, and all the pretended advantages which fhe was given to hope both for her felf and her people, the Queen was immovable in the refolution fhe had taken to put an end to the war. Prince *Eugene* continued fome time longer in *London*, expecting to prevail upon the Parliament: but in this he did not fucceed, and was obliged to return to *Holland*, without reaping any advan-tage from his journey; having acted a part not very fuitable to a Prince who had hitherto ac-quired fo much glory, and fo high a reputation for his military accomplifhments.

Being returned to *Holland*, he, in concert with Penfionary *Heinfius*, left nothing unattempted to

engage

engage that Republick not to agree to the congrefs, which was already appointed.   1712.

All thefe intrigues did only delay the departure of the Plenipotentiaries, and thus engage
the difagreeing powers to make another campaign, which the Court of *France* and that of
England were willing to avoid. It was a long
while before the *Dutch* refolved to name their
Plenipotentiaries, and agree upon the place of
congrefs. At laft they complied with Queen
Anne's defire, who had chofen the city of *U-
trecht*. The Minifters of *France* fet out for that
place on the fixth of *January*, and on the twenty ninth the congrefs was opened.

The *French* Plenipotentiaries made offers for
obtaining a general peace. Thofe of the Allies,
to elude them, and prolong the conferences, gave
no direct and determinate anfwers, and only
made in writing exorbitant demands, which they
intitled *fpecifick articles*; demands which they
would have had no right to make, had their armies been in the heart of *France*. They made
no doubt but that fuch propofals would break
the congrefs. But the *French* Plenipotentiaries
behaved with great moderation and wifdom, and
did not give into the fnare: they remonftrated
with great force, that enough had been written,
and that they ought to negotiate with each other,
as was ufually practifed upon the like occafions.

In the mean time, as it appeared that the
conferences were carried on very flowly, both
fides

1712. fides made the neceffary preparations for taking the field. The King had already given orders, that his army fhould be in readinefs, and had appointed Marfhal *Villars* to command in *Flanders*, and Marfhal *Montefquiou* to ferve under him. Marfhal *Harcourt* was to act in *Germany*. And as during the winter he had been attacked with an apoplexy, his Majefty named Marfhal *Bezons* to affift him, and to take his place, in cafe his health did not permit him to act. Marfhal *Berwick* had the command of the army in *Dauphiny*.

What we have faid above, fufficiently fhews the efforts which Prince *Eugene* made to penetrate into *France*, and by new conquefts to engage the Allies to decline a peace, or at leaft not to agree to it, but upon conditions fo burthenfome to *France*, that we could not accept them. For this purpofe, he undertook the fiege of *Landrecies*, a place which, after the conquefts the enemy had already made, was one of the principal keys of the kingdom. To hinder this place from being relieved, he formed a retrenched camp at *Denain*, whereby he maintained a communication with *Marchiennes*, which the Confederates called *the high-way to* Paris. Thefe meafures were not ill taken, but the defign of them was too unjuft to fucceed. Marfhal *Villars* forced the retrenchments at *Denain*, routed the troops which guarded them, obliged the enemy to raife the fiege of *Landrecies*, and took *Marchiennes, Doway, Quefnoy,* and *Bouchain*.

Thus

Thus all the projects against *France* were de-
feated; and this was the issue of the boasting promises which some of the Allies had made to their
Confederates. The action at *Denain* happened
on the twenty fourth of *July*. A week before,
Marshal *Villars* and the Duke of *Ormond* had
published in their respective camps a cessation of
arms between *France* and *England*. The rest
of the Allies, except the Emperor, at last con-
sented to treat of a peace; and for this purpose
to hold conferences at *Utrecht :* and now they
were not so haughty, and paid that regard to
the Plenipotentiaries of *France* which was due
to them.

It was agreed upon, as the first preliminaries
to the peace, that the King of *Spain* should renounce the Crown of *France*, and that the
Dukes of *Berry* and *Orleans* should renounce
that of *Spain*, in order that these two Crowns
might never be united under the same Prince;
and that *France* should acknowledge Queen
Anne as lawful Sovereign of *Great Britain*; and
admit the succession to that Crown as it was settled on the House of *Hanover*. Accordingly,
that *France* should give no manner of assistance
to the Chevalier *St. George*; and should even
refuse him the Asylum which he had hitherto
enjoyed in the kingdom. In effect, that Prince
retired to *Lorrain*. After these two points had
been agreed upon, the articles of peace were
settled in the conferences which were held at
Utrecht.

As

1712.   As for this year's campaign in *Dauphiny*, the
King had ordered Marſhal *Berwick* to ſtand upon the defenſive; and though his army was ſtill
inferior to that of the enemy, yet he ſtopped, as
he had done in the preceeding campaigns, all the
paſſes in *Savoy*, *Dauphiny*, and *Provence*.

On the fifteenth of *Auguſt* the Earl of *Peterborough* arrived at *Turin*, being ſent to the Duke
of *Savoy* by the Queen of *England*.   At his firſt
audience he had a conference with his Royal
Highneſs for above two hours.   He had afterwards ſeveral audiences, wherein he negociated
with this Prince concerning the advantageous
terms which *France* granted him in the treaty of
peace, at the ſollicitation of her *Britiſh* Majeſty.

Towards the end of this campaign, Marſhal
Berwick detached, according to the orders ſent
him from Court, twenty battalions and ten ſquadrons of dragoons, under the command of the
Chevalier *d'Asfeld*, to march into *Catalonia*.
Count *Thaun* having advice of this, and no longer fearing any attempt from our army, ſent the
German troops to *Rivoli*, and from thence into
winter quarters.   He went afterwards to *Turin*,
where the Earl of *Peterborough* returned a ſecond time, to continue the negociation he had
begun with the Duke of *Savoy*.   On the ninth
of *October* Count *Thaun* repaired to *Milan*, and
after giving the neceſſary orders in that place, he
ſet out for *Vienna*.

Marſhal *Berwick*, having aſſigned to his troops
their quarters, went to *Grenoble*; and while he

was

was preparing to fet out from thence for *Ver-*
failles, he received an order from the King to
go and head the army which met in *Catalonia*,
with an intent to raife the blocade of *Gironne*.
General *Wetzel* had blocked up this place almoft during the whole campaign, and preffed
it clofer on the fifteenth of *October*. The *Ger-*
mans feized *Pontamajor* on the river *Ter*, by
which poft our troops muft neceffarily pafs, when
that river is not fordable : at laft, they ruined
the mills without the town, and cut off the water from thofe which were in it. The Marquis
of *Brancas*, the Governor, was fhut up there
with a garrifon of twelve battalions. Having
found means to give notice of the fituation in
which he was, Count *Fiennes* advanced, according to the order he had received from Court,
and attempted to throw fuccours into the town,
that it might be faved from falling into the enemy's hands, till Marfhal *Berwick* fhould come
to relieve it.

For this purpofe he entered the *Lampourdan*
with fifteen battalions, including the militia, and
fome fquadrons, taking with him a train of eight
fmall field pieces. He had a fufficient number
of troops to raife the blockade ; but having
made the enemy believe that he intended to force
their retrenchments, whilft he fixed their attention on one fide, and kept them in awe by can-
nonading them, he fent on the other fide fifty
fat bullocks and a hundred fheep, and four hundred foot to recruit their battalions, the whole
escorted

 eſcorted by three hundred horſe; and this convoy had the good fortune to ford the river, and
get ſafe into *Gironne*. After this ſucceſs, he ſet
out on the firſt of *November* to aſſemble his
troops in *Rouſſillon*, where he put them into
quarters, expecting the arrival of the regiments
which Marſhal *Berwick* had ſent from *Dauphiny*. Theſe troops, with the former, were to
compoſe an army, with which he might enter
Catalonia, attack the enemy, and oblige them
to raiſe the ſiege of *Gironne*.

This place had ſuffered exceedingly by the
want of ſeveral things. It muſt be ſaid to the
praiſe of the townſmen, that they voluntarily
ſhared in the diſtreſs of our troops; far from
concealing their proviſions and money, they offered them of their own accord, and kept no
more for themſelves than what was neceſſary to
ſave them from ſtarving.

Notwithſtanding this, our troops were reduced
to eat the moſt loathſome things; and what is
much to be admired, none of them expreſſed
the leaſt inclination to deſert, though they had
many opportunities of doing it. The Marquis
of *Brancas*, by his polite and winning behaviour, had gained ſo much eſteem, affection,
and confidence not only among his troops, but
among the townſmen, that the latter lent him,
beſides other things, four hundred thouſand livres for the uſe of the garriſon.

General *Staremberg*, who by his great ability,
had found means to ſupport himſelf in *Catalonia*
with

with a very few troops, notwithſtanding the retreat of the *Engliſh* auxilaries, and the ſuſpenſion of arms made with the *Portugueſe*; knowing to what extremity *Gironne* was reduced,
and the preparations which were made in
France to relieve it, he came to the camp before that place in the beginning of *December*,
and cauſed retrenchments to be made at all the
avenues. Having advice that Marſhal *Berwick*
was arrived on the ninth at *Perpignan*, where
he aſſembled his army in order to enter *Catalonia*,
he judged that he muſt now uſe the utmoſt diligence: accordingly he made ſeveral aſſaults
upon the red fort, and that of the *Capuchines*,
which were ſituated on the eminences of the
town, expecting that the garriſon being weakened, would make but a ſlight reſiſtance. He
had prepared ladders for ſcaling ſome parts of
theſe forts; and hoped, that after he ſhould
make himſelf maſter of them, the townſmen
would oblige the Marquis of *Brancas* to capitulate: but the *Germans* found every where the
troops which defended them more reſolute than
they had expected. Theſe attempts being defeated, General *Staremberg* applied himſelf wholly to cauſe the paſſes which lead from the *Lampourdan* to *Gironne* to be retrenched. Mean
while, Marſhal *Berwick* loſt no time. The troops
which were to compoſe his army, were marching
from *Dauphiny*, *Provence* and *Languedoc*, and in
the mean while he gave the neceſſary orders for
their ſubſiſtence, and for a convoy ſufficient to

revictual

1712. revictual *Gironne*. The rains, which fell in the months of *November* and *December*, swelled the rivers so much, that they retarded the march of these troops above a fortnight. However, the Marshal's orders were given, and obeyed so opportunely, that part of the provisions which had been embarked arrived at *Roses* some days before *Christmas*. Much more bread and bisket were baked than the army could consume in a fortnight: these were carried by mules towards *Gironne*.

On the twenty sixth of *December* the Marshal set out from *Perpignan*, and passed the night at *Boulon*, on the river *Tech*, four *French* leagues from *Perpignan*. This was the place appointed for the meeting of the army. Here he found that some regiments were not yet arrived; among others, the regiment of foot of *Egrigni*, and that of *Caylus's* dragoons. This army was to consist of twenty thousand men. It had a train of thirty pieces of artillery, with engineers, and five Lieutenant-generals, *viz.* Mess. *Arennes, Asfeld, Dillon, Fiennes,* and *Silly*.

At last, on the twenty eighth at break of day, this army began to march. It filed off in three columns, and went over the *Pyrenees* at three different passes. The *Catalan* Miquelets, who guarded them by General *Staremberg's* order, abandoned them as soon as they perceived from the tops of the mountains the first motions of the *French* army. The latter encamped on the

same

fame day at *Jonquieres*, at the bottom of the mountains, in the *Lampourdan*.

Here it was that Marfhal *Berwick* caufed a great many copies of an ordinance of the Court of *Madrid* to be diftributed, forbidding upon pain of death all the fubjects of *Spain* to furnifh either with money or provifions the enemies of the two Crowns; forbidding befides, the *Catalans* to keep arms in their houfes, or to give any af-fiftance or harbour to the rebellious Miquelets, who fhould be found in arms againft his Catholic Majefty, *Philip* V, their only lawful Sovereign. By the like ordinances, and by the ftrict and fpeedy punifhment of thofe who had broke them, Marfhal *Berwick* had fome years before fuppref-fed the revolt of the kingdoms of *Arragon* and *Valencia*.

On the twenty ninth, the *French* army ad-vanced as far as *Figuieres*, which is only four miles from *Caftella d'Ampurias*, on the gulph of *Rofes*. Here they continued on the thirtieth. From hence Marfhal *Berwick* fent feveral parties to fcour the country, get intelligence of the enemy, and difperfe copies of the ordinance a-bove mentioned. On the thirty firft, they left the highway to *Gironne*, along which General *Staremberg* had made his principal retrench-ments, expecting that Marfhal *Berwick* would come to him on that fide, and they paffed the *Fluvia* at *St. Perez de Pefcador*, which is only half a league from the fea.

On

1712. On the same day our troops encamped at *Armentieres*, between the *Fluvia* and the *Ter:* they continued their march along the sea-side, and passed the *Ter* without opposition at *Toroella de Mongri*. The Marshal left a detachment at *Berges*, on the left of the *Ter*, to serve as an escort to the convoy designed for *Gironne*.

1713. General *Staremberg* perceiving that all his precautions were rendered useless, and that whilst he endeavoured to hinder us from sending provisions into *Gironne*, he would expose his own army to the want of them, unless he speedily secured *Ostalric*, the only place by which he held a communication with *Barcelona*; judging besides, by the march of the *French* army, that Marshal *Berwick* would not fail to move to the river *Tordera*, which makes a kind of circle near *Ostalric*, on the night between the second and third of *January*, he thought fit to abandon the retrenchments of the *Red Coast*. As he had ordered the *Ponta major* to be broke, he caused a bridge to be built at a place called *Santa Eugenia* near *Saria*, and passed the *Ter* about a quarter of a league from *Gironne*; so that marching along the river *Onhar*, he descended between the mountains, to gain the road from *Gironne* to *Ostalric*.

Marshal *Berwick*'s principal design was to send into *Gironne* the convoy which had been appointed for that place: thus as soon as the Marquis of *Brancas* acquainted him that the *Germans* had retired, he advanced the convoy
with

with great speed, and it was received in the 1713. town with the greatest demonstrations of comfort and joy.

General *Staremberg* had retired with so much precipitation, that he was obliged to leave in his retrenchments a great quantity of provisions, several waggons, four pieces of cannon, and a great many tools. At the same time that the Marshal sent the convoy to *Gironne*, he detached Lieutenant-general *Dillon* at the head of some grenadeers and of several squadrons, to charge the enemy's rear-guard. But they had got so far before him, that he could not come up with them; he only took à few stragglers. However, having advanced as far as a defile which Count *Staremberg* had passed, he found two hundred and fifty men who guarded it, to give the enemy time to advance to *Ostalric*. He attacked them with his grenadeers, who killed several of them, made forty prisoners, and put the rest to flight: after which he returned to join Marshal *Berwick*.

The Court of *Spain*, to favour this expedition, had ordered a body of four thousand horse and of ten thousand foot to march through *Tortosa* into *Catalonia*. Provisions had been prepared for these troops at *Penis Cola*; they were to advance, in concert with Marshal *Berwick*, into the plain of *Tarragon*. According to these orders, Prince *Tserclas Tilly* passed the *Ebor* on the first of *January*, near *Tortosa*, and advanced with this army into the Viguiery of *Tarragon*,

on

1713. on the fea-fide. The magazine from whence the army at firſt received their proviſions, had been ſettled at *Vinaroz*; but as they advanced to *Catalonia*, the magazines were brought nearer.

Beſides theſe ſuccours, the Marquis of *Grimaldi de Ceva*, having entered *Catalonia* by *Lerida* with a ſmall flying camp of four thouſand *Spaniards*, retook *Cervera*, and poſſeſſed ſeveral poſts which led to *Barcelona*. All theſe troops environed *Catalonia*, and waited in their quarters for the proper ſeaſon of beginning the campaign, in caſe the negociations at *Utrecht* ſhould not terminate the war in this province, as the Court of *Spain* expected.

Don *Tiberio Carafa*, a Major-general, arrived at *Madrid* on the thirteenth of *January*, with letters which informed the King of *Spain* of the raiſing the ſiege of *Gironne*. His Catholick Majeſty made him Lieutenant-general. At the ſame time, Marſhal *Berwick* repreſented to the King of *Spain*, that it would be proper to publiſh an amneſty for the rebellious *Catalans*, who would the more willingly return to their duty, if they were aſſured of their pardon, at a time when they had great reaſon to fear being abandoned at the peace, which was upon the point of being concluded; that ſuch an act of clemency would prevent the effuſion of a great deal of blood, which could not be avoided, if the rebels were rendered deſperate, by leaving them no hopes of pardon. The King followed this advice;

vice; and accordingly two days after publiſhed 1713.
a decree in favour of the *Catalan* rebels, in which
his Catholick Majeſty granted a general amneſty
to all thoſe who ſhould ſurrender to his General
Officers, and take a new oath of fidelity; ordered that they ſhould be continued in the poſſeſſion of their goods and eſtates, and that whatever had been confiſcated, ſhould be reſtored to
them. At the ſame time, the King declared
that thoſe who ſhould not accept of the pardon
ſo liberally offered them, ſhould be puniſhed
with all the rigour of the laws, as rebellious ſubjects, and enemies to the peace of their country.
This amneſty was printed both in the *Caſtilian*
and *Catalan* tongues, and a great number of copies of it were ſent to the General Officers of
the army, and the Governors and Commanders
of towns, in order to diſperſe them in the country. Nay ſeveral of the Miquelets, who were
priſoners, were allowed to return to their reſpective homes, with the like aſſurances of a general pardon.

Thus Marſhal *Berwick* crowned the glorious
enterprize, which he had ſo happily executed:
an enterprize which had appeared the more difficult, as Count *Staremberg* had taken all poſſible precaution to render impracticable the avenues of a town which he expected to reduce by
famine. But all theſe obſtacles, and all the difficulties which aroſe from the ſituation of the
place, and the rigorous ſeaſon of the year, were
ſurmounted by Marſhal *Berwick*; who, by ſav-

1713. ing a town of so great importance, did as signal
a service as he ever rendered to the King of
Spain, or the King of *France* his master. After
having caused a great quantity of ammunition
and provisions to be brought into *Gironne*, he
set out from *Catalonia*, and came post to *Versailles*, where he arrived on the fifth of *February*,
and was received by the King and the whole
Court with deserved esteem and applause.

The conferences at *Utrecht* concluded at last
in a peace, which was signed on one side by
France, and on the other by the Queen of *England*, the King of *Portugal*, the King of *Prussia*,
the Duke of *Savoy*, and the States of *Holland*.
On the twenty second of *May* it was proclaimed
at *Paris*. The Emperor alone refused to acquiesce in it, though articles for him had been
stipulated in it, and though he was allowed two
months to accept of them. The Chevalier *St.
George* suffered most by this treaty, as he was
thereby excluded from the throne of *England*,
and as all the contracting Powers had entered
into a guaranty of the succession in the House
of *Hanover*. Thus he was abandoned by the
King of *France*, who could no longer assist him,
and he was obliged to leave the kingdom. On the
twenty fifth of *April*, in the preceding year, he
had protested against whatever might be stipulated in the congress of *Utrecht* to his prejudice,
and contrary to the lawful and evident right
which he had to the Crown of *England*.

Marshal

1713.

Marſhal *Berwick* was greatly concerned at the departure of this Prince, and the bad ſituation of his affairs. He expreſſed to him his regret, that being engaged in the ſervice of *France*, he could not follow him, and ſhare in his fate : but he aſſured him that he would always be ready to ſacrifice every thing, as ſoon as there ſhould be any appearance that his ſervice could be of uſe to him.

It was believed at the Court of *France*, that the Emperor had only refuſed to ſign the treaty of peace at *Utrecht*, that he might diſtinguiſh himſelf from his Allies, and imitate the conduct which the Emperor *Leopold* had held upon the like occaſions. It was hoped, that he would not let paſs the time granted to him, without accepting the conditions which were offered ; eſpecially as his Imperial Majeſty was not able, when left alone, to oppoſe *France*. Even the *French* Miniſters had ſo much relied upon this, that they had not taken meaſures for another campaign.

They were miſtaken : for the Emperor, animated by Prince *Eugene*, reſolved to hazard another campaign, in hopes that ſome favourable event would happen which might deliver him from the uneaſineſs it gave him to abandon his pretenſions to the Crown of *Spain*; which he muſt have done, had he accepted the conditions ſtipulated in the treaty between *France* and the other Allies.

E e 4

Prince.

1713. Prince *Eugene*, by whose counsels his Imperial Majesty was guided on this occasion, well
knew that *France* would take some towns during this campaign ; but he hoped that if the Emperor's affairs were not successful on the *Rhine*,
it would be time enough to negociate a peace at
the end of the campaign with Marshal *Harcourt*,
who was to command the *French* army in that
country. Besides, he persuaded himself that
France would then restore the conquests they
might make, and that the King, who so earnestly desired a peace, both for the putting his
finances in good order, and for the ease and relief of his people, who had greatly suffered by
this war, would not give worse terms than those
which he had already offered. This able Prince,
whose political views have always been very ex-
tensive, did not besides despair of seeing great
changes happen this year in *Europe*, by which
perhaps the league against *France* might be renewed. The great age of the King of *France*,
who had only one Prince for his successor, aged
but three years, and the great infirmities of the
Queen of *England*, strengthned these conjectures,
and supported the reasons he had alledged to the
Emperor and his council for continuing the
war.

Accordingly the Emperor employed the two
months which had been allowed him for coming
to a resolution, in making the strongest solicita-
tions to the *German* Princes not to accept of a
peace which he said was disgraceful to the *Ger-*
manick

manick body, but to affift him in carrying on the war with greater vigour.

The Court of *France*, who had relied a little too much upon a peace, had made no preparations for a new campaign, and did not ferioufly apply to make any, till the two months were almoft elapfed. Then it was they were fenfible that the only way of reducing the Emperor to an accommodation, was to carry on the war againft him with vigour. They took meafures for having a ftrong army upon the *Rhine*, and caufed all the neceffary preparations to be made for great enterprizes: but as thefe preparations were begun very late, the expences of them were exceffively great, and they coft three times as much as they would have done, had we forefeen that they would be neceffary.

The Emperor, on his fide, obtained the confent of the Diet of *Ratifbon* for continuing the war, with the remainder of a million of crowns which had been granted him; and they directed four millions more to be paid into the military cheft of the Empire. Befides, the city of *Amfterdam* advanced to the Emperor a million of florins, upon the fecurity of the States General. Thefe fums he thought fufficient to defray the expences of the campaign. *Italy* being included in the treaty of neutrality which had been agreed upon for *Catalonia*, the Emperor was thereby enabled to draw from the kingdom of *Naples*, and the Duchy of *Milan*, a part of the troops which fecured thofe countries, and with thefe

he

1713. he confiderably encreafed his army. After this, his Imperial Majefty publickly declared in the month of *May*, that he was refolved to continue the war, and to command his army in perfon.

The Court of *France* prepared, on the other fide, to anfwer this fort of declaration of war; and as foon as it was certainly known that the Emperor would liften to no accommodation, the King gave his orders for beginning the campaign, and defired that the fiege of fome place fhould be undertaken. Marfhal *Harcourt* was to command the army on the *Rhine*; but as his health did not permit him to accept of that command, his Majefty caft his eye upon Marfhal *Berwick* to fucceed him; believing that Marfhal *Villars*, who had already difmiffed his equipage, would be glad to retire with the glory he had acquired, without expofing himfelf to the fatigues of a new campaign. But Mr. *Voifin*, Secretary of War, reprefented to the King, that Marfhal *Villars* had only difmiffed his equipage, becaufe he had believed, with many others, that the Emperor would acquiefce in the peace, and would not venture to continue againft *France* a war, which he alone could not fupport: that his Majefty finding himfelf obliged to carry on the war againft the Emperor, it was his intereft to give the command of his army on the *Rhine* to Marfhal *Villars*, fince the fame good fortune which had attended him in *Flanders*, and had obliged the *Dutch* and other Allies to accept of the peace, might likewife oblige the Emperor

to.

to agree to it; and as the King could not refuse 1713.
him that command, and the glory of this laft
expedition, without making all *Europe* believe
that his Majefty had reafon to be diffatisfied with
that General.

This reprefentation made an impreffion upon
the King. His Majefty changed his refolution,
and named Marfhal *Villars* to command on the
Rhine, and Marfhal *Befons* to ferve under him.
Marfhal *Berwick* was not difcontent with the
preference given to that General: his defires
were always conformable to the King's pleafure;
and his fole concern was, that he loft this opportunity of giving frefh proofs of his zeal for
his Majefty and the good of the kingdom.

Marfhal *Villars* took *Landaw*, which furrendered on the twenty firft of *Auguft*, after twenty
fixth days from the opening of the trenches;
forced the intrenchments near *Friburg*, the capital of *Brifgaw*, which were defended by a
body of feventeen thoufand *Imperialifts*, under
the command of General *Vaubonne*; and concluded this glorious campaign with the taking of
Friburg. The town capitulated on the firft of
November, after thirty one days open trenches,
and the caftle furrendered on the fixteenth.

Thefe conquefts brought the Emperor to a
peace. He named Prince *Eugene* his Plenipotentiary, and ordered him to treat with Marfhal
Villars, to whom the King of *France* had given
the fame title, and the fame orders. The place
of conference was the caftle of *Raftadt*, where
both

1713. both Plenipotentiaries arrived in the end of *No-vember*. The treaty of peace between the King and the Emperor was at laft concluded, and figned on the fixth of *March* 1714. On the twenty third of the fame month it was ratified by the King, and all differences were afterwards fully terminated at *Baden*.

In this interval, the Marfhal of *Berwick* enjoyed an agreeable retirement in the midft of his family. He was now as great and refpectable in a plain and unadorned life, as he had been, when he filled the moft fhining and glorious employments. His life was ever regular and exemplary, his temper even and compofed, and his time undiffipated: no hours were loft or mifapplied; no duty was omitted. Even when he headed armies, and was overwhelmed, one would think, by the multiplicity of affairs committed to him, he never forgot to dedicate to religion and piety thofe hours he had fet apart for them; and particularly, every day repeated the great fervice with fuch an attentive, humble, and devout frame of mind, as edified thofe who were leaft pious, and filenced the greateft libertines.

Towards the end of this year, there remained only the city of *Barcelona* and the *Catalans* to be reduced. That people were ftill in arms, and obftinately refufed to fubmit, and accept of the amnefty which the King of *Spain* had fo generoufly offered them. Never perhaps was there an inftance of fuch an obftinacy. They had no hopes of relief; no mention had been
made

made of them in the treaty of peace at *Utrecht*, 1713.
and much lefs in that at *Raſtadt*; the Emperor
had abandoned them to their deſtiny, and withdrawn all his troops out of *Catalonia*.   Notwithſtanding, we were obliged to reduce them by
force of arms and puniſhments, as will appear
in the ſequel of theſe Memoirs, ſince Marſhal
Berwick had the glory of this laſt expedition.

Towards the end of *February* the King ſent 1714.
him to his Catholick Majeſty with his compliments of condolance upon the death of the
Queen of *Spain*, which happened on the fourteenth of the ſame month, in the twentieth
year of her age. This Princeſs, *Mary Louiſa
Gabriel*, was the ſecond daughter of the Duke
of *Savoy*. On the eleventh of *September* 1701,
ſhe had been married to *Philip* of *France*, King
of *Spain*, by whom ſhe had three ſons, *Lewis
Philip* Prince of *Aſturias*, born on the twenty
fifth of *Auguſt* 1707, the Infant Don *Philip*,
born on the ſeventh of *June* 1712, and the Infant Don *Ferdinand*, born on the twenty third
of *September* 1713.

The death of this Princeſs was univerſally
lamented. Her ſuperior genius, joined with an
uncommon firmneſs of mind, which raiſed her
above all the misfortunes that attended her life,
procured her the admiration not only of the
Spaniards, but of all *Europe*. She was ever intent upon promoting the glory of the King her
huſband, and the intereſt of her people. Her
life, from the time that ſhe aſcended the
throne,

1714. throne, was a feries of calamities. As foon as fhe arrived in *Spain*, the King being obliged to head his army in *Italy*, appointed her Regent in his abfence. In this ftation fhe fhewed a fuperiority of genius uncommon to her fex and her age, for fhe was then only fourteen years old. She beheld a foreign fleet infult the harbour of *Cadiz*, carry off or deftroy at *Vigo* part of the fleet and galleons, which had fled thither for fhelter, and part of their rich cargo, which fhould have ferved to defend her kingdom, fall into the hands of her enemies, and enable them to invade it. It was a fevere affliction to her, that the Duke of *Savoy*, her father, increafed the number of the enemies of the King her hufband. By the events of the war fhe was twice obliged to abandon her palace, and the capital of her kingdom, and to lead a kind of wandering life in the provinces.

This, joined with the treachery of fome of her minifters, the revolt of whole provinces and kingdoms dependent on the *Spanifh* Monarchy, made a deep impreffion upon the mind of this Princefs. However, fhe had fuch a command of herfelf, as to conceal it from the publick. But whilft her firmnefs and courage were univerfally admired, the conftraint fhe had put upon herfelf impaired her health, and at laft occafioned her death, at a time when her affairs began to have a better profpect and all appearances promifed her more happy times.

This

This excellent Queen had chiefly contributed 1714. to encourage and animate her fubjects, to main- tain good order in the government, and to in- fpire both the people and the army with zeal and fidelity. Whilft the King expofed his life at the head of his armies, fhe parted with all her ornaments, and even fome of her neceffa- ries, to fupport him by her liberality. Upon all thefe accounts the people of *Spain* exceeding- ly lamented, and to this day lament the death of that illuftrious Princefs.

Marfhal *Berwick* at the fame time that he received the King's order above mentioned, was likewife commanded by his Majefty to offer his fervice to the King of *Spain* for reducing the *Catalans,* and fubduing the city of *Barcelona.* Accordingly he immediately fet out for *Madrid.* Being admitted to an audience of the King, he fpoke in fuch a noble and affecting manner, that his Majefty and all thofe who were pre- fent were ftruck with it. In this kind of dif- courfe, which is in itfelf fo difficult, Marfhal *Berwick* may be faid to have excelled. He fpoke with dignity; his expreffions were juft and clear, his thoughts and fentiments noble and folid. There was nothing dazzling or fuperfluous in either. Whatever he faid was pertinent, grace- ful, and affecting.

His Catholick Majefty accepted the offer of his fervice againft the *Catalans.* King *Philip* well knew the capacity of the Marfhal of *Ber- wick,* and all the *Spaniards* confidered him as
the

 the worthy fucceffor of the Duke of *Vendôme*, and as a General who by his great talents deferved to be employed in finifhing a work which the death of that great man alone had interrupted. The Marfhal returned to *France* to give his Moft Chriftian Majefty an account of his commiffion: after which he went to put himfelf at the head of the army which was appointed to befiege *Barcelona*. Some time before the King of *France* had fent into *Catalonia* twenty battalions, which were in *Languedoc*, and the neighbouring places; and Mr. *du Caffe* was named to command the fleet appointed to block up the mouth of the harbour of *Barcelona*; but his indifpofition, together with his great age, obliged him to afk leave to refign. He was fucceeded on the twenty fecond of *June* by the Bailiff of *Belle-Fontaine*, a Lieutenant-general.

The *Catalan* rebels who kept the field, continued to ravage the province, and to watch and annoy the flying camps of the *French* and *Spanifh* troops. One of their bodies, confifting of two thoufand men, invefted the city of *Berga*, and even made two affaults upon it. The Duke of *Popoli*, who commanded the army, fent thither the Marquis of *Thoüy*, who put them to flight, and forced them to retire to the mountains which furround the plain of *Vich*, from whence they were afterwards driven by Meff. *Bracamonte* and *Valejo*.

In

In this interval, the *French* troops which were 1714.
arrived in *Rouffillon* paffed the mountains, and affembled at *Figuieres*, where they encamped, waiting for Marfhal *Berwick*, who arrived at *Perpignan* on the thirtieth of *June*, being accompanied by the Earl of *Tinmouth*, his fon by the
firft marriage, my Lord *Lucan*, the fon of the
Countefs of *Sarsfield* his firft wife, Meff. *Silly,
Geoffreville, Asfeld, Firmacon*, and fome other
General Officers. At *Montpelier* he had received a courier from *Madrid* with the patent of
Generaliffimo of his Catholick Majefty's armies.
He arrived next day at *Figuieres*, from whence
the troops marched to *Barcelona*. They arrived
before that city on the feventh of *July*. At the
fame time all forts of warlike ftores and provifions, which had been prepared at *Collioure*, were
brought before *Barcelona*.

As foon as Marfhal *Berwick* arrived in the
camp, he vifited all the advanced works, with
the Duke of *Popoli* and the General Officers.
He gave orders for the encampment of the troops
which he had brought with him, and fhut up
the *Barcelonians* as much as poffible within the
town, that they might have no communication
with the volunteers of the country. He had
under his command fifteen Lieutenants-general,
eighteen Marfhals de Camp, and twenty two
Brigadeers, either *French* or *Spaniards*. The two
Kings had allowed him to chufe the regiments
and the General Officers, who were to ferve in
this fiege. The Duke of *Popoli*, after having

F f refigned

1714. refigned the command of the army to the Marfhal, returned to *Madrid*, where he received fome days after the order of the *Golden Fleece*. Mr. *Orri*, who had for feveral years adminiftered the treafury of the King of *Spain*, and had been fent to the camp before *Barcelona*, with all the neceffary powers to treat with the befieged, having had no fuccefs, returned to *Madrid* with the Duke of *Popoli*.

All the difpofitions being made, Marfhal *Berwick* opened the trenches on the night between the twelfth and thirteenth of *July*, on the eaft fide, where the befieged did not expect to be attacked. The trenches were mounted by a Lieutenant-general, a Marfhal de Camp, and two Brigadeers; ten battalions, and five hundred horfe, befides two thoufand five hundred pioneers to work in the night; and much the fame difpofition was made during the whole fiege. The trenches were advanced within three hundred and eighty fathoms of the counterfcarp: about two of the clock in the afternoon the befieged made a fally, being headed by their brave *Matadors*, feveral of whom were killed upon the fpot, or were taken prifoners and hanged.

On the fame day, the deputation fent a trumpet with difpatches for Mr. *Bellefontaine*, who refufed to receive them. The Marquis of *Villaroël* fent another, with a letter directed to the Marquis of *Guerchy*. The latter carried it unopened to Marfhal *Berwick*, who returned it to the trumpet, and threatened to caufe him to be

hanged,

hanged, if he returned any more to the camp; 1714.
adding, that the rebels muſt only have recourſe
to the mercy of the King. A few hours after,
ſome ladies from the town came to the camp,
and preſented themſelves at the door of the General's tent, in order to intreat him to grant
them an aſylum : but the Marſhal would neither ſee nor hear them, and immediately ſent
them back to the town; ſaying, that when he
ſhould be there, he would hear them. A Marſhal de Camp, a Brigadeer, a Colonel, and five
Captains, eſcaped from the town on the ſame
day, and ſurrendered at diſcretion. They brought
an account that the regular troops were diſpoſed
to ſurrender, but that the people were more obſtinate than ever; that they were employed in
throwing up a multitude of retrenchments, and
declared that they would rather be buried in the
ruins of their houſes, than ſubmit.

All the time till the twenty fourth, was employed in carrying on the works to the covered
way. On the twenty fifth, being the Marſhal of
Berwick's birth day, after having cauſed the maſs
to be ſaid by the Vicar-general of the army, and
the artillery to be bleſſed, he ordered a royal
battery of ſeventy four pieces of cannon, and
twenty four mortars to fire upon a long courtain
extending from the baſtion of the new port to
that of *Santa Clara*; at the ſame time that ſixteen other cannons fired from two batteries upon a redoubt nigh the ſea. So great a fire had
the effect which might well be expected from

it;

 it; the bullets did a great deal of mifchief in the town, and frightned the inhabitants.

This occafioned a general affembly, wherein they refolved to perfift in their revolt. *Pinos*, a gentleman, and one of the moft obftinate of the rebels, fpoke in that affembly in fuch a haughty manner, as intimidated thofe who were inclined to fubmit. The ravings of *Baffet*, Grand-vicar of Cardinal *Sala*, Bifhop of *Barcelona*, which he vented under the name of revelations, feduced others. They made a decree, which they diftributed by their emiffaries, who in the night eafily went out, and returned on the fea-fide. In this writing they gave notice to the rebels in the country of the condition to which the town was reduced, and of the danger with which it was threatened; they commanded all the inhabitants of towns and villages, who were above fourteen years of age, to take arms for the defence of their liberties, upon pain of being treated as enemies to their country. The Marquis *del Poël*, and the Chevalier *Armengol*, went throughout the whole country, to put this decree in execution. The Captains of the Miquelets had the infolence to accompany this writing with an order from them, expreffed in fuch terms as the moft famous and renowned Generals would have hardly ufed: they commanded all the inhabitants of the cities, towns, and villages of *Catalonia*, who were fourteen years of age, to take arms, and repair to them, under pain of being burnt in their habitations.

On

On the thirtieth in the evening the Marſhal 1714. of *Berwick* went into the trenches. They were mounted by Lieutenant-general *Dillon*, Mr. *Vi-cintillo*, Marſhal de Camp, and the Brigadeers *Courten* and *Deſmarets*. Every thing was in rea-dineſs, and the ſignal was given: whereupon four companies of grenadeers on the right, and as many on the left, attacked the covered way, which runs from the baſtion of the new gate, to that of *Santa Clara*; and without firing ruſhed in, and put to ſword all thoſe who were in it. The pioneers followed at a very little diſtance, and preſently made a lodgment, being favoured by the fire of the troops in the trenches, who ſupported this attack.

The beſieged came in great numbers to re-cover the counterſcarp; but our grenadeers were ſo freſh, that the former were repulſed with great loſs. This attack was made with ſo much valour on the ſide of the beſiegers, and was ſo weakly defended on that of the beſieged, that the former loſt but a few men. The batteries continued to fire in breach upon the two baſtions and the courtain; and the miners were ſet to work under them.

To prevent any bad effect which that inſolent writing above mentioned might have produced, Marſhal *Berwick* cauſed a Manifeſto to be print-ed at *Gironne*, and to be fixed up in the towns and principal places of *Catalonia*, forbidding all perſons to diſtribute or have any regard to that writing; and ordering all the *Catalans* who ſhould

F f 3

be

1714. be found in arms, to be hanged upon the spot, without any other form of process; and all the places which favoured the rebels, to be pillaged and burnt. In consequence of this order, which was dated the sixth of *August*, one and thirty rebels were hanged: they had been taken by Mr. *Bracamonte* from a company of two thousand men, commanded by the Chevalier *del Poël*, whom he had defeated at a defile, in his return from *Berga*, whither he had been carrying a convoy of provisions: four hundred of these rebels were killed upon the spot.

After we had taken the covered way, we were informed by some deserters of the state of the forces of the besieged, and of the measures they had taken for making their defence; of this we shall here give an account. There were still in *Barcelona* two thousand regular troops, horse and foot; besides the militia, the townsmen, and, since it must be owned, the Monks and Ecclesiasticks; for they had all taken arms for the defence of the town. The Marquis of *Villaroël* had the principal authority: Don *Joseph Antonio Morli*, commonly called *Ponton*, was Lieutenant-general: it is true, he had left the town, and had come to our camp as a deserter; but his place not being filled up, it was suspected that his escape was concerted with the Marquis of *Villaroël*: for which reason Marshal *Berwick* had sent him to *Peniscola*, till the town should be taken. Don *Joseph Bellever*, sirnamed *Joseph Petz*, commanded the infantry, with the title

title of Serjeant-general of Battalia. He likewife
commanded the city troops, which made a regiment, confifting of fix battalions, of five hundred men each.

When the people were called together by the
alarm-bell, this multitude was named the general affembly of the *Somettani*; importing, that
they entirely fubmitted to the orders of their
Chiefs and Commanders. The Chevalier *Ra-
manat* was General of their horfe; *Baffet* commanded the artillery, and difcharged the office
of firft engineer. The Captain of the bombar-
deers was named *Bruno Tornoze*; and *Pareras*
was the Captain of the miners.

The town regiment above mentioned, confifted of fuch of the common people, as were
fitteft to bear arms; they were diftributed into different quarters, and ferved by turns with the
other troops. Three places were appointed for
the meeting of the troops, one from *St. Catha-
rin* to the *Sea-Chapel*, the fecond was at the palace, and the third at the *Mercy*; fo that thefe
different bodies could fpeedily come to the places
where they fhould be wanted for the defence of
the town. The troops which guarded the half-
moon of the new gate had a reinforcement always at hand, at the convent of *St. Peter*. Thofe
which defended the half-moon of *Santa Clara*
had their reinforcement at the place of *Enllui*.
Thofe which guarded the breach had theirs at
the place of *St. Peter*. Thofe of the eaft baftion
at the ftables of the *Leucata*. Befides, there

were

1714. were three hundred horfe ready to march wherever they fhould be wanted, and an hundred
more, which made a piquet, in the garden *Co-
nari*, without the old town.

By order of the Council, a lift was made of
all perfons above fourteen years of age; and they
were commanded to take arms, and repair to
the places where they fhould be wanted, as
foon as ever they fhould hear the found of the
alarm-bells either of the Cathedral, or of other
churches. If any perfon failed to obey, he was
dragged to prifon, and examined by the council
of war.

The *Barcelonians* had made an entrenchment
from the new port to the gibet, which ftands
near the eaft baftion; and had pulled down all
the churches and houfes between the convent of
· *St. Auftin* and the fiefh-market, which had likewife been demolifhed. That part of the entrenchment which was oppofite to the breach made
by the befiegers, was finifhed from the gate of
the covered way. There they had made a great
place of arms, furrounded by a ditch, twelve
foot deep, and ten foot broad. They had likewife raifed a good ftone wall, with lime and ce-
ment, upon each of the fides which faced the
breach. Here they had planted five pieces of
cannon, charged with cartridge-fhot, in order
to hinder our approaches to it, having much
extended in thefe places the earth of the
wall.

At

At the head of the Junto, or Council of War 1714. of the *Barcelonians*, which they called the *Grand Juſticiary*, was Don *Pedro de Torellas Semanas*, to whom they gave the title of Governor-general of *Catalonia*; but on account of his age, they had given him for his Lieutenant, or Coadjutor, Don *Franciſco de Segoal*. The other members of this Council were Don *Joſeph Pinos*, Count *Coponts*, Count *Placentia*, the Marquis *Semanas*, the Archdeacon *Apre*, Don *Franciſco Finalar*, and Don *Manuel Ferrar*. The Secretary of this Council was one *Verneda*, brother-in-law to the Sieur *Perlas*, who had lately been ſent as their agent to *Vienna*.

The Jurats, or Conſuls of *Barcelona*, had eſtabliſhed another Junto of people of a middle condition; this Junto was ſtiled the Council of the Finances, as they had the care of paying the troops, with the town money. Thoſe who compoſed this Council, took money arbitrarily wherever they could find it; and if they were informed that any perſon concealed money, they ſent for it immediately, and threw the owner into priſon, to puniſh him for not diſcovering all that he had. This they had done ſeveral times. What has been ſaid, ſufficiently ſhews that tho' the beſiegers were maſters of the covered way, they had ſtill ſeveral great difficulties to ſurmount; for we muſt not judge of this ſiege, as of that of a town defended by regular troops. The *Barcelonians* were rebels, who, by their obſtinacy,

1714. ftinacy, had reduced themfelves to defpair ; and
this principle alone urged them to act with the
utmoft fury *.

On

* The author, being mifled by his prejudices, wrongs the
Catalans throughout the whole of his narrative. They were a
people who had enjoyed feveral rights and immunities, while
Spain was fubject to the Houfe of *Auftria*. As they had a juft
value for their privileges, they were defirous to fecure them for
themfelves, and tranfmit them fafe to their pofterity. Accordingly, in the year 1705, having received feveral affurances
from Mr. *Crow*, Queen *Anne*'s Minifter at *Genoa*, from the
Earl of *Peterborough*, and Sir *Cloudefly Shovel*, that if they would
acknowledge *Charles* III as King of *Spain*, and renounce the
Houfe of *Bourbon*, her *Britifh* Majefty would ufe her utmoft endeavours to procure the eftablifhment and confirmation of their
rights and privileges, and the fettlement of them on a lafting
foundation ; the *Catalans* acknowledged and received that
Prince as their Sovereign, raifed men and money for his fervice,
and during a war, which abounded with extraordinary turns of
fortune, gave fignal proofs of their unfhaken fidelity and zeal
for the caufe they had efpoufed. After King *Charles* came to
the Imperial Crown, and *Spain* was at laft given up to the Houfe
of *Bourbon*, the *Catalans*, far from being guided by a fpirit of
obftinacy and rebellion, as this writer would have it, were willing
to acknowledge King *Philip* V for their lawful Sovereign. At
the fame time, as they hoped to be protected by the Emperor,
a Prince for whom they had expofed their lives and fortunes, and
as they relied upon the repeated affurances they had received
that *England* would never abandon them, they infifted upon the
enjoyment of their former privileges. The inhabitants of *Barcelona*, being fummoned by the Duke of *Popoli* to furrender to
King *Philip*, anfwered, *That though they would rather die than
be flaves, yet if their antient liberties were confirmed, they would
open their gates, and receive him with joy.* But the *Catalans*
being abandoned both by the Emperor and by *England*, the Court
of *Spain* would be abfolute. What happened afterwards, how
vigorous and heroick a defence the *Catalans* made againft the
joint efforts of *France* and *Spain*, what miferies they underwent,
how many of them perifhed by the fword, how many were hanged, or fhot to death, and how many perfons of figure were
thrown into dungeons, there to lead the remainder of their
lives,

On the firſt of *Auguſt*, as a new proof of the 1714. rage and fury with which they were fired, ſeveral women and children planted upon the breach a ſtandard, in the middle of which was painted a death's head, intimating that they would rather die than ſurrender. On the third, they made two ſallies to interrupt the works of the *Spaniſh* miners, who were employed at the left flank of the baſtion of *Santa Clara*; they killed two of them, and took four priſoners: but the *French* miners who were employed on the other ſide, and thoſe who were at the baſtion of the new tower, continued their work; becauſe the *Barcelonians* being charged on all ſides, were ſoon driven back to the town with the loſs of ſixty nine men, who were killed. Mr. *du Puy Vauban*, Lieutenant-general, and Chief of the engineers, received upon this occaſion a muſket-ſhot, which entered his ſhoulder-blade and came out on the ſide of his breaſt. Though this was not a mortal wound, yet he could never be thoroughly cured of it, eſpecially as that brave man had already received a great many muſquet-ſhot. He was a near relation of the late Marſhal *Vauban*. On the fifth, the beſieged returned, to the number of a thouſand men, on the ſide of the *Capuchins*, and ſurprized a redoubt guarded

lives, will appear in the ſequel. And here we cannot forbear lamenting the fate of a brave unfortunate people, who fought and ſuffered merely for their liberties and privileges, and have immortalized their name by the noble, though unſucceſsful ſtand they made againſt uſurpation and arbitrary power.

by

 by an hundred men, eighteen of whom they killed, and they made the reft prifoners; but the grenadeers having advanced to them, drove them from the redoubt, and forced them to return within the town.

On the fame Day, the Marfhal of *Berwick* ordered fome of the batteries to be changed, and brought nearer the town; and the next day a battery of fix pieces of cannon began to fire upon the baftion of *Santa Clara.* Soon after, four batteries raifed upon the covered way, fired alfo in breach upon the fame baftion, and were employed in ruining it, and in making a paffage over the ditch. The mines being finifhed and charged, on the eleventh the trenches were not relieved, but the troops which fhould have mounted them, joined the reft towards the evening. On the twelfth at break of day, Marfhal *Berwick* came to the trenches, and all things being in readinefs for attacking the two baftions, the two mines were fprung, and had all the fuccefs that could be expected. Some time after fix companies of grenadeers mounted the breach, and having driven off thofe who defended it, took poffeffion of the angle of the baftion of the new gate; but the workmen not having arrived in time enough to make the lodgments, thefe grenadeers were twice obliged to defcend to the bottom of the breach, in order to fhelter themfelves from the great fire of the enemy: whereupon Marfhal *Berwick* fent fix other companies of grenadeers, who likewife mounted the breach

of

of the baftion of *Santa Clara*, and there lodged 1714.
themfelves; but as the gorge of this baftion was
retrenched, and as it was commanded by a
thick wall to which it was joined, and by the
eaft baftion, our grenadeers were unable to fupport the continual fire of the cannon, bombs,
and mufquetry of the befieged; and after having repulfed three brifk attacks, they were at laft
obliged to defcend to the bottom of the breach,
and to cover themfelves with gabions.

This action lafted above an hour; the fire was
very hot on both fides, and killed a great many
men. Our batteries play'd inceffantly all day and
part of the night, in order to hinder the befieged
from repairing the breaches. On the thirteenth,
the troops which had mounted the trenches the
day before were not relieved, and were joined
by the ten battalions which were to fucceed
them. There was a defign to renew the attack.

In effect, about ten of the clock in the evening,
twenty companies of grenadeers, commanded by
Mr. *Sauve-bœuf*, Brigadier and Colonel of the
regiment of *Blaifois*, and under him Mr. *Pola-
ftron*, Colonel of the regiment of the Crown,
mounted the affault. The befieged, who had
expected this attack, were fo well prepared for
it, that the fight continued from ten in the
evening till fix in the morning, when at laft
the befiegers drove away the rebels, made a
lodgment, and maintained themfelves, after the
Barcelonians had attacked them eight times
with

 with the utmoſt vigour in the ſpace of eight hours.

This action was one of the hotteſt and longeſt that ever were ſeen upon the like occaſion. What was moſt extraordinary, a great number of Monks and Eccleſiaſticks came to the breach, and fought with bayonets at the mouths of their muſquets, againſt the grenadeers of our army. The next day the beſieged, not to give us time to compleat a lodgment upon the baſtion, where Mr. *la Motte*, Lieutenant-colonel of the regiment of the Crown, had maintained himſelf during fourteen hours, notwithſtanding the continual fire which his troops bore from divers places which commanded that poſt, returned at noon with almoſt all the forces of the town, and charged our grenadeers ſo furiouſly, that the latter were forced to abandon the baſtion, and return to the covered way, though all the piquets of the left were ſent to ſupport them.

It never appeared more remarkably how dangerous it is to fight againſt a furious people, who, without any knowledge or experience in the art of war, and being neither inſpired with a ſenſe of their duty, nor animated with a deſire of acquiring glory, are nevertheleſs able to deſtroy many brave men. It was computed that in the ſeveral engagements at the breach, there were on both ſides above fifteen hundred men killed or wounded ; two thirds of that number on the ſide of the beſiegers, and a third on that of the beſieged.

This

This number had been much more confiderable, if the front of the attack had been wider;
and if the troops which attacked and defended
the breaches could have extended themfelves in
the engagement.   The Marquis of *Sauvebœuf*,
Mr. *de Verger*, Brigadeers of the Engineers, the
two Captains of grenadeers of the regiment of
the Crown, the three Captains of the regiment
of *Normandy*, and their Lieutenants, were killed
in this action.   The Marquis of *Polaſtron*, Mr.
Doze, Captain of the grenadeers of the Regiment of *Artois*, and feveral other officers, were
wounded.   The *Barcelonians* loft Count *Joſeph
Matas*, Don *Carlos Ribera*, Don *Geronimo Salvador*, Don *Magin Ninet*, Don *Franciſco de la
Vega*, Don *Geronimo Generes*, Mr. *Llinas*, and
one of his fons.   Among the wounded were the
fon of *Berard*, and the Marquis of *Montenegro*.

After the befiegers had been obliged to abandon the two baftions of the front of the attack,
the *Barcelonians* caufed two *Te Deums* to be fung
in the town, and were inceffantly employed in
fortifying their retrenchments both behind the
breaches, and behind the intrenchments which
they had made at the avenues of the old town.
They made battlements and embrafures at all
the neighbouring houfes, and filled them with
the city troops, that by their fire they might
favour the retreat of their men, in cafe they
fhould be forced to abandon the out-works.

On the night between the eighteenth and
nineteenth, four barks laden with provifions
entered

1714. entered the town; the fleet not being able to hinder them, for want of vessels that could sail close to the shore. Thus the besieged received refreshments from time to time during the siege; and the more easily, as the *Majorcans*, in concert with the *Catalans*, had a magazine near the coast beyond the *Lobregat*, in an old tower, near *Castel de Fels*, where the vessels of *Majorca* unladed in the night time, and those of *Barcelona* went afterwards to take the provisions which had been brought thither. This intercourse continued more than six weeks, without our having perceived it; because that tower had been uninhabited for above a century, and had neither doors nor windows; besides, we trusted to the inhabitants of the neighbouring places, who appeared faithful and zealous for the service of the King of *Spain*, whilst they held a correspondence with the rebels of the country, and of *Barcelona*. This correspondence being at last discovered, the magazine was plundered, and the houses of these inhabitants were burnt. Afterwards thirty barks were armed, in order to give chace to those who should enter the harbour: had this precaution been taken sooner, the siege would not have lasted so long. The Miquelets, commanded by the Chevalier *del Poël* and the Sieur *Armengol*, having gathered together a body of about eight or nine thousand men, formed a design of throwing succours into *Barcelona*, and of forcing one of the quarters of our camp, in concert with the besieged, who were

to

to make a sally at the same time. Marshal *Ber-* 1714.
wick having notice of this, kept upon his guard.
He sent out detachments under the command
of the Duke of *Montemar* and the Marquis of
Arpajou. On the twenty second, the Marquis
of *Thouy* came up with the Chevalier *del Poël* on
the heights of *Sanranat*; and at his first fire, the
Miquelets betook themselves to flight. The next
day, having separated his troops into three bodies, he surrounded the enemy, and killed a
great number of them: those who were taken
in arms were shot to death.

On the thirtieth, the detachment commanded by the Duke of *Montemar* defeated a body of
the rebels near *Piera,* three leagues from *Mar-
torel.* The next day, being the last of *August,*
they were again attacked and defeated near the
glass-house, between *Monferrat* and *Inqualada* :
so that in these four different actions, that great
body of the rebels was entirely dispersed, and no
longer attempted to disturb the siege. The detachments, after having scoured the country for
ten days, returned to the camp, and left the
Marquis of *Thouy* and Count *Fienne,* to keep in
awe the rebels of the flat country. Mean while,
Barcelona was battered by sixty two pieces of
cannon, a great number of mortars and patte-
rero's, which considerably increased the former
breaches, and made new ones.

On the second of *September,* two trenches were
opened in the ditches, from the foot of the counterscarp, as far as the breach. But next day

G g

there

1714. there happened so furious a storm, which lasted twelve hours, that the trenches and the mines were brought under water, and the works retarded: however, all this damage was soon repaired.

And now there came out of the town above three hundred men, women and children, crying, *Mercy, mercy, God save King* Philip V. Immediately after, a greater number of them appeared; and if we had been willing to receive them in the camp, or to permit them to retire, very few people would have remained in the town. But Marshal *Berwick* ordered them to be sent back.

On the sixth, Don *Joseph Pelz*, their Serjeant-general of Battalia, appeared upon the top of the breach with a white flag, and desired to speak with the commanding officer upon duty in the trenches. This was to answer a summons, which the Marshal had given him some days before to surrender, in order to avoid the dangers to which a longer obstinacy would expose the town and the inhabitants; offering at the same time to preserve their lives and effects. The Chevalier *d'Asfeld* advancing to the foot of the breach, *Pelz* told him, that the inhabitants of *Barcelona* had deliberated upon the Marshal's proposal; that they were resolved not to listen to it, chusing rather to perish with their arms in their hands, than to submit. Marshal *Berwick's* view in giving that summons, was to save the town from being plundered, and to

preserve

preferve it for the King of *Spain:* but finding 1714.
the inhabitants were obftinate, as the breaches
were by this time as wide as could be defired,
he refolved to give a general affault, and not to
wait for the effect of the new mines which he
had ordered to be made, and had been over-
flown by the heavy rains of the ninth inftant.
For this purpofe he made fuch difpofitions as
he thought would fecure the fuccefs of this expedition, which he knew would be very difficult and hazardous. The befieged did not expect this affault till the mines fhould be fprung.

Lieutenant-general *Dillon*, having under him
Meff. *le Guerchois*, and *del Caftillo*, Marfhals de
Camp, and Meff. *de Refves, Balincour*, and
Alba, Brigadeers, had the command of the attack of the right and the center, with twenty
battalions, twenty companies of grenadeers, and
five hundred pioneers. Mr. *Dillon* commanded
himfelf the centre, with the Brigadeers *Balincour* and *Alba*, thirteen battalions, and three
hundred pioneers; and gave the command of
the right to Meff. *del Caftillo* and *Refves*, with
the other feven battalions and two hundred pioneers. The attack on the left was given to the
Marquis of *Silly*, Lieutenant-general, who had
with him Mr. *Ribadeo*, Marfhal de Camp, Mr.
l'Echerene, the Vicount *del Puetto*, and the Marquis of *Pleffis-Chatillon*, Brigadeers, ten battalions, ten companies of grenadeers, fix hundred
dragoons, and three hundred pioneers. Marfhal
Berwick commanded in perfon the body of re-
G g 2

ferve,

1714. ſerve, conſiſting of fourteen companies of grenadeers, nine battalions, and three hundred
pioneers.

All theſe troops being drawn up over againſt
the places which they were to attack, and the
pioneers being furniſhed with all the neceſſary
tools for making lodgments; on the eleventh,
at half an hour after four in the morning, the
ſignal was given, *viz.* the firing of twelve guns
from the great battery, and of eight bombs
which were not charged: whereupon the troops
and pioneers marched with the grenadeers at their
head. Mr. *Reſves* attacked the baſtion of the
new gate, where the beſieged had caſt up three
retrenchments: after making ſome reſiſtance,
they abandoned the baſtion; for they perceived
that the beſiegers advanced at the ſame time a-
long the courtain, to ſeize the gorge of the baſtion. An hundred and fifty of their men, who
had not retired ſo ſoon as the reſt, were put to
the ſword; and we made our ſelves maſters of
the baſtion, the gorge, and the head of the
great intrenchment, which run to the baſtion of
St. Peter.

General *Dillon,* with his ſeven battalions,
mounted the great breach of the center; 'at the
ſame time, that Mr. *le Guerchois* mounted that
of the angle in flank of the baſtion of *Santa Cla-*
ra. They carried the whole intrenchment which
was behind the monaſtery of *St. Auſtin,* with
part of the convent, putting to the ſword all the
enemies whom they met. As it was known
that

that this place was mined, the troops were for
some time in fear; but their fear soon vanished,
when it appeared that the mines had been over-
flowen by the rains which had fallen some days
before. In these two attacks we lost but a few
men.

The Marquis of *Silly*, who commanded the
attack on the left, likewise divided his ten battalions into two bodies. Mr. *l'Echerene*, who
commanded one of them, mounted the breach
of the angle in flank of the bastion of *Santa Clara*,
on the side of the great tower; at the same time
that Mr. *Ribadeo*, with the five other battalions,
mounted the breach of the angle in flank, opposite to the east bastion. They made themselves
masters of this bastion, the curtain, and the intrenchment, from the wind-mills of the old wall
to the flesh-market. The besieged had in this
bastion a retrenchment, which would have been
impenetrable, if our troops, by the circuit they
made, had not seized the gorge of the bastion;
so that after having bore the fire of eight pieces
of cannon charged with cartridge-shot, they
forced the enemy, and put to sword all the rebels they met. Upon this, six hundred dragoons, supported by three hundred carabineers,
scaled the redoubt of *Eulalia*, which the enemy
abandoned, after having fired three cannons
charged with cartridge-shot. An hundred dragoons were left to guard this redoubt; the rest
passed by the breach of the east bastion, and occupied that side of the stables which is called

 Locata.

1174. *Locata,* The infantry likewife advanced, feized the ruins of the church of *Santa Clara,* and of the chapel of *St. Martha,* and drew near the great retrenchment, which was not yet finifhed. From thence they drove the enemy, and penetrated as far as the herb-market, giving no quarter. Here Mr. *Silly* ftopped the infantry. It was with great difficulty he could hinder them from entring feveral lanes, filled with ditches and ruins, where feveral of our men had infallibly been loft, for want of being fupported. He cauf-ed the entry of thefe lanes to be cut, and lodgments to be made in the houfes oppofite to them.

The befieged finding we advanced no further, neither on the right nor on the left, took courage again, and to make their laft effort, rallied in great numbers, divided into feveral bodies, and by eight of the clock in the morning recovered the baftion and monaftery of *St. Peter,* part of that of *St. Auftin,* as well as the fouth baftion, the palace, and the houfes of the plan of *Enllui,* and even attempted to recover the breaches, by fpringing two mines, which did fome damage to the *Walloon* troops.

Thefe efforts brought on a new engagement with the troops commanded by General *Dillon,* wherein they fired very brifkly. And now the body of referve, which was in the ditch, mount-ed the breach of the courtain, from the baftion of *Santa Clara,* to that of the new gate. Mar-fhal *Berwick* likewife fent for fome battalions

from

from the camp, with fome companies of grenadeers; fo that on this day forty nine battalions
and forty four companies of grenadeers fought
againft the *Barcelonians.*

The ftrefs of the engagement was at the baftion of *St. Peter*, which was this day taken and
retaken eleven times, and occafioned a very
great effufion of blood. Here the befiegers fuffered the greateft lofs, becaufe the precaution
had not been taken to fecure the abbey of *St.
Peter*, when the rebels abandoned it: for the
fire from the abbey played on all fides upon the
baftion: the *Spanifh* and *Walloon* guards, which
were pofted there, could hardly defend themfelves, or attack, without being quite expofed to
the enemy's fire. For the fpace of twelve hours
they gave moft extraordinary proofs of their valour. One battalion remained under the command of a Sub-lieutenant, all its other officers
being killed. The Chevalier *Montolieu*, a Captain, who commanded a battallion, was moft
univerfally lamented. His youth, his pleafing
behaviour, his wit and valour, had gained him
univerfal efteem and affection. He feemed to
have had thoughts that he would die; for he
had made his laft will, and fettled his affairs a
week before this action. As he did not conceal
it, feveral of his friends rallied him upon that
account: he bore their raillery with an eafy,
chearful air. When he was going to mount the
affault, he made a fhort fpeech to his dear *Walloons*, and afterwards fought like a lyon: at laft,

                    having

1714. having loſt two thirds of his battalion, he received a ſhot, and fell upon a heap of *Walloons* who were killed round him.

All theſe poſts were not retaken, and the *Barcelonians* driven into the new town, till four of the clock in the evening. And now they beat the chamade, and hung out ſeveral white flags. Whereupon Marſhal *Berwick* foreſeeing that it would coſt the lives of a great many men, to force the reſt of the town againſt a numerous, obſtinate, and furious people, after having twice refuſed to hear them, at laſt relented, and granted a ſuſpenſion of arms. About eight of the clock in the evening three deputies came from the town: they were Don *Juan Franciſco Ferrat*, on behalf of the regular troops; Don *Jacinto Oliver*, for the townſmen; and Doctor *Durand*, for the clergy. The negotiation laſted four and twenty hours. They diſputed much on the words *ſurrendering at diſcretion*. At laſt the capitulation was concluded in the evening of the twelfth, on the following terms.

1. That the inhabitants ſhould ſurrender at diſcretion to the Catholick King, *Philip* V, their lawful Sovereign.

2. That under the King's good pleaſure, the lives of all the inhabitants, without exception, ſhould be ſaved.

3. That the town ſhould not be plundered; and that in lieu of the pillage, each battalion ſhould be allowed a certain ſum of money, according

cording to the laws of war, when a town is taken by affault.

4. That the town fhould pay a certain fum
of money to the officers and foldiers belonging
to the artillery, to preferve the bells, which by
the above mentioned laws belonged to them.

5. That the *Barcelonians* fhould on the fame
day put fort *Montjuich* into the hands of the befiegers.

6. That they fhould immediately furrender
the town and caftle of *Cardona*, in the condition
in which that place then was, the garrifon of it
being in their pay, and that the faid garrifon
fhould be fafe as to their lives and effects.

7. That they fhould difpofe the *Majorcans*
and all the *Catalans*, who had taken arms at
their folicitation, to fubmit to the mercy of his
Catholick Majefty.

8. That all thofe who had ferved in the regular troops fhould have leave either to lift in
the *Spanifh* troops, or to retire where they
pleafed.

By virtue of this capitulation, fort *Montjuich*
was delivered on the fame evening to Mr. *le
Guerchois*, who took poffeffion of it with a
French garrifon of eight hundred men. It muft
be obferved that this capitulation was not put in
writing. Marfhal *Berwick*, in order to engage
the *Barcelonians* to do their duty, only gave them
a verbal promife, and obliged them to depend
upon his honour.

As

1714.   As soon as the besieged beat the chamade, the Marshal dispatched the Duke of *Montemar* to carry the news of it to the King of *France*, and when the capitulation was agreed upon, he sent the Marquis of *Broglio* to the King of *Spain*. Such is the detail of a siege, which was one of the bloodiest that ever were seen, and wherein extraordinary feats of valour were done on both sides. The *Barcelonians* would certainly deserve great encomiums, if their cause had been better; but their conduct is inexcusable, after they saw they were abandoned by the Emperor, and no mention was made of them in the treaties of *Utrecht* and *Rastadt*. Thus having supported a siege for three months from the opening of the trenches, they returned to the obedience which they owed to their lawful Sovereign.

Marshal *Berwick* gave the command of the town to the Marquis of *Guerchi*, till the King of *Spain* should name a Governor. In this place were found an hundred and eighty three pieces of cannon, and thirty two mortars. On the thirteenth, at five in the morning, the keys were delivered to that Marquis, and an hour after he took possession of all the posts, and there placed the necessary guards. The garrison consisted of fourteen *French* battalions and of the *Spanish* horse. The next day the Miquelets and the *Catalan* volunteers, who before made a part of the garrison, were disarmed and sent home with pass-ports, after they had taken the oath of fidelity, and promised to behave for the future

like

like faithful subjects. The following days the townsmen were disarmed. They endeavoured to impute their fault to four of their Chiefs, who, said they, had usurped the authority, and had`escaped by sea whilst the town was capitulating.

What was most surprising, and which ought partly to be attributed to the exact discipline which Marshal *Berwick* maintained among his troops, was, that on the fourteenth all the shops were opened, the merchants resumed their trade, and the artisans their work, with as much liberty and safety as they had done before the siege. In consequence of the articles agreed upon, the town and castle of *Cardona* surrendered at discretion, and the rebels of the country retired to their respective homes; so that peace and tranquillity seemed to be restored throughout all *Catalonia*.

But it was necessary to render that peace and tranquillity durable, and to prevent new disturbances. For this purpose it was fit to punish the *Barcelonians*, by making some examples of those who had had the greatest share in the rebellion, and had occasioned so much blood-shed, and the loss of so many brave men. Accordingly Marshal *Berwick* seized upon all the monasteries, and placed guards in them; afterwards he published an order that all the inhabitants should carry their arms to the town-house; this was forthwith obeyed. He dissolved all their councils and tribunals, both civil and military: he established a new counsel with the title of the

superior

1714.

1714. fuperior government, and a new tribunal, with that of the tribunal of the adminiftrators: he gave to the latter, as a mark of their dignity, fcarfs of crimfon gold cloth, inftead of the velvet robes which the officers of the deputation wore in the time of the revolt. After this, he made his publick entry into *Barcelona*, and lighted at the cathedral church, where he caufed *Te Deum* to be fung.

He afterwards ordered the principal Chiefs, fecular, ecclefiaftical and religious, who had moft contributed to foment and fupport this revolt, to be apprehended, and to be fhipped off for different prifons in *Spain*, where they were to end their days. He permitted each of them to take a fervant, and allowed their families to fupply them with whatever fhould be neceffary. Thefe are the names of fuch as were apprehended.

The Marquis of *Villaroël*, Generaliffimo, who was wounded and confined to his bed, was imprifoned in his own houfe. The Marquis of *Pinos*, who was likewife wounded, and died fome days after. The Marquis *del Poël*, and the Chevalier his brother, who had made themfelves known by the cruelty they had exercifed upon the *Walloon* troops againft the laws of war: for in the infurrection in the beginning of the year, having furprifed two battalions of *Walloons*, and two battalions of *Spanifh* troops, they carried them prifoners to the caftle of *Genebret*; and afterwards bringing them out ten by ten, fhot them to the number of feven hundred men.

This

This was the chief reason why the *Catalans* sel- 1714.
dom or never after received any quarter : The
Chevalier *del Poël* was taken at *Arens de Mar*,
as he was making his escape ; both he and his
brother affirmed that they had commissions from
the Emperor, but they were never able to produce them. *Baffet*, who commanded the artillery, *Sebaftien Dalman*, a rich merchant, who
had raised a regiment of horse at his own expence, which he named the regiment of Faith.
Simon Sanchez, a Lieutenant-colonel. *Gaëtant
Antillon*, a Major of the same regiment. *Jo-
feph Belever de Balaguer*, Serjeant-general of battalia, Colonel of the regiment of foot of the
Rofary. *Felix Belever*, his son. *Francis Villa*,
Lieutenant-colonel of the same regiment. *Francis Favez*, Colonel of the regiment of infantry
of the deputation. *Raymond Favez*, his son,
Captain of grenadeers. *Nicholas Alexandri*, Major of the same regiment. *Juan-Jofeph de Tor-
rez*, Colonel of the regiment of *Valencia*. *Francis Mayans*, Sub-lieutenant-colonel. *Bardez*,
Captain of the company of affaffins, called *Matadors*. The Commander of *Cardona*, General *Armengol*, and the brother of *Nebot*. Don *Navarro*,
a monk of the order of *Mercy*, whom the King
of *Spain* had named Bishop of *Albarazin* in *Arragon*, and who notwithstanding had joined the
Barcelonians. Father *Torrens*, a dominican, who
preached, and pretending to be a prophet, had
several times assured the people with a fanatick
tone, that an army from heaven would come and
refcue

1714. refcue the town; and three Monks of the fame order, who preached and prophefied in like manner.

By virtue of a power which Marfhal *Berwick* had received from the King of *Spain*, he publifhed a decree on the fecond of *October*, by which he banifhed for ever out of *Catalonia*, and all the dominions of the Catholic King, with orders not to return thither upon pain of death, feveral Ecclefiaftics and Monks of divers orders, to the number of about fixty, who had not only been accomplices in the rebellion, but had likewife encouraged the people by their particular exhortations and publick preachings. Part of thofe exiles went by *Rouffillon* and *Languedoc* to *Rome*, in order to be abfolved from the irregularities they had been guilty of by taking arms. Others embarked at *Barcelona* in order to fail for *Italy*, and were taken by the *Algerines*. Soon after, Marfhal *Berwick*, in order to banifh all animofities and antipathy between the *Catalans* and *Caftilians*, publifhed a new decree, forbidding the *Catalans* on pain of death to infult the *Caftilians*; and forbidding the latter, and all other *Spaniards*, on the like pain, to upbraid the *Catalans* with the name of rebels.

The Earl of *Tinmouth* carried to the King of *Spain* the colours and ftandards of the *Barcelonians* and *Catalans*, to the number of fixty. His Catholick Majefty received him gracioufly, and gave him the order of the *Golden Fleece*, but fent back to Marfhal *Berwick* thefe colours, in order

to

to be burnt by the hand of the hangman in the 1714.
publick place of *Barcelona*, as well as the robes
of thofe, who having fet themfelves up for Magiftrates of the deputation, had fupported and directed affairs in the time of the revolt. The Marfhal immediately caufed this order to be put into
execution. His Catholick Majefty, to reward the
important fervices of Marfhal *Berwick*, affigned
him a penfion of a hundred thoufand livres *per
annum*; and likewife fent him a fword enriched
with diamonds of a very great value. Befides,
he gave the collar of the *Golden Fleece* to Lord
Lucan, with a company in his life-guards

After having executed all his Majefty's orders,
and having eftablifhed the tranquility of *Catalonia*, Marfhal *Berwick* fet out for *Madrid*, where
he arrived on the twenty eight of *October*, and
met with a moft favourable reception from his
Moft Catholick Majefty. He had feveral private conferences with the King, and with the
Duke of *Popoli*, the Prince *Pio*, the Marquis of
Grimaldi, and the Prefident *Orri*, concerning
the affairs of *Catalonia* and *Majorca:* after which
he returned to the Court of *France*.

The Royal Family had loft another Prince;
Charles of *France*, Duke of *Berry*, died at *Marli*
on the fourth of *May*, in the twenty eighth year
of his age, without leaving any children by
Mary Louifa Elizabeth of *Orleans*, his wife. In
the year 1713 he had a fon, who was ftiled
Duke of *Alençon*, who lived only twenty two
days, and the Princefs of whom the Duchefs of
Berry

1714. *Berry* was delivered on the sixteenth of *June* of this year, died next day. Thus the King of *France*, in the seventy second year of his reign, after having seen a numerous posterity, was obliged to make a Will for settling affairs during the minority of the Dauphin, his great-grandson, who was only five years of age.

This induced his Most Christian Majesty to make an edict, by which he legitimated the Duke *du Maine* and Count *Toulouse*, and called them to the succession of the Crown, failing the Princes of the Blood. This edict was regiftred in Parliament on the second of *August*, in the presence of the Duke of *Enguien*, the Prince of *Conti*, two Ecclesiastical Peers, and seventeen Dukes and Laick Peers. This edict was followed by another declaration, importing that the legitimated Princes should take the quality of Princes of the Blood in all judicial acts, and should be treated accordingly.

This year was remarkable for the death of *Anne*, Queen of *England*; whereby the design which was formed for advancing the Chevalier *St. George* to the Crown of *Great Britain* was rendred abortive; and that Crown, by virtue of an Act of Parliament passed in the reign of King *William*, devolved on *George Augustus*, Elector of *Hanover*. Accordingly, that Prince set out from *Hanover* on the thirty first of *August*, arrived at the *Hague* on the fifth of *Sepember*, and on the twentieth made his publick entry into *London.*

We

We shall pass swiftly over the following years, 1715.
during which Marshal *Berwick*, enjoying that
retirement and tranquility which the peace procured him, was solely employed in discharging
those duties of private life, which are noways interesting to the publick. We shall only mention the principal events which happened at that
time, that we may not lose the thread of these
Memoirs. In this year, with the permission of
his Catholick Majesty, he yielded to the Earl of
Tinmouth, his son by the first marriage, the title
and rank of Grandee of *Spain*, with the Duchies
of *Liria* and *Xerica*. Whereupon the Earl retired to *Spain*, where he fixed his abode, and
took the title of Duke of *Liria*. On the seventeenth of *October*, the Duchess of *Berwick* was
delivered of a son, who was named *Edward*:
and now the Marshal had three sons and one
daughter by the second marriage.

But these private satisfactions were soon disturbed by the loss which *France* suffered upon
the death of the greatest of its Kings. *Lewis* XIV,
born at *St. Germains en Laye*, on the fifth of
September 1638, in the twenty third year of the
marriage of *Lewis* XIII, having ascended the
throne on the fourteenth of *May* 1643, after
the longest and most glorious reign, died on the
first of *September* of this year, aged seventy six
years, wanting five days. Marshal *Berwick* and
all good Frenchmen lost in him the best of masters, arts and sciences their greatest protector,
Europe one of its chief ornaments, and the Ca-

tholick

1715. tholick Religion its defender. The fevere and long trials which he underwent in the end of his reign, difcovered his piety, and manifefted his greatnefs of foul, more than his moft fhining fucceffes. His whole life was diftinguifhed by wonderful events. But furely what is moft to be admired, he feemed to be raifed as much and more above other men, at a time when he was going to be mixed and blanded with the mean-eft of them, as in any other part of his life. All the Princes of the earth, even thofe who are more remote from us by their manners than by the diftance of place, paid him homage by the moft folemn embaffies; and his auguft name ftill procures refpect and efteem to the *French* in the moft diftant countries. Thofe Kings who at-tempted to difpute with him the prerogatives of his Crown, were obliged to make him the moft authentick reparation. The unfortunate Kings found an Afylum in his palaces; and it ought not to be reckoned amongft the leaft of the trials and afflictions of this humane Prince, that he was obliged to abandon them. There was fome-thing marvellous in his misfortunes, as well as his profperities; and it may be faid without flat-tery, that he was at all times, in all fituations, in publick as well as in private, by the air of majefty which graced his perfon, as well as by the talents of his eminent genius, his fagacity, the qualities of his mind, and his chriftian vir-tues, the greateft Prince that ever wore a Crown.

His

His death happened whilst he was employed 1715. in taking measures for making his people enjoy the advantages of the peace which had been lately concluded. This was what he had chiefly at heart, and what he frequently recommended to the young Prince whom he left behind him, and to all those whom he had chosen for taking care of his education. If ever the discernment of *Lewis* XIV was necessary, it was at this conjuncture, when he was to form a successor whom he could no longer instruct himself.

But his discernment of the characters of men was always so just, that we had reason perfectly to acquiesce in the choice he made upon this occasion. We feel the happy effects of it to this day; and *France* has had the good fortune for more than these twenty years, since the death of that great King, to be governed by his spirit and genius, and to see the glory of the *French* name, and the felicity of the people, perpetuated under his successor *Lewis* XV.

Philip, Duke of *Orleans*, having been acknowledged Regent of the kingdom, gave in appearance a new form to the government, by the difrent councils which he established. The superior genius of this Prince, who kept all the Courts of *Europe* in awe, and the measures he took both at home and abroad, maintained the publick tranquility, and we could not perceive that we lived in the time of a minority. But a further detail of these measures would be foreign to our present subject. Let us give an account of the

share

1716. share Marshal *Berwick* had in the war against *Spain*, which was concluded in one campaign.

The enterprizes which alarmed the Regent of *France*, were formed and conducted by Cardinal *Alberoni*, Prime Minister of his Catholick Majesty. The finances of *Spain*, which had been in great disorder, were soon improved under the ministry of that Cardinal. He put them under such good regulations, that *Spain*, which in the late war was unable to defend itself against its enemies, became on a sudden formidable, and in a condition to make enterprizes. As soon as that Minister had put things into such a situation, he formed three projects of such a nature, that the success of any one of them would have been sufficient to immortalize his ministry, and transmit his name to the latest posterity.

His first design was to reunite to the Crown of *Spain* the States of *Italy*, which had formerly belonged to that Monarchy, and had been yielded to the Emperor in the late peace. And as it was to be feared, that by virtue of the quadruple alliance, which had been lately concluded, *England* and *France* would join the Emperor against *Spain*, whenever the Emperor should be attacked; he resolved to give a diversion to these two Powers at home, which might disable them from assisting the Emperor.

For this purpose he took measures for making a descent upon *Scotland*, and raising an insurrection there in favour of the Chevalier *St. George*. He made several preparations for supporting

porting

porting thofe who fhould declare for that Prince, 1716.
being perfuaded, that by thus intangling the
King of *England* at home, he would oblige him
to employ his forces in that civil war, and hinder him from fending troops to defend the interefts of a foreign Prince. As for *France*, he
formed a defign of fomenting in that kingdom
another kind of infurrection, by means of the
malcontents, whom he thought to be more
numerous there than they proved to be, becaufe
he judged only by the circumftance of a minority.

Thefe three enterprizes were to break out
at the fame time; and there was no fufpicion of
them. We were indeed informed of the preparations which *Spain* was making to equip two
fleets, one for the ocean, and another for the
Mediterranean; but the defign of them was not
known. We were only aftonifhed to fee that a
kingdom, which was thought deeply in debt,
and fhould have endeavoured to recover its former ftrength, was fo foon in a condition to act,
and to equip fleets.

We did not remain long in doubt: the papers
which Prince *Cellamare*, the *Spanifh* Ambaffador
in *France*, fent to the Court of *Madrid*, being
ftopped and feized, upon I know not what fufpicions, difcovered the whole affair. Whereupon this Ambaffador was fent back, and the
projects of Cardinal *Alberoni* went no further.
Perhaps they would not have mifcarried, at leaft
foon after their birth, if that Cardinal had not

1716. been oppofed by a Prince fo penetrating, active, and refolute, as the Regent of *France.* The Duke of *Orleans* had no fooner notice of this project, than he put a ftop to it; and he thought himfelf engaged to punifh fome of thofe who had given into the fcheme of Cardinal *Albe-roni.*

1718.   The enterprize in *Scotland* had no better fuccefs.   The fleet which had fet out from *Cadiz,* was difperfed by a ftorm, and could never land in *Scotland.*   The fleet which was appointed for *Italy* could not land its forces, in order to feize the *Milanefe,* becaufe the Prince who promifed to affift in that expedition, did not believe himfelf ftrong enough, and failed in his promife. The *Spaniards* landed in *Sicily,* and made themfelves mafters of that kingdom; from whence the Emperor had afterwards much difficulty to drive them.

Notwithftanding all thefe difappointments, *Europe* learned to know the extent and elevation of the genius of Cardinal *Alberoni*; and though the publick commonly judges of things by the fuccefs of them, yet the glory of fo vaft a project, when it mifcarries by accidents which can neither be forefeen nor avoided, is not diminifhed by the ill fuccefs of it.   From this, *Spain* might know its own ftrength, and where its refources lye.   Large dominions want an able hand, to form and put in motion a mafs very often fhapelefs and confufed.

The

The Regent, provoked at the defign of the 1719.
Spanifh Minifter, which ftruck at his authority,
proclaimed war againft *Spain* in the beginning of
the year 1719. In *December*, the year preceeding, the King of *England*, being no lefs provoked
at the ambitious and turbulent practices of Cardinal *Alberoni*, had likewife declared war againft
Spain.

The Regent, wanting a General for the ma-
nagement of this war, caft his eye upon Marfhal
Berwick: at the fame time he made him a
Member of the Council of the Regency. His
Royal Highnefs having fent for him, faid to him,
*My Lord Duke, his Majefty gives you the com-
mand of his army againft* Spain: *Upon this you
will probably lofe your penfion of an hundred thoufand livres, which you have from his Catholick
Majefty; but the King will make up your lofs.
Sir,* anfwered the Marfhal, *I fhall always have
a juft value for the confidence which his Majefty
will be pleafed to repofe in me: I will obey his orders. If upon this occafion I lofe the penfion of an
hundred thoufand livres, I fhall be lefs concerned
for that lofs, than I am defirous of giving proofs of
my zeal for the fervice of his Majefty, and the
advantage of the kingdom.* A few days after he
fet out for the army, which met on the fide of
Bayonne. Upon his arrival, he was informed
that the *Spanifh* army was already affembled.

The war began with the fiege of *Fontarabia*,
which lafted but a fhort time, the *Spaniards*
making only a faint refiftance. After the taking

H h 4

of

1719. of this place, *St. Sebaſtian* was attacked, and likewiſe carried : whereupon the Marſhal moved with his army towards *Rouſſillon*; and croſſing the *Pyrenean* mountains, made a very extraordinary and ſurprizing march. He attacked and carried the two forts and places of the caſtle of *Urgel*. After this, he beſieged *Roſes*; but the rains falling continually, and moſt of the veſſels which carried the proviſions and ammunition for the army being deſtroyed in a ſtorm, he was obliged to raiſe the ſiege, and abandon that enterprize. Thus ended this campaign, which put an end to the war.

1720.   In the beginning of the year 1720 a peace was concluded between *France* and *Spain*, and the towns which had been taken from the latter were reſtored. Cardinal *Alberoni*, who was looked upon as the principal cauſe of this war, was ſent back to *Italy*.

The ſyſtem of Mr. *Law* (or the *Miſſiſſippi*) had taken its birth in the year 1718, had triumphed in 1719, ſuffered ſeveral changes in 1720, and at laſt in the year 1721, expired by the change of Bank-bills into Bills of Liquidation.

The plague which broke out at *Marſeilles* in the month of *July* 1720, after having made great deſolations in *Provence*, and greatly alarmed the whole kingdom, ended in the year 1721. Marſhal *Berwick* had been ſent into *Languedoc* for the ſecurity of that province. He there formed lines, blocked up all the paſſages where the
plague

plague might enter, and even burnt fome vil- 1720.
lages, which there was no hopes of purging from
the contagion. His ftrictnefs and rigour put a
ftop to the imprudence of fome, and to the ava-
rice of others, and thus prevented the progrefs
of that dreadful calamity.

In the beginning of the year 1715, *Lewis* XIV
had given audience to the *Perfian* Ambaffador in
the moft pompous and magnificent manner. This
Ambaffador's name was *Mehemet Rizabec*. He
was Governor of the province of *Erivan*, and came
folely to complement his Majefty upon his late victories, for which he was fo famous and renowned in the Eaft. The King was feated upon a
throne, placed at one end of the great gallery of
Verfailles; and all thofe who were prefent owned
that the Court never appeared fo fplendid *.

In the year 1721 *Lewis* XV gave likewife a 1721.
magnificent audience to *Cellibi Mehemet Effendi*,
Ambaffador from the Grand Signior, who came
to complement him upon his acceffion to the
Crown, and to propofe fome regulations for commerce. His entry into *Paris* was very fingular:
he entred it on horfeback, with detachments
of the King's houfe. This Ambaffador was a
man of wit and judgment. He efpecially admired the learning of the *French* with whom he
had occafion to treat, and was fenfible of the

* This was a mere farce, contrived, as it is faid, by the *Je-
fuits* to flatter *Lewis* XIV. Soon after the death of that Prince,
the trick being difcovered, the mock Ambaffador retired private-
ly to *Normandy*, from whence he embarked for *Dantzick*; and
he has never been heard of fince.

difad-

difadvantage which the *Turks* lye under by the averfion they have for the fciences, the ftudy of which would polifh their manners, and render their Empire illuftrious. Accordingly, when he returned to the Porte, he imparted thefe fentiments to the Grand Vifier, and occafioned the fetting up of a printing-houfe in *Turkey*, by means of which one might at leaft more eafily learn the languages.

The following year was remarkable for the difgrace of Marfhal *Villeroy*, who was ordered to retire to his government; for the encampment at *Montreüil*, of which Marfhal *Villars* had the direction, as being the oldeft Marfhal of *France*; for the coronation of the King, which was done at *Reims* on the twenty fifth of *October*; and for the demand which the Duke of *Orleans* made in the name of his Moft Chriftian Majefty of the Princefs *Mary Ann Victoria*, Infanta of *Spain*, to be married to the King.

The Regent married at the fame time two of his daughters, one to the Prince of *Afturias*, and the other to Don *Carlos*. But the great youth of the Infanta, and the impatience of *France* to fee a Dauphin, occafioned that three years after this Princefs was fent back to *Spain*. She was afterwards married to the Prince of *Brafil* in *Portugal*.

In this year Marfhal *Berwick* married Lady *Henrietta* his daughter to Meffire *John Baptift Lewis* of *Clermont d'Amboife*, Marquis of *Renel*. This marriage was made on the feventh of *September*.

The

The difgrace of Mr. *le Blanc*, Minifter of War, the death of Cardinal *du Bois*, and fome months after, the death of the Regent, occafioned a great many intrigues at Court in the year 1723. The unanimous regret of the military body for the difgrace of *le Blanc*, might comfort him till he was fully juftified by the Decree of Parliament, which acquitted him in the year 1725.

There was little talk of the fecond, after the firft report of his death. But *France* will always reckon *Philip* Duke of *Orleans* among its greateft Princes; and if in enumerating thofe uncommon qualities with which he was endued, and particularly in giving a character of his uprightnefs and honefty, we pafs over fome things in filence, this will only occafion his being more greatly lamented.

On the fifteenth of *January* 1724, *Philip* V, King of *Spain*, abdicated his Crown in favour of the Prince of *Afturias*, who took the name of *Lewis* I. This Prince reigned but a fhort time; for he died on the twenty firft of *Auguft* following. It was with great difficulty that the King his father was prevailed with to reafcend the throne; he was made fenfible that his confcience was concerned in not expofing *Spain* to the danger of a minority; and he yielded to the earneft folicitations of the Junto, and of the whole kingdom.

Louifa Elizabeth of *Orleans*, the confort of *Lewis* I, returned to *France*. The fame year the

the King gave the Baton of Marſhal of *France* to the Duke of *Roquelaire*, the Duke of *Grammont*, the Marquis *Alegre*, Count *Broglio*, Mr. *du Bourg*, Mr. *Madavi*, and the Duke *la Feuillade*.

His Majeſty made a promotion of ſixteen Knights of the order of the *Holy Gboſt*, among whom was Marſhal *Berwick*: They were inſtalled on the thirtieth of *June*. The views of *France* were at laſt ſatisfied by the marriage of their King with the Princeſs *Mary*, daughter of *Staniſlaus*, King of *Poland*: And this Queen having brought forth a Dauphin on the fourth of *September* 1729, the joy of the people was ſo great, and, if we may ſay it, ſo exceſſive, that the King was obliged to employ his authority to put a ſtop to the expences which the towns and communities laid out upon that occaſion.

In the year 1726, *Lewis* XV compleatly reeſtabliſhed the form of government, as it had been ſettled in the reign of *Lewis* XIV; and the better to ſecure the advantages of it, and follow the model which he propoſed, he placed at the head of affairs the late Biſhop of *Frejus*, who was made a Cardinal much about the ſame time. Let abler pens tranſmit to poſterity the glory of a Miniſter admired by all *Europe*, and who may be placed, without any diſadvantage, among the moſt renowned Stateſmen.

In the month of *April* 1730, his Majeſty gave the government of *Straſburg* to Marſhal *Berwick*. Next year his ſon *Francis Fitz-James*
had

had given him the abby of *St. Victor* of *Paris*, vacant by the death of Cardinal *Gualteri*; and on the eleventh of *March* 1732, Lady *Louisa* his daughter was married to *Joachim Lewis de Montague*, Marquis of *Busoles*.

After a peace of twenty years, the face of affairs changed, and the principal Powers of *Europe* came to a variance. As in this war Marshal *Berwick* gave the last proofs of his military skill, and of his ardor for the interest and glory of the kingdom, we shall here give a particular account of it.

In the year 1726, a particular treaty had been made between the King of *Spain* and the Emperor, which is well known by the name of the treaty of *Vienna*. This treaty was the work of *Riperda*, and had no other effect, but that of raising its author to the dignity of Duke, Grandee, and Minister of *Spain*, that his fall, no doubt, might be the greater. For whether that Duke wanted merit to support so sudden a fortune, or whether he abused his grandeur, he was soon obliged to seek a retreat; and he made so bad a choice, that his retreat increased his dishonour. He thought no asylum safer for him than the Court of the King of *Fez* and *Morocco*; and in order to maintain himself there, and to give no umbrage, he made no scruple to sacrifice his religion. The treaty of *Vienna* not having taken place, the two Powers treated at the same time, but without acting in concert, with *Victor Amadeus* King of *Sardinia*. It has been pretended,

that

that this Prince entred into engagements on both
fides, which afterwards he found himfelf unable
to fulfil, and · that he knew no other way of
extricating himfelf out of this dilemma, than to
abdicate his Crown.　Expedients muft have been
very fcarce and very difficult, if that Prince could
find no others.　Be it as it will, after having fo
often inclined the fcale to the fide which pleafed
him beft, he went off the fcene in the year
1728, and refigned his whole authority to his
fon, the Prince of *Piedmont*, who foon knew
how to gain the refpect and admiration of all
Europe.　*Victor Amadeus* repenting foon after
of having taken this ftep, endeavoured to re-
fume the regal authority.　He accordingly went
to *Turin*, and demanded of the Minifters the
inftrument of his refignation ; but it was refufed
to him : and this occafioned his confinement.
He died in his retreat in the year 1733.

In the fame year died *Frederick Auguftus*,
Elector of *Saxony*, and King of *Poland*.　The
death of this Prince furnifhed a pretence for the
war which we are going to relate.　King *Auguftus* had no fooner expired, but the Primate
of *Poland* fummoned a Diet to elect a new King.
At the fame time (this was in the month of
March) they were informed that the Emperor
affembled troops on the fide of *Silefia*, which
made the *Poles* apprehend that there was a defign to invade the liberty of their fuffrages : they
believed that they had fufficiently fecured themfelves againft any violence by the oath they had

taken

taken not to chufe for their King any foreigner, or any perfon who was not defcended from the family of the *Piaftees*, that is, the defcendants of the firft Kings of *Poland*. Soon after, it was known that the Emperor had made a league with the *Czarina*, to oblige the *Poles* to give their fuffrages to the Elector of *Saxony*, the fon of the late King. Upon this, the *Poles* judged that no time muft be loft; and having agreed to chufe for their King, *Staniflaus*, who had been already elected in the year 1704, by the recommendation of *Charles* XII, King of *Sweden*, they wrote to the King of *France* to demand his protection.

Upon the firft notice of the favourable difpofitions of the *Poles* with regard to King *Staniflaus*, he fet out incognito for *Warfaw*; and at the fame time the King of *France* wrote a letter to the Primate of *Poland*, wherein he affured the Republick of his protection, and that he would fupport the liberty of their fuffrages in the approaching election of a King. Mean while, in the month of *Auguft*, the *Czarina* fent troops into the Duchy of *Courland*, affuring the Republick that her fole defign was to fupport them in the freedom of their election. Thefe affurances impofed upon no body. The King of *France* now thought fit to declare war againft the Emperor: but this affair was conducted with the utmoft fecrecy.

On the feventeenth of *Auguft*, Marfhal *Berwick*, who was named Generaliffimo of the army in *Germany*, fet out for *Metz*. At the 1733.
fame

1733. fame time another army was fent to pafs over the *Alps*, in order to enter *Italy*, where Marfhal *Villars* was to command, under the King of *Sardinia*, though it was not yet known what thefe troops were defigned for.   On the fourth of *September*, the Senate of *Poland* publifhed a Manifefto, wherein they protefted againft the violence which was intended to be offered them in their election, and prohibited all correfpondence with ftrangers, and every Palatine to quit the kingdom. At laft, King *Staniflaus*, after having paffed thro' *Germany*, whilft it was imagined that he was at fea, arrived at *Warfaw*; and on the twelfth, was unanimoufly proclaimed King of *Poland*. The declaration of war which *France* made againft the Emperor, did not appear till the fifteenth of *October*.   It was dated the tenth.   In the following month appeared the Emperor's anfwer, to which the declaration of war of the King of *Sardinia* was a reply : that Prince, with the King of *Spain*, united himfelf with *France*, and complained of feveral grievances.

Marfhal *Berwick* having affembled his army near *Strafburg*, detached on the twelfth of *October* twenty companies of grenadeers, and a thoufand fuzileers, under the command of the Marquis of *Dreux*, Lieutenant-general, and of the Chevalier *Givry*, Marfhal de Camp, to pafs the *Rhine* upon a bridge of boats, which he had caufed to be made below *Strafburg*.   This detachment paffed over the village of *Avenheim*, and was followed on the thirteenth by the whole

army,

army, which had paſſed the *Rhine* on the four-
teenth upon a bridge that had been made below
fort *Kehl.*

Immediately the Marſhal ordered this place to
be inveſted. The following days were employed
in ſettling the quarters of the army, and in making all the neceſſary preparations for this ſiege.
The head quarters were at the village of *Bun-
heim,* the right at the village of *Golſhſchir,* which
covered a ſecond bridge laid over the *Upper
Rhine,* and the left at the village of *Auden-
heim.*

On the night between the nineteenth and
twentieth, the trenches were opened by the
Marquis of *Puiſegur,* Lieutenant-General, Mr.
la Billarderie, Marſhal de Camp, and the Marquis of *Oudetot,* a Brigadeer; two thouſand pioneers ordered for the trenches, were ſupported
by the three battalions of the regiment of *Navarre,* the three companies of grenadeers of the
regiment of the Marine, two of that of *Richelieu,* one of the regiment of *Bourbonnois,* a detachment of a hundred gens d'armes, and four
hundred and fifty troopers or dragoons. On the
ſame night a firſt parallel was made between the
Rhine and the *Schourne,* and three boyaus were
carried forward upon the capitals of the front of
the horn-work.

On the night between the twentieth and twenty firſt, the Duke of *Noailles,* Lieutenant-general; the Chevalier *Givry,* Marſhal de Camp; and
Mr. *Genſac,* Brigadeer, relieved the trenches:

I i

during

1733. during this night and the preceeding, the works were advanced two thousand five hundred fathoms. The next day the trenches were relieved by the Prince of *Tingri*, and the Counts *Guitard* and *Mideburg*. The besieged, who had not yet fired from the beginning of the siege, made this night a great fire of their artillery and musquetry; but they could not hinder our troops from lodging upon the advanced lunet.

On the night of the twenty third, we made a lodgment in the two little counter guards, situated between the advanced lunet and the demibastion of the right of the horn-work. The trenches were relieved by the Marquis of *Dreux*, the Marquis *la Fare*, and Mr. *Buckley*; they were advanced within fifty fathoms of the covered way, and some of our troops lodged themselves upon a lunet of earth, which the besieged had not had time to finish. In the following night the Marquis of *Nangis*, the Count of *Saxe*, and the Count of *Bavaria*, carried on a sap between the *Rhine*, and the right branch of the horn-work. On the twenty fifth the besieged attempted to interrupt it; but our grenadeers obliged them to retire, and the sap was continued under the command of Mr. *du Guat*, the Marquis of *Clermont*, and Mr. *Chenclette*. The Duke of *Duras*, Mess. *Fiavicat* and *Hosanully*, made the following night a lodgment in the counterscarp of the demibastion of the right of the horn work, and employed the miners at the right branch of that work. But in the evening of the twenty eighth,

eighth, General *Phal*, Commander of the place, 1734. beat the chamade, and capitulated. Marſhal *Ber-wick* ſent his ſon-in-law, the Marquis of *Renel*, Colonel of the regiment of *Santerre*, to carry the news of this to the King. The regiments of *Genſac* and *Rouërgue*, entered the fort on the firſt of *November*, where they were to continue as a garriſon: and Mr. *la Fitte*, commander of the third battalion of the regiment of *Navarre*, was appointed Governor of the place.

The Chevalier *Givry*, with ſix battalions and a regiment of dragoons, went on the ſecond to *Huningen*, to cauſe the bridge of that town to be rebuilt; and next day the Marſhal ſet out with a part of the army from the camp at *Sundheim*, came to *Bichem*, afterwards to *Lintenaw*, and arrived on the fifth over againſt fort *Lewis*. The reſt of the army marched under the command of the Duke of *Noailles*, who after having encamped at *Bichem*, moved on the fifth to *Stolhoffen*, where he placed his center at *Selinguen*, his right at the village of *Stolhoffen*, and his left at that of *Hugelſheim*. The bridge and communication of fort *Lewis*, with the iſle of the Marquiſate, and the work which was to defend it, were ordered to be rebuilt.

On the ninth, Marſhal *Berwick* made a general review of the army, where were Count *Charollois*, Count *Clermont*, the Prince of *Conti*, the Prince of *Dombes*, and Count *Eu*. After which the troops went into winter quarters.

I i 2 *Landau*,

   Marſhal *Berwick* returned to *Straſburg*, from whence he went to viſit fort *Lewis*, *Huningen*, *Landau*, and *Befort* : from thence he ſet out for *Verſailles*, where he arrived on the twenty ninth. Upon his arrival, he aſſiſted at ſeveral councils, which were held for ſettling the operations of the enſuing campaign.

In the month of *March* he repaired to *Straſburg*, and having aſſembled the army, he divided it into three bodies, which moved in the beginning of the following month. Count *Beliſle* was detached with one of theſe bodies, and ſent to *Treves*, of which place he made himſelf maſter.   After this, he ſent fourteen companies of grenadeers, and three hundred dragoons of the regiment of *Suſa*, commanded by his brother the Chevalier *Beliſle*, a Brigadeer, to ſeize *Traerbach*. They forced the barriers, broke open the gates with petards, and made themſelves maſters of the town, where they took ſeveral priſoners. Count *Beliſle*, after having given his orders in *Treves* for the ſubſiſtence of the troops, advanced to *Iſmenac*, where he encamped to be at hand to beſiege the caſtle of *Traerbach :* and as ſoon as he received the neceſſary artillery, he beſieged that caſtle, which ſurrendered after four days from the opening of the trenches.

The Duke of *Noailles*, with the ſecond body of troops, encamped on the eighth of *April* at *Saint Vandel*. He extended his quarters from the *Soar*, as far as *Keyſerlautern* ; his head quarters were at *Homburg*. Marſhal *Berwick*, who

was

was at the head of the moſt conſiderable body, 1734.
marched likewiſe on the eighth, and encamped
the following day, his right at the *Little Holland*,
and his left at *Spires*. At the ſame time he
cauſed the poſt of *Marientrault*, and the caſtle
of *Newſtadt* on the *Spierbach*, to be occupied,
in order to ſettle a communication with *Keyſerlautern*. Here the Duke of *Buckingham* arrived
from *Verſailles*, having obtained the King's per-
miſſion to ſerve in his army as Aide de Camp to
Marſhal *Berwick* his uncle.

The Marſhal having left his army under the
command of Mr. *d'Asfeld*, came on the firſt of
May to fort *Lewis*. The troops which followed
him, or were diſperſed in divers parts of *Alſace*,
encamped there on the ſame day. The Duke
of *Noailles* likewiſe arrived there, with the body
he commanded on the ſide of *Homburg* and
Keyſerlautern, to cover the ſiege of the caſtle of
Traerbach.

The next day, the whole army paſſed the
Rhine upon a bridge which had been built in
the night. The Duke of *Noailles*, with fifteen
companies of grenadeers, an hundred carabineers
of the life-guards, and two regiments of dragoons, having under him Mr. *Vitry* and the
Count of *Saxe*, Marſhals de Camp, went to
encamp, his right at *Iffretzheim*, and his left at
Santwir. On the third he marched in the high-
way which leads from *Raſtadt* to *Dourlach*, and
croſſes the lines. He placed his left at the height

of

1734. of the village of *Murfch*, and his right at the great
farm, fituated in the plain, near a league from
a wood. This farm feparated us from the lines,
and kept a confiderable part of them from our
fight. Before he arrived in that place, he feveral times caufed his foremoft troops to halt in
battalia, to give the reft time to open, and be
within reach of fupporting each other, in cafe
the enemy fhould attack them; for it might naturally be fuppofed they would come out of their
lines, was it only to reconnoitre us. However,
they fuffered our troops to advance within half
a league of their lines, without appearing. There
was reafon to believe, that thefe lines were, or
would foon be abandoned; but the Duke of
Noailles having fent about thirty *Huffars*, fupported by fome fmall detachments of dragoons,
to fcour the wood, it appeared that the enemy
were far from intending to retire: on the contrary, they were preparing to defend their lines,
and we faw them working in their fhirts, to
make embrafures, and put the parapets in good
condition. In this incurfion our *Huffars* took
nine hundred fheep which paffed near a redoubt:
the enemy fired fome mufquet-fhot and three
cannons, but this did not hinder the *Huffars*
from keeping their prey. We were now well
perfuaded, and had reafon to be fo, that the
enemy would not abandon their lines, without
making refiftance. Never was any work of that
nature raifed with more care, or difpofed with

greater

greater art. They had employed fix months in making thefe lines, and it was judged from fo many precautions and preparations they had made, that they had put their truft in them, and flattered themfelves that they would fhut up our entry into *Germany* by a barrier which they deemed infurmountable.

Thefe lines took their name from *Etlingen*, a fmall village belonging to the Prince of *Baden*. They were terminated on one fide by the mountains of *Keppelenfberg*; from thence winding fometimes over the tops, fometimes over the fides of feveral of the *Black Mountains*, they defcended into the plain which extends to the foot of *Sommerberg*, and ended at the banks of the *Rhine*, in the neighbourhood of *Taxe-Landen*; fo that if we reckon their windings, they were at leaft ten leagues in extent. That part which run from the mountain of *Keppelenfberg* to the beginning of the plain, was a retrenchment after the manner of the *Turks*: the enemy called this kind of work *Palankas*. They are trees laid chequer-wife, and twifted together. Thefe trees formed a rampart about ten yards thick, which appeared almoft impregnable. The other part, which covered the plain, confifted of a parapet, with its banquette and ditch. Here they had made in feveral places wells, which were fupplied from the river *Albe*, and from a brook that wafhes the village of *Malfch*. Laftly, along this vaft retrenchment were places of arms, re-

doubts,

 doubts, demi-lunes, a swallow's tail, and a horn-work.

The Duke of *Noailles*, after having attentively observed the strong and the weak sides of the lines, went himself about four of the clock in the afternoon to give Marshal *Berwick* an account of it.   After they had conferred together, the Marshal was of opinion that the lines should be attacked at the heights; and the Duke of *Noailles* had the charge of the attack.   Whereupon he repaired to the village of *Malsch*, situated at the foot of the *Black Mountains*; and whilst he was making his first dispositions, he sent to reconnoitre the roads by which he could march.   The Count of *Saxe*, who well knew the country, went on one side, and Mr. *Galeau*, a partisan, went on the other.   The next morning, at break of day, he set out himself with an hundred carabineers of the life-guards, and the two regiments of dragoons of *Orleans* and *Vitry :* and whilst he marched on the right in a road between woods and precipices, the Count of *Saxe* led on the left, by another path, the column of the infantry, at the head of whom marched all the grenadeers commanded by the Chevalier *Marcieux*. The piquets were supported by the brigade of *Piedmont*, and that of the marine, commanded by Mr. *Herouville*. All these troops composed eleven battalions and six squadrons, besides the hundred carabineers of the life-guards.

The

The two columns arrived at the same time *1734.* on the top of the mountain, where they found a small plain very convenient for their forming into battalia. Here they were expofed to a hurrican, which lafted above fix hours, and was followed by fo thick a fog, that they could hardly fee one another at the diftance of four paces. As foon as the fog was difpelled, they went to reconnoitre the enemy, and to fee if their retrenchments had ditches in that place, and required fafcines. When they were well affured that fafcines were not neceffary, the Duke of *Noailles* made the neceffary difpofition for the attack.

He put five companies of grenadeers in front, fupported by five others, after whom the pi-quets marched in the fame order, being follow-ed by eleven battalions, which fupported the former, and marched in columns at a confider-able diftance, to avoid confufion. Upon the right and the left of the infantry, marched the hundred carabineers of the life-guards and the dragoons. As our troops paffed through a wood of high trees, the enemy did not perceive them, till they were coming out of it, when they were within an hundred paces of the re-trenchments.

The Duke of *Noailles*, who marched at the head of the firft battalion of *Piedmont*, ordered the fignal to be given, and immediately the fol-diers rufhed forward, crying out, *Long live the King.*

 King. The *Imperialists* were headed by an officer, who expreſſed a great deal of coolneſs. We heard him diſtinctly ſay to his men: *Be not afraid, God will be for us.* They ſuffered our troops to approach, and then made three diſcharges upon them with the mouths of their pieces almoſt at our breaſts. The firing was briſk on both ſides; but at laſt our troops mounted the retrenchments. Whereupon the enemy betook themſelves to flight, and threw themſelves into a wood not far off, leaving us intirely maſters of their lines. The firſt thing we went about was, to make in the lines the neceſſary openings for the march of our cavalry, and of the reſt of our troops. It muſt be owned, the enemy did not expect to be attacked; they had in that place only about five or ſix hundred men, ſupported by about an hundred horſe: the reſt of their troops, to the number of ten thouſand men, were diſperſed into diſtant places, and eſpecially in the principal works.

As ſoon as they were informed that we had forced their retrenchments, they thought fit to retreat; and about four of the clock in the afternoon, they entirely abandoned their lines, though they had very ſtrong works, and ſuch as we could not have taken but by means of our cannon. On the ſame day, Prince *Eugene* dined in the lines at *Carleſrouch,* a country ſeat of the Prince of *Dourlach,* where he expected the arrival of a conſiderable part of the troops, which

came

came from *Germany*. There were already upon their march fourteen battalions and seven regiments of horse, which made about forty two squadrons. Prince *Eugene* being informed, that the *French* had forced the retrenchments at the heights of the *Black Mountains*, he sent orders to retire, and countermanded the troops which were coming to join him; thus we continued masters of all the lines, which we had taken without much difficulty.

This advantage was owing to the prudence of Marshal *Berwick*; never was any project concerted with greater art, or executed with more conduct. Whilst the lines were attacked at the heights, and the army extended it self in the plain to attack them in front, Mr. *d'Asfeld* passed the *Rhine* at the isle of *Nekerlaw* near *Manheim*, with thirty two battalions and forty squadrons. Thus the enemy found themselves pressed on all sides, and obliged to separate. It must likewise be owned, that the particular attack with which the Duke of *Noailles* was intrusted, was well conducted, and supported with valour; all the separate motions which his troops were to make, were perfectly well timed; and it had been very hard, if such well concerted measures had not been successful.

Marshal *Berwick* continued in the camp of *Bruchsall* ever since the tenth of *May*; on the fifteenth he went to *Kislock*, the enemy who had a detachment of foot and horse at *Epingen*,

incefinceſſantly annoying the rear-guard of the army. On the twelfth of *May*, Prince *Eugene* had ordered ſome troops to advance towards *Rottemburg*, and he ſeemed to have a deſign of marching to that ſide: but he did not quit the camp of *Heilbron*.

The Duke of *Noailles*, whom the Marſhal had ſent out from the camp at *Bruchſall* on the ſixteenth, with the Marquis of *Nangis* to ſcour the country near *Quizheim* and *Epingen*, with a detachment of ſixteen hundred foot, and twelve hundred horſe, returned to the camp on the twentieth. Mr. *Guadt*, whom the Marſhal had ſent to ſubject the country of *Wirtemberg*, and put it under contribution, returned from *Phortzheim* to *Graben*, with the troops, which he commanded, excepting ſome detachments which he left at *Dourlach*, and other poſts. Count *Beliſle*, who had ſet out on the ſame day from the camp at *Traerbach*, with thirteen battalions and fourteen ſquadrons, arrived at *Spires* on the twenty ſixth. Laſtly, Mr. *d'Asfeld*, with thirty two battalions and two regiments of dragoons, marched on the twenty third to inveſt *Philipſburg*; after having made two bridges over the *Rhine*, one at *Gnaudenheim*, and the other at *Oberhauſen*; he immediately began to caſt up the lines of circumvallation, and to prepare every thing for the ſiege of that place. As theſe lines were of a very great extent, they could not be finiſhed ſo ſoon as had been expected.

On

On the twenty fourth, the Chevalier *Marcieux* made himfelf mafter of a redoubt, which was only a thoufand yards from the place. On the fame day we began to unfhip, and bring to the camp, the artillery and ammunitions which were arrived from *Strafburg*, at the bridge of the *Upper Rhine*.

On the fecond of *June*, the Marfhal left the camp at *Kifloch*, and marched with the whole army towards *Philipfburg*. He fent the greateft part of his infantry into the lines; they confifted of fourteen brigades, making fifty two battalions. He kept for himfelf a body of referve, confifting of twenty nine battalions, and nineteen fquadrons. A part of the cavalry were encamped on the right, from the *Upper Rhine*, to the brook of *Scelz*; and on the left, from the *Lower Rhine*, to the fame brook. The reft of the cavalry was divided into two bodies, one in the *Spirebach*, under the command of the Duke of *Noailles*; and the other at *Graben*, under that of Mr. *Guadt*.

On the third, the trenches were opened by the four battalions of the regiment of *French* guards, under the command of Mr. *d'Asfeld* and Mr. *Gaffion*. Two thoufand four hundred pioneers were employed in that work; and none of them were killed, becaufe the befieged, not having perceived that we were opening the trenches, did not fire. By the fourth in the morning the works were finifhed.

Count

1734. Count *Belisle* having been charged with the attack of the fort on the bridge of *Philipsburg*, had opened the trenches before it on the first of *June*, and on the third in the morning our troops had lodged themselves on the faliant angle of the covered way of that fort; and finding the enemy had entirely abandoned the place, they entered it.

On the fourth, the trenches before *Philipsburg* were relieved by the Duke of *Noailles*, and Count *Laval Montmorenci*. The parallel which had been begun the night before, was continued; some boyaus of communication were opened with the two parallels, and they began to raife two batteries of five pieces of cannon, each upon the front of the great attack, over againft the morafs of *Staremberg*. The Prince of *Tingri*, and Count *Aubigné*, during the night of the fifth, caufed the parallels to be compleated in the whole length and top of the eminence facing the body of the town; and the boyaus of communication between the parallel were finifhed. It extended by the right as far as the redoubt of the Capuchins, and by the left as far as the burnt mill.

The Marquis of *Guerchi*, and the Marquis of *Balincour* formed, in the night of the fixth, a new attack with twelve hundred pioneers. A parallel was opened, the right of which was carried as far as the *Rhine*, and the left to the caufey of the Capuchins; and the trenches were carried on towards the advanced ditch of the

horn

horn-work. The works were advanced near 1734. three thoufand yards, the enemy not being able by their fire to interrupt them.

The two batteries which had been raifed upon the front of the great attack, two others of ten pieces of cannon, and one of fix mortars, which had been placed in the fort of the bridge of *Philipfburg*, began to fire on the feventh in the morning.

On the fame day the Marquis of *Dreux*, and the Duke of *Bethune*, mounted the trenches. The enemy, to the number of a hundred men, having fallied out of a redoubt which was upon the advanced ditch, were repulfed by two companies of grenadeers, who made themfelves mafters of the redoubt. The Prince of *Ifengheim*, the Marquis of *Clermont*, and Mr. *Atros* mounted the trenches on the tenth. In the night at the right of the attack of the *Lower Rhine* we continued the works, begun the night before, to drain the morafs which covered the horn-work; and they were finifhed with fo much fuccefs, that there remained in the morafs only fix inches of water, upon a fpace of forty five foot. In the fame night we finifhed the parallel which extended along the morafs.

On the eleventh, the trenches were relieved by the Duke of *Duras*, the Chevalier *Rocofel*, and Count *Berenger*. The Prince of *Conti* was there at the head of his regiment. A company of grenadeers of the regiment of *Richelieu* was commanded to advance, in order to reconnoitre

a re-

1734. a redoubt which was on the banks of the *Rhine*, from whence the enemy fired very briſkly.

Marſhal *Berwick* went every day to the trenches to view the works which had been made, and to give orders for making others. He excelled eſpecially in that part of the art of war; and it is agreed, that he conduƈted a ſiege better than any General of his time; he gave to the engineers themſelves the moſt pertinent and proper direƈtions.

On the eleventh, in the evening, after having examined the works, he ordered the ſap to be begun, and the trenches to be carried forward more direƈtly to the place. The ſap was well advanced, but the trenches were not, as he had ordered; and this was owing to a diſpute which aroſe between the two engineers who were to conduƈt the work. One pretended that the trenches would be ſcoured by the enemy's cannon, if they were carried on to the place intended by the Marſhal, and would have them continued, by turning to the left. The other maintained, on the contrary, that if the trenches were advanced on the left, they would be too much expoſed to the grazing of the enemy's bullets. The diſpute continued till next morning, without their agreeing. Whereupon notice of this was carried to the Marſhal, who would judge himſelf of the matter, and ſee in what condition the ſap was, which had been begun.

The

About feven of the clock in the morning, he 1734.
went on horfeback, being accompanied by Lord
Edward his fon, the Earl of *Clare*, and feveral
officers, to the trenches, and from thence to the
place which occafioned the difference between
the two engineers. In vain did they reprefent
to him the danger to which he expofed himfelf,
confidering the great fire of the befieged. His
intrepidity prevailed againft all their remonftrances; and here he was killed by a cannon
ball between Lord *Edward* and the Duke of *Duras:* the former was covered with the blood of
his father, and the latter was wounded by a
ftick out of a gabion, which the bullet had broke
to pieces.

The death of this illuftrious General, whom
France will ever rank among her greateft Commanders, was not only lamented by all the officers and foldiers, but by the whole kingdom,
even at a time when the advantages we gained
on all fides did not fuffer us to perceive how
great occafion there was for fuch able Generals.
There have been few for whom the troops
have had fo great a veneration, or in whom
they have put fo much confidence, as in Marfhal *Berwick*. He refembled Marfhal *Turenne*
even in the manner of his death: both were
equally confpicuous for their virtue, prudence,
probity, and valour; the fedatenefs and prefence
of mind of the one feemed to have been tranf-
mitted to the other; and even their humours
were perfectly like.

K k   They

1734.

They say, that in order to succeed, especially in war, we muſt always have before our eyes ſome great model, which muſt be choſen conformably to our genius and perſonal diſpoſitions. The great *Condé* ſet before him *Julius Cæſar* at the head of his armies; Marſhal *Turenne* copied *Paulus Emilius*; and *Charles* XII imitated *Alexander* the Great. The *French* have no need to ſeek for models either among the antients, or among foreigners. Had they only thoſe whom we have had occaſion to mention in theſe Memoirs, that would ſuffice to ſupport the honour of the *French* name. It is to be wiſhed, that Marſhal *Berwick* may be imitated by ſucceeding Generals: could his glory ever be equalled, it certainly can never be effaced.

F I N I S.

1. THE Works of Mr. *Thomson*, finely printed on a super-
fine Royal Paper, in 2 vol. 4to.
N. B. The second Vol. in 4to may be had to complete Gentlemen's Setts, who subscribed to the Author for the Seasons.

2. A complete Collection of the Historical, Political, and Mis-
cellaneous Works of *John Milton*, correctly printed from the original Editions ; with an Historical and Critical Account of the
Life and Writings of the Author ; containing several Original
Papers of his, never before published ; and a large Alphabetical
Index. By *Thomas Birch*, A. M. F. R. S. in 2 Vol. Folio,
beautifully printed on a fine Paper, and adorned with a curious
Head of the Author, engraven by Mr. *Vertue*, from a Drawing
by Mr. *Richardson*.

3. The *Oceana*, and other Works of *James Harrington* Esq;
collected, methodized and reviewed ; with an exact Account of
his Life prefixed, by *Toland*. To which is added, an Appendix,
containing all the political tracts wrote by this Author, omitted
in Mr. *Toland*'s Edition.
N. B. There's a few of the last two printed for the Curious
on large Paper.

4. A general Dictionary, Historical and Critical : In which
a new and accurate Translation of that of the celebrated Mr.
Bayle, with the Corrections and Observations printed in the late
Edition at *Paris*, is included ; and interspersed with several
thousand Lives, never before published.
 The Whole containing the History of the most illustrious Persons of all Ages and Nations, particularly those of *Great Britain*
and *Ireland*, distinguished by their Rank, Actions, Learning,
and other Accomplishments.
With Reflections on such Passages of Mr. *Bayle*, as seem to
favour Scepticism and the Manichee System.   By the Reverend
Mr. *John Peter Bernard* ; the Reverend Mr. *Thomas Birch*,
F. R. S. Mr. *John Lockman*, and other Hands.   To be com-
prized in 9 Vols. Six of which are already published.

5. The *Roman* History ; with Notes, Historical, Geographi-
cal, and Critical ; and illustrated with Copper-Plates, Maps, and
a great number of authentick Medals.   Done into *English* from
the Original *French* of the Reverend Fathers, *Cartrou* and *Rouille*,
by *R. Bundy*, D. D.   To which is prefix'd, a New and Con-
nected Summary of the Work.   In 6 Vols.
N. B. There are only 3 Setts of the large Paper remaining
of those that were printed, which may be had at fifteen
Guineas in Sheets.   Those Gentlemen that want any Vo-
lumes to compleat their Setts, may have them of the said
A. Millar.

6. *Eurydice*, a Tragedy, acted at the Theatre-Royal in *Drury Lane*, by Mr. *Mallet*.

7. An Enquiry into the Nature of the Human Soul; wherein the Immateriality of the Soul is evinced, from the Principles of Reason and Philofophy, in 2 Vol. 8vo.

    " He who would fee the juftest and precifeft Notions of God
      " and the Soul, may read this Book; one of the moft fi-
      " nifhed of the kind, in my humble Opinion, that the
      " prefent Times, greatly advanced in true Philofophy, have
      " produced. "

    Warburton's *Divine Legation of* Mofes *demonftrated*, p.395.

8. The Hiftory of the Troubles of Great Britain: Containing a particular Account of the moft remarkable Paffages in Scotland, from the Year 1633 to 1650; with an exact Relation of the Wars carried on, and the Battles fought by the Marquis of Montrofe. (All which are omitted in the Earl of Clarendon's Hiftory.) Alfo a full Account of all the Tranfactions in England during that time. Written in French by *Robert Monteth*, of *Salmonet*. To which is added, the true Caufes and favourable Conjunctures which contributed to the Reftoration of King Charles II. Written in French by *D. Riordan de Mufcry*. Tranflated into Englifh by Captain *James Ogilvie*. The Second Edition.

9. The Hiftory of the Church under the Old Teftament, from the Creation of the World: Wherein the Affairs and Learning of Heathen Nations before the Birth of Chrift, and the State of the Jews from the Babylonifh Captivity to the prefent Time are particularly confidered. *Folio*.

10. The Hiftory of the Propagation of Chriftianity, and the Overthrow of Paganifm: Wherein the Chriftian Religion is confirmed; the Rife and Progrefs of Heathenifh Idolatry is confidered; the Overthrow of Paganifm, and the fpreading of Chriftianity in the feveral Ages of the Church is explained; the prefent State of Heathens is enquired into; and Methods for their Converfion propofed. In 2 Vols. 8vo. The Third Edition corrected, with Additions.

11. The World Unmask'd: To which is added, the State of Souls feparated from their Bodies: being an Epiftolary Treatife, wherein is proved, by a variety of Arguments, deduced from Holy Scripture, that the Punifhments of the Wicked will not be eternal; and all Objections againft it folved. With a large Introduction, evincing the fame Truths from the Principles of Natural Religion. In one Volume 8vo.

12. The Tea-Table Mifcellany: or, a Collection of Scots Songs, 9th Edit. being the compleateft and moft correct of any yet publifh'd. Adorned with the Head of the Author.